# Types of International Society

# Types of International Society

EVAN LUARD

THE FREE PRESS
*A Division of Macmillan Publishing Co., Inc.*
NEW YORK

Collier Macmillan Publishers
LONDON

The Free Press
A Division of Macmillan Publishing Co., Inc.
866 Third Avenue, New York, N.Y. 10022

Collier Macmillan Canada, Ltd.

Library of Congress Catalog Card Number: 75–43173

Printed in the United State of America

printing number

1 2 3 4 5 6 7 8 9 10

**Library of Congress Cataloging in Publication Data**

Luard, David Evan Trant
  Types of international society.

  Includes bibliographical references and index.
  1.  International organization.  2.  International
relations.  I.  Title.
JX1954.L82      301.5'92      75-43173
ISBN 0-02-919450-4

# Contents

# Foreword

For many years scholars engaged in the field of international relations have been exploring, amid much mutual recrimination, new ways of approaching the study of that somewhat amorphous and intractable discipline. This book is a modest contribution to that unfinished, and perhaps unfinishable, search. It proposes a new model or framework for the study of international relationships, as an alternative to those based on systems, games, bargaining, decision-making procedures, communications analysis, and the other multifarious methods of approach which have been suggested in recent years.

Briefly, it proposes that the most fruitful approach to this subject is through a form of international sociology: the study of separate historical societies of nations, with the aid of sociological techniques and concepts, in order to discover the essential variables which distinguish one such society from another, and determine the relationships within them.

It has long been recognized that sociology has a part to play in the study of international relations. But the assumption has usually been that the discipline can help us to understand the various social forces at work *within* states influencing the behavior of their governments. The present book is based on a somewhat different assumption. It is concerned not with the narrower society within nations (the subsystem, in one variety of jargon), but with the wider society of states as a whole. The approach is founded on the belief that such societies of states possess many of the characteristics of smaller human societies, and are governed by many similar forces. Thus the concepts and techniques which have been applied by sociologists and others to narrower societies, and the theories which they have built on them, may have a useful application in the study of international society.

This assumption colors the vocabulary of the book as well as the method. It has been fashionable in recent literature in this field to apply a variety of terms to the world stage as a whole. At one time hopeful analysts habitually referred to the "international community," but, as has long been recognized, there is reason to doubt whether the aggregation of states possesses those common values and assumptions which are, by definition, the essential condition of the community. More recently it has been customary to refer to the international "system," but this term too is avoided here because, as the author seeks to show, its use is equally question begging. It carries with it the presumption, if only unconscious, that the working of international societies is in some ways analogous to that of a mechanical system, with the same automatic, self-regulating, and self-preserving characteristics—a presumption which the untidy, complex, and sometimes self-destructive nature of international society scarcely supports. What each such aggregation unquestionably is, however, is a society, a relatively permanent association of nations and other groups, linked together by ties of intercourse, trade, and diplomatic relations, not necessarily—any more than other societies—always peaceful, still less tightly organized and integrated, but possessing some common customs and traditions, common expectations concerning the relationships and behavior to be expected among its members, even, in many cases, common institutions for discussing common problems. For this reason the term "international society" is used throughout this book to describe such an association; and a number of assumptions that have been made concerning human societies are tested in relation to such associations of states.

Much of the book consists, therefore, of a study, according to this framework, of a number of historical associations of states, to discover what they have in common and how they differ, and what are the essential factors which have governed relations within them. Whether this represents a contribution to the "scientific" or "traditional" schools of international relations must be for the individual reader to judge—unless he is as indifferent on that violently debated issue as is the author himself.

# Types of International Society

# PART 1

**International Sociology as an Approach to**

**International Relations**

# Chapter 1.  Theory and Practice in International Relations

## 1.1 Does International Relations Need a Theory?

Writers on international relations have for many years, in innumerable learned articles, books, and doctoral theses, bewailed their discipline's private shame. They were, they complained, like generals without an army; priests without an altar; bankers without capital. Unlike respectable members of the academic profession, they were without a "theory."

At first sight their sensitivity over this deprivation has been a little excessive. Even those most determined to conceive their discipline as a "science" need scarcely have felt too conscience-stricken. There is, after all, no general "theory" of chemistry; there is no "theory" of metallurgy; no "theory" of engineering or physiology. There are observed results of carefully planned experiments, and certain conclusions, specific or general, that have been drawn from them. But there is nothing corresponding to a universal "theory" in the sense demanded by many practitioners of international relations: a corpus of abstract generalizations, commanding universal or widespread assent, serving as the foundation for all inquiry.

Those less convinced of the essentially scientific character of the discipline need perhaps feel even less concern, for most nonscientific disciplines are even more manifestly deficient in this respect. There is no "theory" of history. There is not even any widely accepted "theory" of sociology (though this is not for want of trying by some well-meaning practitioners of that craft): there are a great many works about society and societies, including some which seek to draw general conclusions, usually disputed and highly controversial, about the nature of societies in general, or which propose some new methodology, but this is scarcely "theory" in the sense demanded by many writers on international relations. Political theories there are in the greatest abundance, but it is significant that these are increasingly discarded and despised by those very students of political science most determined to be scientific. Why then should there be a theory of international relations?

3

This is a question which many students of that discipline, bemused and bewildered by the unending flow of learned, if sometimes arid, argumentation on the subject produced in those vast factories of erudition, the North American universities, must sometimes have asked themselves with some desperation. The skeptical European mind, approaching the discipline more often from a background of history or law, has shown itself unconvinced of the urgent need for all-embracing theory. But the doubt is today, and with some reason, being felt increasingly insistently by a number of U.S. academics as well.

In introducing what might be regarded as in some sense a theory of international relationships, it may be worth seeking first to answer this question, if only in self-justification. On the face of it, the task of students of international relations is simple and straightforward. It is to examine the course of relations among states, both past and present, in a reasonably systematic way, to make comparisons and analysis, and to see what conclusions can be drawn. In this sense the subject would be, in approach if not in method, most comparable to history, which equally examines selected sets of events, though more varied in subject matter, for an essentially similar purpose. A writer of history does not require to be armed with a theory to be licensed to participate. And those who have sought to produce theories of history, such as Toynbee or Spengler (not to speak of Marx), have not provided altogether encouraging precedents. For, to the average reader at least, what they have usually sought to do is not dispassionately to survey historical events to determine whether any consistent pattern could be found, but to bend and batter the facts of history in order to fit them into the particular matrix already preordained for them. If international relations were to seek, or still more to discover, a theory, would it not find itself obliged to crib, cabin and confine events into a similar chosen framework?

Even if one regards international relations as a branch of political science, a widely held and respectable thesis (provided one knows what political science is), it is not self-evident that a theory or even a theoretical framework is required. Does political science itself require a theory? Politicians may require a theory, or at least an ideology, though even this is disputable. But the purposes of politicians are quite different from those of political scientists. Political philosophers may benefit from a theory, but these too are a wholly different species, widely believed to be on the point of extinction. The political *scientist,* it may be held, is no more required to have a "theory" than any other scientist. He needs only to observe and record political life and draw what conclusions he can on the most systematic and methodical basis available. Similarly, the student of international relations needs only to observe and record behavior within the international system, and equally will draw what conclusions he feels possible.

This is a healthily skeptical view of the role of theory in international relations, with which the present writer feels a good deal of sympathy. To consider its validity, however, we must first consider a rather more basic question: What is the object of the study of international relations? If one regards its aim as to develop a theory about the behavior of states, then by definition it requires a theory. This would be, however, a highly idiosyncratic conception of the purpose of the discipline, which even the most dedicated theoretician would scarcely seek to defend. Without embarking on an analysis of the voluminous and generally inconclusive writing undertaken on this subject in the last twenty years, we can perhaps content ourselves with a fairly neutral definition of the object of the study, which would perhaps command fairly widespread assent. The basic, minimum, object of the study of international relations is to improve our understanding of international society. Even this begs a few questions and could do with further definition of some of the terms used, but it will do for the present. The main test of theory, therefore, will be whether or not it contributes to improving understanding of international society as a whole.

But even if we accept this definition of its purpose, it is necessary, in considering the role (if any) of theory, to answer another basic question: What *is* a theory of international relations, or what should such a theory be?

## 1.2  What Is Theory?

The word "theory" is used by writers in the social sciences in a wide variety of meanings. These range from conclusion to premise, from concept to cause, from analytical framework to inductive generalization, from a set of assumptions to a set of deductions. Without examining these various alternatives in detail it is possible to analyze at least five major uses of the word.[1]

First, it may mean a set of propositions about the correct way of studying a subject, rather than about the subject itself. For example, we can talk of the structuralist "theory" in anthropology, or the behaviorist "theory" in psychology. These are basically theories about theory; about the kind of theory, or way of studying a subject, which is most useful. They could perhaps be defined as *approaches,* but they are approaches that contain underlying assumptions: The behaviorist seeks to study behavior not only because he believes that this is a more reliable indication of mental states than introspection or psychological analysis, but because he thinks that action is more important than thought as a subject of study. In international relations it might be said that the quantitative method, or the decision-making approach—the study of the way decisions are reached by national governments and other international actors—represent theories of this type: theories about the right way to look at the subject rather than about the subject itself.

1. For discussions of types of theory in international relations, see W. T. R. Fox, ed., *Theoretical Aspects of International Relations* (Notre Dame, 1959); S. Hoffman, ed., *Contemporary Theory in International Politics* (Englewood Cliffs, 1960); C. A. McLennan, *Theory and the International System* (New York, 1966); K. Knorr and J. Rosenau, eds., *Contending Approaches to International Politics* (Princeton, 1969). For a discussion of the meaning and use of theory in the social sciences generally, see P. S. Cohen, *Modern Social Theory* (London, 1968).

Second, the word "theory" can be applied to a broad set of general propositions, usually stated as a priori principles, and held to be true of all places and all times.[2] These generalizations are taken as the initial starting point, the assumptions, sometimes very simple, on which subsequent research is based. In psychology broad assertions concerning the dominance of particular motivations, such as the will to power, the sex drive, or some other factor, are theories of this kind. In international relations assertions concerning the primacy of the desire for national power or the search for overseas markets, as motivations among states, belong to the same type. Such broad propositions may be used as the core of a general "system," or simply as a source of explanation for state actions. Since most people like to have a relatively simple, easily conceived system of explanation of the universe—and since many writers would like to think they have discovered the principle that can explain almost everything—many theories of this kind have been developed. To assist in this purpose, the theories are often highly simplified: the will to power is not simply an important motivation among individuals, but the only motivation; the desire for power among states is not simply an important motive, but always the most important. These might be unkindly described as *slogan* theories, seeking a simple shortcut to explanation; because of their attractive simplicity and all-embracing character, theories of this kind have a wide appeal and are perhaps of all the best known.

Third, theory may be used to refer to a set of propositions of a more relative type: a series of discrete generalizations, drawn from observation, yet held to possess a considerable degree of universal validity.[3] Here the approach is essentially empirical and the method is usually inductive. In international relations the generalizations would be based on careful observation of the behavior of states in contemporary practice, rather than on a priori views about the nature of states and their motives. In psychology, conclusions based on the study of salivation in dogs that animal behavior is a series of conditioned reflexes could be regarded as "theories" in this sense. In international relations the proposition that states in the modern world are most likely to exhibit restless and aggressive character in neighboring areas conceived as essential to their own security might be given as an example of this type of empirical theory. Essentially we are dealing here with conclusions rather than with premises (as in the previous case).[4] We might call these *generalization* theories.

2. Cf. H. Morgenthau, in *Theoretical Aspects*, ed. Fox, pp. 15–28. "Historically and logically, a scientific theory is a system of empirically verifiable general truths, sought for their own sake . . . a theory of politics must seek to depict the rational essence of its subject matter."

3. These are the theories that come closest to a scientific theory of the strictest kind: a universal statement asserting a causal relationship, based on, and verifiable by, empirical observation. But many scientific theories are not of this pure kind even in physical science, and they exist still less frequently in the social sciences where the necessary testing and proof of a causal relationship is rarely attainable. For discussion see Cohen, *Modern Social Theory,* pp. 4–8.

4. It is arguable that the word should be used in this sense only when such propositions remain *hypotheses,* not when they have been proved and widely accepted. In the physical sciences one could

Fourth, a theory may be not so much a statement or proposition as a set of analogies or comparisons. These may be described as *metaphoric* theories, which explain one set of phenomena in terms of another. The object is to pinpoint essential characteristics by drawing out resemblances. In politics, for example, for thousands of years there have been theories which have sought to explain the state in terms of an organism, or living thing, which has its own life and can grow or decay. In recent times many theories have sought to compare the state with a "system," conceived in mechanical terms, with a set of "inputs" and "stimuli" leading through a series of transmission lines and automatic responses to corresponding "outputs," and with a mechanism for "feedback" to provide information for self-adjustment.[5] In international relations there have been similar theories seeking to analyze the international society by analogy with such a mechanical system, or with games, with bargaining situations, and so on. The difficulty about all such models, as we shall see in a moment, is that they inevitably introduce a measure of distortion. To think of the state as an organic structure, or of international society as a system with feedback, may promote one or two useful insights and comparisons, but in the long run it can only be misleading. For it inevitably leads to the assumption that *all* essential features of the analogy employed must be present in the real society or system which is being analyzed: that the state *does* have a life of its own independent of its members, for example; that international society *does* possess a feedback mechanism making for automatic adjustment; and so on. These are assumptions that derive from the metaphor employed rather than from the evidence of the real world. In other words, the metaphor takes control; the image displaces reality. If you want to study international society, it may be simpler to study international society.

Fifth, theory can be used in a still looser way to refer simply to a framework for analysis. Whatever concepts or categories are used—and any descriptive system must make use of some such concepts, must choose particular factors to describe or analyze—together represent the framework, focus, or "theory." Such a set of concepts is a means of sorting out the random facts and phenomena with which we are faced in any particular field: a system for organizing the material. On these grounds it can be (and has been) said that in every study of politics or international relations there is at least an *implicit* theory; at least a selection of what features are felt to be important; at least assumptions about what are the events and factors which *need* to be described or discussed. This represents a loose use of the word "theory," which in its normal sense implies something more than this: a thesis, a set of statements about underlying principles, a set of basic causes and variables,

---

reasonably talk of Newton's "theory" of gravity or Einstein's "theory" of relativity in the age in which these were first produced, but once established, physicists would more likely refer to them as being "laws." Theory implies, in this sense, a tentativeness which is gradually lost as it becomes more widely accepted. This is also the usage of everyday life: "I have a theory about this."

5. See, for example, D. Easton, *A Systems Analysis of Political Life* (New York, 1965); idem, *A Framework for Political Analysis* (Princeton, 1965).

even a coherent and *explicit* hypothesis which can be explained and justified. Marxist writings represent an example of a theory in this sense (though they also perhaps demonstrate a theory of the second type we have identified—general a priori propositions concerning the forces at work in human history). By focusing attention on such concepts as "class," "class struggle," "relations of production," "contradictions within society," surplus profit, "revolution," and so on, they encourage a particular way of considering and analyzing the phenomena of political relationships. Similarly, in writing on international relations, studies which focus primarily on strategic relationships and the balance of power, on geopolitics, on the internal social structure of states, or on economic dominance and dependence, each in their own way imply a set of theoretical assumptions. A theory of this sort may promote a different way of looking at the subject, and emphasize different material for study and analysis. Theory in this sense can be looked at as a map which provides the essential landmarks and so enables us more easily to find our way around the confusing maze of the untidy and disorganized world.

One way of distinguishing between these highly different types of theory is to identify them by what they seek to do. Roughly speaking, the first seeks to *guide research;* the second to *explain;* the third to *generalize;* the fourth to *compare;* and the fifth to *focus.* In practice many theories do not necessarily belong exclusively to one category or another. But in principle at least the types are distinct and distinguishable.[6]

Theories may be subdivided in other ways. For example, theories can be general or partial: in international relations they can relate to the behavior of states in all their aspects (e.g., a theory that states will always seek to maximize power in every action), or only to certain aspects of their behavior (e.g., a theory relating to states' strategic conduct or economic activity). Second, they can be absolute, in the sense of valid for all periods and all societies, or relative to particular times or systems. They can be theories relating to the wider society (the international system as a whole) or to the narrower (the nature and conduct of national states as such). Finally (and more significantly), they can be inductive or deductive, either leading from direct observation of phenomena to conclusions based on that observation, or proceeding from a statement of general propositions to logical conclusions drawn from those propositions.

The kind of theory we favor will depend on what we want theory to do for us. If

---

6. It is sometimes said that there is another type of theory, "normative theory": that is, a theory which is prescriptive rather than descriptive, related (in the case of international relations) to how states should behave rather than how they do behave. Yet is is doubtful whether this can really be regarded as a separate category, for almost any of the types of theory we have already outlined could also be normative. Prescriptive conclusions could be drawn from approach theories, slogan theories, or any other kind. Moreover, in most cases normative propositions, representing guides to action, are commands, categorical imperatives, rather than theoretical concepts or hypotheses. The ten commandments constitute a set of normative propositions, but they could scarcely be described as a theory. In other words, any normative principles which are associated with political or other theory are properly conclusions derived from theory, rather than the theory itself.

you want a set of conclusions, you will not choose the type of theory which is a set of premises. If you want a map to help you to find your way around, you will not adopt a metaphoric theory designed to compare rather than to reveal, and so on. In other words, there may be room for many different types of theory, designed to perform different types of function. The existence or validity of one type of theory does not necessarily prove that another type is wrong. Once again the only ultimate test is: Does the theory assist us in understanding international society as a whole?

In this sense, it is well to be aware of some of the major dangers which surround theories. For though they may be used, like electricity, to perform useful services, throwing light where there was darkness, they have to be handled with some care if they are not to blind or shock and so lead us to disaster.

One widespread danger is that, by the very act of focusing attention on certain features or factors, theories may close the eye to others that are equally if not more important. We may have needed to be reminded by Marx of the importance of economic factors in determining political and other relationships, or by Freud of the importance of sex in influencing human behavior. But we might be ill-advised if led to believe (like some of their more ardent followers) that these are the *only* factors at work, and that all others can be safely ignored. Sometimes a theory or a theorist have become well known precisely because they have distorted and exaggerated, and in so doing have alerted the world to an important truth previously neglected. Their particular distortion may need later to be supplemented or replaced by some new theory that will reveal yet another previously neglected facet of the truth, perhaps corresponding more fully to the needs, intellectual, social, or political, of some subsequent age.

A second danger is related to this. A theory's use of a concept or a principle in a purely *descriptive* sense may gradually be transformed into a *prescriptive* meaning. The concept of class struggle as a description of an important dynamic force within society is transformed, consciously or unconsciously, into a *recommendation* of struggle by particular classes or parties within society. Recognition of the profit motive as a description of an influence on action commonly observed within the capitalist system becomes in time transformed into a *recommendation* that that motive be appeased, encouraged, and extolled. The description of the maximization of "national interest in terms of power" as the main objective of national policy within the international system is transformed by degrees into a *recommendation* of that goal for all states within the system. In some cases the "is" and the "ought" have been inextricably confused from the beginning: Machiavelli describes the action of all princes as self-seeking and ruthless in order to justify his own recommendation of self-seeking and ruthless behavior to his own prince.

Conversely, a concept which is first used in a prescriptive sense, as a desirable goal, comes to be converted into a description of what must happen. The goal of the greatest happiness of the greatest number, from being a desirable end to be promoted in every possible way, comes to be thought of as the inevitable outcome of human behavior; "perfect competition," as a desirable state of affairs, is translated into "perfect competition" as the inevitable condition of the capitalist economy; "equilibrium" as a desirable aim of policy for governments within the international system gradually comes to be transformed into "equilibrium" as the inevitable outcome of state behavior.

But the third and final danger for all theories is even more basic. Almost every theory must oversimplify. By the very fact of reducing reality to its simplest terms, of seeking to abstract from the complexity of brute facts in order to explain them away in elegant and parsimonious terms, theories must omit all that is inessential and inconvenient. In a sense, the point of the theory is to oversimplify: to organize, to sort out, to present a framework which points up the main landmarks while ignoring or underplaying the tangled undergrowth; to show the wood without too many of the inconvenient trees. A map which showed every shrub, stick, and stone in the area would be confusing rather than illuminating. A framework which sought to encompass every possible variable, and to account for every exception and qualification that could be conceived, would be too complex to be useful.

But unless this tendency is clearly understood, the theory may not merely simplify but mislead. The theory that political events are conditioned only by economic forces and the class struggle may lead to a more accurate understanding of some political societies, but to gross misjudgments of others. The theory that man is mainly motivated by the sex drive may lead to better clinical analysis of certain psychological conditions, but to a total misreading of others. The theory that nations, in seeking their own security, will inevitably act to promote their own power may lead to a better understanding of some national behaviors, but to a total misconception of others. Most theories attempt to explain almost everything in terms of a few basic variables or forces, and in the process of simplifying the analysis they often simplify reality as well.

This does not mean that all theories must distort more than they clarify, and that the search for theory should be abandoned. Our test must remain as before: Can a theory help us in our understanding of reality, and illuminate what would otherwise remain obscure? Let us bear in mind these dangers, therefore, in considering what kind of theory may be of value in helping us understand international relationships.

## 1.3 Theories of International Relations

So far we have concluded that the test of a theory is whether it improves understanding, and we have examined some of the *types* of theories which may be held in political and social science, and some of the dangers which attach to them. Let us now look at some of the theories that have actually been propounded by those engaged in the study of international relations in recent years, and consider how they assist in the analysis of international society.

Theories of the first category we identified, relating to the methodology of the discipline, are, in the case of international relations, of three types, corresponding to different levels of analysis. Some writers have held that the way relationships among nations should be studied was by examining the nature of *man*. Confucius and Mencius in ancient China, for example, believed that whether wars occurred depended on the righteousness or otherwise of rulers; by educating the rulers it might be possible, therefore, to eliminate war altogether. Other reformers in other ages have felt that wars result from the wickedness of human beings generally, so if only these could be purged and purified, and all feelings of hostility and prejudice eliminated, war could be abolished. The belief that the ultimate cause of war is man's psychological makeup, especially innate aggressive urges, has been particularly common within the last fifty years. It has been encouraged both by psychologists, some of whom have sought to show that much human behavior is conditioned by a basic "aggressive" impulse, and by ethologists, who have sought to show that much human behavior was conditioned by the same drives and impulses as those of animals. It is implicit in the concept (enshrined in the UNESCO charter) that wars begin "in the minds of men" and often result from nationalist propaganda and ideological beliefs glorifying the state and national power. Such theories propose that international relations should be approached at the lowest level: through the avenue of individual psychology. While, as we shall see later, the study of human psychology certainly has a role to play in this discipline, it may be doubted that it is sufficient in itself. The inconvenient fact is that it is not only bad or aggressive men who become involved in making war, any more than it is only totalitarian and militaristic states. Individual aggressive urges have innumerable outlets alternative to war itself. To account for war, it would seem necessary not only to examine the nature of men themselves—who live sometimes in peace and sometimes at war—but also the nature of the international environment within which wars break out.

A second approach has contended that the most significant way of considering international relations is to examine the nature of *states*. Examination of domestic pressures, systems of government, and political structures will tell you, it is held, the type of foreign policy each nation will pursue, and therefore the whole structure of their relationships. These theories concentrate on the individual unit or member of society, rather than on the international society as a whole. They focus attention on such questions as the system of government, the class structure, and the national elites, rather than on the external challenges to each state or the character of the international environment as a whole. Writers such as Rousseau and statesmen such as Woodrow Wilson have held that democratic nations will normally be peace loving and cooperative while autocratic governments will be aggressive and expansionist (a contention scarcely supported by the history of the last fifty years or so, during which some totalitarian states, such as Spain and some Asian and Latin American states, have been almost entirely uninvolved in external war, while some nations that are impeccably democratic have been several times so involved).

A weakness of such theories is indeed that it is difficult to find any consistent correlation between the internal character of states and their external behavior. States which *change* governments or systems often continue to pursue the same policies as before. Such theories thus have much the same weaknesses as theories of individual psychology of a century or more ago. Those, too, tended to assume that individuals' behavior was determined purely by internal factors—disposition and character—and took little account of family background, relations with parents, peer groups, and society as a whole, which modern psychologists would regard as much more important in conditioning human behavior. In both cases, concentration on the internal character of the individual without reference to the *social* environment which shaped it can be seriously misleading.

An example of an approach theory which concentrates on study of individual units, rather than of the system as a whole, is the so called "decision-making theory."[7] This has attempted to analyze the procedures for reaching foreign policy decisions within states, and the various forces that may bring their influence to bear: the bureaucratic procedures involved, the agencies consulted, the influence of pressure groups, the effect of press and public opinion, and so on. This no doubt has its interest and, if conclusive results could be obtained, even some importance (for example, if it could be shown that different types of decisions were reached according to the procedure used). Most of the writing in the field so far, however, has been highly generalized, describing the kinds of factors which *might* influence governments rather than those which have influenced them in particular situations. Only one study has examined a particular set of decisions in detail, and even this was inconclusive in its result.[8] Moreover, even more detailed and concrete studies seem unlikely to show that the particular procedures used in reaching decisions have a crucial influence in determining the responses made to particular situations, threats, or challenges. What students of international relations are really concerned about is what decides the policy decisions, not how they are reached—quite a different question. And such a study requires analysis of the other two levels, individual psychology and the international environment generally, as well as group decision-making procedures.

Any theory is thus likely to prove unsatisfactory if it ignores the dominant influence of the environment as a whole: the character of the international system, expectations current within that system concerning acceptable types of national behavior, the effect of demands for national power, influence, and wealth within that system, fear of the actions of other states, the balance of military power, and many factors that cannot be adequately analyzed by concentrating on the nature of individual governments or states alone. The third type of approach theory is concerned with this wider *international society*. Examples of this type are those theories which conceive of the system as governed by the balance of power principle,[9] equilibrium,[10] or the needs of the "system."[11] The implications of such theories is that the needs and nature of the system in a sense impose their own

7. R. C. Snyder, W. H. Bruck, and B. Spain, eds., *Foreign Policy Decision-making: An Approach to the Study of International Politics* (New York, 1962).

8. C. D. Paige, *The Korean Decision* (New York, 1968).

9. H. Morgenthau, *Politics Among Nations* (Chicago, 1948).

10. M. Liska, *International Equilibrium* (Cambridge, Mass., 1957).

11. M. Kaplan, *System and Process in International Politics* (New York, 1957); A. M. Scott, *The Functioning of the International Political System* (New York, 1967).

internal logic on the individual members: States must act in a certain way to protect the balance of power, to preserve equilibrium, to sustain the system. They might therefore be compared with psychological theories which hold that all human behavior can be accounted for exclusively by environmental factors, and that innate characteristics are of no influence at all.

This approach may have more to commend it than the last, but it is almost equally unbalanced. Though there can be little doubt that the behavior of states is conditioned to a considerable extent by the nature of international society and the drives it instills, it would be as false to eliminate consideration of internal forces as it would be to ignore the influence of the external system. As in individual psychology, both factors count, and the important point is to determine the relative importance of each in any given situation.

Methodological studies of this kind have their role in clarifying our approach to the subject and sharpening the tools of the discipline. But by concentrating attention on particular factors, or at a particular level, they tend to downplay or ignore others. They have rarely been systematically applied to concrete situations. And being concerned primarily with method rather than with matter, it seems unlikely they will in themselves do much to deepen our understanding of the concrete factors underlying relations among states in particular situations.

The second category of theory which we defined—those based on a few a priori generalizations or concepts—has many representatives in international relations writing. The bald assertion of Marx, Lenin, and their followers that war results from economic conditions generally, and especially from the search of capitalist producers for foreign markets, is one instance of this method at work. Rather than examining the wars which have taken place over a particular period, leading to a conclusion about their causes, these make an initial assumption— capitalist nations need markets abroad and must make war to acquire them—from which all else stems. It is then not a very far jump to asserting that all wars everywhere result from this cause, or that no wars can ever take place among socialist states because among them the major motivation for war will have been removed. The inquiring observer may be puzzled to find that a considerable number of wars have other causes, or that many capitalist states do not make war for markets. Such theories tend to reflect the central preoccupation of their authors with a particular theme or motivation, and any evidence which does not conform with it is conveniently ignored. They do not usually, therefore, serve as a very persuasive basis for examining the causes of war, or of international behavior in general in the modern world.

Another example of this a priori type of theory is the well-known and influential thesis sometimes known as the "realist" theory, associated especially with the name of Hans Morgenthau. The theory is based primarily on the somewhat dogmatic assertion, laid down in the first pages of that author's best-known book, that "statesmen think and act in terms of interest, defined in terms of power,"[12] an assumption which, he asserts, "allows us to retrace and anticipate . . . the steps

12. Morgenthau, *Politics Among Nations*, p. 5.

statesmen—past present or future—have taken or will take on the political scene." The weaknesses and fallacies of this type of reasoning have been pointed out by many writers.[13] They derive in part from the ambiguity and imprecision of the concepts of "interest" and "power" that are used throughout, but never adequately defined. They derive from the failure to distinguish between power as a means and power as an end. They derive from the failure adequately to account for many aspects of national behavior (and almost all the behavior of some states) that are not concerned with "power" in the normal sense of the word. For to say that such other behavior—cultivating friendly relations, economic strength, or cultural influence, representing a large part of the activity of most states—seeks power, but by other means, is to rob the word "power" of all its meaning. The only valid meaning of that word is either armed strength or the general capacity to coerce other nations. Each of these is desired mainly as a means rather than as an end, and even then only as one among a large range of alternative means. A more basic weakness of this theory, however, derives from its very character as a statement of a priori truths. Although Morgenthau states that "the character of a foreign policy can be ascertained only through the examination of the particular acts performed and of the foreseeable consequences of those acts,"[14] in fact his hypothesis is merely stated baldly at the outset, in the words already quoted, as if it could not seriously be questioned, and is never adequately demonstrated in subsequent pages (stimulating though many of these undoubtedly are).

This is a typical example of a theory which exerts impact simply as a thesis, a challenging statement of a characteristic, if extreme, viewpoint, rather than through the persuasiveness with which that thesis is argued. It depends for its effect on the reiteration of two key concepts. All theories of this a priori type suffer from the defect of being based on what is, in the eyes of their author, a revealed and undeniable truth which therefore scarcely needs demonstration, while to their readers that truth may be very far from evident. By *assuming* what most people wish to see proved, they beg the very questions which are of fundamental importance to the discipline. Certainly the theories of this type which have been produced so far have proved largely unconvincing to many of their readers, if only because they proceed from theory to reality rather than vice versa.

The third type of theory we characterized, that which consists of inductive conclusions, demonstrated, or said to be demonstrated, by the evidence assembled concerning the facts of international society, has been rather more fruitful. Quincy Wright's classic "Study of War"[15] might be given as an example of this category: The basic facts concerning the phenomenon of war are reviewed and analyzed and an attempt is made to draw general conclusions. Other examples could be found in some of the foreign policy studies of the interwar years and more recent times, and

13. Hoffman, *Contemporary Theory*, pp. 30ff; I. Claude, *Power in International Relations* (New York, 1962); K. W. Deutsch, *The Analysis of International Relations*, (Englewood Cliffs, 1968), p. 46.

14. Morgenthau, *Politics Among Nations*, p. 5.

15. Quincy Wright, *Study of War* (Chicago, 1942).

in the writers on geopolitics, such as Harold and Emily Sprout. A number of more recent works fall into the same category. But it is not a method which has as yet been systematically exploited, nor can it be said that many widely accepted generalizations or laws have been discovered through its use.

It does, however, seem to be the method most likely to yield fruitful results. Sustained and systematic examination of the behavior of nations in particular situations, comparative study of particular types of relationships (say between block leaders and their allies), examination of types of economic domination, studies of economic relations among states in general (so far a field almost completely ignored), could assist in building up a significant body of "theory" of this kind. One possible reason for the comparative poverty of writing in this field at the present is that there has tended to be a wide gap between those authors writing on theory and those undertaking empirical case studies, national, regional, and international. The former have often too little knowledge of the case histories, and the latter too little interest in theory.

There is, however, one type of empirical approach that has become only too widely adopted in the past decade, the use of the so-called "quantitative" method: studies said to be designed to insure objectivity by relying, so far as possible, on purely "quantitative" evidence. Practititioners of this school contend that their methods permit systematic examination of the international system, free from bias or slipshod methods, directed at specific and researchable questions of a kind which may bring out the important variables. If the discipline of international relations is to acquire any worthwhile academic standing and self-respect, they hold, it is essential that it develop techniques, concepts, and procedures that will enable it to reach demonstrable conclusions rather than relying on mere impressions, guesswork, and unfocused records of events. And in reply to the charge that, by rigorously avoiding all normative judgments, and merely measuring the status quo, they imply a conservative attitude of acceptance, they insist that they themselves are concerned only with methods: the uses made of their research are matters that are outside their control.

It is not the purpose here to retread this already rather heavily trampled ground.[16] So-called quantitative methods are now widely used in this field, as in all other social sciences. But the important point is that, whatever their merits, they cannot, however rigorously employed, insure that the conclusions reached provide any significant improvement in our understanding. This will depend on the choice of what is to be measured. Efforts to count the number of letters that pass between two states, the number of Ph.D. students working on international studies, or the number of times delegates at a UN committee rise from their seats to talk to other delegates (all matters which have been the subject of painstaking research by workers in recent times), however impeccable the methodology, provide conclusions of somewhat dubious value. The relevance of the answers, as always, depends on the relevance of the questions asked. Many of these studies seem, to

16. For an exposition of rival views on this question, see Knorr, Rosenau, *Contending Approaches.*

some at least, to be devoted to answering questions which are at worst irrelevant and at best insignificant. Indeed, the obsession shown by some with confining themselves to countable phenomena can only be regarded as an example of method become madness: total absorption with a technique which, however useful on occasion, should be the tool rather than the master of research.

Devotion to this method seems to reflect an assumption that there is a close correlation between "science" and statistics, reliability and number. In all social studies there do exist areas for which number, counting, and calculation are not merely important but essential: for example, where it is necessary to know how many students entering universities have parents of a particular kind of occupation or social background, or how many of those voting for a particular political party belong to a particular profession or interest group. Even in the field of international relations there are some areas of which this is true. Yet a general belief that to make a discipline "scientific" only quantitative data are relevant or reliable is totally contrary to the experience of science itself. Many scientific studies do not depend primarily on numbers but on description and analysis—not on *counting* the number of times monkeys groom each other every day but on *describing* those actions and suggesting reasons for them. And this is still more true of the human as opposed to the physical sciences. Psychological research does not depend on counting the number of times a child cries or laughs in a day, but on studying and describing his behavior and seeking to understand the reasons for it. Even in politics, though you learn something by knowing the *number* of people who vote for a particular party, you learn more by considering why they do so, about which numbers will tell us little. Similarly, in examining the relations among states you learn something by counting—say, the distribution of UN votes—but far more by studying the motives that underlie the action—such as *why* the votes are as they are, an area in which statistics will be of little assistance.

In all these cases what really matters is the *relevance* of the phenomena which are examined. Counting the number of Ph.D. theses on international themes undertaken in the universities of a particular country may tell you how far that country is internationally minded, but it may only tell you something about the number of universities or postgraduate students there, or about academic fashions at any particular time. To count the number of times delegations in a UN commit-tee get up from their seats may tell you how active their governments are as initiators in the UN, but it may only tell you how sociable are the individual delegates, how bored by other delegates' speeches, how well equipped with funny stories, and so on. Ironically, for this reason quantitative methods, which pride themselves on their reliability and objectivity, are often the least reliable or objective, for they depend crucially on assessments of relevance which are the most affected by subjective assumptions.[17] They could lead, for example, in a

17. One of the curious features is that in nearly all these cases the use of more straightforward techniques would not only lead to more reliable conclusions (because less biased by the initial choice of phenomena to be counted), but would have reached them far more easily and quickly. It was not neces-sary to sit through 200 meetings of the UN's Fifth Committee over several years to find out that Canada,

recent case, to the conclusion that after 1962 the process of integration had halted within the European economic community, since it was held (admittedly by a faulty calculation) that the growth in intracommunity trade had run down after that time. If, however, the choice had been made to count, instead of the growth in trade, the number of schoolchildren who had traveled to the other countries of the area (an equally arbitrary choice), an exactly opposite conclusion might have been reached, but one much closer to the truth.[18]

It is perhaps the fourth type of theory, the metaphoric type, based on analogies or concepts drawn from another discipline, that has been most widely used in recent writing on international relations. There can be no attempt here to consider all of these studies, but it may be worth looking at the more important of them.

One type has examined negotiation and bargaining among states, and sought to make use of concepts and conclusions drawn from the world of games, or more accurately from the theory of games (which is somewhat different). This theory was developed thirty or forty years ago with respect to business organizations and economic competition. Its application to international politics thus removed it still one stage further from its ostensible subject matter: the strategy of games. Its use in this context has some of the assets and all of the disadvantages of other metaphoric theories. It may enable us to understand more clearly what might be a rational course for a government to take in a certain kind of world, but that world is so remote from the real one that the conclusions are of only academic interest. Within it, it is assumed, the behavior of governments is closely analogous to that of the players of competitive games. They are, for example, engaged in a struggle with one or a few antagonists in isolation, rather than a complex interrelationship with many; their aim is always ''victory,'' to ''defeat'' their opponents at all costs; they plot their strategies to this end; they do this in a way that is single-minded, rational, and ruthless, and they wholly ignore intangible extrinsic factors such as domestic opinion, the influence of pressure groups, allies, world public opinion, the interests of their opponents, morality, their conception of a world society, and other factors which may have importance in the real world of international

---

as the country which left its seat most often, played a leading role in discussion of secretariat and financial affairs. Any UN delegate could have told this in half a moment, and a glance at the resolutions themselves would have given the same information. Indeed, straightforward studies of influence in the UN, based on inquiry and interviewing among UN delegates, have provided far more complete and reliable information about the way political influence is exercised and mobilized in the UN than all the painstaking enumeration of bodily movements in a UN committee under the quantitative method, and take a fraction of the time to produce. Moreoever, such studies provide more reliable information precisely because they use some evidence that is *not* measurable, such as the impressions and views of those actually involved in these bodies. To decide to confine oneself to countable phenomena is to exclude others that are not countable, but may be more relevant.

18. Similarly, the choice of *categories* can crucially affect the reliability of results based on such methods. Thus a recent study was able to conclude, on the basis of counting speeches and votes in the UN on particular subjects, that between the mid–1950s and the early–1960s East-West issues in the UN increased in relation to North-South issues, a conclusion that anyone who knows the UN would realize was the opposite of the truth. Such a conclusion was only possible by categorizing colonial issues as being East-West issues, rather than North-South, a categorization which most people would regard as entirely wrongheaded.

relations. The theory thus ignores most of the *social* factors, influences, and aspirations arising from the society of states, which in practice play a vital role in determining the behavior of states in international society.[19]

The assumption of a wholly self-regarding competitive strategy may be no more lifelike in relation to the behavior of nations than it would be in calculating behavior among individuals. Like other metaphoric theories, therefore, this grossly oversimplifies. If all governments did behave totally rationally and totally ruthlessly, the study of international relations would in many ways be simple: It would be far easier to calculate their likely course of action than it is in the real world. In real life, which is what concerns most of us, governments have more complex motives: They seek friendship and confrontation with the *same* nations, they *are* influenced by opinions abroad as well as opinion at home, by differing views of different departments and pressure groups, by the irrational hopes, fears, and prejudices of individual leaders, by traditions and habits derived from the past, and many other factors which may conflict with the single goal of defeating an opponent for its own sake. They can also be influenced by persuasion and concessions, as well as by threats and coercion, a possibility which most such theories totally ignore. Moreover, antagonists are not (as in games of chicken, or "prisoners' dilemma") totally cut off from each other, but are mutually interacting. The distortions are almost endless. Here too therefore, the metaphor may take over. By encouraging the notion, even if only subconsciously, that other states do and will behave ruthlessly and solely self-interestedly, such theories promote the conclusion that one's own government must do so. They become self-fulfilling prophecies.

Much the same is true of theories of bargaining and deterrence. Though it may be useful for nations, in situations where they are involved in a genuine bargaining posture (for example, in some arms control discussions), to understand the basic principles of bargaining, most international relations situations are not of this kind. Even in genuine bargaining situations, very often intangible, psychological factors are involved which these theories ignore. Here too irrational factors play a large part. Threats or warnings, which ought to produce a certain response in a rational opponent, may sometimes produce the contrary effect: they may provoke rather than deter. Again, such theories will lead to the conclusion that deterrents or threats are "rational" when undertaken by a large power against a small though clearly unreasonable when made by a small against a large one. By its assumptions, therefore, such a theory maximizes the importance of the factors of power and fear, and omits many others: the expectations of other states, for example, the tradition of intercourse among states, the desire for reputation as a reasonable and reliable member of the international community, the impact of home public opinion, not to speak of moral attitudes generally. This, therefore, is another

19. One basic difference that is ignored is that in a game, especially a zero-sum game, you cannot compromise or do a deal, you can only win or lose. In international relations there are rarely all-out victories, nearly always deals of one kind or another

model based on oversimplified assumptions (sometimes recognized, yet nonetheless distorting).[20]

A still more widely employed type of metaphoric theory is that which can be called, in a general way, systems theory: theories that assume that the international society can be compared with a mechanical system. The phrase "the international system" has been in use since the eighteenth century. But in modern times it has been used in a more consistent way to create an analogy with the functioning of a machine, complete with capacity, regulatory process, feedback, self-adjustment, and so on. A number of writers have used this analogy more or less systematically. In doing so, however, they rarely do more than translate fairly elementary and well-known facts about the nature of international society into the language of mechanical engineering. Perhaps the best-known work of this type outlines six possible alternative models of the international system, with differing distributions of power within them, and postulates the rules of behavior that would be necessary among the units to maintain each system.[21]

Such an approach, like all other metaphoric theories, suffers from a simple but basic defect. The validity of the conclusions depend entirely on the assumptions which are built into each model. Those assumptions, as most of their authors admit, are highly oversimplified, and bear only a passing resemblance to any international system which has actually existed: in some cases they are gross distortions of the real world. They thus tell us nothing about reality, but only about the imaginary world which has been postulated within each model. Four of the models used in Kaplan's book do not even purport to resemble any international system which has actually existed, and the other two (the "balance of power" and the "loose bipolar" systems) are defined in a way that effectively makes them almost equally remote from any real-life system.[22] The conclusions based on these underlying assumptions can therefore hardly be regarded as particularly illuminating.

Another shortcoming is that this, like most other metaphoric systems, introduces automatic distortions that derive from the metaphor employed. The concept of feedback, for example, immediately establishes the assumption that there must exist some *automatic* process for the retrieval of information, or for self-adjustment, an assumption which is then built into the model. To discover the working of real systems, it seems likely, once again, that the study of the real world, the information gathering and decision making actually used by gov-

20. For another critical examination of current bargaining theory see Deutsch, *Analysis of International Relations*, pp. 128–130.

21. The six types of system are: balance of power, loose bipolar, tight bipolar, universal international system, hierarchical international system, and unit veto system.

22. Of the six rules laid down, for example, to define the balance of power system, only two can reasonably be said to have held good for any real international society, and then only among certain nations and at certain times. But at the same time many other principles underlying their behavior, and many of the most important motives among their governments, are totally ignored in the model and therefore equally distort the conclusions.

ernments, will give a more accurate account of the way an international system operates than a study using prejudicial language derived from a foreign discipline.

There is another built-in distortion. By focusing attention exclusively on the "system" and the needs of that system, such theories induce the assumption that the behavior of individual components, that is, nations and governments, must be conditioned by that system rather than by any internal decisions or motives of their own. In distinguishing the relative weight to be attached to the influence of the external environment and of the internal forces within each state, these theories thus balance the scales overwhelmingly and unjustifiably in favor of the former. For this reason such theories are, at least by implication, highly conservative, for they encourage the assumption that, since it is the system which determines actions, nations must simply learn to live within the system and to play the rules more skillfully than their rivals.

Again the theory makes no allowance for variations among the motives of *different* members of the system. It takes little account of the different *means* that may be employed to achieve even the same ends; for example, coercive or concessive, political, military, or economic, threat or persuasion, and so on. It tends to assume that there is no significant difference in the way the game is played between governments, between regions, between different periods, according to different weapon technology, different communication systems, or different conceptions of international law and morality. Finally, perhaps more basic than any of these, the theory does not *tell* us anything: The conclusions it draws are entirely tautological, derived from the assumptions built into the model in the first place. What you take out depends on what you put in. The fact is that such models will give accurate results only if every significant detail of the real world were built into the model; in this case it might be simpler to study the real world itself.[23]

Many of these criticisms apply not only to systems theory, but to any kind of metaphoric theory. They will tell us more about the subject of the metaphor than about the international system itself. For example, the type of theory which seeks to compare international relationships with those within an economic system can find tempting analogies between the forms of competition, contest, and bargaining which take place in the economic marketplace and those which occur in dealings between nations,[24] but introduces distortions of its own. The assumption that nations carefully calculate their actions to maximize profit; that "power" is a currency which can buy followers; that war in real life is easily comparable to a trade war; all these distort reality rather than illuminate it. The differences between the two types of systems are profound. And even the ways in which governments calculate their interest in the two cases are totally diverse. Thus there is a likelihood, in this as in other cases, of importing false assumptions or concepts, derived from the metaphor, into our view of international society.

Finally, there are some writings on international relations which belong to the

23. Professor Kaplan himself admits that "the absence of properly collected data does not permit incautious statements concerning 'fit' between theory and reality." But it is after all reality we are mainly concerned to know about.

24. Perhaps the most successful attempt of this kind is the brief essay by C. P. Kindleberger in

fifth type of theory we identified earlier: those intended to provide a conceptual *framework* for analysis rather than a bold set of propositions concerning the nature of relationships in international society. Such theories could have a significant role to play in developing a more sophisticated and carefully defined conceptual framework for the study of international relations. They have, however, so far been relatively sketchy and unsystematic in scope. They do not get very far beyond the traditional type of analysis in terms of balance of power, competitive influence, contests among ideological and economic interest groups, and so on, which has been current for many years. Such works have not for the most part attempted any systematic survey and classification of the phenomena of international relations, nor attempted to draw general conclusions relating to them. And it is perhaps towards a more systematic analysis of this kind that the discipline now most needs to proceed.[25]

This type of theory faces one fundamental difficulty: how to find the framework, how to identify the concepts and factors that are of most fundamental importance in the analysis of international relationships in a way that will command general consent? Even a theory with this relatively modest aim must hope to point up, in its choice of concepts and categories, certain key forces and variables whose significance has not been adequately recognized in the past. There has, perhaps, in recent years been some increase in cross-fertilization. Concepts drawn from other disciplines such as anthropology and social psychology have come to be employed more widely. Yet this has so far been on a somewhat scattered and unsystematic basis. And it cannot be said that there is so far any system of classification or categories—in other words, any theory of this fifth and limited type—which has begun to command widespread support among writers in the discipline.

All the types of theory we have identified, therefore, are represented in one form or another in modern writing on international relations. Each may have a role to play in increasing or deepening understanding. Yet it would be difficult to say that any of these writings has produced a widely accepted theoretical foundation, or has helped us much in answering the basic question with which we began: Does international relations need a theory, and if so, of what sort? It is to a consideration of this question that we must now once more return.

## 1.4 Theory and Practice

There is one basic characteristic of a good deal of the theoretical writing of the past twenty years which has aroused a certain degree of doubt, even despair,

---

*Theoretical Aspects*, ed. Fox., pp. 69–82. See also R. Tanter and R. Ullman, eds., *Theory and Policy in International Relations* (Princeton, 1972).

25. One of the better works of this type is K. J. Holsti, *International Politics: A Framework for Analysis* (Englewood Cliffs, 1967).

among some of those who have studied it, and has therefore encouraged a negative answer to our basic question.

A large proportion of the writing in this field has appeared so remote from the real world of international relations, as it has been practiced in modern times, that there has been some doubt about its value. It has usually been pitched at such a high level of abstraction that it has often been difficult to detect any close relationship between the language employed and the world of international affairs that has been under study. If this is theory, it has been felt, we do not need it. In other cases attention has been focused on minute observation of one or two small aspects of relations among states, and here too there has been some skepticism as to the wider relevance of such endeavors. And it is precisely this question of relevance which, in many fields of intellectual activity, from philosophy to the physical sciences, must be the ultimate test. However valid or well-proved a particular study or piece of research may be, does it relate to the *significant* aspect of the subject under consideration?

This is the first test we must apply to theory in this field: the test of significance. Is the subject matter discussed, the factor measured or studied, really the vital variable in determining the nature of the system, or in measuring behavior, which it is said to be? Is decision making, bargaining, systems maintenance, really the factor determining relations among states? Is the theory concerned with *general* factors influencing international relations or only with particular details?

Second, there is the test of significance in another sense. Is the theory concerned with the *real* world, with concrete phenomena, or is it at a level so lofty as to be hopelessly abstract and so irrelevant? The more abstract are the terms employed in any theory, the more certain we may be of saying something that cannot be refuted, but the less significant or new what is said will often be. A considerable proportion of the statements made in many textbooks on international relations are of this uncontroversial but essentially unilluminating kind. To say that "communication is an essential part of virtually every interaction process in the international scene" (to take a typical sentence from a recent work in this field) is no doubt true, but it does not seem to tell us much that we did not already know about the way international relations are undertaken. Virtually every sentence of this particular work, and of many others like it, share this somewhat empty character because they rigorously avoid the concrete and specific.

Another condition for a theory, therefore, is that there should be a clear relation between theory and practice. While we should not necessarily follow Marx in thinking of theory as a guide to action, we may nonetheless wish a theory to have some relationship to the real life situations we observe in our own international society. At the very least, we shall hope that it will assist in explaining the nature of that society and the behavior of nations and men within it. It may not invariably give us *more* information, but it must at least assemble, label, and focus information in a way which adds to our previous comprehension. It must give us a new insight, and a new comprehension, of the fundamental factors which influence conduct within international society.

A third condition is related. Our theory should be derived directly from observation, rather than from introspection or a priori logic. The causation should be fact-theory, rather than theory-fact, inductive rather than deductive. This is a condition of *persuasiveness*. The theory must convince us that it derives naturally from the facts of the universe as we have perceived them, rather than being an a priori invention which subsequently may or may not be proved by reference to certain carefully selected facts. This is virtually the reverse of the methodology now advocated by some writers of the ''scientific'' school in international relations. That methodology, based on stating a hypothesis and subsequently testing it, is indeed one that appears the reverse of scientific. In the physical sciences it may well be a valid method of proof (and not all science is proof) to state a hypothesis in specific terms before it is tested, though even here it has probably been arrived at in the first place, consciously or unconsciously, as the result of a prolonged period of observation. But even in the physical sciences this is primarily a method of setting out a proof, rather than of undertaking research. Newton did not formulate the theory of gravity as a hypothesis and then shake the apple tree to make the apple fall; he saw the apple fall, whether literally or metaphorically, and derived the theory of gravity from that fact. Darwin did not think up the theory of the Origin of Species and then sail round the world to find the evidence for it; he saw a great deal of evidence on his voyages and then built up the theory on that basis.

But in the social sciences, the priority of observation is all the more essential. For here the evidence is so confused, causation so complex and difficult to identify, and reliable experiment so difficult to undertake, that to state the answer before producing the evidence can only *appear,* whatever the reality, as a gross case of begging the question—of assuming from the outset what has to be proved. And indeed, in a number of works written on this principle, this is precisely what appears to have occurred. It is never difficult, among all the varied and sometimes conflicting evidence thrown up by international events, to discover some facts to support almost any theory that may be propounded. To *appear* convincing, as much as to possess objectivity, therefore, a straightforward examination of the evidence before any attempt to draw conclusions will usually prove a more persuasive method. It is this, the empirical approach, which is in reality the more scientific, and it is one of the oddities of some recent writing in this field that ''empirical'' becomes almost a term of abuse, identified with old-fashioned, square, unmethodological, and unscientific, and *contrasted* with the ''scientific'' method, with its highly unscientific and question-begging methodology.

But the final and most important condition which our theory must fullfill if it is to increase understanding, or to appear persuasive, is that it must take account of *all* factors. It is not enough to be relevant. It must be comprehensively relevant. It is not enough to show the relevance to the child's behavior and attainments of his environment, though much may indeed be explained in that way, if the effect is to blot out and ignore the relevance of heredity. It is not enough to find the biological evidence of human behavior if in doing so psychological, sociological, and much other evidence is ignored. *All* relevant facts must be accounted for.

It is in this respect above all that much recent writing on international relations is unconvincing. It has indeed identified many significant areas of study, and uncovered hopeful methods of approach. But much of it has tended to focus attention on a single facet of the international system, and to raise this to the level of a single key variable which can explain *everything:* the balance of power, the system of decision making, communication, the structure of the system, and so on. All of these may be important, but they are each only partial factors. The relations of states do not consist entirely of power relations. If they did, the analysis of their relationships would indeed be simple (and some of the simple theories concerning the balance of power, or bargaining principles, which have proved so unfruitful in practice might have had a greater relevance). The system of decision making may have some importance in determining the way states behave, but it seems unlikely that it is the *only* factor affecting a state's decisions, or the only aspect of international relations worth researching. It is precisely the complexity, many-sidedness, and irregularity of international relationships, and the many interacting features and forces which affect them—economic, political, and cultural, as well as military, interpersonal relations as well as intergovernmental, international companies and international opinion as well as national parties and pressure groups, informal understandings, agreements, and conventions as well as formal treaties and alliances, individual contacts and influences as well as national and group contacts—which give international relations their peculiar character and present some of the special difficulties (and fascination) of studying them.

This means that we must first seek to identify those areas of knowledge which are of prime relevance in providing a better understanding of international relationships. It is to the consideration of what those areas are that we must now turn.

# Chapter 2.   The Relevance of History

## 2.1 History and Social Science

The most important type of evidence to be taken into account in any persuasive theory of international relations, it is here suggested, is that provided by history. Most writing in this field has made some use of the evidence of history. Some of the earliest contributions to the study of international relations were mainly historical. Some were of the kind now somewhat disparagingly described as "diplomatic history": detailed accounts of particular episodes or phases of recent international relations. Others were studies of particular international institutions, such as the history of international organizations, international law, or war.[1] Still others were more wide-ranging histories of international politics during a particular period, usually with some attempt to draw conclusions or morals, such as E. H. Carr's two studies of international relationships during the interwar period.[2]

The recent fashion, however, has been to downgrade the importance of history as a source for international relations studies. Work of this kind has sometimes been regarded as the clumsy and uncertain groping of an infant discipline before it had achieved its mature status as a "science."[3] It has been held that the historical method is wholly different from that of international relations, being concerned merely with the competent ordering of facts rather than the more ambitious attempt at wide-ranging generalization of the latter discipline; with simple narrative rather than with broad conclusions. One writer has declared that:

1. See, e.g., L. Woolf, *International Government* (London, 1923); Q. Wright, *Study of War* (Chicago, 1942).
2. E. H. Carr, *The Conditions of Peace* (London, 1942); and *The Twenty Years' Crisis, 1919–39* (London, 1946).
3. Cf. C. McClelland, in *International Politics and Foreign Policy,* ed. J. N. Rosenau (New York, 1961), pp. 28–32; M. A. Kaplan, in *Contending Approaches to International Politics,* ed. K. Knorr and J. N. Rosenau (Princeton, 1969), p. 56; D. Vital, in ibid., p. 154; K. Thompson, "Towards a Theory of International Politics," *American Political Science Review* 49, no. 3, pp. 733–35.

The common method of the historian is to immerse himself as completely as possible in the data, and to work intensely until an arrangement and pattern of the materials become impressed upon his mind. The process of selection and interpretation, is, of course, a form of generalizing, but it is usually very limited and highly individualized. . . . The historian is frequently repelled by general statements which come from other fields and which are intended to explain the phenomena of a large number of time-place areas. . . . While historians *do* use theory, they have not, as a rule, accorded it much attention or respect.[4]

It is possible that not all historians would recognize this somewhat patronizing definition of their approach. Most historians are, for example, increasingly concerned with the methods of sociology, economics, art history, and other disciplines. Others might claim that, even as here described, the historical method could sometimes be a more convincing procedure for the drawing of general conclusions than the hypothesizing of the social scientist, who starts out with a thesis and then proceeds to find evidence from one source or another to support it. The historian could well hold that it was more reliable to concentrate first on an accurate assembly of the facts before seeking to order them into a theoretical framework, rather than to begin with the theory. And he might even claim that, if our test is the improvement of understanding, historical studies of particular events and periods can often do as much or more to increase our comprehension of the factors which have mainly influenced the course of international relations than the more schematic, but also, more question-begging, methods of the "scientist." The main reason for the downgrading of history is that it is the social scientists who have mainly dominated international relations studies in recent years. They have been brought up in other techniques, often derived in the first place from the study of national political systems: quantitative methods, survey techniques, systems analysis, content analysis, and so on. They have assumed these are the ones appropriate for international relations. In some cases they seem almost to be more concerned with the development of these *techniques* for research than with the actual stuff, the facts, of international relations.[5] They have usually had little training in history. They have sometimes appeared to despise the use of historical research, for any purpose other than testing, for the very reason that it was the method primarily used by earlier scholars.[6]

4. McClelland, in *International Politics*, ed. Rosenau, pp. 29–30.

5. "All that remains is for those in the scientific camp to shift from the digital to the analogue computer and recognize that every serious scholar's work is on the same continuum." J. D. Singer, in *Contending Approaches*, ed. Knorr and Rosenau, p. 86.

6. It is one of the unappetizing features of the protracted, bitter, and frequently childish wrangling which takes place between the so-called "scientific" school and others in the field of international relations, that the issues are frequently presented in highly tendentious terms: for example, as a struggle between "science" and "traditionalism," between "method" and "intuition," between "rigor" and "imagination" (to quote Professor Singer in ibid.) The important difference between the two schools, however, does not concern method ("nonscientists" are not necessarily either traditional, intuitive, or unrigorous). It concerns the relevant subject matter to be researched and analyzed. What arouses some disquiet among many works of the scientific school is the triviality, and apparent irrelevance, of the

Many of those brought up in the traditions of political science have therefore held that straightforward historical study was not a fruitful approach. It could not "prove" anything. "Unless scientific procedures are followed," it is said, "to the extent that subject-matter permits, intuitions cannot be fortified and science cannot grow. . . . To conduct . . . an investigation requires systematic hypotheses concerning the nature of the consequences of the variables. Only after these are made can past history be examined in a way that illuminates the hypotheses."[7] History for such writers comes in only at the end, almost as an afterthought, to verify assumptions that have already been made; in practice, the bulk of the space in most works of this type is devoted to describing the methodology and setting out the hypotheses, with the room allowed for describing the historical evidence for the hypotheses alarmingly small.[8]

The rather low place accorded to the study and knowledge of history in the contemporary approach to international relations is shown in its unimportant position in the teaching of international relations in most universities. Many courses and hours are devoted to the study of theoretical writings, but relatively few to the study of international history. Many books and articles are recommended to students on the current controversies concerning methodology, but relatively few on the relations among states in the eighteenth century, say, or on the history of diplomatic practice or of international law. The student is thus frequently expected to write at a relatively sophisticated level on some of the widest and deepest theoretical problems of international relationships at a time when his knowledge of international history remains almost nonexistent.[9]

International relations is thus in some ways somewhat at the stage in which sociology was thirty or forty years ago. At that time almost all books written on that subject were concerned, not with society and societies, but with sociology: the proper method of *studying* society and societies. Just as sociology has today progressed to more concrete examination of particular societies, social problems, and social situations, so international relations may now be in a position to proceed, on the basis of the techniques and concepts so far developed, to a more

---

"researchable" subjects chosen, their refusal to recognize that important new knowledge and insights may be revealed by other methods, together with considerable intolerance of all who do not share their own views.

7. Kaplan, in *Contending Approaches,* ed. Knorr and Rosenau, pp. 43–47.

8. In Professor Kaplan's well-known study, *System and Process in International Politics,* (New York, 1957), for example, the greater part of the book is devoted to discussing methodology. Virtually no space is given to testing the model systems described against historical facts, which perhaps partly accounts for the wide divergence, already noted, between the rules proposed for particular systems and those that have in fact operated in particular periods of the past.

9. The antihistorical bias of much of the teaching and writing in international relations of modern political science is accepted by some of the "scientists" themselves: "The fact is, unhappily, that the charge of being ahistorical is far from unfounded, and an appreciable fraction of the modernists do indeed restrict themselves to the study of only the most recent past or the more trivial problems. . . . Almost all training in political science (with perhaps the exception of political philosophy) is weak in historical depth. . . ." Singer, in *Contending Approaches,* ed. Knorr and Rosenau, p. 80.

systematic study of particular international societies. It seems unlikely that this can be done except on the basis of detailed and systematic historical research.

## 2.2 History as a Raw Material

Whatever techniques are used in analyzing it, history will always be the primary and basic *raw material* of international relations study. There is, after all, nothing else to study. All international relations of which we have knowledge are a part of history, even if only of last year's history. Any convincing hypothesis, theory, or concept can only be based on the knowledge derived from history.

It has often been recognized that in international relations, even more than in the other social sciences, experimentation and testing in the normal sense are impossible. Sociologists can set up small group situations which are not altogether remote from those which occur in real life. Psychologists can undertake tests of memory, perseverance, or conditioned reflexes, not only in rats but in human beings. But the student of international relations cannot experiment in any meaningful way with international situations. Simulation models, war games, and similar methods may have their value as *training,* in developing in a student a better awareness of the factors which decision makers must take into account in some international situations. But they cannot give us any information about the real world of international relations. Any conclusions drawn from them are only circular, deriving automatically from the rules and assumptions built into the model in the first place. These assumptions will always be infinitely more simple than the immensely complex situations of real life, with the huge range of influences which come to bear on each decision maker, ranging from the furthest point on the international horizon to political pressures in the home country, from the influence of conflicting interest-groups and personal animosities in the cabinet room to friction in his own home. If we want to identify the significant influences, and the amount of weight to be attached to each, we shall have to look at the real world itself, and not at imperfect copies of it: that is, at the evidence of history (including contemporary history).[10]

The evidence of history must always be used with caution, since the essential variables of one period or system are not necessarily those of another. There will always be important differences in the international environment, in domestic political pressures, in the motives and attitudes of those mainly involved, from one period to another. But it is precisely here that history can help. It may enable us to identify with greater precision the factors which have caused certain governments

10. It is somewhat surprising that, among the wide variety of techniques and methods used in the modern study of international relations, the systematic questioning of ex-diplomats and ex-statesmen, for example, about what were in their experience the decisive motivations and objectives in the formation of the foreign policy of their own and other governments, has not been more widely employed.

to behave in a particular way at a particular time, what determined the nature of the system, what were the crucial influences in each period. By noting and comparing the *differences* between the behavior, reactions, even the language of governments in different ages, we may detect some of the basic divergences between different international societies, and so the factors that determine their character (it is such a comparison this volume seeks to attempt). This in turn may enable us to consider whether the generalizations widely used in the discipline, concerning the "balance of power," the importance of economic motives, the tendency among nations to pursue power, have an absolute validity, or whether they are relative to other factors, if they have been truer in one period than another, and why. Whatever type of theory is being built, therefore, inductive or deductive, a set of generalizations or a framework for analysis, it will require constant and detailed testing against the reality of history in this way.

Above all, history can provide a much greater *volume* of knowledge about the factors determining the behavior of governments than we can usually have about the present. There are records of cabinet discussions and other documents (so far extraordinarily little used by students of international relations); these are not usually available for contemporary events, but can give a close insight into the factors that influenced important foreign policy decisions of the past. There is the evidence of the speeches and subsequent reminiscences of statesmen who were personally involved in important events of history: these too can provide important indications of the factors and influences which were mainly at work when particular decisions were reached (though in this case it will be important to take account of bias, faulty memory, vanity, and wishful thinking in interpreting these accounts). Finally, there is the record of events themselves: the pattern of history which itself, if analyzed in sufficient detail, can provide illuminating evidence concerning the significant variables, influences, and motivations at work within the international political system at each period.

If assembled and analyzed on a sufficiently systematic basis, these could together provide the raw material for the kind of framework for analyzing international relations which we are seeking; in other words, for improving our understanding of the behavior of nations within a given international society. A really detailed study, for example, of European politics in the ten years between 1904 and 1914,[11] or between 1929 and 1939, based on all three sources described above, but more sharply focused on particular problems than historians' studies, could undoubtedly lead to a much clearer understanding of the basic factors at work in that period, including much that would be relevant to the understanding of the behavior of nations in other periods. A systematic analysis of foreign office and cabinet records of the major governments of the nineteenth century, with the aim of analyzing the dominant motives and considerations governing policy decisions, could help resolve some of the problems concerning the central and crucial

---

11. L. Albertini's *Origins of the War of 1914* (London, 1952) provides the historical raw material for this but without the type of analysis international relations study requires.

questions of the discipline: those involving the motivation of states. So far this kind of work has been done only by historians, without the focus, concepts, and framework of international relations specialists. It is only when we possess a sufficient accumulation of thorough, detailed and carefully focused studies of this kind, using the appropriate concepts and so asking the appropriate questions, that we are likely to be able to reach any valuable generalizations about the underlying factors determining international relationships.

## 2.3  The Lessons of History

The evidence provided by history in this way can offer two main benefits. First we can learn, in the simplest and crudest way, the *direct* lessons history can teach. Direct lessons might be drawn, for example, from tracing the development of particular institutions, such as war, diplomacy, international law, or international institutions. In this way one might be able to discover the factors which mainly influenced the development of each—the patterns of their growth, reasons for growth, reasons for change, historical consequences, and above all the different roles or functions which each has played in different international societies. Again, the development of the system of relatively fixed alliances in the period after 1870 could be analyzed and compared with the preceding system, where alliances were far more transitory in nature. The factors in the international situation leading to the outbreak of war before 1914 could be compared with those leading to the outbreak of war in 1939. The relative success of policies of appeasement or deterrence in different periods of history could be compared; the reasons for the failure of the League of Nations could be analyzed and applied to the UN; the comparative success of policies of disarmament and arms competition in avoiding war in different periods could be assessed; and so on.

These are all examples of relatively direct conclusions which might be drawn from history, each of which could have an important bearing on general theoretical conclusions. Such studies can be deliberately focused to provide conclusions especially relevant to theory. They could be directed to comparing, for example, attitudes toward the balance of power, domestic and external political pressures, national security, international rules of conduct and so on, in differing international societies. Comparison of the different ways in which foreign policy is formulated in different countries and in different periods of history may lead to conclusions about the influence of methods of decision making on the type of policy conducted. Correlation of the level of arms in different periods with the incidence of war for the same periods may help us in reaching conclusions about whether the level of arms influenced the incidence of war. Thus any hypothesis or theory that depends on assumptions on such questions can be tested against empirical studies.

But the relevance of history may be more indirect. For example, an examination of the doctrines of international law in different periods may yield conclusions about differing conceptions of national rights and duties within these periods. Knowledge of the past evolution of a particular institution or practice, such as the UN Security Council, or diplomatic usage, may lead to conclusions about the way they may evolve in the future. In a sense a knowledge of the past is the essential background to all judgments about the present. Any study confined to the modern international system alone will lack the perspective required to draw worthwhile generalizations. Our knowledge of history may help us to judge what is relevant and what is irrelevant, to see which correlations are valid and which are not. When generalizations are made about the operation of a bipolar system or a balance of power system, it may be useful to judge the plausibility of these against the evidence of more ancient societies (such as that of the city-states in Greece, or the Warring States in China) as well as those of modern history.

One reason why there have not been more systematic attempts to draw conclusions from history in this way is that so few historians have been engaged in the discipline of international relations; when they have been, it has been in almost total isolation from the work of the political scientists. Even so, it is arguable that in some cases it is the works of historians[12] which have provided the most revealing insights for international relations specialists—sometimes more so than the work of those more directly involved in that field. Though such works may not analyze the essential variables so systematically, they do often examine many of the same problems which have been the concern of those involved in international relations studies, and their conclusions are of direct relevance to the research of the latter.

In attempting to build up a systematic body of theory in this field, therefore, the lessons of the past are as important as those of the present.

## 2.4 History as the Basis for Comparison

The final advantage of the historical approach in the study of international relations is that it enables us to *compare*.

This function is particularly important in attempting to develop a theory of international relations. Some of those involved in this task assume that there are certain absolute rules which govern the relations among states at all times and in all places.[13] In the words of Professor Morgenthau quoted in the preceding chapter,

12. For example, such works as E. V. Gulick's *Europe's Classical Balance of Power System* (Ithaca, 1955); A. J. P. Taylor's *Germany and the Struggle for Mastery in Europe* (Oxford, 1954); and W. L. Langer's two volumes on *European Alliances* and *The Diplomacy of Imperialism* (New York, 1951 and 1956).

13. It is one of the disappointing features of Raymond Aron's otherwise brilliant *Peace and War* (London, 1966) that throughout he makes general and unqualified statements about the behavior of nations, as though these were unvarying attributes and propensities which did not change significantly from one international age to another.

they seek "empirically verifiable general truths, sought for their own sake, which can depict the rational essence of its subject matter." This view seems to be based on the idea that there are certain fundamental characteristics of states and their relationships that do not change significantly from one age to another.

The assumption of the present work is precisely the opposite. It is that nations, like individuals, are socially conditioned; their character varies radically accordingly to the international society to which they belong, and to the international social pressures which therefore influence them. Their behavior will alter widely from one age to another with changes in that environment. For a theory of this kind history is especially important, for it must be concerned above all with *comparison*. We are concerned to identify the variables which have mainly influenced the character of different international societies, and so the behavior of nations within them. Only by examining different systems in different periods can we trace the main factors differentiating them and causing the differing behavior of states within them.

Certain features occur in every international society, yet can also differ significantly from one to another. These include the system of communications, the weapons technology, the system of diplomatic intercourse, economic relationships, methods of political influence, institutions, and international rules. In tracing the changes that take place in each of these, and correlating them with changes of other kinds, it may be possible to reach significant conclusions about the role of each factor. It may even become possible to analyze the causes of basic transformations of the system. One factor which may be particularly significant, and about which we shall be especially concerned, for example, involves widespread patterns of belief about the legitimate aspirations and goals of states, about the obligations of states, about the authority to be accorded to international institutions, and so on. Another concerns the sociological structure of each unit within the system. The changes noted in these two factors can be examined in relation to changes in the other features mentioned earlier; patterns in the development of international law, for example, may be correlated with changes in social structure or external relationships.

Another point that will concern us here is the variations in the *speed* of change of different factors. For example, we will wish to see whether changes in communication, and therefore in personal contacts, outpace changes in traditional conceptions of relations among states, diplomatic procedures, rules of war, and so on. We may wish to compare the pace of changes in weapons technology with ethical conceptions about the nature or legitimacy of war; to compare changes in economic relationships with changes in political relationships; and so on. In this comparison we shall wish to notice where there are *vestiges*, attitudes and ideas inherited from a previous international society, which continue to exert a considerable influence on thought, even though their original cause may have largely disappeared.

In a word, just as anthropologists may need to select certain key variables, such as the kinship system, marriage rules, religion, stratification, and so on, in undertaking their examination of particular contemporary societies, so international relations theory may need the aid of certain key concepts in a *historical* comparison of international societies.

Even if our interest in international relations were directed entirely at one international society, say the present, the study of the past would still be important. For at all times the past is an important part of the present. International actors today are at least to some extent prisoners of their predecessors, acting always in the shadow of history. They are brought up in traditions, memories, and practices inherited from earlier times which will vitally affect the way they look at the world and the way they behave. Thus to understand the underlying causes of actions and attitudes today, we may need to study those of the past. Only by a better understanding of previous international societies are we likely to be able to improve understanding of our own.

# Chapter 3.　The Relevance of Psychology

## 3.1 The Psychology of Individuals

Our theoretical framework, however, must take account of *all* relevant factors. And there is another discipline whose findings may be important to us in studying international society: the study of psychology.

This results automatically from the fact that all those ultimately involved in international relationships are human beings. Government leaders who make the decision to declare war or to enter into negotiations, diplomats and foreign office officials who compile the reports which influence those decisions, ordinary citizens who urge their governments to stand firm or to seek revenge, traders and directors of multinational corporations exercising their influence behind the scenes, are all human creatures, subject to the normal passions and prejudices, frailties and foibles, of other human beings. In any attempt to discover the basic factors at work determining relations among states, the psychological factors which influence human attitudes and decisions are thus important to us.

It is true that, in many of their actions which affect international relationships, such individuals may be performing a collective role on behalf of their group, and will thus be influenced by collective relationships, collective ambitions, and collective attitudes, rather than by individual drives. But here too psychology is important in helping us to understand collective sentiments and drives, what binds men to groups, why they conceive the interests of their group in the way that they do, why they choose one decision rather than another for their group, how the groups see each other, and how far individual reactions may diverge from group reactions. Here it is the findings of social psychology we shall need. At a wider level still, psychology can tell us something about the nature of mankind as a whole, the basic motivations and drives within men, and so of how they may behave as members of an international society.

The importance of psychology for any theory of international relations was at one time taken for granted. Even in classical writings on the subject, a consideration of psychological factors is at least implicit. In Kant's *Perpetual Peace* and Rousseau's *A Lasting Peace Through the Federation of Europe,* for example, assumptions are made about human nature: that the character of man is such that, given the right institutional framework, human societies can live in peace with one another on a lasting basis. Conversely, the writings of Machiavelli and Hobbes are based on opposite psychological assumptions: that man is by nature competitive, insecure, weak, treacherous, and potentially violent, so that only a tightly organized state, under a supreme absolute ruler pursuing a policy of ruthless self-interest at home and abroad, is likely to be able to maintain its position within international society. Forty or fifty years ago there was still greater interest in psychological factors. A considerable number of books then sought the basic causes of war among states in human psychology.[1] The establishment of UNESCO after 1945 to root out the causes of war by improving understanding and communication among states reflected this point of view.

With a few exceptions, recent writing in international relations has been little concerned with psychological factors. There has been a small amount of writing by social psychologists.[2] Study of psychological factors does not figure widely, if at all, in current teaching of international relations. And a large proportion of the writing in this field seeks to abstract from any consideration of individual, or even group, feelings and motives. The state or the system are the basic units under consideration.

There are a number of reasons for this. First, national behavior is often seen as the action of "states" or "governments" conceived as abstract entities rather than sets of individual human beings. Second, there is a general assumption in much of the writing that most of the decisions reached by governments, at least in the modern international system, are rational, based on a clear appreciation of national interests and the intentions and capabilities of other nations: it is thus sufficient to understand those interests and capabilities, without regard to the psychology of individuals, to know how nations will and should behave. Third, widespread acceptance of the "systems" approach, and so the assumption that the behavior of states is largely conditioned by the external system, especially the power relationships within it, downgrades the human factor: personal psychological traits and even group pressures become of minor significance in relation to the more basic external forces emanating from the system. Fourth, the assumptions of the realist school that most state actions can be explained by the propensity of states to pursue security and power, regardless of the type of government or leadership involved, encourage a somewhat similar disregard for individual psychological factors. Fifth, even advocates of the "decision-making" approach, and similar microsys-

---

1. For example, E. F. M. Durbin, *Personal Aggressiveness and War* (New York, 1939); J. Dollard et al., *Frustration and Aggression* (New Haven, 1939); M. May, *A Social Psychology of War and Peace* (New Haven, 1943); R. West, *Psychology and World Order* (London, 1945); T. M. Newcomb and E. L. Hartley, eds., *Readings in Social Psychology* (New York, 1947); T. H. Pear, ed., *Psychological Factors in Peace and War* (New York, 1950); O. Klineberg, *Tensions Affecting International Understanding* (New York, 1950). These are only a few among a considerable number of such works in that period.

2. For example, H. C. Kelman, ed., *International Behavior: A Social Psychological Analysis* (New York, 1965).

tem studies, though they do not discount psychological factors altogether, tend to assume that decisions are influenced far more by institutional factors such as the relationship between government agencies, procedures for consultation, systems of communication, and the influence of pressure groups, than by any feature of individual psychology.

Finally, and perhaps more important than any of these, there is once again the fact that most writing in this field is undertaken by political scientists. These have little experience in psychology. Their training in modern political science often does not incline them to attach high importance to psychological factors in international any more than in national politics (again a striking difference from the situation thirty or forty years ago). It is thus perhaps not altogether surprising that they have not afforded a large role for the findings of psychology within their theories.

But the evidence of psychology is important to international relations theory, and at three different levels which correspond to the three levels of analysis we have already identified. At the lowest level of analysis, the psychology of individuals within a nation, especially of leaders and other decision makers, and the influence of this on their perceptions of international society and on decisions in foreign policy, is significant in its effect on international relationships. Group psychology, above all that of the nation, and the effect of group loyalties such as nationalism in determining the course of international relations, is important in analyzing the moods and actions of national states. Finally, the psychology of humanity as a whole, the degree to which men are influenced by an "aggressive drive," and the effect of this in leading men to warfare, is important at the level of analysis directed to studying the system as a whole. Evidence at all three levels may be important in helping us to answer some of the most fundamental problems of international relations: What are the factors which lead men to make decisions in favor of war in certain situations? How far are their perceptions of their own situation at moments of crisis realistic and rational, or distorted and emotional? Are some kinds of individuals or groups more peaceful than others? What kinds of institutions within or among nations are most likely to lead to a more peaceful and harmonious international society?

Let us consider each of these levels in turn. The psychology of *individuals* can be important in determining international relationships in a number of ways.

First, there can be little question that the course of international relations can be considerably affected by the mental attitudes and ways of thoughts of particular decision makers who play a leading role in the conduct of international affairs: dictators and other personal leaders, foreign ministers, members of a cabinet, diplomats, and senior civil servants. The character of an individual prime minister or foreign minister (say Palmerston or Bismarck), of a nationalistic ruler (Napoleon III or Kaiser Wilhelm II), the intransigent but influential foreign policy adviser (such as Holstein or Vansittart), the autocratic or obtuse ambassador (Stratford Canning or Neville Henderson), all these can have a considerable or direct influence on the course of history. Where individual rulers wield a high degree of personal power, psychological factors are obviously especially vital. The mentality of such men as Frederick the Great, Napoleon, and Hitler, to name only a few, has clearly had an important effect, not only in determining the foreign policy of their own countries, but in influencing the international system as a whole in their day. Even in recent times, the control of foreign policy in most states is in the hands of a tiny group of individuals, and in many cases of a single autocrat. The personality of a Nasser, a Sukarno, a Khrushchev, or a Mao has had a decisive influence on contemporary international relations. Even in democratic countries, differences between the personalities of an Eisenhower or a Kennedy, an Adenauer or a Brandt, an Attlee or an Eden, can exert a considerable impact on foreign policy, and so on the international scene as a whole. The understandable desire of most writers on international relations today to abstract from the individual case, to be able to reach broad generalizations, has no doubt encouraged the neglect of personality factors of this kind. This does not prove that they are of no significance.

Sometimes it may not be so much the influence of a particular leader which is the decisive factor, but that of a group of leaders, in one or a number of countries at a particular moment in time. If, in June–August 1914, for example, individuals of different attitude and temperament had been in power all over Europe, how much difference would it have made to the decisions reached? If Germany and Austria had had chancellors of stronger personality, more willing to resist the urgings of their generals and to impose their own will on events, would the outcome have been different? In a more general way, if some national leaders seek to protect national interests by negotiation alone, while others determine to protect them by armed force, is this only from differences of circumstances, or are personalities also significant? Are some, by temperament, more inclined to think in terms of achieving their aims by *coercive* means, by pressure, bluster, or force, and others to think naturally in terms of securing them *concessively,* by bargaining, persuasion, and goodwill? These are important questions which have a considerable bearing on the central problems of international relations. Yet they tend to be ignored by much writing in the field.

Again, we need to know if there are differences in the attitudes and personality traits of individuals in entire national *groups*. It may be important to know, for example, whether there are differences between the personality profiles and attitudes of military and of civilian leaders, or between young officers and older ones, and whether these may be of importance in accounting for differences in foreign policies. Should the differing external policies of conservative and progressive parties be accounted for partly by reference to personality factors, as well as to intellectual beliefs, just as many political writers tend to associate highly authoritarian political beliefs with a particular type of personality?[3] Leaders and leadership groups might be analyzed and an attempt made to correlate attitudes on

3. T. W. Adorno, et al., *The Authoritarian Personality* (New York, 1950); M. B. Smith, J. S. Bruner, and R. W. White, *Opinion and Personality* (New York, 1956).

external affairs with other personality factors. There are a number of other contrasting psychological traits which may have an influence in determining foreign policy attitudes and behavior: inflexibility against imagination (Dulles and Mendès-France), caution against risk taking (Stalin and Khrushchev), cynicism against idealism (Clemenceau and Wilson), egotism against considerateness (Palmerston and Salisbury), ambition against humility (Napoleon III and Louis Philippe). Leaders (or advisers) possessing flexibility and imagination are more likely to be able to adjust their foreign policies to changing circumstances than those who are inflexible or highly ambitious. Those who are cynical are less likely than those who are idealistic to put much faith in the assurances of other states, or in the effectiveness of international institutions. These traits will influence not only the leaders' own policies but the entire international system of the age.[4]

A number of writers have attempted to identify the fundamental personality traits which influence political attitudes within states. Harold Lasswell showed in his early books[5] some of the factors related to early upbringing and childhood experiences which affect political attitudes, including attitudes to foreign countries and peoples. A study undertaken at the University of California tested a somewhat similar thesis on a more scientific basis.[6] Professor Eysenck, the British psychologist, concluded that there were two fundamental scales according to which all individuals could be measured: one indicating the level of authoritarianism as against liberalism, the other measuring conservatism (resistance to change) as against progressivism.[7] In general, high scores in authoritarianism and conservatism (which are not always associated together) are likely to be correlated with a high degree of nationalism, hostility toward other nations, and hostility toward international organizations. A more systematic attempt to correlate attitudes on foreign affairs with personality factors—for example, seeking to show how far foreign policy attitudes were related to the influence of national and international society as a whole, to early childhood experiences and training, particular social classes, or to innate elements of personality—could be of importance for the study of international politics.

The findings of psychotherapy and psychoanalysis may also be relevant. The concept of *projection*—the imputing of feelings, attitudes, and aggressive intentions present in oneself to other people—might be shown to take place among nations as well as among individuals. That is, the members of one nation may attribute to the members of another the aggressive attitudes which they feel themselves. The concept of *paranoia,* the belief in a complex conspiracy of hostile forces all around, often associated with delusions of grandeur, may be reflected on

4. The only attempt known to the present writer to trace the influence of statesmen's personalities on their foreign policy is contained in P. Renouvin and J. B. Duroselle, *Introduction to the History of International Relations* (New York, 1964).

5. H. Lasswell, *Psychopathology and Politics* (Chicago, 1930) and *World Politics and Personal Insecurity* (New York, 1935).

6. Adorno et al., *Authoritarian Personality*.

7. H. J. Eysenck, *The Psychology of Politics* (London, 1955).

the international scene, not only in the abnormal behavior of a Hitler or a Stalin, but in the more common belief among many national leaders in such things as "communist conspiracy" or "capitalist encirclement," in the hysteria of the McCarthy era in the U.S. or in the "antirevisionist" witchhunt in China. The finding that the aggressive feelings of individuals frequently result from a situation of frustration could also be shown to have application to the behavior of nations; for example, the aggressive nationalism of prewar Germany, Japan, and Italy might be accounted for partly by their sense of frustration that the previous settlement had not accorded them the international status they believed to be their desert.

Such findings concerning individual attitudes and sentiments are important to the theory of international relations for a number of reasons. They can help to test the validity of a number of partial theories. Strategic theory, theories of threat and deterrence, can be judged only by reference to the findings of psychology on individuals responses to threats: If it could be shown that a threat sometimes evokes an irrational response, a mood of resentment and hostility, rather than a sober assessment of interest and a decision to submit or to treat, some of the assumptions of strategic theory might have to be rethought. We might have to conclude that the uttering of certain types of threats in certain situations may be irrational, just as the angry flashing of headlights to counter the headlights of an oncoming car may be irrational, though understandable. In both cases the reaction may only blind the respondent and make him more likely to do damage. Similarly, decision-making theory can be tested against psychological knowledge of the factors which mainly influence decisions within small groups. For example, evidence that members of such groups are more influenced by the attitudes and information they take in from their everyday institutional environment than they are by what they hear within occasional mixed consultative groups might indicate that there is more likely to be agreement between representatives of a foreign office and a defense department if contacts are taking place all the time and at every level, than if they meet only at rare intervals within the cabinet room.

These findings of psychology will be particularly important if we conclude that, as is suggested in this work, the culture of the international society as a whole is one of the most important factors determining foreign policy attitudes and behavior. The findings of individual psychology will then be important in determining exactly how such influences are brought to bear on the citizen and how they vary from one international society to another in their effect.

## 3.2 The Psychology of Groups

The second type of psychological evidence which is relevant for the theory of international relations is group psychology: study of the attitudes and mentality of whole societies, races, and above all, nations.

Here it is relevant to know first whether there are basic *differences* between the foreign policy attitudes of different races or nations. Though the old-fashioned stereotypes of "national character"—"arrogant Germans," "cynical French," "perfidious British," "suspicious Russians," or "militaristic Japanese"—are fortunately now largely discredited, it remains of interest to know how far there are in fact significant differences in attitude among peoples of different nationalities: whether there is any variation, for example, in the average level of aggressiveness, insularity, hostility toward foreigners, or sense of racial superiority among members of different nations. If significant differences were found on any important foreign policy attitude, it might then be possible to see whether there is a correlation between this and the foreign policies pursued by that state. Similarly, it would be of interest to know whether attitudes of this kind were the same among the mass of the population as among elites and decision makers. Finally, there could be value in knowing if there were variations in attitude between different types of decision-making groups: for example, between foreign affairs and defense department officials within the same nation.

Again, there would be advantage in knowing how such attitudes vary over *time*. If the same tests were repeated, say, every five years among the same populations, we could see what changes there had been in that time. This in turn could make it possible to judge how far these were correlated with changes in the external situation of a country, the tone and content of mass media, changes in the international environment as a whole, changes in leadership, or other factors. We could assess whether, as some have supposed, an increase in contacts and communications among groups automatically causes mutual images to become more favorable. Such evidence is particularly relevant to any study which seeks to analyze and compare different international societies, for it might help us to assess which group attitudes and emotions vary from one age to another, and which are relatively fixed and unvarying in all international environments.

One type of information which would be relevant here would be a comparison among *nations* on the conservative-progressive, authoritarian-liberal scales we mentioned earlier. If these are fundamental scales of personality, as has been suggested, are there differences between the proportion of, say, Russians and Americans, Africans or Chinese, exhibiting liberal or authoritarian, conservative or progressive attitudes? And if there are such differences, do they really derive from basic genetic differences or are they the result of cultural factors influencing personality type?

Clearly group psychological attitudes vary, like those of individuals, not only from people to people, but from situation to situation. This makes it necessary to try to disentangle the effect of the two factors. How far is the behavior of Germany in the 1930s to be attributed to the fact that Germans were involved, and how far to the *situation* (defeat in war, forced disarmament, forced admission of war guilt, reparations payments, and national humiliation) that preceded this involvement? Are there particular types of situations—such as when a vital communications link is threatened, as for Britain in 1956 or for Israel in 1967—which arouse an especially violent group reaction? There is some evidence that there do exist clearly defined group emotions which correspond to different group situations. The collective *humiliation* of a nation through defeat (as of France in 1940, China in 1895–1898, or Germany in 1918), a collective *threat* to security (as to the Soviet Union in 1956 and 1968 or to the U.S. in 1962 and 1965), a collective *insult* (as to France in 1870), a collective *challenge* (as to Austria in 1914), can arouse group reactions of a very powerful and surprisingly homogeneous kind among the populations concerned, regardless of nationality—reactions not unlike those which might be seen among individuals in comparable situations.[8]

It is, of course, not surprising that nations often behave in much the same way as individuals might in similar situations. For nations are composed of individuals, each of whom conceives the situation of his nation almost as a personal situation, a threat to the nation is a threat to himself, a humiliation to the nation is a humiliation to himself. And it is natural that he will seek to respond in his collective capacity in much the same way that he will in his personal capacity. He must ward off the collective threats, avenge the collective humiliation, respond to the collective challenge. A single decision maker, a small group in a cabinet, or an entire population may therefore sometimes feel and behave in a strikingly similar way in similar situations. But there will still be some differences, both within and between nations, and we need to know the reasons for these.

A fair amount of surveying of group and class attitudes on foreign affairs has been undertaken by some social scientists.[9] The Norwegian social scientist, Galtung, found in comparing foreign policy attitudes among social classes that the "central" strata of society, that is, those high in education, knowledge, occupation, wealth, and status, were not significantly different from those elsewhere in the *content* of their opinions on the main issues. But they were more pragmatic and gradualist on ways of achieving goals, as against the absolutist demand among the rest for everything now; they were more consistent in attitude than those at the periphery (who were probably less able to see the relationship between two different questions); were more aware of means; and were less willing to conceive of goals without regard to the means and the costs.[10] This more "rational" approach is perhaps what might have been expected among a more intelligent and knowledgeable section of a population, but it is the type of finding which can assist understanding of the psychology of groups engaged in international relationships. For the most part, such surveys have not been sufficiently sharply focused on the kinds of questions that are of interest to the international relations specialist to

8. For a study of group psychology and its relation to international relations, see Kelman, *International Behavior*. See also Evan Luard, *Conflict and Peace in the Modern International System*, (Boston, 1968), pp. 54–59.

9. For example, B. Christianson, *Attitudes Towards Foreign Affairs As a Function of Personality* (Oslo, 1969); L. Free, *Six Allies and a Neutral* (Glencoe, 1959); J. N. Rosenau, *Public Opinion and Foreign Policy* (New York, 1964); Yale Political Research Library, *West European Attitudes on International Problems, 1952–61* (New Haven, 1963); J. Galtung, "Foreign Policy Opinion As a Function of Social Position," *Journal of Peace Research*, 1965. Many opinion poll results have been published in *Public Opinion Quarterly*.

10. Galtung, "Foreign Policy Opinion."

assist in the formulation of theories. They certainly have not yet determined whether there is any correlation between the attitudes revealed among populations and the foreign policies pursued by governments. Nor have they yet identified significant differences among important groups—for example, among foreign office officials, defense department officials, politicians, businessmen, trade unionists, supporters of different ideologies, or parties in one or a number of countries.

If we are concerned with international societies and what determines their shape, as here, group attitudes of this kind are obviously of special importance. This applies especially to the most significant group attitude affecting relations among states in modern times, that known as "nationalism." Powerful nationalist feelings have often been regarded as one of the main factors influencing the likelihood of war between states. It has been held that in most countries the social environment generally, the exaltation of "patriotism" and national duty, symbols such as the flag, the crown, the uniform, and the national anthem, the slogans, pressures, and traditions surrounding the nation, have served to promote fanatical loyalty to the citizen's own state and irrational hostility toward others. A study of this phenomenon could show some of the processes by which nationalistic mentality and attitudes are inculcated; in other words, the process of socialization which takes place in different types of national and international society.

Nationalism is clearly largely a *cultural* factor, the strength and force of which depends on influences within each national culture, the influences of the educational system, the mass media, the speeches of political leaders, and so on. But it may also be influenced by the wider international culture, the traditions and expectations of the international society as a whole: nationalism in one country is influenced by the intensity of nationalism in others, and the example of nationalistic attitudes and actions in the world as a whole. Such factors influence not only the intensity of nationalist and other group loyalties but also the form they take. National ambitions can be channeled by the international culture in many different directions: into demands for military adventures, or for higher economic growth; for a bigger air force budget, or for a bigger educational budget; for successes on the football field, or for successes in the arts; for military expansion, or political, economic, or cultural expansion. It is here that the difference between international societies of different periods or places may be greatest in its effect, guiding and channeling national ambitions in particular paths. It is thus important to us in this study to know what determines the differing directions in which different societies promote national ambitions.[11]

Nationalism is, however, only one of a number of group loyalties and attitudes which affect international relations. In the sixteenth and seventeenth centuries the loyalties of religion were in many ways more important than those of nationality. In Greek times, and again in recent times, ties of ideology were as significant as

11. For a discussion of different types of nationalist feelings, see W. C. Olson, in *The Theory and Practice of International Relations,* ed. W. C. Olson and F. A. Sonderman (Englewood Cliffs, 1966).

allegiance to city or nation. In the early years of this century class loyalty could be almost as important as national allegiance. And increasingly today there are loyalties to the continent, or to the race, which can overlay and sometimes counteract those to the nation (compare Egyptian patriotism and Arab nationalism). It is the exact mix and relative intensity of these different loyalties, and the different ways in which they can influence the same individual which may need to be studied in determining the character of a particular international society.

This leads to a still wider psychological problem. Even if, as this evidence suggests, neither aggression nor nationalism are necessarily universal and unvarying attributes of human nature, is *some* form of group loyalty an essential consequence of all social existence? And must this inevitably lead to sentiments of hostility, or even acts of hostility, toward other groups?[12] Even if nationalism were to decline as a significant element in inducing conflict within the international society, therefore, must it inevitably be replaced by some wider loyalty (regionalism, for example) which could be just as significant a cause of conflict in the future? Or are the wider loyalties which exist today, to ideology, race, or continent, themselves only the product of temporary cultural conditions which do not necessarily presuppose permanent group hostility, let alone armed conflict between the relevant groups?

In devising any general theory about the working of the international system, it is essential to take into account such evidence as the drives, emotions, and frustrations of groups. Strong evidence that group attitudes and actions were heavily influenced by irrational factors, such as feelings of insecurity or hostility to other groups, might lessen the plausibility of those theories—such as strategic and games theory—which presuppose a rational response by one group to another. Strong evidence that the main factor conditioning group sentiments and beliefs concerning national conduct derive from the international rather than the national environment would lend greater plausibility to those theories which stress the macrosystem rather than the microsystem. Strong evidence that leadership groups are more influenced by prevailing moods among their populations than by conceptions of the power balance in reaching decisions would affect the validity of "balance of power" theories. Evidence that there were significant differences between the degree of hostility toward other nations felt by the populations of different countries, and that these were correlated with standard of living or with the involvement of their nations in war, would have significant implications for theory.

Any attempt to consider and compare the working of international societies therefore requires some study of group attitudes and sentiments as well as those of individuals.

12. Cf. N. Grodzins, in *Theory and Practice*, ed. Olson and Sonderman, p. 64. "Loyalties are a part of every individual's life because they serve his basic needs and functions. They are a part of his indispensable habit patterns. Loyalties provide him with a portion of that framework through which he organizes his existence. . . . Without the aid and comfort of these group ties, an individual will find existence impossible."

## 3.3  The Psychology of Mankind as a Whole

There is still a third type of evidence which psychology can provide that is important in the study of international relations. This is that which relates to the psychological makeup of humanity as a whole.

Political theory has always been influenced by differing conceptions of the "nature" of man. In earlier times most such theories began with statements, more or less dogmatic, concerning that nature: man was "by nature" social or antisocial, cooperative or competitive, "good" or "bad," and so on. These presuppositions conditioned, or at least justified, the conclusions drawn concerning the type of political system which men therefore required. Mencius believed that man was good and favored one system of government, Han Fei-tsu believed that he was bad and favored another. Aristotle believed that man was a social (or "civic") creature and favored one form of government, Plato that he was potentially antisocial and favored another. Such presuppositions concerning man's nature are equally important in relation to international relations.

It has, for example, been widely declared that men possess natural "aggressive" drives, and that these are the fundamental cause of war among states. Some of the classical writing in this field is based on such assumptions, whether explicitly or implicitly. From Han Fei-tsu to Hegel, from Hobbes to Herbert Spencer, there have been many who have felt that man's natural instinct to fight made war an inevitable feature of his existence, and that governments must frame their policy on the assumption of a never-ending struggle for survival among nations. In modern times, too, psychological theories of aggression have sometimes been used to show that organized warfare was a natural condition of man.[13] The findings of animal ethologists have been used, often with scant regard for scientific method, to show that men inevitably share the tendencies of (some) animals to engage in a ruthless struggle for survival, or that there exists among them a "territorial imperative" which dictates an implacable struggle among humans for living space. Such studies have exercised a certain fashionable appeal. But they are based on the highly simplistic assumption that there exists a direct analogy between the nature of animals and of humans, and so between human societies and animal societies. There is in fact no evidence that the behavior of other species can provide any guide to the behavior that is "natural" to man. Even if there were, those species most closely related to man, the primates, provide precisely the opposite conclusion: They are mainly neither "aggressive" nor warlike in their normal existence. They never initiate conflict with other species. Being mainly migratory, they can certainly not be termed to have in any proper sense a "territorial" instinct (any more than can the simplest, gathering human

13. For a survey of this literature, see E. B. McNeil, "Psychology and Aggression," *Journal of Conflict Resolution* 3 (1959):195–293.

societies which we know today). Finally, there are few animal species which, like men, systematically kill other members of their *own* species. Far from reflecting animal "nature," therefore, it is the abnormality and *unlikeness* to animals of human behavior in this respect which requires explaining.

Nor do the findings of psychology provide any better foundation for the belief that men's "aggressive" characteristics, assuming they exist, must inevitably find expression in organized warfare. The degree to which men exhibit aggressive tendencies varies widely. It appears to depend on a number of factors, including early childhood experiences, parental affection, peer-group socialization, and the social environment as a whole, as well as immediate situations. Many individuals show very low aggressive drives. If aggression is present at all, it is more likely to take the form of careerism or cantankerousness than a desire to kill other human beings. Often it is sublimated into other channels altogether. Thus whatever "natural" tendency men may have toward aggression, there is nothing that suggests that that tendency must find expression in organized warfare (the outbreak of which is in any case wholly outside the control of the vast majority in most societies). The fact that there are many primitive societies which are known to have lived in a state of peace, a number of modern nations which have existed for centuries without war, and still more individuals who never fight in war, is itself sufficient proof that there is nothing in man's "nature" which inevitably condemns him to a state of war.

This suggests that war is in fact a *cultural* factor, which derives from the influences, traditions, and institutions of the human environment over the past two or three millennia, rather than from any feature of man's innate disposition. Organized warfare has, during this period, been sanctified as a recognized institution. It has come to appear as a "normal" activity. In certain national situations of grievance or resentment, where "wrongs" have been inflicted or "rights" denied, war has been accepted as a natural and acceptable response. This implies that simpleminded generalizations concerning man's "inevitable" tendencies, whether to war or to peace, cannot have validity. For man may be capable of many different natures according to the character of the society into which he is born and the socialization to which he is subject. Since the individual today suffers many pains and penalties in war, and gains from it very few satisfactions, it is highly improbable that he is "naturally" impelled to it. If, nonetheless, war is made, it is more likely to be because of *external* influences coming from the international society within which men live.

Such conclusions, like those which may be reached concerning group motives and attitudes, are important for any attempt to build a satisfactory theory of international relations. Just as political theories have from time immemorial been based on particular conceptions of man's nature, so must international theory take account of the best available knowledge concerning the nature of man and of groups. If it is true that man's nature is not necessarily warlike, that it is the influence of the international environment which determines the likelihood of war, a relevant theory will be concerned with the study of that environment and its influence on national actions. This will involve detailed study of historical international societies, and the varying types of influence they have brought to bear on individual and group motivations.


## 3.4 Psychology and Sociology

The findings of psychology thus have much the same kind of importance for international sociology as they do for other forms of sociology. Society can no more be understood without some understanding of individual humans than humans can be understood without an understanding of the society which molds them. An international society, like any other, depends on the individuals who comprise it.

All three main areas which we have identified in which the findings of psychology are important to us—understanding of the differences between *individuals* in their attitudes and actions in the field of foreign affairs, knowledge of *group* drives and aspirations within states, and understanding of the psychological factors that are basic and common to all *humanity*—are relevant to the central problems with which international relations theory is concerned. They are particularly important in relation to the basic question which we considered earlier: What is the relative importance of factors which derive from each particular national unit and of those from the international society as a whole in determining foreign policies and international relationships? In part, this is a purely empirical problem: How far *are* national decision makers influenced, in the decisions they make, by factors coming from the outer world, or by those coming from the domestic scene?

We are likely to find that in most cases both sources are important. The two are in any case closely interrelated. The domestic pressures which may influence a government have themselves been influenced by stimuli coming from abroad. The external threats may themselves have been promoted by factors within the domestic society of the threatener. At root the problem we are concerned with here is the motivation of those involved. And in studying international society the study of dominant motivations is clearly of special importance.

Second, a satisfactory theory of international relations must be concerned with the way in which the international society, and the part each nation must play within it, are *perceived* by members of each national society. Why does a threat from one country in some cases give rise to an act of submission, and in others to a hardening of attitude? How much is the perception due to the immediate situation (say, the murder of an Austrian archduke) and how much to the long-term situation (the challenge by Serbia to Austria's position among the Southern Slavs)? How far do factors determining a country's foreign policy (economic poverty or a national territorial claim) remain the same for any type of government, and how much will their effect vary from one government to another? How far is each nation *expected* to perform a particular role–dominant or submissive, superpower or satellite–

within the society? On all these questions an improved knowledge of the way in which foreign policy situations and national roles are perceived, both by individual decision makers and by populations as a whole, will be important.

Third, knowledge from the field of psychology is particularly important in the study of the process of socialization: the process by which individuals are made subject to the pressures and norms of their society, in this case the international society as a whole. Here we need to know how individuals acquire their conception of the national behavior which is thought normal, or acceptable, or moral, within a particular international context. And in examining the differences between different international societies, we shall be particularly concerned to discover how this process of socialization has varied from one to another, and what its effect has been on national behavior within each society. Have some been more successful than others in instilling accepted norms or rules of conduct among states, and if so for what reasons?

Any adequate theory of international relations must therefore take account of all these different aspects of human psychology. In considering the chief international systems of earlier times, it will be important to keep all these factors, dominant motivations, expected roles, and prevailing norms clearly in mind.

But to understand adequately the forces at work in the society we will need the help of still another discipline, whose findings will be of even more direct importance to us.

# Chapter 4.    The Relevance of Sociology

## 4.1 Inner Society and Outer Society

Writers on international relations have long recognized that sociology is one of the disciplines which has a distinctive contribution to make within the field. Some have declared themselves concerned, for example, with the study of "societal" factors, that is, factors within individual nations and other groups that affect their international behavior.[1] Others have been interested in "historical sociology," a comparison of different types of society *over time,*[2] to consider what kinds of internal systems, demographic forces, or domestic pressures, have led to what kinds of policies.

International relations, however, as we have seen, is concerned with two types of society. It is concerned with national societies and the influence which various forces within those societies can have on the decisions of governments and the interactions of states. But it is also concerned with a wider society: the society *among* states.

So far the concepts and techniques of sociology have been used almost entirely to study the former field. Those concerned with "societal" factors have defined these as factors which derive from domestic sources *within* a society.[3] In the words of one writer, "these 'societal factors' are those which occur within the individual 'units'—usually nations, but sometimes also large segments of a nation or certain groupings of nations."[4] Raymond Aron, in speaking of "historical" sociology, suggests:

> A comparison may be made of the way in which foreign policy is determined in the U.S.A. or Great Britain, of the differing parts played by Congress and Parliament, and of the influence of the press. In the same way we may show, or at least attempt to show,

1. Cf. J. N. Rosenau, *International Politics and Foreign Policy* (Princeton, 1969), pp. 174, 261 ff.

2. R. Aron, in *Contemporary Theory in International Relations,* ed. S. Hoffman (Englewood Cliffs, 1960), pp. 200–8.

3. Rosenau, *International Politics,* pp. 261–62.

4. H. C. Kelman, "Societal, Attitudinal and Structural Factors in International Relations," *Journal of Social Issues,* 11, no. 1 (1955):42–56.

the special conditions imposed in the conduct of foreign policy by a democratic form of government (the policy-makers probably have less tactical freedom). . . . The method of historical comparison can and must be used to test the correctness of the theories advanced to explain phenomena by reference to geography, population or economics.[5]

Studies of internal factors of this kind can certainly assist us. They could tell us, for example, about the effect of high unemployment within a state in stimulating nationalistic sentiments (as is said to have happened in Germany between the wars). Comparative study of foreign policies in different types of national society—relatively democratic and relatively authoritarian, more developed and less developed, industrial and agrarian, elitist and egalitarian—can be used to show how far these have caused significant differences in the international behavior of governments. Sociological research can provide information about the role of different ideologies in molding attitudes to foreign affairs. The impact of population pressures on governmental policies could be examined. Finally, and perhaps above all, the relative importance of different kinds of domestic pressure groups and opinions in influencing the actions of governments can be measured and assessed.[6] All of these have a contribution to make to the analysis of relations among states. It is not, however, the only use of sociology and sociological concepts that is possible in international relations research. And it is not the type of use which, in the present author's view, is most helpful in improving our understanding of international society as a whole.

For, as we have seen, the international system is itself a kind of society. Whether or not it is a "community," as some allege, it is at least an association of nations, groups, and individuals, in regular communication with each other, engaging in formal and official relationships as well as unofficial contacts, having economic, cultural, and social, as well as military, interrelationships, with its own traditions of intercourse, expected norms of behavior, and its own institutions for mutual discussion of common problems. It has, in other words, many of the essential features of the small-scale human societies which have long been the subject of study by anthropologists and sociologists.

Such a society is as subject to systematic analysis with the techniques of these disciplines as any domestic society. Its somewhat undeveloped structure makes it perhaps more analogous to some of the simpler societies studied by anthropologists and sociologists than it is to the sophisticated political systems of developed states. Because, however, it is political scientists, brought up in the tradition of that science, who have studied it, it has so far been mainly the concepts and techniques developed for the study of domestic politics in advanced societies which have been applied to it. But it is the techniques and concepts of the former disciplines that seem in many ways more appropriate to its study. Such sociological concepts as "status," "role," "dominance," "stratification," "elite," "socialization," "norm," and "authority," to mention only the most obvious, have a

5. Aron, p. 201.
6. See, for example, J. N. Rosenau, *Public Opinion in Foreign Policy* (New York, 1964).

clear application to this wider society. And the sociological and anthropological theories that have been built up around them may well have considerable value in analyzing the way in which international societies operate.

International sociology has a double meaning here. In a sense it can be regarded as a simple extension of traditional sociology. For the whole world today could be regarded as one single, immensely complex, variegated, subdivided, yet at the same time interconnected, society, of vast size and many-sided character. International elites and interest groups, international parties and political creeds, multinational companies and intergovernmental organizations, world movements of opinion, transnational media, ideological alliances and regional organizations, all play their part within that society, just as exactly corresponding elements do in narrower national societies. The size and the variety of the groups involved complicate analysis, but it remains in its essence a single society, today increasingly interlinked by personal contacts and a common communications system. It is thus not unreasonable to hope that a new discipline of international sociology might help in the analysis of the working of that society.

But the international system can also be regarded as a society in a different sense: a society of states. The essential units or "actors," to use the jargon currently popular, are the 140 or so national states which enter into relations with each other, and represent the important initiators of action and wielders of power within that society. These themselves, it is true, consist of individual human beings in direct relation with each other. But because of the solidarity in feeling and consistency of attitude that exist among most of their members, because they are controlled by a single authority deputed to act, or effectively acting, on behalf of the whole population, it is rather the *collective* actions and relations of the entire units, than those of the individual human beings, which are of concern to us. These states form something like a viable society among themselves. That society has its own institutions, rules, traditions, and expectations quite distinct from those among individuals in each society. And it is therefore this society above all with which international sociology will be concerned.

For this society of states can be studied as a factor distinct from, though itself a part of, the world society of individuals. Stratification among nations, for example—the class structure dividing nations according to wealth, power, influence, and status—is a factor largely independent of stratification among the human populations in the world as a whole. The struggle for dominance and authority among nations can be examined as a phenomenon quite distinct from the corresponding struggle taking place among individuals within the same world community. The role of institutions and norms in establishing some regularity in relationships within the society of states is quite distinct from their role in influencing relationships within national societies.

These are two alternative pictures of the same society, and international sociology may study either picture. It can also study the relationship between the two types of world society: how far relations among individuals, for example, among economic organizations, affect the relations among states; how far the formal relationship entered into by governments condition the relations possible among the organizations and citizens within them; how far individuals conceive of their relationships with those in other nations as being *mediated* by the relationships of governments, or as totally independent of the views and policies of those governments. For the moment, and until a fully transnational society has come into existence, our study must be primarily of the society of states which dominates international relationships. And we need next to consider how that society should be studied.

## 4.2  The Outer Society

At first sight there are such huge differences between world society and a domestic social system that it might seem meaningless to attempt to analyze it according to traditional sociological techniques. Its size, its complexity, its diffuseness, its lack of recognized authority or social cohesiveness, its lawless and violent character, all seem to remove it to a different realm altogether.

All these differences, though they are real, on examination prove to be differences of degree rather than of kind. Its size is self-evidently greater than that of any individual state, but not disproportionately larger: If it is possible to apply sociological techniques to a nation such as China, with 800 million people of many races, provinces, and cultures, it is not self-evident that they cannot be used in a society whose population is only about four times that size and whose distances, in traveling time, are far smaller than were those of China only two or three decades ago. It is complex and diffuse, certainly, but this is true of all modern large-scale industrial societies—world society is far less different in kind from the U.S. than the U.S. is from the small-scale primitive societies studied by anthropologists. It is subdivided into relatively enclosed and heterogeneous compartments, but this again is true of a number of national societies, particularly federal states such as Switzerland, the Soviet Union, and Yugoslavia. It is lawless and violent, certainly, but so are many national states and many primitive societies, to only a slightly lesser extent.[7] There is no widely accepted consensus concerning how this society should be ordered, but this too is true of many modern societies where there is widespread dissension on basic values. There is no authority capable of law enforcement, but this is equally so in a large proportion of primitive societies, which may have procedures for *pronouncing* on violations of order but no means for insuring the fulfillment of those pronouncements.[8] There is little social cohe-

7. See R. D. Masters, "World Politics as a Primitive Political System," *World Politics,* 16, 4 (July 1964): 595–619. Much of this article is directed to showing the resemblances between a primitive society and the modern international system.

8. See L. Mair, *Primitive Government* (London, 1962). For an excellent demonstration that law can frequently exist, even without enforcement powers, see W. D. Coplan, "International Law and Assumptions About the State System," *World Politics,* 17, 4 (July 1965): 615–634.

siveness, but this too is the case in very many societies, especially large modern states, in which there are many subcultures and subgroups sharing few common beliefs.

There are of course significant differences between world society and the type of society mainly studied by sociologists. In most national societies, even where there is no basis of common *values,* there exists at least a limited consensus concerning how disputes and differences on such points should be *resolved;* at the lowest there is a willingness most of the time to live and let live. In the world society even this is sometimes lacking. However, in this respect, too, the difference is only marginal. On the one hand, even within national societies, there are today significant groups (minority ethnic groups, revolutionary political movements, and others) who are no longer prepared to accept the traditional norms and traditional means of resolving differences—who will no longer live and let live, who use violence to express their discontents. On the other hand, in the international society there is increasing acknowledgment, at least in large sections of it, of the illegitimacy of violence as a means of securing change, even an embryonic willingness to concede the legitimacy of international understandings as the means for determining certain issues. Authority is undoubtedly weaker and more widely challenged in the international society than in the national, but this is a difference of degree rather than of kind. In certain specific areas—for instance, the allocation of broadcasting frequencies, the drawing up of international health regulations, the maintenance and enforcement of international navigation standards, the determination of international monetary problems—a considerable degree of authority has already been vested in international bodies, with virtually no dissent; conversely, authority in national states is also sometimes disputed. Integration may still be much weaker in the international society than in the national, and may be growing more slowly, but it is nonetheless increasing rapidly, since many of the same factors (trade, travel, and communications) which bring it about at the national level also operate within the wider society.[9]

Thus, though this is perhaps an unusual, indeed a unique, type of society, it is a society nonetheless, and not so dissimilir to smaller societies that some traditional sociological concepts may not have some relevance to it. Let us then consider the applications which some of these concepts may have in this sphere.

## 4.3 The Concepts of International Sociology

If we accept the thesis that there exist "societies" of states with their own traditions, rules, expectations, and institutions, and that they should be studied on

9. It is one of the weaknesses of much of the study done in recent years (for example, by Professor Deutsch and others) on integration that it concentrates so much on *relative* speeds of integration within the national state and at regional or international levels. Unless national integration is accompanied by aggressive expansion abroad (which is not normally the case) it is not the *relative* rate of integration, but the absolute rate at each level, which is important. And this is increasing both at the regional and international level, probably at an increasing speed, unaffected by national integration.

this basis, which are the concepts which will be of special importance to us in examining these societies?

Before analyzing the key social factors that will concern us in this study, let us first look at some general sociological ideas. To some extent almost all the concepts devised by sociologists for the study of smaller societies, can be used in examining international societies.

For example, the concept of *authority* has relevance for us, though its application here is limited. Within most international societies, including even that of the present day, international authority has been so weak in relation to that of the members of society (the nations) that its significance is questionable: the characteristic of international societies is that power is decentralized there. The difference is not an absolute one, however. There are many primitive societies in which there is no central authority with powers of enforcement.[10] Conversely, even in the international society, lip service at least is paid today to the authority exerted by world bodies: in Article 25 of the UN Charter almost all states of the world have expressly acknowledged the authority of the UN and their own obligation to obey its decisions under certain circumstances. Authority within an international society is not unlike that of a body of elders, or a revered chief, within a primitive society, whose influence is based largely on intangible factors, involving respect for the office, rather than on the ability to call on armed power to enforce his judgments. The authority which is exerted within a diffused and highly decentralized society is different from that to which we are accustomed in tightly organized national states, but it is a type of authority nonetheless. And the same methods of analysis which have shown their value at the national level may have their application here too.

The concept of *legitimacy* also has its application within the international society. It has indeed been applied for centuries in the relations *between* states. Governments acknowledge the legitimacy of other governments by entering into diplomatic relations with them. The international society, equally, accords or denies legitimacy to particular governments by its decisions concerning membership of international organizations. The eagerness with which this is demanded by certain governments (and opposed by others) is an indication of the importance such decisions hold in their eyes as a mark of legitimacy. A nation that has been admitted as a member of the UN can be regarded as a bona fide member of the international system, even if individual governments continue to boycott it. It provides, in a sense, a definition of membership of the international society, a mark of respectability. And the fact that it is a mark which is valued and acknowledged, that membership in such organizations is almost universally desired, is evidence not only of the legitimacy of the member governments in the eyes of others, but of the legitimacy of the organizations themselves in the eyes of all.

Again the concept of *status* operates within the international society as in smaller ones. A large and powerful state will normally be accorded a certain position of dominance in its dealings with others. The five largest European states

10. See J. Middleton and D. Tait, eds., *Tribes Without Rulers* (London, 1958).

in the earlier nineteenth century became "the powers," accorded by the rest a special position within society and coming together at frequent intervals to resolve the important issues of the day. Similarly in the League Council, in the UN Security Council, and the corresponding councils of many of the specialized agencies, a permanent seat has been accorded to the largest and most developed states: a visible symbol of status that is coveted by others. But status may be acquired by means other than power or size. During the Chou dynasty in China, the Chou state possessed, as we shall see, a revered status and authority that was disproportionate to its power or importance: status was based on the traditional authority of the dynasty. In the middle ages the Pope had a status that was not dependent on military power but on spiritual authority. And in modern times nations may acquire status through liberal sentiments (Sweden or Canada), wealth (Saudi Arabia or Iran), technology (the U.S.), generosity (the Scandinavians and the Netherlands), benevolent neutrality (Switzerland or Ireland), or for other reasons.

But *class*, among nations as among individuals, does not necessarily correspond to status. Class is related above all, in the international society, to the size of a state, especially its military power or, sometimes, its wealth. Traditionally nations have been divided into "great" powers and small. The great powers have been those able to coerce the smaller. Today wealth has become more significant than before, though primarily because of the influence it brings. And because nations at a similar level of economic development have not only a common economic status, but a common *interest*, for example in relation to the policies of international organizations, or on questions of trade and development, they become increasingly organized, like classes within states, to struggle for their common interests within the international society. So the group of 77 is created in the UN to struggle for the rights of the poor. Such a class division, in modern times at least, has displaced divisions of other sorts, based on ideological or historical association. The class struggle is in a sense fought out at the world level, and becomes in the international society as dominant and overriding a concern as it had been in national societies.

Another factor of importance, in international as in domestic societies, is the *socialization* that takes place within them. On the international level the socializing forces are very weak. Unlike the socialization which occurs within states, where the individual is directly influenced by parents and peer groups, by priests and pedagogues, by the press and other media, it is here mainly indirect. Images of an international society existing beyond the national are only gradually instilled. The idea of an international authority is one which emerges for the individual only slowly in the course of reading about international events generally. Insofar as they occur at all, these conceptions of the international society arise much later in life, usually in adolescence or even after adulthood, and for this reason make a far smaller impact than the conceptions of the nation instilled in early life. Slowly, and then mainly among a small elite, through the reading of speeches, news, history, or today through the viewing of films and television, a vague conception of an international society, and of the kinds of national conduct within it which are acceptable or taboo, begins to be formed. Insofar as any explicit instructions, dos and don'ts, are made on such questions—for example, by international bodies or law courts—they are made only indirectly, to governments in the first place, rather than to individuals, and for this reason too are weaker in effect. Moreover, insofar as any idea of an international society with purposes and norms of conduct of its own is established, it is only superimposed on loyalties and attitudes toward the national state which have already been far more deeply imprinted. Finally, the lack of any visible sanction which can be wielded by the international society to secure compliance with its norms also means that its perceived authority is weak. For all these reasons, socialization of individuals into the wider society is much feebler and more indirect than that which occurs within national states. Yet it none-theless occurs. And with the increasing number and saliency of international communications—for example, press items and television programs relating to foreign opinion and to decisions by international bodies—socialization into the international society is constantly being marginally strengthened.

Resulting from this socialization process are the *attitudes* and *loyalties* of individuals toward the wider society. These will be drawn partly from the domestic scene within, and partly from the international stage without. Because the impressions derived from these sources are generally similar for individuals within the same nation, attitudes and loyalties will be somewhat similar for all its members, though there will be variations according to the psychological factors we examined earlier, and to education and position. Thus it is collective motives, collective ambitions, collective desires for revenge or justification, instilled by a common socialization and a common national experience, that are often the essential factors within the international society. The attitudes and motives of individual decision makers will usually reflect the attitudes and motives of their population, not so much because they are controlled or directly influenced by those populations, but because they share the common sentiments and views of a people to which they themselves belong. Thus, though many of the international *events* which are perceived are the same for all nations—the murder of an Austrian archduke, the invasion of the Rhineland, the war in Vietnam—because of differences in the domestic environment in each state, different speeches by different statesmen, different editorials in the press, different initial prejudices and sympathies, *perceptions* of them, reactions and long-term attitudes, will vary considerably from one population to the next, even where interests do not radically differ.

These are only a few examples of some concepts which have been used by sociologists in analyzing small-scale societies and which have a clear applicability to the society of states as well. Those mentioned so far, however, are of a relatively general kind. They are unlikely to provide the key ideas we need to guide us in our analysis of individual international societies. A systematic study will have to be more clearly focused on those social factors that are of special importance in determining the character of the society as a whole.

It is a *series* of such factors that we are seeking. It has long been recognized among anthropologists that no single category, material culture, institution, or kinship system can alone give an adequate understanding of the essential nature of each society. The significance of the material equipment can be totally transformed according to the type of social organization, religious beliefs, kinship system, system of authority, above all the dominant value structure. Similarly, the significance of the power relationships within international societies, or relative technical development, will depend on the basic motives and objectives of the units, the type and effectiveness of the norms established, the communication system, the interrelationships normally existing among members, and above all the value system currently held. It is thus no more possible to distinguish and classify different types of *international* society according to a single factor, such as power relationships ("balance of power," bipolar, or multipolar), communications systems, decision-making procedures, and so on, than it is to classify primitive societies according to a single factor, such as material equipment or kinship system. It is the mix among the various elements within each society which will give it its specific character.

## 4.4  The Key Factors

So far in this book we have sought to show four things: that in seeking a theory of international relations we seek a system of analysis, a set of concepts that is relevant and empirical, above all one that will improve our understanding of the way international society works; second, that such an analysis must be partly historical in approach, since only this will enable us, by *comparing* different systems of international relations, to discover which are the most significant variables; third, that such a study will require evidence from psychology, since only this can help us to understand the attitudes and decisions of human beings, whether individual leaders, groups, or mankind as a whole, which ultimately determine the behavior of nations and other elements within the system; finally, and above all, we have concluded that such a study needs also to make use of sociological techniques, since international relations take place in a society of a kind, which can profitably be analyzed by methods similar to those used in studying other societies.

It is necessary now, in the light of these considerations, to set out the basic framework of the analysis which is to follow.

Our object will be to examine a number of different historical societies of states, and to consider them especially from the point of view of international sociology, as just described. In order to analyze them on a comparable basis, we shall adopt the same basic framework for examining each different international society.

For this purpose we need first to identify the key factors that determine the character of each society. What are the factors that are of prime concern to us as the differentiating features between societies?

One feature that will certainly be of special importance is the nature of the *elites* within each society: the dominant groups which are able to shape the policies, especially the external policies, of their governments.[11] Clearly the character of these has a vital importance in determining the type of decisions reached and so the nature of the international society. Usually these groups have a somewhat similar character among all the different members of society; the elite groups within eighteenth-century Europe, for example, the sovereigns themselves, together with a relatively small class of statesmen, royal advisers, and other politically influential forces, were relatively similar to each other throughout Europe, had substantial contacts across frontiers, and were able to develop a measure of mutual understanding. In the nineteenth century the elite groups, that is, the ministers and their advisers, were representative of a somewhat different strand of opinion within society, but yet remained a limited and relatively homogeneous group throughout Europe (even in Britain, which, with France, was one of the more democratic members of the system, nearly all foreign secretaries until the end of that century were members of the peerage). Similarly, in China during the multistate period, though the social background of the main decision makers changed considerably during the course of the age, it remained generally similar among the different members of the system. In all these cases there was probably a greater homogeneity among the attitudes and ideas of those in different countries holding similar positions than there was between themselves and those of more humbly placed members of their own nation. It is clear that in each case it is the aims and ambitions, the attitudes and assumptions, of this relatively small group that are mainly important in shaping the foreign policy of their own nation, and so the character of the whole system. It is thus important to know which are the dominant social forces exercising influence on national policies in each international society, and the values and attitudes which govern their approach to foreign policy.

Next, and in consequence, a vital factor will be the *motivation* of these ruling groups and elites, especially those motivations directed to the international society. Clearly such motivations will vary to some extent among individuals within the same elite group, and we considered in the last chapter some of the personal factors which may be significant. But in general we shall find that there are widely shared group motives which do not vary much among members of the same elite in the same nation, or even among the elites of different nations within the same international society. The desire for national security, the desire for national status, for national prosperity, for influence, for good name, for stability will probably be common goals in almost all societies. But their *relative* importance may vary considerably from one society to another. Moreover, certain motives— for dynastic success, for overseas colonies—are specific to particular ages. The *dominant* national motives at any one time will be of great importance in determin-

---

11. In this case the sociological term (elite) is used in relation to the individual society, rather than the wider international system. This is an exception to the general rule under which we shall be applying sociological concepts to the wider international society. Elite in the wider sense (elites among states, such as the "powers" in nineteenth-century Europe or the superpowers today) will be considered under the heading of "stratification."

ing the character of the society as a whole. To show this at its crudest: It is obvious that where the dominant motive of states is to acquire territory, and there remains no unoccupied land, the character of the society is bound to be one of constant mutual conflict. On the other hand, if the dominant motive is economic prosperity, and this can be satisfactorily acquired by internal growth and mutual trade alone, there is more chance that the society may be a peaceful one (though perhaps equally beset with disputes). These are, of course, extreme and therefore unreal examples (in practice both motives are felt in most societies in varying degrees). But they help to make clear the special importance of studying the dominant motives among states in seeking to analyze the character of the society which they inhabit.[12]

Third, also important will be the dominant *means* employed. These will be related to dominant motivations. For example, in a society where dynastic power—authority for a particular royal house—is the goal, dynastic marriage and dynastic compacts may become important instruments of policy. In a society where ideological expansion is a widely held motive, as today, propaganda, international political movements, puppet parties, subversion, coups, and similar means may become the favored instruments of policy, and so give the international society an entirely different character. But the means adopted, even for the same goal, will also vary according to the available instruments: the military technology, the economic bribes and threats, diplomatic leverage, and so on, which are at hand. This, however, is rarely decisive (military weapons may be discarded because they are *too* powerful, because of stricter observance of international rules, because other means to procure change are more effective, and so on). Finally, the means adopted may vary in a more fundamental way from one society to another. They may be primarily *coercive,* designed to achieve goals by force, or primarily *concessive,* designed to achieve them by negotiation, bargaining, give and take; this too may influence (or reflect) the character of the society as a whole. The choice of means will thus tell us much about the character of each society.

Fourth, societies will vary also according to the *stratification* within them: the relationships in size, military strength, economic power, political influence, and so on, among them—in other words, the degrees of dominance and dependence which exist among the members. One aspect of this is the number and relative

12. Particularly decisive in this connection is how far the external goals are *incompatible* or exclusive (as is the demand for territory, assuming no nation is willing to give it up peacefully): where they are, the satisfaction of those motives must inevitably lead to conflict. The commonest kinds of incompatible claims are those related to expansion. Expansion may be military, economic, political, or cultural. Wherever expansion, in any of these forms, is resisted by other states at whose expense it is to take place, it must inevitably lead to conflict situations. This applies particularly to military expansion, since this is the case where it is most certain to be resisted. Thus an international society in which expansion is a widely held national motive (like China during the Warring States period) will inevitably be competitive and warlike in character. Even in a society where political expansion replaces military expansion (as is perhaps increasingly the case today) there may be conflict over the allocation of political influence in particular areas (as, in recent years, in Vietnam and Cuba, Greece and the Congo). Economic expansion likewise can lead to conflict, as where two imperialist powers are in competition for the same territory, or where foreign investment by one country is met by nationalization by another.

strength of the "great powers" within a system. This can vary from the situation, as in Roman days, when there was only one great power, incomparably stronger than all other nations with which it was in contact, to that of the early Chou dynasty in China, when there are said to have been 1,700 small states, of widely varying strength and size, all vying against each other. Between these two extremes there have been societies having two great powers (as over the last thirty years); three (as in the early seventeenth century, when Spain, France, and Austria were the three dominant powers); four (as in Italy in the late fourteenth and early fifteenth centuries, when Milan, Venice, Verona, and Florence were the dominant powers); five (as in the first half of the nineteenth century in Europe); and six (as at the end of that century, when Italy, at least in theory, joined the other great powers). Sometimes there have been two distinct levels of power (or international classes), one of stronger powers, another of weaker, as in nineteenth-century Europe when the "powers" enjoyed an acknowledged superiority or authority and prestige over the rest. Occasionally there are three or four separate classes of nations of hugely differing size, military power, and economic strength, as is the case today. Stratification, in international as in other societies, can be based on varying criteria. Indeed, one of the features distinguishing different international societies is how far they rank nations purely by military strength (as in the nineteenth century); by economic power (as increasingly today); by cultural contribution (as was partly the case among the states of ancient Greece); or by other factors.

Fifth, international societies may be distinguished according to their *structure*: the type of interaction which takes place among their members. A basic factor here will simply be the extent of the contacts and relationships within the society, in any or all fields. This will depend on distance and communications. Where travel even between neighbors takes several weeks, as in ancient China or dynastic Europe, the structure of the society will be clearly different from that in a society where neighbors can reach each other in a few hours. In the former case an envoy will probably need to be entrusted with considerable authority to negotiate ("full powers"), while in the latter the smallest detail of the negotiations will be reported to the capital at home and exact instructions sent. This in turn means that control over foreign policy will be more highly centralized in the latter case. Again, military relationships will be transformed according to the communications available: if it takes many days or weeks to reach a neighboring country, a threat of invasion or attack or even a guarantee against attack will be far less immediate in effect than in a society where nuclear weapons may be dropped on the other side of the world at a few minutes' notice. This in turn can transform the nature of alliance and the need for self-sufficiency. In 1938 a guarantee by Britain to Czechoslovakia against attack, even if Britain had been prepared to give it, could have been only of psychological value; however well-armed Britain was, she could not save Czechoslovakia from being conquered, only offer to fight Germany to recover her territory after the event. Today an alliance and a guarantee of that kind, by the U.S. to Europe, for instance, has a much more real and immediate meaning, since missiles and long-range aircraft give the opportunity to fulfill a defense undertaking even to a relatively remote ally (this will favor defense over attack generally and so could reduce external conflict). But distance has another importance, for it will affect the degree of *concern* felt about events in other parts of the world, whether on strategic, political, economic, cultural, or human rights grounds. In the middle ages other countries were seen largely as *objects* to be acquired or attacked according to choice, but not known, understood, or valued, and scarcely felt to be inhabited by humans at all. In the nineteenth century the inhabitants of European countries began to feel some degree of concern on violations of human rights in other European countries, but not elsewhere in the world: Liberals in Britain and France deplored the existence of authoritarian regimes in Turkey and Russia, but not in Asia, Latin America, or Africa. But the structure of a society will be determined not only by the number of units and the distance between them, but also by the system of diplomatic relations established. For this serves to mediate, influence, and modify the messages received from other parts of the society. Finally, there is the regulatory system: balance of power, sphere of influence, and so on. All of these structural factors may be more important than the types of government which exist in individual states. Just as the individual in society will react in generally similar ways to similar stimuli, according to the behavior pattern the society imposes, so, within a given international society, nations will react in generally similar ways, regardless of their internal structure, according to the structure of social relationships.

Next, an important feature in each society will be the *roles* performed by individual member states within them; for example, those of "great power," ally, competitor, enemy, client state or satellite, trading partner, buffer state, neutral, aid donor, aid recipient, and so on. Some of these roles are *traditional* for the nation concerned, in the sense that they have been handed down from one generation to the next (just as the role of priest or medicine man may be transmitted from generation to generation within a smaller society): The Swiss role as a neutral is a traditional one that has lasted for nearly two centuries, and is unlikely now to be reversed by any Swiss government in the near future. Other roles are short-term, *adopted,* as the U.S. deliberately adopted the role of isolated outsider between the two wars and of world policeman for a period after them, or as India adopted the role of neutral during the 1950s. Some roles, as among individuals, are virtually forced on a nation by its external circumstances: Upper Volta can scarcely choose to become an aid donor, nor the U.S. to be an aid recipient. Some are literally imposed by force: Czechoslovakia has been compelled to be a client state of the Soviet Union, as the Dominican Republic has been, less brutally, by the U.S. The important point is that the role adopted to a considerable extent determines behavior. In adopting the role of rebels from the neighboring superpower, Albania and Cuba have adopted at the same time certain forms of behavior pattern: defiance and provocation of the hated neighbor. In some cases, as among individuals, there may be a considerable degree of role conflict: The U.S. and the Soviet Union may both be, and perhaps sincerely, anticolonialist in their views, yet are compelled to adopt relationships which are semi-imperialist toward small countries in strategically sensitive parts of the world; China may strongly support revolution in words and even in sentiment, but find it inconvenient or impossible to support it in individual cases. And so on.

Next, international societies, like narrower societies, have been obliged to develop their own methods of social control. In the absence of coercive powers, they have employed *norms* of conduct to regulate behavior among their members. International society, despite frequent assertions to the contrary, has never been characterized by a state of anarchy. The word might possibly be used to describe the relations of certain primitive tribes at particular periods, but cannot be used to describe the international societies we are concerned with here. All groups of nations in regular contact have in practice adopted certain rules defining the conduct which could usually be expected among their members. These expectations influence not only what one state expects of others, but what it expects of itself; the bounds of behavior which it regards as *normal* or reasonable. Such norms are not necessarily always obeyed; but neither are they in smaller societies. They nonetheless exist, and exert some influence on conduct.

Because no overwhelming coercive power is available to international societies, such norms of conduct have a particularly important role to play there: rules are the only rulers. These norms are of a number of kinds: practices (ad hoc forms of behavior adopted between two or more states), customs (traditional forms of behavior which have become more widely accepted within the international society), rules (principles of international behavior which have acquired a more binding character), and laws (written rules which have acquired a still more compulsive character within international society as a whole).[13] They are for the most part still fragmentary, disputed, and uncertain. But each type exerts some influence on the behavior of governments within any international society, despite the fact that there is no power of enforcement available to international authorities.[14] Though the norms apply to the behavior of *states,* they need to be apprehended, internalized, and put into practice by the individual human beings within those states who act on their behalf.

The influence of the norms is indirect in influencing perceptions. All four types—practices, customs, rules, and law—have had some influence on the relations among states within most of the societies which we will examine. Even international law (rules which have been set out in documentary form, such as treaties, judgments of the International Court, or international conventions which have received general endorsement) has had some influence, though it is doubtful

13. For a more detained discussion of these types of international norm, see Evan Luard, *Conflict and Peace in the Modern International System* (Boston, 1968), pp. 41–51.

14. The legal system "does more than direct or control the actions of its members through explicit rules backed by a promise of coercion. The legal system functions on the level of the individual's perceptions and attitudes by presenting to him an image of the social system—an image which . . . contributes to social order by building a consensus on procedural as well as substantive methods." Law is thus a "primary tool in the socialization of the individual." Coplan "International Law," pp. 616–17.

how far it is *felt* as law and so absolutely binding, in the way that the laws of the state are so felt, since it cannot be enforced. Societies of states vary in the way in which norms of each kind are regarded, in the balance which exists among them, and in the content of the rules laid down. We therefore need to examine the type of norm which exercises influence in different international societies.

Next, international societies, like narrower ones, have also relied on *institutions* as a means of social control. Institutions of a kind have existed in most international societies. Some have relied on the use of ad hoc conferences, called from time to time to resolve particular difficulties, as in Europe before the nineteenth century. More advanced societies have established such conferences on a more institutionalized basis, so that there exists a recognized channel for raising grievances and securing redress; this was roughly the situation in nineteenth-century Europe. Next, there may be provisions for the submission of disputes to arbitration or mediation; this occurred at times in ancient Greece and over the past two or three centuries in Europe. Finally, there may be full-scale international institutions in the modern sense, permanent organizations to which all or most members of the society belong, as has been the case at least since 1918. There may also be *specialized,* or functional, organizations for performing particular purposes (for example, for running postal services or considering trade questions), and *regional* organizations embracing the countries of a particular continent or area. The character of a society will vary according to the relative importance of different institutions of this kind. And the institutions themselves may vary according to their degree of universality, legitimacy, influence, and power. The types of institutions may affect the adaptability of each international society, its capacity to adjust, to react to challenges, and to resolve peacefully internal conflicts and contradictions.[15]

Finally, we shall find there is one further factor we need to consider, possibly more important than any of these—almost indefinable yet nonetheless real. Just as many anthropologists have concluded that the character of a primitive society depends ultimately not on any easily defined component such as material technology, kinship system, religion, and so on, but on an indefinable factor related to attitudes, belief systems, and values, in a word its ideology, so, among international systems, we find a similar factor which will ultimately determine much else in the society. International societies which were similar, for example, in terms of power structure, military technology available, diplomatic system, and economic relationships, might nonetheless vary enormously according to how far they were basically competitive or cooperative; their units expansive or inward-turned; tradition-based or achievement-oriented; conceiving of national glory and status in terms of territory conquered, or of cultural achievement, or of material standard of

15. This is not to say that, from a sociological point of view, a society should be judged solely according to how far it is peaceful or warlike. For conflict may itself be one of the mechanisms employed by society for adjustment and self-regulation. But if it is considered that war is an unsatisfactory, wasteful, and dysfunctional way of achieving this purpose, institutions may be judged according to their capacity to bring about adjustment on a less violent and less unpredictable basis.

living. Thus, just as primitive societies may be typed according to how far they are tradition-based or contract-based, role-oriented or achievement-oriented, Apollonian or Dionysian, "communities" or "societies," so international societies may vary on somewhat similar dimensions.

The basic ideology which prevails may reflect the aspirations and motives of ruling groups within each unit rather than those of the ordinary people. It may reflect their interests as well as their beliefs. It may reflect unconscious traditions of the wider society, rather than the conscious demands of the narrower. But it will in any case express prevailing expectations about the wider society and the relationships which should occur there, and that will determine actions within it. We must thus, in examining individual international societies, be above all concerned with considering the nature of this prevailing ideology, the set of assumptions and beliefs which exists among its members.

Having defined these as the key variables determining the character of an international society, let us now go on to examine historical international societies in the light of this analysis.[16]

16. It is not, of course, suggested that the international societies here discussed are the only ones that have ever existed. But they are the only ones for which there are adequate historical records of international relationships and possibly the only ones where relations among a considerable number of states were close and constant enough to establish a fully developed society. (The reader who prefers a more straightforward historical approach may wish to read consecutively the sections dealing with each period from each of the next nine chapters, rather than the more analytical framework here presented.)

# PART 2

## The Key Factors in International Society

PART 2

The Report on International Society

# Chapter 5.   Ideology

Anthropologists, sociologists, and others, in studying domestic societies, have been particularly interested in considering and comparing the basic belief systems held among different societies. These are often of special importance because they may influence many other factors, types of authority, religious practices, kinship systems, institutions, methods of law enforcement, and so on. In examining international societies, we should similarly look first at the fundamental beliefs and values which determine attitudes, motives, and many other features of each.

The word "ideology" may be used to denote this prevailing set of beliefs, values, and concepts. The importance of ideology in this sense has long been recognized by sociologists. Even Marx, though dismissing values as a form of superstructure laid above the basic network of economic relationships by the classes in authority, accepted the power of ideas (for example, class-consciousness) in changing and ordering society. Durkheim believed that an "organic" society would be distinguished by the common pattern of beliefs which held it together and which conditioned the thinking and behavior of its members. Many modern sociologists, such as Talcott Parsons, have accepted the significance of ideas and values in influencing the relationships undertaken by individuals within a community. And anthropologists, even more than sociologists, have acknowledged the importance of ideas and beliefs in determining the essential character of a society.

In international societies too there is normally a prevailing set of beliefs which largely determine the action of its members (that is, the states). These are, it is here suggested, more decisive in molding conduct than some of the factors more commonly studied by students of international relations (such as power relationships, diplomatic systems, international law, and so on).

Clearly, international societies are societies of a very special kind, with a special kind of ideology. First, we are thinking here of societies which are extremely *diffuse:* their members (the nations within them) may have contacts which are relatively tenuous and sporadic. Each of these nations is itself a society, moreover, having its own domestic ideology. These domestic ideologies may vary widely from each other (as well as from those of the international society). It is

67

only the *international* expectations, assumptions, and beliefs, those governing relationships between states, that represent the "ideology" with which we are concerned.

Second, as within states, the ideology is not necessarily totally consistent for all states within the society. Some may be more socialized, more governed by it, than others. Others may be deviant members and less under its influence (though a state is not necessarily deviant in making war, for the ideology may *expect* the making of war in certain situations). But normally it will have some influence among all its members.

Third, we are concerned here mainly with beliefs about *relationships:* those regarded as proper and normal among the members of the society. It would be possible, for example, to have an international society where there prevailed a "feudal" ideology; that is, expectations of relationships among states comparable to those between lord, knights, and vassals in the feudal system. This would imply a kind of hierarchy among states, with some small states subordinate to middle-sized states, which were themselves subordinate to the largest of all. Acts of submission, or payment of tribute, would be performed by some states in return for protection or other services by the larger state. Though it is not possible to point to an international society that applied this principle exactly, the relationship between China and her tributaries in the eighteenth and nineteenth centuries came close to being a feudal relationship, as did some of the relations existing in the ancient Chinese multistate system to be examined shortly (see pages 203–205 below). And the "protectorate" in the nineteenth century was virtually in a vassal relationship to the protecting power.

In some cases the conception of an expected relationship among states may derive from some aspect of ideology which determines all else. Thus an expectation that territorial conquest is a natural ambition of every state implies a belief that their relationships will (assuming no state willingly desires to be conquered) be marked by continuing conflict and rivalry, since a universal ambition of this kind must at least lead to frequent competition among the stronger states for territory. This, as we shall see, was to a considerable extent the situation in the ancient Chinese multistate system, and, in a slightly different form, in the dynastic competition of medieval Europe.

These are examples of ideologies that are basically competitive. But there can be others which are predominantly cooperative. Sometimes the two may even coexist. Between 1815 and 1914 the ideology of nationalism promoted a bitter competition among states, yet there existed at the same time a highly developed system of consultation among the very powers which were most strongly competing, to find the means of accommodation between them (see page 330ff. below). What this example shows is that, in international society as in domestic societies, the prevailing ideology is not necessarily a single or simple concept. It is a complex of beliefs and values, including assumptions which can modify or complement each other.

Sometimes the international ideology reflects the domestic ideology. In the era between 1914 and 1974, for example, domestic societies were preoccupied by concern over different political ideologies. These rivalries and differences were reflected in somewhat comparable rivalries and differences between states within the international society as a whole. So the concern with the ideology became in a sense the "ideology" of the wider society too. Something of the kind occurred in ancient Greece during the time of the city-states there. In such a situation interstate and intrastate conflicts become merged, and each state may expect to find supporters (because they are supporters of the same ideologies) within the territories of other states.

The ideology exercises its influence in determining *expectations*. The goals held by the ruling groups in each nation are influenced by the prevailing ideology, which they find in the international society as a whole. For example, the general acceptance of the assumptions of sovereignty in seventeenth- and eighteenth-century Europe encouraged and induced *demands* for sovereignty among those who might not otherwise have conceived them. In nineteenth-century Europe nationalistic ambitions did not derive only, or even mainly, from the *internal* motivations of ruling groups but were stimulated by the prevailing *assumptions* of nationalism existing within the wider international society. Thus a country like Japan, emerging into that society, borrowed the current ideology it found in the existing international society and became more nationalist than any.

This is to suggest only that nations, like humans, are social beings, intensely influenced and molded by the external culture in which they exist, as well as by spontaneous, individual attitudes and motives. And we shall find that, while all the factors we have described are important, it is above all changes in the widely held attitudes, the ideology, of the outer society which determine the changing motives and demands of individual governments. They thus determine the character of the entire society. And it is changes in this fundamental ideology that are chiefly responsible for the transition from one type of international age to another.

These beliefs which determine actions are not necessarily held by every individual in each state within the society. Many individuals may have little conception of the wider society, and give little thought to it. It is above all the beliefs among those who determine the actions of each state, the dominant elites within them, that is of importance in determining the character of the society as a whole. And it is for this reason that in the following chapter we shall consider the changing nature of the controlling elites in different international societies, and the relationship of this change to the ideologies which are held. One of the points we shall need then to consider is how far the ideology determines the elite, and how far the elite determines the ideology.

Having undertaken this cursory examination of the meaning of "ideology" when applied to an international society, let us now proceed to consider a number of individual societies and the various ideologies which have determined conduct within them.

## 5.1 The Ancient Chinese Multistate System (771–221 B.C.)

The earliest international society of which we have detailed knowledge existed in China between 771 and 221 B.C. Among Chinese the period has traditionally been divided into two main periods, known as the "Spring and Autumn Period" (Ch'un-chi'iu), named after the annals of the period, which have survived,[1] from 721 to 481 (or 464); and the Warring States (Chan Kuo), from 463 to 221. Though there are qualitative differences between the two periods, which we shall discuss, they represent in most ways a single phase of Chinese history and a continuous international society, and will thus be treated here as a single entity.

In theory this was one single state at first, a semifeudal system. But already by the beginning of the period the Chou monarchy, established roughly four centuries earlier,[2] was in a state of dissolution. The feudal fiefdoms, given by the founder of the dynasty in the early days to relatives and other helpers, had made themselves virtually independent states. Lip service was still paid to the concept of a single kingdom, traditional ceremonies were still performed, but the effective power of the Chou kings had disappeared.[3] The individual states now went their own way as essentially sovereign nations, making war against each other, and even against the Chou king on occasion. "Royal authority was slight beyond the boundaries of the royal domain and the power of the king depended largely on his ability to retain the goodwill of the feudal lords."[4] Especially from the time of the removal of the royal capital to the east, near the present Lo Yang, in 771 B.C., when our period begins, the system was in effect one of competition among a considerable number of independent states. But the vestigial role still played by the monarchy and the memory of an earlier age when there was a united China gave a special character to competition in this society.[5]

There were two highly distinctive features of the system. One was the large number of separate units which were originally members. The second was the ruthless process of mutual annexation and absorption which brought a rapid

---

1. This work is in fact the annals of only one of the states of the system, Lu, a state whose rulers were descended from the royal family. Lu was the state where Confucius for long acted as an adviser to the ruler, and by tradition he was responsible for compiling the annals. Most of the detailed information of the period comes, however, from another ancient work, the Tso Chuan, a commentary on the Spring and Autumn annals.

2. According to the traditional chronology, the date assigned to the beginning of the Chou dynasty is 1122 B.C. For a discussion of the varying modern estimates, see H. G. Creel, *The Origins of State-Craft in China* (Chicago, 1970), pp. 487–93.

3. After the beginning of the Spring and Autumn Period "there was virtually no king in China . . . and the lord of each feudal state did what was right in his own eyes." J. Legge, *The Chinese Classics,* vol. 5 (Oxford, 1893), p. 113.

4. Creel, *Origins of State-Craft,* p. 53.

5. R. L. Walker, *The Multi-State System in Ancient China* (Hamden, 1953).

decline in their number. There are said to have been 1,700 states, mainly very small, in the tenth century (when the feudal system was still partially operative). By 720 B.C. there were only about 170 significant states, by 480 there were only 13, and by 400 there were 7. Finally, in 221, Ch'in absorbed all the others and established the first Chinese empire, so bringing the society to an end. Thus while at the beginning of the period there were more states than in any other known international society, toward the end there were less. The society was therefore characterized by the highly *expansive* character of state behavior, on a scale unique in world history, and the perpetual reduction in the number of states that resulted.

Another feature was the explicit acceptance of a leadership principle among the states. A number of states rose in turn to acquire the role of "hegemon." This was a position generally acknowledged in a substantial part of the society. In the north, near the Yellow River, where most of the states formed from the original Chou kingdom were situated (including the Chou domain itself), a kind of northern league was established. The title of leader within this group was secured in turn by Ch'i in the northeast, then by Sung, Chin, and Ch'in. Ranged against this Chou league for most of the period was Ch'u, a powerful state of the southwest on the Yangtsze River, which progressively absorbed a number of the smaller states surrounding it and formed an alliance system of its own. Between the two regions were a number of states, Cheng, Sung, Chen, and others, which fluctuated between the two alliances. There were also local rivalries between different pairs and groups of states. Finally, especially from the sixth century onward, there emerged a number of powerful states on the periphery. These were of barbarian origin but increasingly influenced by Chinese culture and techniques: Wu in the southeast, Yueh in the same area, and above all Ch'in in the west. Each of these became for a time dominant powers. By 400 B.C. there were only seven significant states left: Ch'u, Ch'i, Sung, the three parts of the former Chin that were now independent (Han, Wei, and Chao) and Ch'in, the final conquerer of the system.

A key element in the prevailing ideology of the system was the assumption of systematic territorial expansion. The philosopher Mencius recounts the actions of the king Hwuy of Leang, who "for the sake of territory tore and destroyed his people," and was "so intent to secure the victory he urged on his son, whom he loved, till he too was killed."[6] Mencius complained that in his age (about 300 B.C.) the ministers revered were those who said that they could "enlarge the territories of their sovereigns and built up their army and treasure . . ." while "in the ancient days they would have been called 'robbers of the people.' "[7] He and Confucius and other philosophers of the day perpetually denounced the unscrupulous acquisitiveness of the rulers for territory.

The tendency is equally clearly revealed in the history of the period: the record of systematic annexation. The Spring and Autumn Annals record over 200 "invasions," about 100 "incursions," 40 "entrances by force," and 29 "extinctions"

6. *The Works of Mencius,* VII, i, 1.
7. Ibid., VI, ix, 1.

in less than 250 years.[8] Ch'in and Ch'u are believed to have absorbed 30 to 45 other states each by 400. In the Tso Chuan one officer of Chin is recorded as having told a ruler that Chin's greatness is "owing to its absorbing of . . . territories. If it had not encroached on the small states, where would it have found territory to take:"[9] The dominant aim everywhere became

> the external expansion of state power. . . . Expansion was at the expense of the weak. At first small feudal cities expanded to absorb surrounding territory or buffer areas. Then the stronger cities began to take over the weaker. . . . The more powerful states continued the expansion process by absorbing the weaker ones which had become the new buffer areas. . . . State expansion meant a constant decrease in the number of states and this trend continued until it produced the eventual unification of China.[10]

This does not mean that the contest was altogether without restraint or rules. There were clearly known and accepted rules of the system, which we shall consider later in examining norms. These rules, however, did not forbid war as such. They rather specified the conditions under which war could be initiated and conducted. Especially in the early part of the period there was an elaborate code, comparable to the rules of chivalry in medieval Europe, specifying the courtesies to be extended to enemies, when they should be spared, when they should be killed, even when they could be attacked. The code was thus not altogether unlike that which emerged in Europe, between the Middle Ages and the nineteenth century: It was designed to *civilize* war, not to ban it. As in the Middle Ages, military daring came to be especially prized: "Like the 'chivalrous knights' of medieval Europe, many of these aristocrats considered war a game and valued reckless courage and the killing of men as ends in themselves; yet at the same time it included a code of proper conduct in fighting."[11] Only during the time of the Warring States (from 460 onward) did this code begin to become debased, and methods of war became increasingly ruthless and unrestrained.[12] At that point "war became a business. Military organization and techniques were altered and became more efficient. The contest was one for the survival of the fittest. The strong ruthlessly overran and absorbed the weak."[13]

The fact that some states behaved in this way inevitably affected the rest.

> Throughout the period the policies, both internal and external, of the states had to be formulated on the basis of the expectation of violence. In the absence of higher

8. Legge, *Chinese Classics*, Vol. 5, Tso Chuan, index.

9. Ibid., p. 114. As Legge pointed out, the way in which Ch'u and Ch'in, two of the dominant states, proceeded "was by extinguishing and absorbing the smaller states adjacent to them, and by a constant process of subjecting the barbarian tribes."

10. Walker, *The Multi-State System*, p. 98

11. Creel, *Origins of State-Craft*, pp. 257 ff.

12. "This was a time of dissension marked by increasing rivalry, diplomatic intrigues, and bloody warfare. Under these pressures the religion, the mores and the political procedures, of earlier times deteriorated and in large measure collapsed. Ibid., pp. 47–48.

13. K. S. Latourette, *The Chinese, Their History and Culture* (London, 1946), p. 51.

authority, war was the final arbiter. . . . Thus the major concern of the rulers and their ministers was the quest for state power and the maintenance of a constant state of military preparedness and alertness. . . . Security and power were the concern of the day.[14]

The concept of neutrality, a *recognized* disengagement from the system, was for this reason scarcely known; states ''which attempted to remain neutral usually suffered extinction at the hands of one of the power blocks, which saw them as the means of swinging the balance in its favor.''[15]

The process of interstate struggle promoted the development of patriotic feeling. Before the period began there was a situation, perhaps somewhat similar to that in feudal Europe, in which loyalties were divided between the immediate lord and the Chou king, the ultimate ruler. But with the decline of the Chou power and the increasingly intensive struggle among the states, feelings of loyalty became concentrated on the individual state. According to one study, there was ''a gradual transference of the symbol of loyalty for the peasant from the feudal lord directly over him to the person of the prince of the state and the state itself. The very fact that the states were sovereign, and insisted on maintaining that sovereignty, contributed to local pride.''[16] Official histories of the individual states, inspired by the rulers, strengthened this feeling and the sense of identity of the individual state. Pride in the amount of territory ruled came to be felt as much by the ministers, and even by many ordinary citizens, as by the rulers themselves, and influenced their behavior accordingly. A citizen of Chin is said to have declared, ''If by my death the state of Chin wins security and the ruling family is firmly established, why should I live?''

This prevailing image of international society was reflected in the writings of the age, especially those of the so-called Legist, or realist school (which was adopted as official doctrine in Ch'in, the ultimate conqueror). Believing as they did that force must be the ultimate basis of government within the states, the Legists were inclined to extend this doctrine to the external relations of states. The *Book of Lord Shang* declared:

> What is the cause of one's reputation becoming respected and one's territory wide, so that one attains sovereignty? It is because one conquers in war. . . . From antiquity to the present time it has never happened that one attained supremacy without conquest, or that one came to ruin without defeat. He who succeeds in making a people delight in war attains supremacy.[17]

Even the Confucian Hsun Tzu had to accept that ''he who can neither annex territory nor hold on to what he had will surely be destroyed. He who can hold on to territory will invariably be able to conquer more. When one can both acquire and hold on to territory, there is no limit to the amount one can annex.'' So the

14. Walker, *The Multi-State System*, p. 101.
15. Ibid., p. 101.
16. Ibid., pp. 35–36.
17. *Book of Lord Shang*, 14, 18, trans. J. J. L. Duyvendak (London, 1928).

expectation of warfare and annexation made some regard military expansion almost as a moral duty as well as a political aspiration in this society.

This then was a society in which prevailing expectations tolerated continual and unscrupulous struggle, maneuver, intrigue, and warfare to expand the territory of the individual state. The ideology was one of unrestricted competition, expressed above all in territorial ambition. As in other societies, expectations of the behavior of *others* determined policy as much as a country's own aims. The knowledge that unscrupulous aggrandizement was to be expected in some encouraged it in their neighbors. Rulers and statesmen *inherited* the expectations current among the society as a whole. And the influence that any one of them might achieve in seeking to change those conventions—as Mencius and Confucius discovered—was small against the strength of the pressures deriving from the dominant ideology of the society as a whole.

## 5.2  The Greek City-States (510–338 B.C.)

The society of states which grew up in Greece between the sixth and fourth centuries B.C. had some similarities with that existing in China at about the same time. It too consisted of states mainly of a similar language and culture. It too possessed a very large number of separate units (well over 300) of widely varying size and power. It too included a few powers at the fringes of the system, originally of alien culture yet becoming increasingly assimilated with it, one of which finally conquered all the rest. It too divided, as time went on, into two main alliances, incorporating or dominating many of its members. It too was characterized internally by the emergence of an increasingly articulate middle class, acquiring a growing power within each unit. And it too became, with the passage of time, increasingly competitive and unrestrained in the use of force, ending finally in a time of troubles during which conflict was endemic throughout the entire system.

The differences between the two, however, were perhaps more significant, for these were related to their governing ideology. The dominant principle of the Chinese society, as we have seen, was the ceaseless demand for territory and the process of systematic annexation which resulted from it. Territory was not a dominant concern in the Greek society. Though there were territorial disputes (for example, between Sparta and Argos, between Thebes and Athens, between Corinth and Megara), these were not the issues over which the major wars were fought. At the end of the major conflicts—for example, after the Peloponnesian War—there were usually few major territorial changes. What did occur were changes in the political complexion of *governments,* changes that had an interstate as well as an internal significance. Even the dominant states, such as Athens and Sparta at the time of their maximum strength did not attempt to extend their frontiers significantly at the expense of their neighbors. Rather, they sought a dominant influence over the policies, internal and external, of their satellites and allies. Sparta used her dominance after 404 to insure the rule of oligarchic governments, just as Athens had used hers in favor of democratic governments 50 years earlier. Each (like ideological superpowers today) knew that this favored their own *state* interests as well as their own political viewpoint: Oligarchic governments would in general be more favorable to Sparta in their policies, just as democratic governments would to Athens.

There was a second major difference from the Chinese society. Ideology was important in itself. It was not simply a screen that concealed state ambitions. The political viewpoint of a government was of importance in its own right in this intensely political age. But, as today and indeed in all ideological ages, ideology and state interests were closely interlinked. Both between and within cities there was a complicated nexus of interest; an oligarchic faction in almost every city stood to gain from a Spartan victory, if only because it might bring them to political power, while Sparta could in return gain equally from a revolution that brought such a faction to power. In consequence, as Thucydides put it,

> Practically the whole of the Hellenic world was convulsed, with rival parties in every state, and democratic leaders trying to bring in the Athenians, and oligarchs trying to bring in the Spartans. . . . In time of war, when each party could always count upon an alliance which would do harm to its opponents and at the same time strengthen its own position, it became a natural thing for anyone who wanted a change of government to call in help from outside. In the various cities these revolutions were the cause of many calamities.[18]

This close relationship between interstate relations and internal conflicts within states, the presence of factions within eah state favorable to another, was something quite unknown within the Chinese society. It made the Greek system above all a fluid transnational society, with the links between states as powerful as those within them. In this it resembles the two later ideological societies that we shall consider: the age of religious wars in Europe and the modern world society.

Of course ideology could often be used (as in recent years) simply as the rationalization or mask for state objectives. When the delegate of Corinth called upon the Peleponnesian states to fight on behalf of "freedom," he meant freedom for Corinthian colonies from Athens. When 50 years later Thebes and Athens demanded "independence" for the Greek states, they meant independence from Sparta. When Sparta demanded "autonomy," she meant an autonomy which might break up the federations threatening her own power. All of these various abstract nouns (like those sometimes used by ideological factions today) provided noble-sounding justifications which could sometimes win the support of sympathizers in other cities, but often concealed the purposes of individual cities. They were the slogans necessary in a society in which the ruling forces were both highly educated and highly concerned about political principles.

Yet the crude reality was that, as they knew, they were usually fighting for one set of masters rather than another. "Leaders of parties in the city had programs

18. Thucydides, *The Peloponnesian War*, III, 81.

which appeared admirable—on the one side political equality for the masses, on the other safe and sound government by the aristocracy—but in professing to serve the public interest they were seeking to win the prizes for themselves.''[19] For the superpowers the rule of such politically sympathetic factions could provide the substance of control by proxy. This was thus a system of *indirect* control quite different from the Chinese practice. It was adopted partly because of the difficulty of control by direct occupation, but mainly because of the high expectation of local autonomy which generally prevailed and the presence of ideological factions in every city.

The dominance of ideology also accounts for the frequency and bitterness of internal conflicts, fought out with a savagery known at almost no other time except perhaps in the Thirty Years' War in Europe (in another age of ideology). It is scarcely surprising that civil wars are common where political passions are deep. And it has often been remarked that in all ages civil wars have been conducted with even greater ferocity than other kinds. Because of the importance of ideology, because of the division of the entire Greek world into political factions, and because of the deliberate instigation of internal conflict by the great powers, civil wars broke out at the smallest provocation and were fought with a fanatical intensity. As Thucydides put it:

> In their struggles for ascendancy nothing was barred: terrible indeed were the actions to which they committed themselves, and in taking revenge they went further still. They were deterred neither by the claims of justice nor by the interests of the state: their one standard was the pleasure of their own party at that particular moment. So, either by means of condemning their enemies on an illegal vote or by violently usurping power over them, they were always ready to satisfy the hatreds of the hour. . . . As for the citizens who held moderate views, they were destroyed by both the extreme parties, either for not taking part in the struggle or in envy at the possibility that they might survive.[20]

This fanaticism and cruelty in the methods employed is a feature we shall encounter in other ideological ages to come.

Another direct consequence of the importance of ideology was the lack of any strong tradition of state loyalty. This could be expressed in the converse form: The lack of state loyalty made possible ideological commitment to an outside state. Which is chicken and which egg is not particularly important. The significant point is that in all international societies these two factors, commitment to ideology and commitment to state, are inversely correlated. There has perhaps been no other international society in history in which individuals were so ready to transfer loyalty from one state to another, or even directly to betray their own state, as among the Greek cities. The war histories of the period are full of accounts of the gates of one city being opened clandestinely by a dissident faction to another city which was besieging it; for example, Plataea was betrayed to its archenemy Thebes

19. Ibid., 83.
20. Ibid., 82.

in this way at the beginning of the Peleponnesian war, Megara to Sparta a few years later in 424. It was common for exiled or disgruntled leaders not merely to go to live in another city but to give it their service and support. Even Alcibiades, perhaps the most militant and rabidly anti-Spartan of the Athenian leaders, had no compunction, after his disgrace in Athens, in going over first to Sparta herself, giving her every advice and assistance, next to the Persian satrap, archenemy of the Greek cities in Asia Minor, and finally to Athenian oligarchic rebels (despite the fact that he had once been an ultrademocrat).

Nor was there any more loyalty to Hellas as a whole. A considerable proportion of the Greek states, including Thebes, Argos, and others with proud histories, had no scruples about ''medising''—offering allegiance to the Persian king—at the time of the Persian invasion. Still more remarkable perhaps was the fact that some of the greatest leaders of the Greek forces in the war against Persia—Pausanias, Cleomenes, and Leotychidas among the Spartans, and Themistocles among the Athenians—were later condemned as traitors, apparently with reason, for having offered their services to Persia or another foreign power. Finally, during the closing stages of the Peleponnesian War, both Athens and Sparta were prepared at different times to sell the freedom of the Ionian states for the sake of a Persian alliance. All of these reflect the loose nature of allegiance at the time (far looser than in the recent ideological age, where, except among a small number of fanatics, state loyalty remains high).

There was another factor affecting the expectations and values of the society. This was the way in which the individual units were conceived: in terms of peoples rather than of places. While we say Sparta and Corinth, they more often spoke of the Lacedomonians and the Corinthians.[21] This encouraged a slightly different conception both of men's relationship to each other and of their duty to the state. They thought of themselves as men first, grouped only by geography, rather than as members of some superhuman state to which all citizens owed unconditional loyalty, regardless of the way it was governed at any one moment, as became common in later centuries. This too was typical of a loosely oriented transnational society.

Another effect of a society with strong ideological commitments, together with strong great-power domination, was the development of relatively well-recognized spheres of influence. The Athenian Empire, originally an alliance but increasingly held together by brute force (as the treatment of Naxos, Thasos, Melos, and other rebel states too clearly demonstrated), represented one such sphere, including much of northeast Greece and Ionia. The Peloponnesian states to the south, over most of which Sparta normally held hegemony, represented another. Persia exercised sovereignty in much of Asia Minor, as did Syracuse eventually in Sicily. Sometimes a smaller area was dominated in the same way: Thebes became the center of gravity for Boeotia, as Argos did in Argolis and Mytilene in Lesbos.

21. Even the conception of the Greek people as being one seems only to have emerged in the sixth century. See V. Ehrenberg, *From Solon to Socrates* (London, 1968), p. 174.

Toward the end of the period the issue of federation therefore became one of the dominant concerns of the society, strongly upheld by Thebes and opposed by Sparta. Thus, over and above the struggle between ideologies, and that between the great powers who espoused them, was another on the issue of regionalism: To what extent was it natural, right, or even inevitable that the cities should shed their autonomy in a local group or federation?

Still another factor governing loyalties was the division among races: between Dorians and Ionians. To some extent this corresponded with that between the big alliances. Most of the Ionians were pro-Athens and most of the Dorians pro-Sparta. There was also a clear geographical link. Most of the Peleponnesians were Dorians and most in mainland Greece and the islands were Ionian. But this was by no means exact and the colonies in particular cut across any clear geographical distributions. This was a factor known in no other international society (the division among black, white, yellow, and brown "races" today is perhaps closest). Once again it encouraged a transnational attitude to the international society.

Thus cities, federations, races, and huge ideological alliances struggled in a complex interaction. The history of the period reflects this interplay of forces. While it was power rather than ideology which determined events, the use made of the former was influenced by ideology. At the end of the sixth century when Sparta conquered Argos and Athens, she had become the strongest military power of the system and was unhesitatingly given leadership of the Greek states against Persia at the beginning of the next century. However, at this time she was cautious and restrained in her exercise of power. Athens, on the other hand, always more outward-turned because of her commercial and colonizing activities, soon established a wide-ranging alliance (the Delian League) which she quickly transformed into a subject empire. The growing power of this empire soon caused Sparta, Corinth, Thebes, and others to join against her, first between 459 and 446, and later in the protracted and bitter Peleponnesian War between 431 and 404. The period of Athens' crudest imperialism coincided with the period of the finest flowering of her artistic achievement and her most democratic constitution. Indeed, her most ardent democrats were often those most in favor of expansion abroad. It was this external policy which concerned the other states, above all her interventions, not only in her own empire, but in the colonies of Corinth. The real reason for the war was, as Thucydides put it, "the growth of Athenian power and the fear that this caused in Sparta." When eventually Sparta and her allies emerged victorious in 404, Sparta, previously highly restrained in her own policy, became as dominant and interfering as Athens had been before her. The result was that Corinth, Thebes, and even Persia, all formerly her allies, turned against her, joined Athens, and ultimately defeated her. Thebes enjoyed her turn of dominance between 478 and 462, causing eventually the rare spectacle of Sparta and Athens fighting together to resist her. Finally, after a brief resurgence of the power of those two cities, the wheel came full circle with the defeat of all three great powers at the hands of the small states in the middle of the century. Ideology was increasingly forgotten in the implacable struggle of naked power politics. Only the final Macedonian conquest in 338 brought a brief moment of Greek unity, however artifically imposed, and a kind of peace to replace the perpetual warrings of the rival cities.

This then was a society in many ways more complex than that which had existed in China. Its dominant character is perhaps the power of the transnational forces: ideology, party, race, commerce, learning, and culture. With this went the weakness of the ties of the individual to his own state. The relative smallness of the individual cities, together with their geographical closeness and vulnerability, meant that the ruling elites were far more insecure, more dependent on external alliances or intervention, than in most other international societies. All lived in the fear that they might quickly be overturned, either by revolution within or by intervention from without. The society was divided as much into rival parties as into rival states, each competing with the ruthlessness that ideological fanaticism and internal struggles for power alone induce. In the words of Thucydides once more:

> If pacts of mutual security were made, they were entered into by the two parties only in order to meet some temporary difficulties, and remained in force only so long as there was no other weapon available. . . . A victory won by treachery gave one a reputation for superior intelligence. . . . Society had become divided into ideological, hostile camps, and each side viewed the other with suspicion. As for ending this state of affairs, no guarantee could be given that would be trusted, no oath sworn that people would fear to break.[22]

While the short distances and a common language and culture provided some favorable preconditions for a viable international society, the intensity of political and factional fighting, both within and between states, provided some of the least favorable. Expectations here were of ruthlessness and treachery, within states as well as without. It was these expectations, the assumptions, the ideology of the wider society, that largely governed the conduct of individual states.

## 5.3 The Age of Dynasties (1300–1559)

The society of states which emerged in Europe, between the beginning of the fourteenth century and the Treaty of Cateau-Cambresis in 1559 shared some of the features of the two societies we have just considered. Here too there was a very large number of units: many hundreds, if the many small principalities, bishoprics, and cities of Germany are included. Here too there were wide variations in the power available to each. ranging from the overwhelming might attained by the Hapsburg monarchs at the end of the period to the total dependence of the smaller cities of Germany and Italy. Here too there were at the outer edge powerful

22. Thucydides, III, 82.

external forces, such as the Mongols and the Turks, not in any real sense a part of the system, yet exercising at intervals an important influence within it. And here too, eventually, there occurred a progressive concentration of power among the larger members, leading finally to a period in which a single dynasty held in its hands the mastery of half the world, achieving a dominance only a little less complete than that won by Ch'in in China and Macedonia in Greece.

There were, however, vital differences. This society was characterized above all by one leading idea, a dominant motive force, which had played virtually no part in Greece and only a small one in China. This was the dynastic principle. The dominant aim and source of policy was to extend the power and influence of the individual dynasty. The control of policy was almost universally in the hands of a single prince, subject only to the advice of a few trusted counselors, who themselves usually shared the ambitions of the dynasty. The same feudal urges which caused their vassals, the great magnates and lesser landowners, to seek title to territory as extensive as possible, especially by marriage and inheritance,[23] inspired the princes as well. Their concern was not with the system of government established in the territories they acquired (as in Greece), nor with securing personal rule there (as in China)—day-to-day control was left largely in the hands of local magnates—but with ultimate dynastic authority and rights.

> Ruling dynasties laid province to province, as the more successful landlords among their subjects laid field to field, by purchase and exchange and foreclosure, but chiefly by marriage and inheritance. Force was employed not to advance a rational interest, but to support a legal claim. . . . In consequence the leading thread in the diplomacy of all this period was dynastic interest. . . .[24]

Dynastic interest dominated personal and state motives and it dictated the character of the international society as a whole.

The importance of this principle may be measured, as in other ages, in the issues for which war was fought. In this age most of the wars were disputes over succession. This was the cause, for example, of the two greatest contests of the age: the Hundred Years' War, fought over the English kings' persistent, if poorly founded, claim to the French crown; and the sixty-five-year struggle in which successive French kings, beginning in 1494, sought to pursue French dynastic ambitions, equally precarious, in Italy.[25] Dynastic claim and counterclaim underlay the almost ceaseless struggle in the Iberian peninsula during the fourteenth

---

23. "The reasons for this lie in the principal aim of the great land-owner: more land. Undoubtedly the main way in which land was sought was by marriage. Except on troubled border-lands war, espoliation of the church, pressure on weaker neighbors, were generally speaking insignificant means of augmenting one's domains; heiresses were in every region a safer and more profitable investment. . . . It is an extraordinary story in which great dynasties were built up, and usually by natural causes (infertility or a large number of daughters) disintegrated." D. Hay, *Europe in the fourteenth and fifteenth centuries* (London, 1966), p. 64.

24. G. Mattingly, *Renaissance Diplomacy* (London, 1955), p. 119.

25. Cf. F. Pirenne, *A History of Europe from the Invasions to the Sixteenth Century* (London, 1939), p. 603: The wars of Charles VIII and Louis XII "were not related to any natural ambition, they were 'wars of magnificence,' which is to say useless."

century in which Aragon, Castile, Portugal, and Navarre fought over each other's crowns. They inspired the two-hundred-year struggle in which the Wittelsbach, Luxemburg, and Hapsburg families contested for the crowns of Bohemia, Hungary, Poland, and Austria, each enjoying two and occasionally three of the crowns at different periods. An essentially similar struggle was waged among the cities of Italy, where such families as the Viscontis, Sforzas, Estes, della Scalas, and Medicis, not kingly themselves, made themselves pseudodynasties, passing authority from father to son and struggling for territory and succession,[26] just like their royal contemporaries elsewhere (so, for example, the first Sforza in Milan had to marry the last Visconti to consolidate his claim, just as the first Tudor had to marry the last Yorkist in England for the same reason).

The power of this principle is also reflected in the decline of the nondynastic forces, which had been so important in the previous era: papacy and empire, civic commune and Hanseatic League, Teutonic knights and Knights of Malta. Or rather, still more significant, these forces themselves borrowed the essential aim and attitudes of dynasticism. The Holy Roman Empire became now just another dynasty like the rest, whose power depended not on a mythical elective "kingship" in Germany and Italy—where Emperors' authority over their nominal vassals was minimal—but on the strength they were able to build up in their personal territories.[27] And in a more literal sense, the empire became a dynasty, being passed from father to son, first by the Luxemburgs and finally by the Hapsburgs, who held it almost without break for 350 years, so that the election, which had previously expressly prevented dynasticism, became little more than a formality. Similarly, the Byzantine emperors, under the Palaeologi, became a hereditary dynasty in which authority was passed from father to son as in a kingdom. Even the popes became dynasts of a sort, not only in the sense that they claimed such territories as Hungary, Naples, and Sicily as papal fiefs, but because they devoted themselves increasingly, from the early fifteenth century onward, to strengthening their temporal authority in the papal states, and even sometimes, like the Borgias, to enhancing the power and territory of their own families, rather than with spiritual concerns. Similarly, republican communes in Italy were replaced by personal leaders, sometimes military in origin, who increasingly claimed ducal titles from pope or emperor. The knightly orders acquired dynastic leaders, as in Cyprus and Prussia. Even the Ottoman Turks eventually formed a dynasty much like those among their western neighbors, except that they were more successful in their territorial acquisitions.

Dynastic principles prevailed partly because the dynasts themselves, the monarchs and princes, were at home steadily extending their own power and

26. "The 'lord' now tried to secure his succession and entered into marriage alliances with the families of other 'lords.' A principate was thus formed and the process could be illustrated from the della Scala family at Verona, the Carrara family at Padua and many others." Hay, *Europe*, p. 168.

27. "The only way in which a future emperor could hope to secure any respect or obedience was to acquire such a territorial power as would make him formidable. . . . Each successive emperor set himself not so much to strengthen the monarchy, as to aggrandize his own family. . . ." R. Lodge, *The Close of the Middle Ages* (London, 1957), pp. 6–7.

authority, and therefore their control of international policy at the expense of their domestic rivals. In England, France, and Scandinavia the foundations of a centralized monarchical system had been firmly laid by the end of the fifteenth century. In Bohemia, Poland, and Hungary, the three great contemporary kings, Charles IV, Casimir the Great, and Louis the Great, during the fourteenth century asserted royal dominance over the feudal magnates (though in each case royal power was to decline again later). Above all, in Spain and France by the early sixteenth century immensely powerful royal authority was established, which enabled the rival dynasts, Charles V and Francois I, to dominate the international politics of the age. Everywhere the decentralizing forces which had dominated under feudalism were slowly overcome and replaced by the centralizing force of the monarchy.

One indication of the dominant force of the dynastic principle is the extraordinary and grotesque configuration of the territories controlled by individual rulers. By their very nature inheritance and marriage were transnational factors which took no account of race, language, or natural frontiers, and indeed were intended to overstep them. Thus territories were added to each other with a fine disregard for geographical propinquity, historic ties, ethnic or cultural affinity, still less popular loyalties. Rulers frequently claimed or acquired territories not only far from their homelands, but deeply embedded in the territories of others. So while England possessed parts of the south of France, a French family (without ruling in France) acquired Sicily, Naples, and Hungary: they were replaced in Italy by a Spanish family and in Hungary by a German. So Luxemburg acquired Bohemia, Bohemia got Hungary, and Hungary got Poland. Denmark got Norway and Sweden; Sweden got Estonia and parts of Russia; Hungary claimed Naples and Naples Hungary. And so on. Perhaps the most spectacular illustration of this process was the huge and polyglot empire ultimately put together by the skillful matrimonial policies of the Hapsburgs, joining Spain and Austria, the Netherlands and Peru, Burgundy and Naples, Portugal and Mexico, Tunis and Milan, among others— territories having nothing whatever in common but their king. An empire acquired by the nuptial bed rather than by the sword did not need to take account of natural boundaries.[28]

Related to this was the general weakness of national loyalty. The peoples of the central European lands not only accepted their wholly foreign rulers, but occasionally invited them in. Many of the lords of Gascony who were French in language and culture eagerly supported their foreign overlord, Edward III, against the French king. The people of Naples are said to have wept for joy when the French forces entered there in 1494. The lack of national feeling resulted almost inevitably

---

28. "The tendency to expand was not delayed by any concept of national unification nor directed by one of natural frontiers. States looked beyond their borders as soon as the minimal internal order needed to support a war economy was gained. And no desire to make economic and national frontiers coincide determined the direction conquest would take, no desire to reach a natural alignment of a mountain range or a river, nor to make frontiers correspond with language or custom." *New Cambridge Modern History,* I (1957): 262.

from the system. Where a territory could be transferred at a moment's notice, according to the conclusion of a marriage or the death of a ruler, from one monarch to another, it was impossible for any people to form a strong devotion to a particular ruling house or to acquire any powerful national identity. Loyalties were still in many cases more firmly attached to the immediate overlord than to the national ruler, still less to the national state. In Italy and Germany particularly, where there existed no dominant state, where authority and loyalties alike were local, national sentiment was minimal.

Only the dynastic principle itself began to transform popular sentiments, and even the nature of the units. The dynasty, by its very successes, made itself a focus of loyalty. In shouting for Prince Hal the English soldiers shouted for England too. At the same time the principle helped rulers to secure national unification. The French kings subjected the remaining fiefdoms, which continued to defy their authority till the beginning of the sixteenth century, by marrying into them. England married Scotland (or rather was married by her). The marriage of Aragon to Castile unified Spain, and the marriage of Spain to Portugal the Iberian peninsula. The Low countries were painstakingly married together by the patient matrimonial diplomacy of their rulers and those of Burgundy.[29] The consolidation of power brought about in this way in turn affected international relations. The effectiveness with which royal power had been so buttressed in England enabled her to challenge France, with three times her population, in the fourteenth century; when, a hundred years later, French royal power had been equally firmly established, France was enabled to resist the challenge.

All this meant that the rules governing inheritance were of major importance. They were, however, extremely imprecise, and varied from one place to another. This multiplied the conflicts which could occur, both within states and between them. Sometimes these concerned the principles themselves, such as that of female succession, the basic issue involved in the Hundred Years' War (though the two monarchs concerned supported precisely opposite principles in disputes occurring at the same time over Brittany and Artois). There were an enormous variety of questions which might arise. Even if a woman could not herself inherit, could she transmit rights to her sons? This was the issue which arose between Ferdinand of Castile and other claimants over Aragon in 1410. Could an illegitimate line inherit? This was the issue which caused prolonged conflict over Castile in the fourteenth century and over Naples in the fifteenth. Should the nearest kin (say a brother) prevail over the direct line (say a grandson)? This was one of the issues in Artois in 1302 and in many other cases. Could a ruler decide his own heir, in

---

29. However, territories could almost equally often be subdivided through inheritance. The Hapsburg possessions were several times split up, for example, in 1358 and 1386, and were only reunited through the extinction of the Albertine line; Milan's territories were subdivided among the three sons of Giovanni Visconti in 1354, though reunited 30 years later; and the huge empire assembled by Louis of Bulgaria was split up after his death among his children of two marriages. The smaller territories of Germany also multiplied for the same reason. It was royal power, rather than royal matrimony, which ultimately produced consolidation.

defiance of the normal rules of inheritance, as Johanna I of Naples sought to do in naming an Angevin heir? Could a mother inherit from her son, as Margaret of Denmark did in 1387? Could a princess, unable to inherit one part of her father's kingdoms, inherit another part under other rules, as Jeanne of Nevarre did in 1316? Could a son born posthumously inherit, as a Hapsburg prince was permitted to do in Austria in 1440 (but was not allowed to do in Hungary at the same time).

All such points were important since they could determine the disposition of huge territories. Any could give rise to a challenge. In Aragon in 1412 half a dozen different claimants were able to make out a reasonable case according to different principles (a committee of nine representing the three parts of the kingdom had to be set up to resolve the issue). Any challenge could be revived and perpetuated among later generations, like the Angevin claim in Naples and the Orleanist claim in Milan, each taken over many years later by the French royal house for its own purposes. A manifestly faulty succession, like that of the Lancastrians in England, was especially subject to challenge later, however long the period that had elapsed. For time was no bar to any claim of legitimacy (Warwick thus contemptuously scorned the Lancastrians' "pedigree of three score years and ten: a silly time to make prescription for a kingdom's worth"). There is no more powerful evidence of the importance of the dynastic principle, and its hold on the minds of populations everywhere, than the ability of pretenders, if they could once convince an audience of the legitimacy of their claim, to challenge a dynasty which might have been in power for generations. This accounts for the sense of insecurity showed by many rulers of the period: Henry VIII was executing, without evidence or charge, any possible contender to his throne, however remote the claim, sixty years after the Tudor succession had been effected.

There was another major difference from other societies. Here there was no clearly defined unit with firm outer boundaries. Each nation was often subdivided into many different layers of authority, with those at each level owing a loose allegiance to the nominal overlord, recognizing lower centers of power beneath it, and entering into independent relations with other states. It was not even always easy to say what was the essential sovereign "unit" within the society, and what the subordinate element: empire, dukedom or vassal, papacy or bishopric, France or Brittany. This might therefore be called a "permeable," soft-shell society, without rigid divisions between each unit, or even clear definitions of what they were. Feudal and semifeudal influences modified the structure. Rather than a collection of theoretically equal and laterally divided states with clear boundaries, such as was to emerge later, this was still a vertically organized and hierarchical society, with influences moving up and down inside the units, as well as out and across. Conceptions of allegiance, duty, and reciprocal obligation of this kind exerted a significant influence on behavior and were independent of the influence of brute power. There was no sharply defined or generally accepted conception of "sovereignty." A state that was nominally a vassal might in practice be powerful and independent (Burgundy, Bavaria, or Milan). A state that was equal in power to another might nonetheless do homage to it for a part of its territory (as the English king did to the French at the beginning of the period). A treaty might be signed either by a sovereign or a vassal, with little clear distinction concerning the distribution of authority.[30]

This was therefore a society of a quite different character from both of those examined earlier. The dynastic principle, which dominated everywhere, determined the motivations of states, the means they employed, and the distribution of power achieved. The control of territory depended not on systematic annexation (as in ancient China) nor on alliances and interventions (as in ancient Greece), still less on the wishes of the populations concerned, but on skillful and persistent matrimony. The greatness of Charles V's Spain was not won by force of arms or personal popularity, but by the marriage policies of his ancestors. The importance of military power came rather in *defending* territories once acquired, or in the prosecution of rival claims for the same territory.

Here too, therefore, expectations played a vital role. Because barefaced and naked aggression, unsupported by dynastic claims, was not permitted by the rules of the system, it was in fact almost unknown. Conversely, where claims did exist, war was assumed inevitable. Because the dynastic principle was built into the fabric of a still feudal society, it had a unique influence on motives within it. A foreign prince might still command loyalty, despite being foreign, simply because he was legitimate. If legitimacy had not been widely respected, it could not have been defended; it was only on these grounds that such conglomerates as the Hapsburg empire could be put together at all. If all the Hapsburg territories had rejected the very conception of foreign rule, they would have been quite impossible to hold. They *were* held, for a time, because the assumptions surrounding the dynastic principle still prevailed. Over the centuries they could not be held because new expectations arose to take their place.

## 5.4  The Age of Religions (1559–1648)

The divisions between one historical age and another are never clear-cut. Some features of the age not yet born will become visible before the previous age is dead: *anticipations* of the future to come. Conversely, various features of an age already finished may remain visible in the subsequent period: *vestiges* of a period now passed. There were some manifestations of an age of religious concern and religious conflict at least a century before the age in which they came to dominate all international relationships. The reformation doctrines of Wycliffe and Hus

30. "Large parts of the political map of Europe presented an intricate puzzle of partial and overlapping sovereignties.... Who was to say which of them were to be granted and which denied the right of negotiating with others? Kings made treaties with their own vassals and with the vassals of their neighbors. They received embassies from their own subjects and from the subjects of other princes, and sometimes sent agents who were in fact ambassadors in return. Subject cities negotiated with one another without reference to their respective sovereigns," Mattingly, *Renaissance Diplomacy*, p. 24.

were not purely domestic in effect. Sometimes they affected international relations, as for example in the Hussite Wars in the early fifteenth century. During the sixteenth century, with the emergence of Lutheran doctrines, the impact of religious factors in the wider society became even more visible, as in the religious wars in Germany in 1545–1555, which briefly merged with the great dynastic struggle of that age between the French and Spanish houses. The crucial point, therefore, is the balance between the various factors influencing international decisions. Before 1559 religion was in general a less important factor in interstate relationships than dynastic and national rivalries. After that year it became for nearly a century the most important influence.

In fact, 1559 represented a surprisingly clear-cut line of division. It finally brought to an end the sixty-five-year struggle between Hapsburgs and Valois for mastery in Italy, initiated by Charles VIII in 1494. It inaugurated a century of Spanish domination of European affairs, and with the death of the French king in the same year, and the ensuing religious conflicts, a period of weakness for France. It saw the opening of a new ideological conflict to replace the dynastic battle: The same treaty which brought the long war to an end included a clause under which Philip and Henry agreed to use their power to convoke a general council "for the reformation and reeducation of the whole Christian Church to true union and concord," and within three or four years the final session of the Council of Trent issued its declaration of war on the dangerous menace of Protestant heresy. In 1559 Philip II arrived from the Netherlands in Spain, never to leave that country again, and initiated an auto-da-fé against all of Protestant religion in that country. In France the year saw the calling of the first great assembly of the Huguenot congregations, which challenged the monarch and the Catholic majority by calling for a considerable measure of self-government for those of their faith. In the same year, too, according to William of Orange, then present at the French Court, Henry II, just before his death spoke of a project by the French and Spanish kings for a joint international campaign to exterminate the new heresy with the help of the Inquisition. And in Geneva in 1559 the academy was founded which was to be the powerhouse of Calvinist evangelism for the following century.

Very soon this confrontation broke into open warfare. In England the suppressed civil war between Protestants and Catholics, each ranged around rival monarchs, in 1559 flared into a Catholic revolt in the north. Within the next decade the first of a series of bitter civil wars between Protestants and Catholics was raging in France; with only a few intervals, they were to afflict that country for the next thirty years. In the Netherlands a revolt which, though in part nationalist, was strongly influenced by religious differences, broke out into full-scale fighting. In Germany the fragile truce erected on the basis of the Peace of Augsburg in 1555 was soon creating as many quarrels as it solved, erupting in 1580, in Cologne, into a period of bitter fighting. Most of Europe became engaged in this new conflict, concerned now not with national or dynastic rivalries, but with the struggle for supremacy between two contending religious doctrines.

Religion was at the center of men's lives in a way it has never been at any time since.[31] A threat to the faith, a change in doctrine, restriction in the right of worship, was a threat almost to life itself and so to be resisted to the death. The simplest solution, that of mutual toleration, was nowhere considered. Within each state it was universally acccpted that only one faith could prevail. The French maxim, *un roi, une loi, une foi,* was generally accepted by Catholics and Protestants alike. The adoption of an alternative faith was not a question of personal choice. It was one of error, wickedness, and sin. So a rival faith had to be not merely opposed but, if possible, wiped out.

Moreover, this was not a series of isolated and separate national conflicts. It was, in a genuine sense, an international religious struggle. Men were, as in ancient Greece or today, almost as concerned about the survival of their faith abroad as at home. Protestants in England helped Protestants in France and the Netherlands. Catholics in France and Spain helped the Catholics of England. German Protestant princes came to the aid of the Protestant cause in the Netherlands. Protestant kings of Sweden and Denmark came to the aid of the Protestant cause in Germany. Conversely, religious minorities looked always for support from the great power of their own persuasion, so English Catholics plotted with the French and Spanish courts, French Protestants signed a treaty with Elizabeth surrendering a French port in return for English aid, William of Orange was willing to sell even the crown of his country in return for English or French military assistance, while the Catholic League in France welcomed in France's traditional enemy, Spain, to keep a Protestant king from the French throne.[32]

Thus, as in the modern world, the main political forces were transnational, and international politics became closely related to domestic factors. And also as in the modern world, the major powers became patrons and supporters of ideological parties in every part of Europe.

Political factions tended to identify themselves with rival international religious sects—the Guise faction in France with the Church of Rome, the Beggars in the Low Countries with Calvinism . . . all Protestant rebels—French, Netherlands, Scottish— looked more and more to Protestant England for help: all the Catholic rebels—French, English, Scottish, Irish—looked to Catholic Spain. By the 1580s the role of Protestant champion was being thrust upon the very reluctant Elizabeth I; that of Catholic champion upon Philip II, who until recently had been hardly less reluctant. Unofficial

31. "For in the minds of most men of these times religion was the dominant concern. . . . What most people wanted now was certainty, to find among all the doubts and challenges a faith, an authority that could be accepted and obeyed. And certainty was most readily provided in the closing ranks of churches that became more and more sharply set apart from another by more and more precisely defined creeds and ceremonies. But separation bred hostility, the more so as all except a few small and despised sects had inherited from medieval christianity a conviction that there could be only one true church and that this church had the right, indeed the duty, to use force to uphold and impose its faith." *New Cambridge Modern History,* III (1968):12.

32. "Many a humble Huguenot felt that he had more in common with his English or Dutch co-religionists than with his catholic fellow countrymen. As always ideology knew no frontiers and it was reponsible for many an unnatural alliance. . . ." C. Petrie, *Earlier Diplomatic History, 1494–1712* (London, 1949) p. 68

and underhand intervention now turned gradually into open war and the various local and national feuds began to coalesce into a new general conflict.[33]

Formal alliances were also largely determined now by religious affiliations. Throughout this period Protestant countries allied with Protestant, and Catholic with Catholic. Since in most cases religious issues were at stake, this was almost inevitable: It was precisely religious solidarity which brought the alliance into being. The leagues among the towns and princes of the Low countries and Germany were formed on the basis of religion. England helped the Protestant cause in the Netherlands, Spain the Catholic cause in France and Cologne; Sweden, Denmark, and England supported the Protestant cause in Germany during the Thirty Years' War, Spain and Austria the Catholics. Even the pope and the emperor, so often opposed to each other in the past, came together now in defense of their common faith. The only exception to this rule was, as ever, France. Just as she had been prepared in an earlier age to make common cause with the infidel Turk to promote dynastic or national interests, so now she was willing to make common cause, in the Thirty Years' War, with heretic Protestants against the archenemy Spain (though even she sought to protect the Catholic interest in doing so, for example by safeguarding the Catholic faith in Bavaria).

A religiously oriented society produced its own methods of state behavior. As in a later ideological society, cold war, or as it was then known "war underhand," that is plotting and sedition, were often used as an alternative to full-scale external war. Because religious beliefs were now more powerful than national or dynastic loyalty, outside powers could always count on a fifth column favorable to its cause in other lands. The devout citizen would feel little loyalty to a ruler of opposite faith, and feel fully justified in seeking to overthrow him. We thus find the same phenomenon as in ancient Greece in another ideological age: limited loyalty to the state. English Catholics felt justified by the necessities of religion in promoting an invasion of their own country from France or Spain, or even plotting the assassination of their sovereign, just as the Protestants of France and the Netherlands sought assistance from England and as the Moriscoes in Spain sought help from the Muslim rulers of Algiers against their Christian masters. This in turn engendered (again as in other ideological ages) a chronic sense of insecurity among governments and a ruthless determination to stamp out those who were at once heretics and a menace to the state. Elizabeth felt obliged to persecute Catholic preachers as a menace to her own throne as much as to the Protestant faith. Richelieu regarded the reduction of the independent power of the Huguenots as essential to building the strength and security of France. Still more insecure was a ruler such as Mary Queen of Scots, in the unique position of professing a religion that was no longer that of a majority of her subjects, a situation that would have rendered her position precarious even without the vagaries of her personal life.

In a situation of ideological conflict there are only two theoretical solutions,

33. *New Cambridge Modern History,* III (1968): 8.

toleration and partition. Since toleration was not an acceptable policy in this age, the solution adopted had to be that of partition. This was the solution which the Peace of Augsburg had sought to implement in Germany (though imperfectly and unjustly, since the Calvinists were excluded from its terms). It was also the solution finally adopted throughout most of Europe in 1648. The nations were divided into those which were Catholic and those that were Protestant, and in most of them the alternative faith was not permitted (even in France, which was at first an exception, this solution was adopted after 1685).

It was a matter of supreme importance which religion was assumed by the ruler of each country, since it was normally he who, directly or indirectly, determined which religion was to be practiced. This could raise problems. If the ruler changed faith, did this mean that his people must do so too? Or, conversely, should he accept the religion of his population: When the Catholic Duke of Cleves died in 1609, both the chief claimants were Protestants, and so could have made their subjects Protestants. This caused the emperor himself to intervene, with a claim to administer the territories himself till the matter was resolved, while most of the Protestant rulers of Europe banded together in opposition. Finally it required the conversion of both the two main claimants, one to Calvinism and the other to Catholicism, to resolve the issue, once again on the basis of partition. Later in Germany some rulers, changing faith, required a similar change in their subjects (though this was not always enforced). In such an age, therefore, a conversion could be the cause of a major international incident.

There were, moreover, other ideological conflicts. The Protestants were almost as bitterly divided among themselves as they were from the Catholics. Both in Germany and the Netherlands, Lutherans and Calvinists were in bitter conflict. In the early years of the Thirty Years' War, the German Lutheran princes showed no inclination to go to the support of their Calvinist brethren in Bohemia. The Orthodox in the East had still less fellow feeling with either Protestant or Catholic, sometimes even siding with the Turks against their fellow Christians in the West. Above all, the ancient conflict between Islam and Christianity, pursued for centuries, was continued with renewed bitterness in this age, both in the Mediterranean and East Europe.

As a result, during the century between 1559 and 1648 there was scarcely a single war in any part of Europe in which religion was not in some way an issue; in most of them it was the central issue. This does not mean that dynastic conflicts totally ceased to be of account. They continued to occur, but always modified by the religious factor (as in Cleves-Julich). Even where dynastic interests counted most, as between France and Spain, Catholics in both would still sometimes stand together against Protestants. Small nations, such as Venice and Savoy, whose existence depended on playing off powerful neighbors against each other, continued in some cases to pursue their traditional policies regardless of religious loyalties. In other cases religion (like ideology in ancient Greece) was used at least partly as a mask: to rationalize and justify policies required by national interest.

Sweden, in championing the Protestant cause in Germany, also promoted her own national interests in the Baltic, as Spain did in seeking to stamp out Protestant revolt in the Netherlands. But this did not mean that Gustav Adolf was not genuinely Protestant, or Philip II not genuinely Catholic. Both were profoundly so (just as today the Soviet Union and the U.S. are genuinely committed to their ideologies, yet may promote national interests by ideological acts). Religion was, in the minds of most, the greatest issue of the day. The fact that it was the major issue over which wars were fought, that it was the center of domestic conflict as much as international, that the *results* of wars, as in the Netherlands and in the Thirty Years' War, often conformed largely with the boundaries of religious allegiance, that it was possible to buy Paris with a mass—all of these are clearly indications that in this age religion was generally seen as the most fundamental issue of international society.

The society thus had much in common with other ages of ideology, in Greece and in recent times. Many of the most important political forces were transnational. Minority groups in every country looked for support to great patrons elsewhere. Superpowers made themselves into champions of one faith or another. Heresy was widely identified with treason. And the dominant concern was not so much with territorial control as with the defense of a particular faith. So Philip II declared that he "would rather lose the Low countries than rule them should they cease to be Catholic." In such a society, inevitably, both the dominant motives and the dominant means employed became quite different from those of previous and of subsequent ages. So *expectations* concerning state actions—those of one's own state as much as those of others—changed yet again.

## 5.5 The Age of Sovereignty (1648–1789)

The end of the age of religions is as clearly marked as its beginning. After 1648 religious issues continued occasionally to be important in the *internal* politics of a number of states (for example, in France in 1685 and in Britain three years later). But between states they ceased to be of significance. They were almost never a major cause of war. Even in the continuing conflicts with the Turks, it was now the control of territory rather than ideology which was primarily at issue. The era of crusade was well past. The religious frontiers of Europe, both in the West and in the East, were now fairly firmly established and were to remain largely unchanged for the next three hundred years.[34]

But the Peace of Westphalia not only announced the end of the age of religions. It also marked and symbolized the emergence of a new type of international

---

34. Cf. *New Cambridge Modern History*, (1961):1. "Although religious events and motives continued to be of vital importance in the history of many European countries—such as France, England and the Hapsburg territories—there were no further changes in the religious frontiers: the European countries and principalities retained the religion which was established there in 1648."

society, different from all those which had preceded it. The beginnings of this could be seen during the long negotiations leading up to it: in the absurd and puerile disputes over precedence, in which the United Provinces for long delayed sending a representative in case he should not be accorded the same status as that from Venice, in which the French and Swedish delegates had to negotiate in separate cities to avoid raising the delicate question of their relative standing, and so on. Similarly, the *separate* representation at those negotiations of the German princes, which was skillfully engineered by France, revealed not only the impending dissolution of the empire but the emergence of a new age of "sovereign equality" in which even the smallest states arrogated to themselves all the rights and trappings of sovereignty. The final acknowledgement in the treaties of the right of these princes to make independent alliances reemphasized their status as indepen- dent and sovereign states.[35] Disputes over the titles to be accorded the different sovereigns—the French objection to the Spanish title of King of Portugal and Prince of Catalonia, the Spanish objection to the French monarch's claim to be King of Navarre, and so on—expressed the same overriding concern for *sovereign* rights.

Perhaps even more clearly symbolic of the new age now being ushered in was the reaffirmation in 1648, in terms more unambiguous than ever, of the principle, first laid down ninety years before, of *cujus regio ejus religio*. In this formula the whole burning issue which had engaged Europe in war for the previous century was now to be resolved. In principle in Germany, and in practice elsewhere, it was to be settled by the simple expedient of according all authority to the sovereign. Sovereigns were given the right to dispose not only of the physical but of the spiritual destiny of their subjects. Exaltation of the sovereign's power could hardly be taken further. The simple formula proclaimed by Hobbes, under which order, peace, and harmony in each state were to be attained by the simple expedient of according unlimited authority to the supreme sovereign power, was here put into practice in the most emphatic form.

The concept of the "sovereign" now became something far wider than that of a personal ruler. In the very year of the Peace of Westphalia, the English parliament proclaimed its own sovereignty over the people by the simple device of executing its previous embodiment, the king. Though elsewhere (and even, within a dozen years, in England once more) the sovereign power usually remained a personal ruler, that ruler was now no longer simply a personal dynast, fulfilling his own desires and interests through his occupation of the throne. He was now the personification of the state he ruled, seeing his own greatness embodied in the greatness of his state. Louis XIV was universally seen as the model and archetype of the sovereign, and he stamped on the age that goal of "glory" which was typical for its rulers. But the glory was that of the state as much as of the ruler. And Louis'

---

35. "By receiving at Westphalia the unfettered control of their foreign policy the member princes of the empire became sovereign. . . . With the final devaluation of the imperial title the Treaty of Westphalia left Europe a collection of sovereign entities." R. Albrecht-Carrie, *A Diplomatic History of Europe Since the Congress of Vienna* (New York, 1958), p. 5.

most famous aphorism, identifying the state with himself, sums up in three words the essential ideology of this society. For the true significance of that phrase was not that it expressed the subordination of the nation to his own power, but that of himself to the interests of the state.

The quest for glory was expressed in many different ways. It was seen, for example, in the constant disputes over status so typical of the age. In every court of Europe there were conflicts over the precedence to be accorded to the ambassadors of the different states. Louis XIV, after a particularly bitter clash between the staff of his own ambassador and that of Spain in London, made it his business to secure for himself diplomatic precedence in all the courts of Europe. There were frequent armed clashes at sea over the demands of one fleet for a naval salute from another—between England and the United Provinces, between France and almost every other state. So Colbert, Louis' great minister, said: "France claims that all other nations must bow down to her at sea and at the Court of Kings." So in a treaty with Algeria in 1681, France stipulated that, whenever a vessel "of the Emperor of France" anchored in that harbor, it was to be saluted with more guns than a ship of any other country. Other countries were little different in their ambitions, though more modest in their attainments. Every state felt that its honor and its reputation, as well as those of its sovereign, was bound up in such disputes.

The competition for glory among sovereigns and their states (increasingly identified with each other even by their subjects) was seen also in new attitudes to territory. Almost every ruler in Europe had territorial ambitions of one kind or another, but these were on behalf of the state rather than of the dynasty. Louis, though often seen as the model, was only one among the many powerful sovereigns of the day who saw the enhancement of their own glory in increasing the power of their own state abroad as well as at home. It is not by chance that it is in this age that so many of the monarchs who, then or later, acquired the appellation "Great" appeared, and that this was applied, not to the genuine reformers and innovating spirits such as Joseph II of Austria or Gustav III of Sweden, but to those who best promoted the territorial aggrandizement and external power of their states: Frederick in Prussia, Catherine in Russia, Louis in France. More clearly than anything this attribution reflected the essential valuations of the age. If a ruler's policies resulted in perpetual wars, this was not held against him, so long as they resulted in the enhancement of the power and glory of the state. In an age of absolutism, when monarchs could often personally control the destinies of millions of subjects, it is scarcely surprising that nations were often identified with their rulers. But it is also scarcely to be wondered that Jean-Jacques Rousseau, searching for the cause of war in the world at the conclusion of the period, laid it squarely at the door of the monarchs themselves. If the sovereigns who made it could be abolished, he understandably believed, then war too could be banished from the universe.

The rulers sought not any territory to which they could lay claim, as had their dynastic predecessors, but territory important to their own state, especially to round out its frontiers. This was the motive behind France's repeated wars on her eastern boundary; the northern wars between Sweden and Denmark, Sweden and Russia, and between Poland and Russia; those between Austria and Turkey and Russia and Turkey; and those between Prussia and Austria. Consolidation of territory became an almost universal aim. The wars were usually fought for limited ends by limited means. Even the conflicts overseas, in North America, India, and the West Indies, were now fought to promote explicitly conceived national interests, whether commercial or strategic, rather than to acquire territory for its own sake. Everywhere it was now the interests of the state, as much as of the ruler and his house, which became the dominant concern.

Associated with this concern for state interests was the *lack* of concern for popular wishes. It is this which distinguishes this society above all from that which was to follow: national sentiments had begun to appear, but not the nation-state, or even nationalism. Indifference to popular wishes over international questions of course reflected attitudes shown equally at home in an age of absolutism. If the mass of the people could not expect any say in *how* they were ruled domestically, how could they expect to have a say in *who* ruled them internationally? Certainly one of the outstanding features of this age is the arbitrary way in which territories were bartered and assigned by governments to suit their own convenience, without any regard for the desires or interests of their inhabitants in the matter. So Belgium and Milan were casually transferred from Spain to Austria, equally alien and almost as remote, Gibralta and Minorca to Britain, Finland from Russia to Sweden, and so on. The concept of "compensation"—that a territorial acquisition by one power made necessary a territorial acquisition by another—was used to justify wholesale transfers of large populations to suit the convenience of the major powers. So Sicily was handed over from Spain to Savoy in 1714, swapped in 1720 for Sardinia, and twenty years after that lumped in with Naples and handed to a Spanish prince. Parma and Piacenza were awarded to the same Spanish prince (Don Carlos) in 1732, transferred to Austria in 1739, and transferred yet again to his brother in 1748, all three rulers being equally alien to the inhabitants. After the war of Polish succession in 1739, the Duke of Lorraine exchanged his own duchy for Tuscany, while the unsuccessful candidate for the Polish throne, Stanislaus, was compensated with the gift of Lorraine, and the elector of Saxony got Poland: All the rulers got something, but all the *territories* acquired totally foreign rulers. So, too, a little later the ruler of Prussia sought to acquire Saxony from its elector by offering in exchange Czech Bohemia (which was not his to give). The idea that on any such question the populations most affected should be consulted would have been thought laughable: a challenge to the very principle of sovereignty that was now everywhere accepted. And the fate of Poland, cynically carved up by the great powers immediately neighboring her, perhaps most vividly demonstrated the indifference to popular wishes so characteristic of this age.[36]

Conversely, although the views of peoples counted for little, neither did the

36. The example of Poland is itself a sufficient refutation of the theory, sometimes put forward, that one of the rules of the "system" in this age was that the individual units while they might be weakened, were never totally destroyed.

laws of inheritance. The assumptions and expectations of the age of dynasts were now dead. It was no longer possible for a ruler, simply through the working of the laws of inheritance, to become master of territories far distant from his homeland (at least in Europe), or of vast empires like that of Charles V. The wars of Spanish, Austrian, and Bavarian succession were fought to prove precisely the opposite. Rights of inheritance, it was shown, even the express and clearly defined will of the previous ruler, might have to be overthrown if they interfered too seriously with the interests and views of the other states—with the "balance of power," as it began euphemistically to be described. The war of Polish succession likewise was fought essentially to prevent the normal rules and procedures for succession from applying, and resulted in the withdrawal of one of the chief candidates for the throne, and in a complex exchange of territories for the mutual convenience of the states participating. The prevalence of wars of succession in this age, therefore, far from making it a dynastic age, as is sometimes suggested, shows rather the opposite. The principle of dynasticism was increasingly resisted and flouted in the interests of the "balance of power" or, more accurately, of the combined will of other states, exerted if necessary by armed force.

The assumptions of sovereignty also destroyed those of the age *immediately* preceding, that of religions. The right of one state to intervene in the religious conflicts of other states was no longer assumed. "Sovereignty" implied the independence of each on such questions. Nor did religious minorities involved in domestic disputes any longer expect support from their coreligionists elsewhere: The Huguenots in France in 1685 had no thought, like their predecessors a century before, that foreign governments might intervene to protect their rights, any more than Lutherans in German states expected it when they had problems with their rulers over religious questions. This was partly because, with increasing toleration, intervention was less necessary. But it was even more because of the universal acceptance of the *principle* of sovereignty, of the right of sovereign powers to exclusive jurisdiction and control in their own states on all questions, including that of religion.

This was connected with another change from the age before. The previous century had been one above all of internal upheavals and civil conflict, not only on religious but also on national issues, as in the Netherlands, Ireland, Catalonia, and Portugal, among others. Its closing year, 1648, was as much a year of revolutions as its better-known successor 200 years later; revolutions occurred in that year in France, Britain, Portugal, Catalonia, and Naples. But in the next 140 years internal conflict was at a minimum. The power of the state which the new sovereigns were building up deterred it, and greater indifference to ideology made it less necessary. This in turn reduced external wars designed to assist in internal struggles. Meddling in the domestic conflicts of others, which had been perhaps the most important source of war in the previous age, now scarcely featured at all.

A final change in this age was equally a consequence of sovereign power: the slow emergence of the concept that sovereigns had some *common* interests, that they belonged to an interdependent system. There was plentiful contact between the courts of different sovereigns and growing understanding between them. There was increasing recognition that the impact of one ruler's actions on others must be taken into account. The need for common action, either through alliances and coalitions, or through mutual undertakings, to maintain a mutuality of advantage, or balance within the system, began to be recognized. This attitude was expressed by Montesquieu in 1748: "The law of nations is naturally founded on this principle, that different nations ought in time of peace to do one another all the good they can and, in time of war, as little injury as possible, without prejudicing their real interest."[37] Though such admirable precepts were not always fully implemented in practice, they reflected the general emergence of the idea of a society of states, in which every member must take account of the views and interests of others—a European "system" which all must help maintain.

The special character of this society thus derives from the combination of a number of factors: the rise in the power of the sovereign at home, development of the territorial as against the dynastic state, competition for status among sovereigns and states, indifference to popular wishes, professionalization of war, development of organized foreign offices and organized foreign policies, general moderation in ends and means. But the central core was the elaboration of the idea of sovereignty and sovereign rights. The absolutism of such a ruler as Louis XIV demanded that within his own territories he could do what he liked, an assumption that was widely borrowed by other rulers in relation to their own. In their mutual relations this implied not simply a competition for glory, but a willingness to recognize the rights of *other* sovereigns, a willingness to do deals, to sacrifice some unilateral gains for others that were agreed, a limitation of ambitions to accommodate the ambitions of others. Sovereigns might have little truck with the ordinary people. With other sovereigns they could do business. So the dominant assumptions of the society, the basic ideology, changed again.

## 5.6 The Age of Nationalism (1789–1914)

The end of the age of sovereignty can be dated almost as accurately as its beginning. The French Revolution represented a challenge to the international order established over the previous century and a half as direct and threatening as that which it posed to the domestic order of states. And while the latter threat was, temporarily at least, overcome, the former could not be undone so easily. For the challenge posed to the international order arose not because of the political changes which the revolution brought in France: Many of these were already reversed by 1794, and most of the rest in 1814. What primarily affected the international order was the *national* revolution which persisted long after the political revolution had

37. Montesquieu, *L'esprit des Lois*, I.

been undone: after the totalitarianism of the Directoire, the conservatism of the Consulate, the police state of the Empire, had given way once more to the restored monarchy in 1814. And outside France, while it was the political ideals of the French Revolution which were most discussed, acclaimed, or denounced, it was the national revolution which won the most effective emulation.

The national upsurge in France, which the revolution quickly became, was defeated by two forces. It was defeated in part by the forces of monarchical sovereignty which it most directly challenged, both domestically and internationally. But it was defeated even more by the forces of *rival* nationalism which it had itself raised up against it: in Britain, in Spain, in Prussia, and in Russia (the persistent failure of Austria, defeated in four successive wars by Napoleon, occurred perhaps partly because that country could not afford, without destroying itself, the outbreak of national spirit which occurred elsewhere). The effect of France's defeat was the temporary reestablishment of a settlement based on the old principles of sovereignty, and a settlement reached by all the old procedures of wheeling and dealing, of "balance of power" and "compensation," and in total disregard of the wishes of populations, which had been typical of the age of sovereignty. So Norway was passed from Denmark to Sweden, Finland from Sweden to Russia, Belgium was handed to Holland, (and large parts of Italy were handed to Austria in "compensation"); so half of Saxony was handed to Prussia and parts of the Rhineland given to Saxony in return; so Poland, Venice, and Genoa were obliterated altogether; all without regard to the views of the inhabitants of these territories, and entirely to suit the convenience of the major powers. But the national sentiments which the French Revolution had evoked were not to be so easily laid aside. And most of the century that followed was devoted to overturning the settlement of Vienna bit by bit, sometimes in peace and sometimes in war, to adjust it to the demands of the new "national principle," the demon which the revolutionary armies had released from its bottle and was now by no means willing to be corked up again.

The nationalism of the period took three main forms. There was the *explosive* nationalism, the demand of minority peoples for independence, which threatened especially the conglomerates, such as the Ottoman Empire, Austria-Hungary, Russia, Norway-Sweden, Netherlands-Belgium, and so on. There was the *integrative* nationalism which sought to achieve unity among peoples previously divided among a number of separate entities, affecting especially the peoples of Italy, Germany, and Poland. There was finally the *competitive* nationalism among existing nations which increasingly influenced the attitudes and actions of all the major states, especially those newly established. Among them these three forces accounted for much of the history of the period.

The whole era can indeed be divided into three relatively clearly marked periods, of roughly equal length, each dominated by one of these three main forms of nationalism. The first, lasting from 1815 to 1854, was marked especially by the effects of explosive nationalism. There were during this time no wars *between* the major powers in Europe and scarcely any even involving one of them (the war of

1828–1829 between Russia and Turkey is the only significant exception). But it was an age of much internal unrest, frequent revolutions, and civil conflicts. Revolutionary movements in Naples and Piedmont, Modena and Parma, Spain and Portugal, Greece and Belgium, Poland and Egypt, and finally, in 1848, in almost every state in Europe, came into violent conflict with monarchical governments and with the principle of sovereignty which they had reestablished: Greeks against Turkish sovereignty, Polish against Russian, Belgian against Dutch, Hungarian, Italian, and Slav against Austrian. This provoked continuing disagreements among the governments of Europe about the correct way to respond to this movement, disagreements which led finally to the polarization of Europe between a Western bloc, consisting of Britain and France, relatively sympathetic to the national principle and unsympathetic to intervention against it, ranged against an Eastern bloc, consisting of Austria, Prussia, and Russia, relatively unsympathetic to national movements and more inclined to favor intervention from outside to suppress them if necessary.

The second period lasted from 1854 to 1878. Now it was integrative nationalism which was the dominant threat to the international order. This was an age of frequent wars among the major powers, six in thirty-four years. All except the first, in the Crimea (even this had as *consequence* the national unification of Romania), were wars of national unification or (in the case of the Balkan wars of 1875–1878) of national solidarity. In consequence major states, such as Germany and Italy, for the first time achieved unification in this period; smaller states, such as Serbia, Montenegro, Bulgaria, and Rumania, became for the first time independent national states. The national principle was now not only being asserted. It was actually being implemented.

In the third and final period, between 1878 and 1914, competitive nationalism became the dominant force and the main threat to the international order. The competition for status, influence, and territory became more intense than ever, especially among new states, such as Germany, Italy, and Japan, which felt they had ground to make up to achieve a status corresponding to their power. Like the first period, it is one in which there were no wars among the major powers. Competition took place as much or more outside Europe as within it, in Africa, Asia, and the Pacific. But these external conflicts were all ultimately resolved, and it was once again in Europe that the tensions between the powers became most acute. This is specially so in the border areas between them, above all the Balkans. Here more than anywhere the newly emergent force of nationalism came into conflict with the traditional force of sovereignty; in the decaying empires of Turkey, Austria-Hungary, and Russia. Here indeed the forces of explosive nationalism (in Austria-Hungary and Turkey), of integrative nationalism (among the Slavs), and competitive nationalism (in Germany and other powers) came together and finally ignited the tinder-barrel which was to bring the whole society to its cataclysmic Armageddon.

It is thus the ideology of nationalism that dominates this international society and gives it its special character. This increasingly challenges and displaces the ideology of sovereignty. The French Revolution's most famous statement of faith, the Declaration of Rights of Man of 1789, declared that "the principle of all sovereignty rests essentially in the nation." So nationalism assimilated the doctrine of sovereignty for its own ends. Similarly, the revolutionaries in Belgium in 1830 declared, in the constitution drawn up in the following year, that "all powers have their source in the nation." Many other of the new constitutions of this age reflected the idea of the nation as the ultimate focus of allegiance and the fount of obligation. The sovereign body, the source of the citizen's rights and duties, is transferred from the person of the ruler, the monarch of the day, to the nation itself.

Everywhere, for a number of reasons, historical, political, cultural, and social, men became more conscious of national identity, national history, national culture, national language. This occurred within already unified national states, as it did among minority peoples or divided peoples. But it was among the latter that it was most powerful, for it was here that those national feelings encountered the most stubborn resistance. To the many existing states which were multinational (such as Turkey, Austria, and Russia) or binational (such as Holland-Belgium or Norway-Sweden), to the divided peoples (in Germany, Italy, and Poland), the national principle, increasingly widely accepted, represented an automatic challenge. And it was this tension between the principle of the nation and that of the state which accounted for a large part of the international history of this period and almost all the wars of the age. Those wars were fought to create new nations by dissecting old states.

There was another way in which the assumptions of the age of sovereignty were challenged. Sovereigns themselves were displaced from the central role. Here too Napoleon symbolized the challenge. The idea of a self-made sovereign, even more of a self-crowned sovereign, a sovereign of common blood displacing a king of royal blood who had himself been executed by his own people, was the most brutal and direct challenge possible to the principle of legitimacy, and one of the chief reasons for the hostility to Napoleon shown by ruling forces elsewhere. The idea of such a self-made sovereign making new sovereigns out of his own brothers accentuated the challenge. But when, years later, a nephew, equally self-made, appeared on the scene, the other sovereigns (though they debated solemnly whether he should be styled as "brother" or merely as "friend") had no choice but to accept him because he was accepted by his own nation. Sovereigns were devalued in other ways. New dynasties were made and unmade in this age with remarkable facility. Three were used up in France in little more than fifty years. The newly established kingdoms of Serbia, Greece, and Bulgaria each got through two before 1914. In Italy and Germany large numbers of princely families were dispensed with altogether, without noticeable inconvenience or even protest. The aura surrounding kinghood everywhere began to fade.

Above all, however, the sovereign's role within the state, even in the absolutist nations, declined everywhere. Control and operation of foreign policy increasingly fell out of their hands altogether. In the previous age the policies of France, Prussia, Austria, and Russia had been those of Louis XIV, Frederick the Great,

Maria Teresa, and William III. They had ministers to *execute* their policy, but the policies were their own. Now the policies of France, Prussia, Austria, and Britain were those of Guizot, Bismarck, Metternich, and Palmerston and their colleagues. And the interests they promoted increasingly were not those of the sovereign but of the nation. Public documents, diplomatic notes, and other official sources speak of the policies and aims, not of the sovereign or the crown, as before, but of "France" or "Russia." While Louis XIV in his memoirs speaks of "his" armies, government, people, or policy, Palmerston and Bismarck speak of Great Britain's or Germany's.

Such changes in phraseology were not haphazard. Statesmen spoke in terms of the nation because they felt in terms of the nation, and in doing so they reflected feelings which were widespread among their population. Though almost no states were "democratic" in the modern sense (that is, enjoyed universal suffrage), there was nonetheless during the course of the century an increase in the *representative* character of government in most countries, and so in the degree of popular influence on policy. Collective ambitions, which had played little part during the age of sovereignty (how could one feel passionate devotion to the cause of a sovereign who was often foreign, or to a state which was often an accidental conglomeration of territories and peoples), were now more powerful and more closely reflected in policy. Nationalism was a popular movement not in the sense that it was necessarily strongly felt by the mass of the peasantry or proletariat, but because it was strongly felt by large segments of the articulate bourgeoisie who in many places began to take over or at least share political power. And while originally nationalism was still for some a means to other things—liberalism, democracy, or conservatism—it became increasingly an end in itself: a dynamic force in its own right which more and more determined policy.

Such sentiments were further stimulated by the conflicts and wars of the age. If Napoleon's armies evoked patriotic fervor in the nations they occupied as well as in France, Bismarck's wars evoked patriotic fervor in Denmark, Austria, and France, even in Britain, as well as in Germany. Larger sections of the people were involved in wars and other national affairs. Populations were increasingly educated. They identified with the fortunes of their own state, experienced together collective pride, ambition, jealousy, humiliation. When in 1661 the French ambassador in London was insulted by the servants of the Spanish ambassador, it was an insult to Louis XIV personally and aroused his rage. When in 1870 Bismarck humiliated France in his famous telegram, it was an insult to France nationally and enraged the whole French nation.[38]

The development of powerful national administrative structures meant that individuals no longer thought in terms of the village, city, or district, but increasingly in terms of national units, and of national governments acting on their behalf. The development of national communications, railways, roads, and the post office

38. The words "patriotism" and "patriot" had not even appeared in the French Academy dictionary of 1694; they were included for the first time in that of 1777.

promoted national consciousness. National newspapers instilled a national viewpoint. Even the philosophy of the age reflected and encouraged this dominant ideology. The vast metaphysical construction of Hegel, exalting the nation into a mystical supreme being so that the Prussian state could be identified with God walking on earth, the ultimate embodiment of right, and the logical end-process of history, Herbert Spencer's adaptation of the Darwinian notion of a struggle for survival to the international sphere, with its belief that only the nation which remained strong and aggressive was likely to survive in the endless competitive struggle for living-space and power, these represented the ideological superstructure for the rule of the nation-state. Even socialism borrowed the assumptions of nationalism: so, though it once rejected state power and denounced the middle-class state as a committee of the bourgeoisie, increasingly it sought instead another nation-state run by the proletariat; "nationalization" became its key concept; and in 1914, for all their internationalist dreams, socialists responded to traditional nationalistic stimuli as obediently and enthusiastically as the bourgeois classes they had despised for so long. The Second International proved only too national.

The governing ideology in this society was thus different from anything that had existed in earlier times. Identification with the state and its aims became more widespread and more intense than in any previous age—provided that the state was a national state and not a multinational empire. A competitive spirit entered into state relationships on a scale not seen since the ancient Chinese society. In this case the competition was not among a small number of rulers and advisers, but of entire peoples. Expectations were changed in a more fundamental way. For in many cases the national sentiment influenced not merely the inhabitants of *existing* political units, but individuals spread among many units, or limited minorities in one. Nationalism therefore represented not merely a powerful motive force *between* the units but a transnational (or rather transstate) influence within them. While it promoted the purposes and the power of some states, it threatened the very existence of others. In either case it represented a force which not only challenged the traditional concepts of sovereignty, but continually threatened the stability of the international order. A new international ideology had brought into existence a society of quite a new character.

## 5.7 The Age of Ideology (1914–1974)

The end of the age of nationalism can be dated relatively clearly. The outbreak of World War I was the climacteric culmination of a century of nationalist rivalries, and it brought a whole world to an end. In its course four of the old empires were destroyed, temporarily or permanently: the Turkish, the Austrian, the Russian, and the German. The *principle* of nationalism survived, and the war's end brought into being a whole new family of nations, especially in East Europe, established on that principle (though these were too small to be fully viable and in a sense only discredited the principle). Nationalist urges were still powerful especially among the defeated or disappointed powers, such as Germany, Italy, and Japan. But in general nationalism lost some of the intensity of earlier years. The jingoism of Palmerston and Joseph Chamberlain, the preoccupation with French glory of Napoleon III and Boulanger, the national ambitions of Bismark, the flag-waving patriotism of Teddy Roosevelt, were never to appear in their old form. Increasingly statesmen began to demand a wider cause than national glory to guide their actions.

At this very moment these wider causes began to be found. Even while World War I was still being fought the process began. So the Western allies felt it necessary to insist that they were fighting not for Britain, France, and other ancient names against Germany and Austria-Hungary, but for respect for treaties, for the integrity of small nations, for self-determination, against autocracy, against militarism, against aggression. Even the central powers, though less insistent on the subject, claimed to be fighting for an equal place in the sun, for legitimacy, for traditional sovereign rights. "The need to induce peoples to continue in their acceptance of the sacrifices demanded of them put a premium on factors other than that of crude power: ideologies laden with moral content. And this became an important aspect of the struggle. . . ."[39]

Two events in 1917 accentuated this trend. The entry of the U.S. into the war brought for the first time the direct participation in world politics of a nation especially disposed to seek a moral justification for its actions, under a leader even more disposed than his fellow countrymen to find such ideological purposes. Woodrow Wilson, in announcing the U.S. declaration of war, proclaimed: "We shall fight for the things we have always carried nearest to our hearts—for democracy, for the right of those who submit to authority to have a voice in their own government, for the rights and liberties of small nations, for a universal dominance of right by such a concert of free peoples as shall bring peace and safety and make the world itself at last free." The October Revolution in Russia in the same year brought a major government under the control of the most powerful and original political ideology of the day. That government too became, for a time, more devoted to the promotion of ideological ends than to national goals. It was willing to denounce the secret agreements and unequal treaties of nationalism; it gave away Finland and other areas. Instead it sought to export revolution. These two powers, soon to become the strongest in the world, became the leaders of the two ideological forces that were to dominate the age that followed. Both retreated into their shell for a decade or so. While the U.S., tired of making the world safe for democracy, sought temporary isolation, the Soviet Union likewise withdrew for a time, to make the state safe for socialism. Each reemerged twenty years later as the acknowledged champions and leaders of the two great ideologies that were to contest the world for the next thirty years.

For a time, however, the ideological contest was triangular rather than bipolar.

39. Albrecht-Carrie, *Diplomatic History of Europe*, p. 343.

Within a few years of the end of the war there emerged new ideological doctrines, equally hostile to both the main rival creeds of U.S.-led democracy and Soviet-led communism. From 1922 in Italy, from 1924 in Germany, a few years later in Japan, there arose powerful political forces, and ultimately governments, proclaiming new right-wing, authoritarian dogmas, demanding the subjection of the individual to the purposes of the state. These borrowed something from each of their rivals (the belief in state action and totalitarian control from the communists, and the claim to represent and to reconcile varying interests within the state, in their case through corporatist institutions, from the democracies). Yet they denounced with impartial fervor the inequities of each. So for twenty years a complex triangular struggle took place among the three, with each party almost equally hostile to both the other two. Because the communist and democratic forces were too mutually suspicious to join forces, a brief, opportunistic understanding was reached in 1939 between the far right and far left, to be followed only two years later by an equally opportunistic alliance between West and East against the authoritarians. But the destruction of their common enemy only led in turn to a new and deeper ideological confrontation between the two victorious forces of communism and democracy which was to dominate the world scene for the next thirty years.

This universal concern with ideology transformed the prevailing image of international society. As always, language reflected this change. Statesmen now denounced not Germany, but "Nazism," not Russia, but "Bolshevism," not the U.S., but "imperialism." The world was still divided into friends and foes, but these were now ideological allies and enemies, rather than rival nations and alliances formed among similar states on purely tactical grounds. The ideological divisions, as in earlier ages, affected not only the external relations between states and blocs, but events within them as well. The ideological struggle of the interwar period, among communists, democrats, and fascists, was fought out as bitterly within each state as between them. The postwar struggle between East and West was fought out in each individual state as well as between the blocs as a whole: indeed, violence was now primarily between domestic factions. As in the Greek system and the age of religions, domestic political struggles and international politics were merged in a single global struggle.

Equally important for the international system were the bitter ideological struggles *within* each bloc and ideological group: between Stalin and Trotsky, between Mao and Li Li san, between Roosevelt and Taft, between Tito and Stalin, McCarthy and Stevenson, Khrushchev and Mao, and so on. All of these disputes within ideologies, like those between them, had an impact on foreign relations. There developed sectional ideologies, increasingly associated with particular nations within a bloc (China, Yugoslavia, France, Cuba, Chile). Many of the main issues of international politics were associated with these disputes: Those between the Soviet Union and China, the Soviet Union and Czechosolvakia, the U.S. and France, Casablanca and Monrovia powers, progressive Arabs and conservatives, Cuba and Brazil, ultimately became almost as important as the divide between the main blocs. So ideological factors influenced the relations of states in a much wider way than in the obvious cold war confrontation.

Such a society was characterized by a number of features. Motives, as in other ideological ages, were not so much territorial as political: concerned not with defeating or destroying states but with the type of government established in existing states. For a time it is true, between the wars, while nationalism remained a powerful force, territory remained an important source of conflict. But from 1945 the objective was not so much to conquer territories (even if strategically vital) but to establish, or to restore, the types of government to be politically reliable. So in many parts of the world the two major powers competed to bring to power governments favorable to their own cause. There was, as in other ideological ages, a complex relationship between the interests of the superpower and the ideology; in defending the ideology, the superpower defended itself as well. Just as Spain as well as Catholicism had an interest in the defeat of Protestant regimes elsewhere, just as Athens as well as democracy had an interest in overcoming oligarchic regimes elsewhere, so now the U.S. as well as democracy had an interest in preventing the coming to power of Communist regimes in every part of the world, and the Soviet Union in promoting it.

Second, as in earlier ideological ages, there is a genuine internationalization within the system. Ideological loyalties have become as important in determining action as national loyalties. Volunteers travel to fight in a civil conflict elsewhere, impelled by ideological rather than national aims: republicans in the Spanish Civil War, white mercenaries in African states, Che Guevara and his band in Bolivia. Conversely, the adherents of one particular political faith will betray their own nation for the sake of that faith. Fifth columns are sometimes again a significant factor in international politics. In a more real sense than ever before there is now a single, integrated world political arena.

Third, the concern with ideology is associated with another basic change. Almost every other international society throughout world history has been characterized by a high degree of territorial instability: frontiers have been fluid and subject to rapid change, mainly through war. In the ideological age frontiers have become more firmly established than ever before and are not now seriously challenged. Even among newer nations this is true. In Africa, despite the total irrationality of the borders inherited from the colonial age, the newly independent governments explicitly endorse them. In Latin America, after a century and a half of conflict, most of the remaining frontier disputes have become of small importance. In Asia the territorial problems are mainly within divided states rather than over international frontiers. Even where there are frontier disputes, between Algeria and Morocco or India and China, they are relatively limited in scope.

But as in other ideological ages, such as the age of religions, this increase in *external* stability is mirrored by an increase in *internal* instability. Though international wars are fewer, civil wars are much more numerous.[40] Between the wars,

40. For statistics and fuller discussion concerning types of war see Evan Luard, *Conflict and Peace in the Modern International System* (Boston, 1968).

well over half the countries of Europe experienced civil wars or coups. After 1945, though Europe became somewhat more stable, the countries of Latin America, Africa, and Asia became even more subject to internal unrest. Almost all of them underwent civil wars or coups or both. This combination of external stability with internal unrest brought about a substantial change in the means which states employ in their relations with each other. The characteristic means of the age became subversion, propaganda, the organization of plots and coups, and other forms of assistance from outside (as in other ideological ages), rather than overt attack. So, in the interwar period, Germany sought to win power for the Austrian Nazi party and to support German nationalist parties in Czechoslovakia and Danzig, Italy and others supported Franco in Spain, while the Commitern sought to encourage and stimulate communist movements in West Europe. After 1945 the Soviet Union secured the accession to power of acceptable governments throughout East Europe, while the U.S. achieved the same in Guatemala, the Dominican Republic, Laos, and other sensitive areas. Propaganda became a major weapon of national policy. Nazis and fascists first perfected the art, but it was developed after the war by Radio Moscow, Radio Cairo, and the Voice of America. Radio stations, as important sources of power, became the first target for attack in any attempted coup.

Fourth, as distances are reduced still further, each state may be affected more closely by happenings elsewhere. Conversely, political events in other countries can be more readily influenced. So major powers must be in a position to influence the internal affairs of countries in their own region: the Soviet Union is concerned to control events in Hungary and Czechoslovakia, the United States events in Cuba and the Dominican Republic, China events in Korea and Southeast Asia, India events in Bangladesh. Developments in military technology bring nations closer in a military sense too: missiles can carry immeasurable destruction thousands of miles in a few minutes. Thus every nation becomes vulnerable as never before and so still more inclined to favor war underhand rather than external aggression. And whether or not the government of a neighboring power is friendly or hostile, whether it may shelter the missiles of an ally or an enemy, becomes a question of supreme concern to every power.

Fifth, as in ancient Greece, the ideological blocs are each dominated by two main superpowers. The gap between the power of the very great and that of their nearest rivals is now greater than ever. The insecurity of the age, caused by the universal ideological struggle and more powerful weapons, induces lesser states to shelter under the protective leadersship of these superpowers. This gap reflects the widening *economic* gap between nations, for only a power of advanced economy can contemplate the manufacture of nuclear warheads, means of delivery, or supersonic fighters and bombers. Partly for the same reason, and because decolonization creates many new small states, there is also a larger gap between the medium powers and the small, of whom there now exist more than ever. So society is more stratified. Yet, conversely, in an ideological age these differences in military power are not always decisive, even in battle (as Vietnam shows). Even a nation which has unmatched power at the highest level may prove itself far from powerful in conditions of guerrilla warfare. Superpowers have other sources of influence—such as their capacity to dispense investment, arms, and aid—but these do not always win friends either.

Sixth, the dominant influence of ideology has another effect seen in other ideological ages: considerable inflexibility in alliances. These are no longer simply arrangements of convenience which can be reshuffled at will to suit the immediate short-term advantage of each state. They reflect the genuine political convictions of each state, and can change only with a fundamental change in the character of the government of that state. Especially from 1945, therefore, large military blocs emerge which, as in no previous age, remain almost totally unchanged in membership for thirty years. Conversely, when an alliance is made across the ideological barriers, as between Germany and the Soviet Union in 1939, among Greece, Turkey, and Yugoslavia in 1954, or between China and Pakistan in 1962, it is relatively short-lived or insignificant.

Finally, foreign relations are affected by a moralistic attitude seen only in such ages: In fighting for an ideology rather than a nation, statesmen, politicians, and even their publics easily convince themselves (as in the age of religions) that they are fighting for right against wrong, for the forces of light against those of darkness. This moral content of the ideological contest means that each side has a moral duty to pursue it to the bitter end in every part of the world.

> Each side looked forward to the eventual supremacy of its system all over the earth. The official communist goal was the liberation of mankind from capitalist oppression. . . . To the ideologists in Moscow . . . the imperialist ruling circles in America were trying to enslave all mankind under the yoke of Wall Street. . . . To the extent that the cold war was to be regarded as an ideological context there could be no geographical limitation to it, and it could properly end only when one side had at last destroyed the other.[41]

This in turn led to a situation of acute mutual fear.

> Each side would insist and would in some measure convince itself, that the other aimed to make itself master of the whole world. . . . Each in attributing this unlimited objective to the other would thereby be led to the conclusion that the struggle could be resolved only by the total defeat of the one side or the other—as in the wars between Rome and Carthage. . . . The objective once again could be nothing less than unconditional surrender.[42]

This struggle for ideological purity also affects relations within blocs. Here too relations are conducted in terms of competition in ideological rectitude. The accusation of ideological error is a weapon used within states, as by Stalin against Trotsky, Mao against Lin Piao, McCarthy against his victims, or between them by China against Russia, Russia against Albania and Yugoslavia, or by the U.S. against Cuba or Chile.

41. L. J. Halle, *The Cold War in History* (London, 1967), p. 158.
42. Ibid., pp. 154–55.

As in every international society, there remain important vestiges of the age which preceded it. New nations established on the national principle ape the national pretensions which they discover among the older nations. More significantly, ideology is still used to promote purely national interests. The doctrine of "national socialism" becomes a rationalization for the furthering of Germany's national interests; the defense of socialism and the "socialist commonwealth" a rationalization for Soviet national interests; the defense of "the free world" a euphemism for U.S. interests. Since the promotion of purely national aims is no longer regarded as respectable, it has to be dressed up in acceptable ideological garments. But even nationalism increasingly becomes in a sense ideological: "After 1919 . . . nationalism had to be joined with militant social radicalism. It had to appeal to the pauperised lower-middle class, to the workers, to the returned soldiers as much as to the more respectable bourgeoisie. This new kind of nationalism was to create a new ideological antagonism in world politics."[43]

In this age, therefore, we find a number of the same features we have encountered in other ideological societies: high commitment to political creeds, relatively low loyalty to national states, especially to national governments, a high degree of internal instability, a high level of transnational influences, intense concern with "hearts and minds" and the means of influencing them, such as propaganda, censorship, and news management, frequent resort to coups and sedition, relatively unchanging alliances, and a moralistic and intellectual, rather than realistic, approach to foreign policy. Associated with these are other features which do not necessarily stem only from the ideological character of the age: high concentration of power among two or three superpowers, considerable caution in the conduct of foreign policy because of the existence of especially powerful weapons, and a sudden decline in distance favoring the rapid mobilization of power in distant parts of the world.

Together they create a noval type of international society. Ideology and state interests are now interrelated even more intimately than in other ideological societies. A country committed to a particular ideology cannot easily change its foreign policy (or, if it does, it may need to change its ideology too, as Yugoslavia, Albania and Cuba show). Conversely, a country with a special state interest or geographical situation cannot easily change its ideology (as Czechoslovakia and the Dominican Republic show). So ideological commitments not only determine state policy, but reflect it. State interests not only follow ideology but determine it. In ancient Greek times, Argos could change both its ideology and its policy at will. Today Guatamala and Hungary, the Dominican Republic and Czechoslovakia have no choice: they can change neither.[44]

We have now examined briefly the main features of a number of international societies. We have seen that they vary widely in such factors as the number of

---

43. R. L. Rosecrance, *Action and Reaction in World Politics* (Boston, 1963), p. 168.

44. The above is not intended as a sketch of the international society existing after 1974; it is assumed the age of ideology is now ending.

members, the elites which control policy, the dominant motives, and the conventions and institutions established among them. We will look at some of these in more detail in the following chapters. For the present it is sufficient to note the contrasts we have observed among each of the various societies' dominant ideology, the ethos or governing principle which determines assumptions and expectations. As in smaller societies this ethos, the pattern of belief, the basic value system, governs almost everything else within the society.

If this is so important, what *determines* that ethos itself? Does it derive from internal domestic factors within each state? Or from external sources in the society as a whole? In a more general way, what *is* it, and how does it operate in influencing the behavior of the society's members?

Clearly the ideology does not derive from internal factors within an *individual* state, for it is something that is common to the society as a whole. As we have seen, it affects every state in generally similar ways: the characteristic attitudes of the dynastic age affected all members of that society equally. But they might still derive from internal factors, which were common to *all* the members. For example, the ethos of the dynastic age could be said to derive from the feudal social structure existing *within* each state, which then influenced in turn assumptions and attitudes toward other states.

Though this may be partly true, it is an oversimplification. The dynastic "ethos" with which we are concerned is that affecting the international society, and is not identical with the dynasticism which operates within states. It includes only those elements of the latter—such as attitudes to the rights derived from marriage and inheritance—which affect the wider world. Even these are only one factor in a complex of interacting assumptions and expectations which make up the international ideology as a whole. Just as Christianity is not the sum total of medieval European societies, or Marxism of contemporary communist societies, so dynasticism is not the sum total, but only the dominant strand (and so the one chosen to label it) of the international ideology of this particular age.

Certainly the dominant ideology will *reflect* some features of the domestic society. An international "age of religions" reflects widespread domestic concern on questions of religion. An age of sovereignty reflects the concern of sovereigns and governments over domestic sovereignty; an age of nationalism reflects the nationalist passions widely held within national states; an age of ideology reflects a concern over ideology that is almost as important domestically as it is internationally. But in all cases it is only the international aspects that matter to us. It is only insofar as they build up a consistent set of assumptions and expectations relating to the *external* world that the domestic elements shape the international ethos.

The general ideology of the international society is made up of influences which emanate, for each individual, rather from the international than the national scene. It is the international expectations and assumptions, those of *other* states, which determine how far concerns that may have been originally domestic are expressed in international relationships. Thus even though some of the attitudes which prevailed in the dynastic society *originally* derived from domestic dynasticism, they became in time modified and transmuted in their effect on the international society as a whole. It was the international influences that determined, for instance, how far and in what circumstances the prosecution of a claim to foreign lands was tolerated, what methods of war were acceptable, what methods of negotiation or settlement could be adopted, and much else besides.

The ethos therefore represents a set of assumptions and expectations, held in the minds of those who mainly influence decisions, concerning the way relationships should be conducted within the international society. It is thus not unlike the ethos, ideology, or value system within narrower societies, which equally establishes expectations in men's minds concerning relationships within the society. Those expectations are important because they influence *motivations:* the essential dynamic force within each society (just as the expectations established by the ethos of a narrower society, say medieval Christianity, have a *social* effect only insofar as they influence motives there). It is nationalist *motives,* the desire to build up the individual nation, to expand its power in relation to that of other states, which gives the special character to the nationalist age. It is religious *motives,* the desire to spread a religious creed to other lands, that distinguishes the age of religions from others. Ideology creates the demands which shape the society.

Yet ideology is more than a collection of motives. It is the whole set of expectations and assumptions, attitudes and concerns, about the behavior of other states as well as one's own. It includes rules and restraints as much as desires and demands. Motives are in a sense the *effect* of the ethos or ideology rather than their cause.

Such an ethos or ideology does not necessarily affect the entire population of each member state, certainly not all to the same extent. All that is necessary for it to operate effectively, is that it influence the dominant elites within each society, especially those that are responsible for action toward other members of the society. We will consider in the next chapter the changing character of these elites in different societies; and we shall investigate how far it is they who determine the character of the prevailing ideology, or whether on the contrary that ideology has an independent life of its own which may in turn affect the elite.

*How* then does the ideology act in influencing attitudes and behavior within society? Like the ideology of any other society, it is instilled especially through interaction. That is, individual human beings in each state, in learning of the wider society in which they grow up, in acting later within that society to deal with other states, in hearing of the precedents, conventions, and procedures traditionally laid down within it, acquire, as do members of a narrower society, beliefs and assumptions about the type of behavior to be expected of its members, and the role which they themselves should play within it. The process is different in the international society in that socialization normally takes place when the individual human being is older, so that the rules and roles acquired are less deeply instilled. Moreover, the influence from the wider society may sometimes be counteracted to some extent by those coming from the individual's own narrower society, so that the cooperative nationalism demanded by the wider society may be counterbalanced by the competitive nationalism demanded by the narrower (this is not unlike the kind of conflict between loyalties to the family and to the state, or to the family and to the tribe, that may be felt in many narrower societies). But there will always be a considerable range of messages from the outer world which, despite these counterpressures, gradually instill into its members the expectations and assumptions that taken together make up the "international ideology."

We have observed a wide range of contrasting ideologies in the different international societies we examined. What are the differences among them? There is a clear distinction to be made between what might be called "cellular" societies, in which there is a relatively hard barrier and low communication between each unit, so that the cross-influences are small; and the "fluid," that is, open and transnational, societies, where contacts between the units are frequent and easy, and loyalties therefore often almost as strong between states as within them. The extreme form of cellular society would be one in which there was virtually no communication between states except in time of war—this would correspond roughly to the classical "billiard-ball" image of international society. This would not necessarily be a totally individualistic society. The states might still recognize certain rules and obligations that affected them, at least in time of war: otherwise it would scarcely be a society at all. But in general it is likely to be competitive rather than cooperative. Such a society has never existed in this extreme form, but the most "cellular" in type is that of ancient China, followed by the ages of sovereignty, dynasticism, and nationalism in that order.

The most "fluid," that is open and transnational societies, as one might expect, have been those associated with ideology: ancient Greece, the age of religions, and the age of ideology. In such times loyalties *between* the units (to the ideology) may be as strong as those within them. In an age of religious concern this influences all state action, abroad as well as at home, and the citizen of one state may feel greater devotion to another state than to his own. But this fluid or transnational character is not necessarily *because* these ages are ideological; it is at least theoretically possible to have an age in which there is intense ideological concern, but directed entirely inward toward the political situation of each individual state, while there is indifference about the political situation of others. Thus the main causation may be in the opposite direction. It is where contact and communication are easy that *concern* about events elsewhere becomes high, the capacity to influence them increased, and ideological competition more intense. This was the situation in ancient Greece, as it has been in the modern world. Under such circumstances the whole international society becomes a single political arena: the system of government in any part of it becomes important to all everywhere.

The other main contrast to be seen among these various ideologies is between those that imply, or cause, a considerable degree of integration or orderly social existence within the international society, and those that imply a competitive, violent, and essential disorderly society.[45] This is not directly related to the differences between cellular and fluid or open societies. A society might have

45. This might be compared with the difference suggested by Ruth Beledict, *Patterns of Culture*, (London, 1935) between primitive societies that are "Dionysian" and those that are "Apollonian."

relatively high barriers between states and yet be relatively orderly; the age of sovereignty was of this type. Conversely, an "open" society could be very disorderly, like ancient Greece. The most orderly societies were probably the ages of ideology, of sovereignty, and of nationalism in that order, while the most violent and disturbed have been the others. This is partly simply the effect of chronology. It is not altogether Utopian to suggest that international societies have become better regulated as time has progressed. There are two exceptions. The age of religion was more disordered than that of dynasties, partly because communications were easier and weapons more destructive, but also because of the nature of the issues fought over. Conflicts between religions created a more profoundly divided society than those of dynastic houses. Second, the age of sovereignty was in some ways more orderly than the age of nationalism. Even this is disputable; there were many more wars in the age of sovereignty, while the age of nationalism possessed far more evolved institutions for resolving international disputes. If the latter was in the final resort more disorganized, it was partly that nationalism represented a more disruptive force *within* many states than was present in the previous age, and partly that the passions of nationalism lent an intensity to international politics, mobilized populations far more totally, and so made war far more destructive than had been the case in the age of sovereignty.

There are many other contrasts that can be drawn between types of ideology, and we shall look at some of these in the final chapters of this book. But we have perhaps shown sufficiently the crucial importance of the basic "ideology," that is the assumptions and preconceptions of each society, in determining attitudes toward other states, and behavior between them: in other words its whole character. In general most members (that is, states) of each society behave in similar ways, irrespective of the differences in social structure or government. The difference between the attitudes and conduct of states in *different* ages is far greater than that between individual states of the same age. The common factor among states of the same age is a common, social ethos, a common pattern of belief about the nature of international society and the behavior within it seen as normal.

In considering other important factors of each society—elites, motives, structure, institutions, and so on—we shall need to consider how far these have been influenced and molded by the dominant ideology, or how far, conversely, it is these that have themselves determined the character of the ideology.

# Chapter 6.   Elites

So far we have looked in general terms at the dominant character of the main international societies of which we have knowledge. Let us now look at some of the individual features of all these societies and compare them. In particular let us seek to determine which, if any, is responsible for determining the nature of the general ideology or ethos that we have just described.

How far, for example, is the prevailing ideology determined by the elites within each society? Or how far does this ideology have an existence that is largely independent, which in turn influences whatever elite is in power at any one time? These questions are related to a more general problem still. How far is state behavior determined by domestic factors, *internal* to each state, and how far by social factors, that is, influences deriving from the international society to which it belongs?

This is a question somewhat comparable to the question of how far human behavior within a society is determined by individual, innate personality traits, and how far by the social ethos of society, the socializing pressures to which the individual is subjected. The simple answer in both cases is that each plays its part. Nobody would suggest that the innate character of individuals in the same society, their inherited traits, cannot influence behavior at all: the effect of the socializing pressures on each individual will vary because of the influence of heredity or of early environmental factors. Most would probably at the same time accept that the socializing pressures also have their influence on behavior, that is, induce socially conditioned responses in particular types of situation, even among those having different innate characteristics. In many situations society tells us what behavior we should adopt, even to some extent what emotions we should feel—when we should be jealous, angry, flattered—in particular situations.

Similarly, in international societies we must expect that both the character of the individual states (and of the elites within them) and the dominating ethos of the society will have an influence in determining behavior. The wider society will, as we have seen in the last chapter, inculcate certain general attitudes and assumptions concerning the relations to be expected among states. This too will to some extent tell governments how they should respond in certain situations, the type of international behavior which is normal and acceptable. And this too will to some

111

extent tell states what emotions they should feel, when they should feel angry, outraged, or revengeful: teach them that desecration of the national flag, violation of a few yards of territory, an insult to an ambassador, should be regarded as an insult justifying national indignation and armed retaliation in one age, while in another they might be accepted with indifference. Yet at the same time the nature of the government, the ruling forces, may also have an influence on responses.

In discussing elites in this chapter, we are considering the *internal* character of the individual members of a society. The elites will not necessarily be the same for all members of the society. A revolution in one state may bring to power an elite which is essentially different from that ruling in others. We shall need to consider how far, if there are variations of this kind, they result in different types of behavior by the states in question.

But usually we shall find that, within any given international society, the elites in control of state policy do not vary enormously from one state to another. In nineteenth-century Europe, for example, the statesmen and politicians who ultimately determined policy belonged to much the same social order, and shared many similar assumptions, throughout the society. They did not even vary very much between authoritarian states, such as Austria-Hungary and Russia, and constitutional and parliamentary states, such as Britain and France. In ancient Greece, similarly, Sparta was an oligarchy and Athens usually a democracy of a sort. Yet those in control of the two states were not in background and way of thought altogether different from each other. In such cases, though the *domestic* ideologies differ, the elites all accept a common international ideology.

For the most part, therefore, we shall be comparing the different elites among *different* international societies, rather than those of different states in the same society. And we shall wish to consider the relationship, if any, between the differing character of elites in different international societies and other aspects of that society.

The elites which matter to us are not always the elites which dominated the society as a whole. Here we are concerned with international elites, the elites which determine foreign policy. We shall thus need to consider the character and the influence of foreign office staffs and ambassadors, as against other types of civil servant; of foreign ministers, where they existed, rather than cabinet ministers in general. This will not usually be a distinction of great importance. Normally the elite which controls a state as a whole will also be in control of foreign policy. But there will sometimes be differences. What we shall wish to see is whether and how the character of this international elite influences the character, and especially the ideology, of the society as a whole.

## 6.1 The Chinese Multistate System (771–221 B.C.)

The most important elite group within the Chinese multistate system were the rulers themselves. Particularly in the early part of the period, these exercised virtually absolute control over policy both at home and abroad. The accounts that have come down to us, for example from Mencius, show that, although the rulers would sometimes consult with a chief minister or even a traveling scholar, such as Mencius himself, it was the ruler who would take the final decision.

The rulers as a class were often related by marriage (this even included the barbarian states).[1] The class of rulers thus became a fairly closely knit status group, acquiring a common attitude to the conduct of international relations. It was they at first who met in the big interstate conferences. As a class they were inevitably especially concerned about their own prestige and that of their states. Like the rulers in most later systems, they felt that the strength and extent of their own state reflected personal glory on themselves. Mencius records the personal shame of King Hwuy that while "in former time there was not a state in the empire stronger than Chin," under his rule its territories had been lost to powerful neighbors, and his hope that "his people might soon become more numerous than those of the neighboring kingdoms."[2] It was to extend their personal glory and to emphasize their independence that the rulers of these states, once dukes, marquises, earls, and so on, finally in the fourth century declared themselves "kings." And it was on the same grounds that they struggled with other rulers unceasingly for supremacy within the system. Their policy was to seek to make their states stronger and so to extend their own prestige.

The second elite group, which became increasingly important as the period progressed, were the ministers serving the rulers. As time went on an increasing degree of political power fell into the hands of such ministers, and especially those of the chief minister (hsiang) of each state. As each state grew bigger, administration became more complex and an increasing degree of power had to be delegated to officials. The growing influence of the official class can be measured in quantitative terms by comparing the figures of those attending the interstate conferences and meetings (hui) at different periods. In the seventh century, 90 percent of the meetings were attended by rulers only, and 10 percent by rulers and ministers. But by 500 B.C. nearly 70 percent were attended by officials only, nearly 16 percent by rulers and ministers, and only 15 percent by rulers alone.[3]

An equally significant indicator is the fact that in 500 B.C. the chief ministers of the various states, meeting together, felt able to repudiate an agreement which had been reached by their own rulers.[4] In a few cases (as in Wu at the end of the sixth century and in Ch'i in the early fourth century) a chief minister became to all intents and purposes the ruler of the state. More often, like skilled bureaucrats in the modern system, they were able to manipulate their rulers from behind the scenes, to get them to implement the policies they favored. This new importance of the official class introduced an element of social mobility into what had been a static society. Even those "from the meanest alleys of poverty could hope to arrive

1. H. G. Creel, *The Origins of State-Craft in China* (Chicago, 1970), p. 213.
2. *The Works of Mencius*, I, V, i and I, III, ii.
3. R. L. Walker, *The Multi-State System in Ancient China* (Hamden, 1953), p. 62
4. Ibid., p. 76

rapidly if they were skilled enough and if they could gain the ear of someone in power."[5] But like statesmen in sixteenth-century Europe, they became as committed as their masters to promoting the ruler's power and that of his state abroad.

Another elite group, though their influence declined as that of the officials rose, was the traditional feudal nobility within each state. The distinction between nobility and bureaucracy is not clearly defined, since many of the officials were drawn from the noble class and in some cases their offices even became hereditary. In Sung the six chief officials were members of the six leading families and formed a sort of council sharing power with the ruler. In Lu in the fourth and third centuries three leading families monopolized almost all power. No wonder Mencius said: "The administration of government is not difficult—it lies in not offending the great families" (IV, 1, b). The Shih, or noble family, often had considerable lands and became almost a state within the state in some cases. Thus, in the early part of the period especially, these big families had extensive power. But their authority declined as time went on, while the power of the officials, by virtue of their abilities and the offices to which they were appointed, increased. Already "by the end of the Ch'un-Ch'iu [i.e., by 480 B.C.] most of the members of the feudal aristocracy were fulfilling merely ceremonial functions. They were completely outnumbered by the growing body of functionaries and were of constantly diminishing importance in the effective direction of affairs."[6] The reforms which Kuan-tzu implemented in Ch'i in the early seventh century were specifically designed to reduce the power of this traditional feudal class and to replace it with that of officials directly appointed or approved by the rulers, and so more subject to their influence.[7] Nonetheless, even during the later part of the period, because of the difficulty of maintaining centralized control in each state, this aristocratic class must have continued to have some influence, especially on questions of peace and war. They still often became ministers or senior officials. And they were at least significant in representing a dominant strand of public opinion within each state which must be taken into account in foreign policies: probably their love of fighting and of the traditional chivalric code sometimes represented an influence in favor of war.[8]

There was also the rising merchant class. The first half of the period saw "the gradual emergence of new social and economic groupings, and a rapid increase in their number and relative importance within the social structure. . . . merchants, artisans, and especially bureaucrats, elbowing the aristocracy for recognition."[9]

5. J. H. Crump, *Intrigues* (Ann Arbor, 1964), p. 4

6. Walker, *Multi-State System*, p. 63.

7. See Crump, *Intrigues*, p. 1: "The tensions of the Warring States period doomed a state relying on entrenched courtiers to do its work to fall behind in the competition . . . The constant cry throughout the period is to 'use men' and the king who 'used men' is described as a virtuous ruler."

8. According to Creel, in the Spring and Autumn period, "the scene is dominated by aristocrats, boasting of their descent, quarrelling (and sometimes fighting) over precedence and points of honour, inter-marrying and cementing alliances in other ways, conforming or pretending to conform, to an elaborate code of aristocratic conduct and criticizing others for failing to do so." *Origins of State-Craft*, p. 333.

9. K. S. Latourette, *The Chinese, Their History and Culture* (London, 1946), p. 51.

Commercial activity undoubtedly developed during this time and it seems probable that in some cases merchant families came to acquire lands and to become eligible for important offices of state. Their sons would become minor officials, and their sons in turn might rise to eminence. "Some of the members of the old aristocratic families sank to the level of the common people, and many new families rose to power."[10] Conversely, ex-officials and ex-ministers sometimes became prosperous merchants, and still remained people of considerable influence (for example, the famous Fan Li, minister of the state of Yueh, who later became a prosperous merchant in Ch'i). It seems doubtful, nonetheless, whether at this stage the influence of such a class was a significant factor in influencing state policies, especially in the field of foreign affairs, on which they could not expect to be consulted.

Fifth, there was the military. It is by no means certain how far this really represents a distinct class, or whether military commanders as such were consulted on questions of policy. In some cases it was the ruler himself who led the armies in war.[11] Other commanders would be leading nobles, rather than a specialized military class.[12] The dominant weapon of the day was the four-horse chariot, and it was only the leading aristocratic families which possessed these, the essential condition of any military command.[13] Even the drivers of the chariots were normally members of the aristocracy. In some of the states there were officials described as "directors of the horses," who seem to have been a kind of minister of war. Of the six officials of the state of Sung, two were the commanders of the left army and the right army, and another was minister of war (director of horses), an indication that military considerations were at least likely to carry considerable weight in state deliberations. But these probably shared the common assumptions of the noble and bureaucratic classes, rather than those of a distinct military elite, which does not seem to have existed. Moreover, despite the prevalence of war, the soldier's arts and accomplishments were never much admired in China, even in this period. Though one of the mythical founders of the Chou dynasty, Wu, symbolized warlike deeds, military leaders in general were not revered at this time, and seem almost never to have won or seized power.

More significant in their influence on foreign policy were the class of philosophers, scholars, and advisers, to which both Confucius and Mencius belonged. These occupied a position without parallel in any subsequent system. In many cases they held no formal position as minister or official. They were merely respected and venerable figures to whom rulers would turn for advice and wisdom. In a sense they may be said to be successors to the old soothsayers and diviners, and in some cases no doubt still used somewhat similar methods and arguments. But by

10. Ibid.

11. Like the ruler of Ch'i, who disappeared altogether during a campaign against Ch'u in the ninth century.

12. See, for example, *Mencius* VII, 8, where the Prince of Lu makes his minister commander of the army.

13. "The principle occupant of a war chariot was undoubtedly its owner and an aristocrat," Creel, *Origins of State-Craft,* p. 280.

the time of Confucius the arguments were usually based on moral and philosophical grounds: only the righteous and benevolent ruler would win the support of his people. Mencius certainly often preached on the evils of war. But he also taught that the righteous ruler would be even more likely to extend his territory, since his reputation would win him support elsewhere as well as at home.[14] The most remarkable feature of this system (which demonstrates how far all the states were felt still to belong to a common society) was the fact that the philosopher-adviser not only had little allegiance to a particular state but would give advice to many states.[15] Such advisers were revered but it seems unlikely from the accounts that their influence was very powerful. The general tenor of the writings is that the rulers of the age were concerned only with state power and interest, or with personal good living, and were largely indifferent to the moral advice they were given.

These then were the main elite groups within this international society and the ones who had most influence on foreign policy. Insofar as one can speak at all of public opinion, it is the opinion of these groups which counted. The mass of the population, the peasants, the rising urban class, and the increasingly large slave population, unable to read and write and having little direct contact with the ruling classes, had no direct influence at all. The only influence they could have would be of a *negative* kind, in that, as Confucius and Mencius never tired of asserting, if their condition was reduced to too miserable a state, they would rise and overthrow their ruler, as indeed happened from time to time (the people of Chü expelled their ruler in 631 B.C., causing a change in policy). There are one or two recorded instances of cases where rulers voluntarily sought the views of their people before taking particular actions. But this was relatively marginal. In general, the policies of the individual states, and so the character of the society as a whole, were determined by the views of the relatively restricted elite group we have described.[16]

Let us return to the question we posed before: How far was the basic character and ideology of the system determined by the nature of the elites and how far was it derived from independent sources? Both the groups which wielded ultimate power, the individual rulers and the small group of ministers they appointed, stood to benefit, in differeing degrees, from the extension of power and territory of their own states. Conversely, there was no power in the hands of the mass of the people, who bore most of the hardships of war. In this crude sense the social structure certainly helped to encourage the prevailing ideology of persistent and unrestrained territorial expansion.

But it would be an obvious oversimplification to suggest that the highly competitive system resulted *automatically* from the type of social structure that prevailed. The state of chronic conflict that occurred, and which stood in consider-

14. cf. *Mencius,* I (Part II), I, 2.

15. Confucius is said to have been searching to find the ideal ruler who would put his doctrines into practice.

16. "Oligarchy was the form of government within the various states. It is mainly about the elite at the top of the very broad pyramid that written sources report," Walker, *Multi-State System,* p. 59.

able contrast to the relatively settled conditions which existed in both the preceding (western Chou) and succeeding (Han) period, could as well be attributed to the excessive autonomy acquired by the feudal lords in the early part of the period, the decline in centralized authority, the increasing incursion of barbarian states on the periphery, and a growing competitiveness within the system, which to some extent most classes accepted (just as the masses in nineteenth-century Europe acclaimed the nationalist wars that they had to fight). The important factor was the growing assumption, shared among all the elite groups, that such behavior among states was *normal*. Once this tradition had been established, similar goals might have been pursued even by quite *different* types of elite if they had come to power. In engaging in a perpetual struggle against each other, the rulers and ministers merely conformed with what had become the accepted norms of the international society. It was thus this tradition, the prevailing *expectations,* in a word the "ideology," which determined conduct, and this was not determined by the internal structure of each state alone: Where that structure differed, where ministers were more power-ful, philosophers more influential, policies were no different.

There is, however, another question that is relevant here. There are two significant trends during the course of this 550 years. First, warfare in general became more common, more ferocious and unrestrained, as time went on (this is reflected in the very name given by the Chinese to the second half of the period). On the other hand, the influence of ministers and officials became greater in relation to that of the rulers. Is there any direct correlation between these two developments? There is some attraction in this view. It is arguable that the restrained chivalric method of warfare in the Spring and Autumn period—for example, the tradition that one did not attack a general who was unprepared—was partly the effect of some fellow feeling and mutual understanding among a limited group of rulers and aristocrats sharing a common tradition, just as the relatively civilized warfare of the eighteenth century, when European monarchs still largely dominated the policies of their states, is sometimes contrasted with the more ruthless methods of the nineteenth century, when ministers and generals had more influence over state policies. Later, when ministers were more powerful, wars were more ferocious. Certainly, the histories continually recount instances in which ministers urge on their rulers the need for warfare against a particular state: "The Intrigues" of the Warring States period, for example, describes many highly subtle and esoteric reasons of state educed as justification for acts of war by such ministers.

The shift in power may have been a factor, but the trend toward more ruthless and unscrupulous warfare probably was promoted far more by other factors: the rise in importance of the barbarian states (Wu, Yueh, and Ch'in), the perpetual reduction in the number of states, the increasing intensity of conflict that resulted, the increasing disregard for Chou authority, and the increasing momentum which the doctrines of maximization of state power obtained (for example, in the writings of the so-called Legists). It was the general character of the system and of prevailing expectations, in other words, the basic ideology, which changed most.

Changes in the internal structure of the states may have contributed to this. But it was the development, among rulers and ministers alike, of the prevailing expectations and assumptions which was mainly responsible for the changes in policies pursued. The influence seems to have been from ideology to elite rather than vice versa.

## 6.2 The Greek City-States (550–338 B.C.)

The elites controlling foreign policy in the Greek city-states differed radically from those in the Chinese society. The concentration of decision-making power in a single ruler, which remained the normal situation in China, even if increasingly modified, was almost unknown in Greece after the age of the tyrants—that is, from around the end of the sixth century. Among the peripheral powers—Persia and its satrapies (which were almost independent for part of the time), Macedonia, Libya, Carthage, and so on—individual rulers often held undivided sway. But these, though they could sometimes influence the Greek system, were not strictly part of it. Among the Greek cities, the authority and influence of a single leader was sometimes such that he could, almost alone, determine policy, and this was as often true in the democracies as in the oligarchies. Even in Athens at its most democratic phase, according to Thucydides, "because of his position, his intelligence and known integrity, Pericles could while respecting the liberty of the people, at the same time hold them in check. It was he who led them, rather than they who led him. . . . So in what was nominally a democracy power was really in the hands of the first citizen."[17]

But in general after the age of the tyrants, in most cities, including the oligarchies, policy decisions were the result of discussion among a considerable group, involving wide-ranging, realistic, and outspoken discussion of the merits or demerits of alternative courses of action (if the historians' accounts are to be believed). And while for the initial decision this would be a relatively restricted group, even in many of the oligarchies decisions on major questions had to be ratified by a much larger body; for example, in Sparta decisions for war had to be confirmed by the Spartan assembly.

The character of the elites involved in such discussions clearly varied according to the constitution of the state concerned. But it would be wrong to exaggerate these differences, for they were mainly of degree rather than of kind. Nearly all cities possessed some kind of representative institutions. Almost all hated and rejected "tyranny." Kings, even where they still existed, as in Sparta, had little personal power except in battle. In almost every state there existed roughly comparable institutions: an assembly of citizens (and even in democracies the citizens were a relatively limited elite); a council (gerousia or boule); magistrates and various other officials, including generals, all exercising various respon-

17. Thucydides, *The Peloponnesian War*, II, 66.

sibilities. The differences between states were in the exact distribution of power among the different bodies, rather than between a state wholly ruled by its assembly and one wholly ruled by a council.

In most of the states by this time the original organization, based on tribes, brotherhoods, and clans, had been broken down and replaced (very deliberately in the case of Athens and Sparta) by new subdivisions based on a different principle, thereby removing the power base of the aristocracy who had once dominated religious, social, economic, and military life. The normal transition was monarchy to aristocracy to oligarchy to democracy, and nearly all the cities had reached one of the last two phases. In many of them there had emerged a substantial middle class of merchants, guildsmen, artisans, and other educated people who saw their interests in economic terms rather than in terms of traditional tribal loyalties. These often formed the bulk of the hoplites in the armies, while the navies were recruited from humbler sections of the populations. Thus education, way of life, and attitudes to foreign policy in a democratic state were not all that different from those in an oligarchy; they were almost everywhere those of an educated middle class. Insofar as the elites differed, it was not so much because of the differing constitutional systems and class backgrounds, but because of the different traditions and economic interests of the states: for example, the adventurous, restless ambition and outward-looking turn of mind of the mercantile urban Athenians, against the cautious, conservative, inward-looking policy of an agrarian, poor, and politically backward Sparta. Differences of tradition and attitude of this kind were more important in determining foreign policies than constitutional differences.

The fact that decisions had to be made by a committee or group rather than by an individual ruler meant that foreign policy was rarely the result of whim or caprice. The policies pursued, however ruthless and aggressive, were not unconsidered. The accounts given by Thucydides of crucial discussions—for example, the decisions of the two camps at the opening of the Peleponnesian war, the debate on the fate of Mytilene, and that on the Sicilian expedition in Athens—though perhaps more polished in style and intellectual in content than the reality, probably reflect reasonably accurately the *type* of debate which occurred. The danger here was thus not so much the caprice of the ruthless autocrat, as in China, but the passions and angers of the mob, especially in the democracies. And archdemagogues, such as Cleon in Athens, knew well how to rouse and play on those passions, and so gave them greater influence.

In most of the cities, therefore, even if formally oligarchies, the newly emerging middle classes played an increasingly important role. Conversely even in democratic states, such as Athens and fourth-century Thebes, members of the

18. "The legal sovereignty of the Cleisthenian demos must be seen against the background of the feuds between various local families and their individual leaders: feuds which persisted because aristocrats were, and remained for a long time the only trained politicians and therefore held or were struggling for power within the democratic constitution." V. Ehrenberg, *From Solon to Socrates* (London, 1968), p. 139

old families continued to play a major part; even democratic leaders such as Pericles and Alcibiades usually came from such families.[18] But within the oligarchies the elderly often enjoyed a more dominant role than in the democracies, since membership of the council was sometimes reserved to those over fifty or even over sixty. This no doubt partly accounts for the more cautious and moderate policy of Sparta as against the expansionist and aggressive course pursued by Athens, with its relatively youthful assembly.

There were of course differences of class interest. These were especially apparent in the democracies. For example, between the landed and nonlanded classes, the former had a great interest in peace.

> The upper and middle classes generally owned land in Attica, in defense of which they fought as cavalry and hoplites and swayed the foreign policy of the state: to them relations with Sparta and her alliance were as important as the conflict with Persia. The lower class owned no land. They found a new and more congenial field of employment in the fleet . . . their future was tied up with naval expansion and with Athens' naval coalition.[19]

There is evidence that the emergence of the new middle and artisan classes, which was particularly pronounced in the prosperous commercial states such as Athens and Corinth, had its impact on foreign policy. The reason that the most democratic states, such as Athens and fourth-century Thebes, were the most expansionist and aggressive was certainly partly because of the emergence of these new classes to power. In some cases they had a direct economic interest in expansion. The merchant class of Athens in most cases used their influence in favor of imperialist policies. Similarly, land hunger among the increasingly overcrowded farmers was partly responsible for colonialism. But these interests were not equally shared. During the Peloponnesian war there was a clear division of interest, remarked by Thucydides, between the wealthier and propertied classes of Athens, who paid most of the taxes for the war, had most to lose through defeat, and bore most of the risk through their service as hoplites, and the common people, who paid little in taxes but gained, indirectly, from the preservation of the empire and the tributary payments, and directly from their navy pay. The former were more inclined to see advantage in seeking terms with Sparta, while the latter were determined to pursue the struggle to the bitter end.[20] The influence of the masses was greater the more democratic the state; thus in democratic Thebes Epaminondas was unable to secure acceptance from his more bellicose assembly for moderate policies toward the defeated Achaeans.

Inevitably, the more democratic the state and the greater its social mobility, the more vulnerable it was to the appeals of demagoguery. Pericles himself recognized the difficulties and dangers he faced in leading his city to war under conditions of

---

19. N. G. L. Hammond, *A History of Greece to 233* B.C. (London, 1967), p. 263.

20. Cf. Thucydides, VI, 24: "The general masses and the average soldier saw the prospect of getting pay for the time being and of adding to the empire, so as to secure paid employment in future. The result of this excessive enthusiasm among the majority was that the few who actually were opposed to the expedition were afraid of being thought unpatriotic if they voted against it and therefore kept quiet."

democracy, and he was proved justified in his belief that Athens would eventually lose because of her own mistakes rather than because of the successes of Sparta. The folly of the Sicilian expedition, undertaken at the instigation of firebrands such as Alcibiades, is one example of the calamitious results of foreign policy decisions largely determined by the multitude. Ironically it was Cleon himself, the chief demagogue, who most clearly diagnosed the dangers of the system:

> Any novelty in any argument deceives you at once, but when the argument is tried and proved you become unwilling to follow it. You look with suspicion at what is normal and are the slaves of every paradox that comes your way. . . . You are simply victims of your pleasure in listening, and are more like an audience sitting at the feet of a professional lecturer than a parliament discussing matters of state.[21]

However, the influence of political structure on state conduct was reciprocal. Not only did a greater degree of democracy bring more adventurist policies; increasingly warlike policies in turn modified the class structure. In many of the states the class system reflected military organization. From the seventh century the rise in importance of the hoplites within the different armies brought an enhancement of the political power of all those who could afford their weapons. The phalanx of hoplites, formed of the nonnoble class, began to replace the cavalry of noblemen, so increasing social mobility and eventually helping to democratize the state. The "citizen" who was able to bear arms in foreign wars became more important than the old leaders of the clans, phratries, and tribes. In Athens, and later in other states, the development of the navy brought further democratization, the sailors being largely recruited from the artisan class and becoming strong supporters of democracy and foreign military adventure. It was this "navy crowd," the thetes, to whom such demagogues as Cleon mainly made their appeal.[22]

The nonenfranchised probably had a different attitude again. The helots in Sparta, the slaves in Athens and elsewhere, had little interest and little benefit from foreign victories. But they also had little opportunity to express their views. In time of grave crisis Sparta held out inducements to her Messenian helots: when her forces were surrounded at Pylos she offered freedom to the helots who would risk their lives by taking food and water to them. But in general slaves and helots often had a greater interest in victory for the enemy than for their own side, a fact that was exploited vigorously, for example in the efforts of Athens to provoke an uprising among the helots in Sparta (Sparta accordingly secured an undertaking from Athens in their treaty of 421 that Athens would not assist a helot uprising).

21. Ibid., III, 38.

22. Hammond, *History of Greece*, p. 369: "The war had also created an opposition of interest between the classes. The cavalry and the hoplites bore the brunt of the casualities, for they led the sea-borne landings, fought the battles and conducted the sieges. The classes from which they were drawn suffered most through the ravaging of Attica, and they paid taxes. . . . Patriotic as they were, they wished to accept favorable terms from Sparta and put an end to the war. The thetes had suffered few casualties in battle. They paid no taxes. They received state-pay as a perquisite of the empire, and they were naturally prompted by patriotic and self-interested motives to extend the empire by prosecuting the war."

The only influence of these classes on foreign policy was therefore negative: The governing classes would be inhibited from taking any action which might provoke them into open revolt.

Apart from the direct influence of individual classes, there was a general, somewhat amorphous, Greek public opinion, which may have had some influence on the decisions reached. Thucydides records that the Plataeans, pleading with the Spartans not to kill them to appease their allies, the Thebans, called on them to "beware lest public opinion condemns you, however superior you may be, for passing an unworthy sentence on good men."[23] It is by no means sure how far in reality public opinion always upheld such a moral viewpoint, still less how far it was heeded. It is striking that in the dialogues recorded by Thucydides, even the arguments of the doves are normally expressed in terms of self-interest rather than morality. Thus Diodotus, in pleading with the Athenian assembly to show mercy for the Mytileneans, bases his argument primarily on the interest of Athens, rather than on the claims of justice: clearly assuming this would carry greatest weight.

How far then did the class structure determine the ideology of the international society as a whole? Undoubtedly the dominance of the middle class, who felt especially the ideological preoccupation of the age and the concern to promote commercial interests abroad, was significant in determining this society's special character. The fact that, in general, the more democratic states and politicians were those most expansionist in policy was partly because the middle class was more strongly represented and their commerical interests were greater. Certainly too the commercialism of the age promoted colonization and imperialism.

But it was the ideological concern that most dominated policy. And this was not directly caused by class structure. It was shared equally by oligarchies and by democracies. The democratic states were perhaps the more ardent and expansionist. But this was not because they were democratic. It was rather that the same causes—rising prosperity, commerce, and the sense of adventure—which had brought democracy also brought the desire for expansion. Athens and Thebes became democratic at the moment of maximum expansion, so that the impetus of expansion was carried forward by the new democratic leaders.

But in general the dominant aims of the society and the methods by which they were pursued—political evangelism and the promotion of ideologically sympathetic governments in other states—were pursued by all the states, regardless of ideology or class structure. The character of foreign policy was determined by the assumptions and expectations, the ideology, of the society generally, rather than by the class structure or constitution of individual states.


## 6.3 The Age of Dynasties (1300–1559)

The ruling elites in the Middle Ages in Europe were of a quite different kind from those considered so far. As in the Chinese multistate system, the dominating

---

23. Thucydides, III, 57.

force was the rulers themselves. They exercised a control of foreign policy that was virtually absolute. Though there were usually counselors to advise the ruler, he usually consulted them at his own discretion: Machiavelli declared that a prince "ought always to take counsel; but only when he wishes, not when others wish."[24] Even when they were consulted their advice was relatively marginal: Froissart recounts how the Black Prince's advisers counseled unanimously against intervention in favor of Pedro the Cruel in Aragon because of his unpopularity among his own people, but how nonetheless the Black Prince overruled them, because "they could not remove him out of that purpose, for his mind was ever more and more firmly set on the matter."

Foreign policy, therefore, was in general personal policy. The launching of the Hundred Years' War was the personal policy of Edward III, just as the French wars in Italy were the personal policy of Charles VIII and his successors. The great monarchs of central Europe, Charles IV of Bohemia, Casimir the Great of Poland, and Lewis the Great in Hungary, conducted their own policies, military and matrimonial, according to their own personal whims, and the success of each depended largely on his own personal character. Ferdinand the Catholic supervised in person all the diplomacy of Spain, keeping all the papers in leather-covered chests, "and when the chests got full, abandoned them casually at whatever castle he happened to be leaving."[25] Even Philip II nearly a century later conducted his own diplomacy (and is said to have been several years behind with his correspondence as a result). There were no foreign ministers, and virtually no ministers of any kind.[26] The dynasts conducted their own personal policies for their own personal purposes.

Machiavelli advises his prince to keep full control of foreign policy for himself and warns against the minister who fails to put the prince's interest first, "for whoever has in hand the state of another must never think of himself but of the Prince and not mind anything but what relates to him."[27] This personal control of policy was assisted by the emerging diplomatic system, since ambassadors and agents were the personal envoys of the rulers: "Such agents could be appointed by an autocratic prince without consultation with anyone. They could be dispatched and recalled at will, and paid out of private and unquestionable funds. They would receive their instructions directly from the Prince and report to him directly."[28]

This virtual monopoly of control by the rulers no doubt partly explains why policy at this time was directed so much toward dynastic interests. But it would be wrong to establish too crude a correlation between the nature of control and the character of the ideology. For dynastic ambitions, being, as we saw, part of the ethos and expectations of the age, were in fact widely shared; perhaps the less the lower one descended within society, but to some extent everywhere. Most

24. Machiavelli, *The Prince*, chap. 23.

25. G. Mattingly, *Renaissance Diplomacy* (London, 1955), p. 139.

26. "If the king was too busy to answer the ambassador's letter, or did not choose to do so, the ambassador got no answer." Ibid., p. 140.

27. Machiavelli, *The Prince*, chap. 23.

28. Mattingly, *Renaissance Diplomacy*, pp. 75–76.

courtiers fully identified with the success of their royal masters, though, as time went on, they increasingly emphasized the interests of the nation as something distinct from that of the royal line. The bourgeoisie welcomed the strengthening of the king's authority, even if they did not necessarily welcome foreign wars for which they might have to pay and to fight. Even the mass of the population, though foreign adventures were entirely remote from their own personal concerns and lives, could be aroused by dynastic ambitions, like Henry V's soldiers in Shakespeare's play, or the French population by Joan of Arc. And certainly those elites most able to influence policy were favorable to dynastic ambitions.

But even the most absolute rulers consulted with some trusted advisers. So Edward III, Froissart said, "often-times desired counsel of his chief and special friends and counselors." Since the counselors were usually hand-picked, and since their fortunes often depended on those of their masters, these were scarcely an independent influence. Many no doubt endorsed all proposals put before them. But they clearly did not always do so. And the class background of advisers widened.

> An almost universal trend of the period was the rise in importance in the councils of kings . . . of humble men chosen for their training in affairs, for their expertise in managing finance or domestic intelligence, above all for their skill in managing men. The old council gave place to a new body . . . disinterested in carrying out his policies—which were after all often hammered out by the councillors themselves. . . . Often in the end they were rewarded by promotion to the nobility, but others were ready to step into their shoes.[29]

Another important elite group in many countries were the big magnates, not necessarily members of the king's council, and far less committed to the king's cause. Sometimes indeed these could be actively hostile to royal foreign policies or even have independent ambitions of their own, as John of Gaunt did in Castile and Portugal, or as the Dukes of Flanders, Anjou, Burgundy, and Orleans did in France. The custom of *apanage,* by which the monarchs invested titles to important fiefdoms in their sons or other supporters, increased these threats to an independent policy by the king at home: By making his fourth son, Philip, Duke of Burgundy in 1361, John II of France created problems for his successors for the next two centuries.

The extent to which foreign policy was directly influenced by these magnates depended in part on the degree of central power the monarchs had attained, and in part on their independent powers of taxation. These two factors could work in opposite directions. English kings were more dependent on Parliament in raising taxation than their French counterparts, but, till the second half of the fifteenth century, had greater authority over their nobles. The central European monarchs had the worst of both worlds, often having unreliable sources of finance and an extremely powerful noble class to contend with. Probably the Spanish kings, at least from the middle of the fifteenth century, had the greatest independence of

29. D. Hay, *Europe in the Fourteenth and Fifteenth Centuries* (London, 1966), p. 114.

action, both in relation to finance and to their nobles, and this was part of the reason for the growth of Spanish power.

In all cases, however, until the kings began to develop unchallenged authority in the sixteenth century, the magnates were extremely powerful and in a position to influence foreign policy. That influence might be used in different directions. In many cases they might favor foreign adventure as a means of acquiring loot, land, and personal glory.

> Outside Italy all Europe was saddled with a class in possession of most of the landed wealth, most of the local political power, and most of the permanent high offices of state, who had no business except war and few peacetime diversions as attractive as conspiracy. Before it attained its zenith, the territorial state had no way of ensuring the allegiance of this class so effective as giving them some foreign enemy to fight. Leading the nobility and gentry to foreign conquests eased domestic pressures. Inevitably writers compared the expedient to a judicious blood-letting which reduced excessive humours in the body politic.[30]

But even if they could find a foreign adventure to release their energies, the king would need to deal with such overmighty subjects with caution. Indeed, it was when they were at war that kings were often most dependent on the goodwill and support of the magnates. The pitiful position of the kings of Castile and Portugal, described by Froissart, when on the point of defeat by their enemies, they called in vain for the support of their vassals, is one illustration of this fact; the domination acquired in France by the Orleans and Burgundy families and in England by Gloucester, Beaufort, and Suffolk during the Hundred Years' War is another. It was probably in wartime above all that this group exercised the greatest influence on their monarchs' policies.

At a somewhat lower level, the knights and the bourgeoisie had a greater interest in supporting the king, if only because they feared the pretensions and the endless warrings of the big bad barons. It has often been suggested that it was common interest between middle class and their rulers which was instrumental in reducing the power of the nobles.

> It was felt that the crown represented the interests of the nation as a whole, in opposition to those of any particular section of the community and this was the secret of its strength. The monarchs thus came to typify the passions and aspirations of their subjects who, realizing the identity of their interests, became aggressive where their interests were concerned.[31]

This middle class had somewhat less reason for common cause with the king in foreign policy, since they were obliged to pay for and fight his wars, often for little appreciable benefit other than the glory of the dynasty. Nor were they in any case able to influence his policies significantly, except insofar as they were represented in parliament, and where parliament voted his funds. Yet even then there was rarely active or effective opposition among them to his adventures. And generally,

30. Mattingly, *Renaissance Diplomacy,* p. 127.
31. C. Petrie, *Earlier Diplomatic History* (London, 1949), p. 9.

as in England and France, opposition occurred on domestic rather than foreign issues.

The new and growing class of royal officials had a far closer common interest with the king. At this period "a new race of public servants, secretaries and ambassadors, had appeared—the discreet and self-effacing instruments of princely authority... adept in pressing the legal and traditional powers of the crown...."[32] Ambassadors, for example were

> not a restricted professional class, devoted to diplomatic careers, but a loosely defined group of public servants and prominent citizens, among whom the honors and burdens of foreign services were distributed by a kind of rotation. Except for a sprinkling of magnates, usually employed only on the most important special embassies, they were mostly from what one might call the upper-middle class, solid respectable burghers, or petty gentry or junior scions of great families.[33]

In their foreign dealings, since these were the creations of the ruler, they were no doubt fully committed to his cause. They may, however, by virtue of their expertise, sometimes have exercised a marginal influence.

The voice of the general mass of the population was of course minimal. But as always they exercised a certain negative influence.[34] In the final resort, every ruler knew he could not push his population beyond all endurance. The insurrections which did occur—the revolt of the Flemish weavers in 1336, that of Etienne Marcel in France and the rural disturbances which followed in 1357—broke out at a time of foreign war and at least partly in consequence of that war, and exercised a considerable influence on the policies pursued thereafter. The Peasants' Revolt in England, though not directly resulting from the war, at least showed Richard II the dangers of neglecting domestic problems for foreign adventures. It is for this reason that Machiavelli told his prince that "however strong your armies may be, you will always need the favor of the inhabitants to take possession of a province."[35] No ruler could ignore such considerations. And though their views were not consulted, their *wishes* must have been often against foreign adventure which, even if successful, brought heavy taxation as well as loss of life.[36]

At first sight it could be held that in this society it is the dominant elite, the

32. Hay, *Europe*, p. 161

33. Mattingly, *Renaissance Diplomacy*, p. 109

34. " 'Everyone knows,' wrote Honoré Bonet at the end of the fourteenth century, 'that in the matter of deciding on war, or declaring it... poor men are not concerned at all.' It was no less true a hundred years later, when royal power had been still further strengthened.... No case had to be laid before a country to call it to arms, and as increasing reliance was placed in professional soldiery, the bulk of the population was ignored. War was waged at the discretion of the king." *New Cambridge Modern History*, I (1957): 26.

35. Machiavelli, *The Prince*, chap. 3.

36. For example, even in the most successful expeditions, such as that of Henry V in France, "it may be doubted whether many of the king's subjects really shared his dream of a continental empire. For one thing the merchants were becoming dimly conscious that England's destiny lay not in France but upon the seas.... While Henry lived the English command of the narrow seas was never again disputed. His policy nevertheless was not altogether popular. The only interest to which it appealed strongly was the Staple." *Cambridge Medieval History*, VIII (1959): 384.

rulers, that determine the international ideology. Dynasts impose a dynastic society. All the elite groups were (as in ancient China) dominated by the figure of the king, and all joined in supporting his dynastic ambitions abroad. But this is an oversimplification, for those ambitions derived not exclusively from the ruler but from all the sentiments and loyalties of a semifeudal society which served to buttress his dominant position. Thus the influence of the nobles was favorable to royal foreign policy sometimes for the reason that they could often gain on a smaller scale some of the same benefits, in loot, land, and ransom, as the king himself. The only serious restraint on foreign adventure was probably the resistance of the bourgeoisie to heavier taxation, but even that group often shared in the general support for dynastic ambitions. The character of the age derives only in part, therefore, from the dominance of one particular type of elite; it derives much more from the assumptions and expectations which were so widely shared among other groups within the society.

## 6.4 The Age of Religions (1559–1648)

There is never an abrupt alteration in the character of the elites determining foreign policy in succeeding international societies. Even if there is a relatively sudden alteration in the attitudes and concerns surrounding international affairs— as occurred, for example, around 1559 (see p. 86 above)—this will not in itself transform the structure of society or the location of decision-making power within it. While, therefore, under the impact of the Reformation there was an increasing preoccupation in Europe with questions of religion from the middle of the sixteenth century, there was no equally sudden change in the social structure of individual states, or the ways in which foreign policy decisions were made there. Nor, conversely, was the change in motivation that occurred *caused* by a change in class structure. There were nonetheless distinct alterations in the balance of authority in almost every state.

Some changes resulted directly from the increasing preoccupation with religious questions. Religious leaders and religious groups could be, in this society as perhaps in no other, a powerful influence on policy. Religious groups were highly organized, often with the special aim of influencing state policy. The Jesuits, for example, the spearhead of the counterreformation, sought in every way to promote policies which would extend the influence of the Catholic church and eradicate Protestant heresy; they were influential in inducing Emperor Ferdinand II to stamp out Protestant belief in Bohemia and Austria. Similarly, on the Protestant side, the Calvinists sought by direct preaching among the people to induce a mood of opposition to Rome and all it stood for; they also exerted a large direct impact on state policy in the Netherlands, the Palatinate, and in Scotland. Individual members of particular religious groups—Coligny, Guise, or Marie de Medici in France, Rizzi in Scotland, Bishop Granvelle in Spain, and Richelieu's grey eminence,

Father de Tremblay—were often able to exercise a profound influence on the policies of their governments. Religious movements and factions, such as the Catholic League in France, or the Bohemian Calvinists responsible for the defenestration in Prague, could have a vital impact on events. Even the traditional religious influences, such as the Papacy, could in the era of the Reformation, and under the impact of popes who were now genuinely religious rather than secular in their ambitions, influence international events in a decisive way, as in the naval expedition against the Turks of 1571, launched under the Pope's blessing, or in the encouragement given by successive popes to Philip II's ambitions against the Netherlands and England.

The influence of elite groups was affected in another way. The authority of the sovereign was qualified and reduced by religious loyalties. Succession was no longer automatic, but often depended on the willingness of the sovereign to conform to majority views. James I, despite his undoubted claims, would not have succeeded in England but for his abandonment of his mother's religion. Henry IV in France, whose dynastic rights where indisputable, was opposed by a substantial majority there until he too changed his religion. In Sweden the rightful heir was prevented from succeeding when he professed the wrong religion. In this way the dynastic principle, which had once been so powerful, was now drastically weakened by the new factor of religion. And in their conduct of foreign policy the rulers could never afford to ignore the deeply held religious views of their subjects, as Mary Queen of Scots found to her cost.

Religion had another effect on the class structure. In most cases it cut completely across traditional class lines. Protestant doctrine found adherents among the ranks of the aristocracy, the bourgeoisie, the craftsmen, and the peasants alike.

> Now for the first time . . . revolutionary movements became nationwide and included classes, or elements of classes, ranging from artisans to princes of the blood. . . . Only religious belief, held either from fanatical conviction or political expediency, could bring together the divergent interests of nobles, burghers and peasants throughout whole kingdoms.[37]

It was these great religious minorities which replaced the big magnates as the principal threat to kingly power, and it is scarcely surprising that royal governments came to regard the subduing of these minorities as a primary objective. Though such opposition forces had little direct impact on the formulation of foreign policy, they had, as popular forces always do, a negative influence: A government threatened by them had to be extremely cautious in foreign policy. The caution shown by Elizabeth in England in relation to foreign affairs, and by Richelieu in France in his early years, derived mainly from this cause: fear of the hidden Catholic menace in the first case, and of the Hugenot power in the second.

The monopoly of power in the hands of the sovereign was reduced for other reasons. The ruler continued in most cases to be the major *single* influence on foreign policy. The vital importance of the sovereign's own views in France was

37. *New Cambridge Modern History*, III (1968): 234.

shown in the effect of the dagger of Ravaillac in bringing a total reversal of France's policies. Queen Elizabeth in England, and even her two Stuart successors, retained considerable independence in determining the external policies of their country. In Spain, even more clearly, the personal view of Philip II was the main determinant of policies. Imperial policy too changed radically according to the character and attitudes of the incumbent, from the conciliatory and tolerant Maximilian II to the withdrawn and half-mad Rudolf or the fanatical Ferdinand II. In Scandinavia the leadership, determination, and world view of Gustav Adolf had a decisive effect not only on Sweden but on the entire course of world events. But such rulers could not have imposed their policies against the religious convictions of their peoples. It was the fact that these rulers reflected the religious passions of their subjects which determined the religious character of the ideology in this age.

Other influences from elsewhere were also important. Elizabeth's policies were considerably modified by the clear-sighted and realistic advice she received from Cecil, Walsingham, and others at her court. In France a minister such as Coligny, in spite of his religion (or because of it), was able to exercise a powerful influence, while later Sully and above all Richelieu took the conduct of foreign policy largely into their own powerful hands. Even in Spain, the home of absolutism, the solitary power of Philip II was increasingly diluted under his weaker successors, and a minister such as Olivares was virtually in control of Spanish policies during the Thirty Years' War. In Sweden another chief minister, Oxenstierna, shared responsibility and power with his king to such an extent that it was he, rather than any member of the royal family, who took over the reins, especially in foreign policy, on the king's death in 1632. Far more than in the age of dynasts, the power of the monarch had to be shared with his chief advisers. While religious sentiment was in their case strongly tempered by considerations of state interest, they often reflected the general religious preoccupations of their time. Once again it was not the change in political structure but the change in general belief that was decisive.

Another important influence was that of military leaders. In an age that was almost continually at war it was inevitable that military commanders were sometimes in a position to have a decisive control over policy. Wallenstein in the empire, the Dukes of Alba and Parma in the Netherlands, were sometimes able to bring about significant changes in their masters' policy if it could be shown that military success depended on them. Similarly, the powerful governors of distant provinces, who were more closely aware of the situation on the spot than those at home, could have a considerable say in determining the policies pursued. The consolidation of royal power depended crucially on delegation to powerful officials of this kind, and this entailed taking some account of their views on important policy issues. If the great magnates in opposition to the king had less influence than in earlier times, the great officials in his service had more than ever before.[38]

The common people had as little influence as ever. In England, with the rise of

38. E.g., "The Spanish viceroys satisfied their distant masters with public directives and private bribes, and governed much as they pleased." Ibid., 272.

the burgher class, public opinion of a sort exercised some influence on royal authority. James I's long flirtation with Spain between 1604 and 1620, across the religious boundary, was brought to an end partly by the wave of popular and parliamentary enthusiasm for the cause of his son-in-law, the elector Palatine, after the outbreak of the Thirty Years' War. Parliament prevented Charles I from playing a more active role in that war in 1626–1630, by the simple expedient of refusing him the money to do so. The middle class had still greater influence in the United Provinces than in England. Elsewhere, where the power of the purse was not in the hands of parliament, such direct means were not available, but public opinion of a sort could nonetheless sometimes exert an influence. Sometimes, in an age of conflict between religious extremists, a middle viewpoint emerged—as among the Politiques in France, or among the northern rulers in Germany—calling a plague on both the more extreme houses and demanding nothing so much as peace and order. And certainly the religious views of the broad mass of the people were a factor which could never be left wholly out of account, if only because they might be exploited by those so minded.[39]

How far then was the changed character of this international age the effect of a change in social structure? In a period in which the major issues are ideological rather than political, concerned with the next world rather than this, there is bound to be some shift in the influence of different groups. The preachers and churches acquire influence, largely because of their sway with the sovereigns and chief decision makers. The great magnates lose it, because of the decline in their own power. But the change in foreign aims and policies is not so much the effect of any alteration in social structure as of changes in attitude and belief *throughout* international society, shared by all classes, kings and magnates, priests and people alike.

Traditional class allegiances and class differences indeed become *less* important because they are overlaid by religious differences which influence all classes and appear of far greater moment. Thus the ideology or ethos cannot be regarded as merely a "superstructure" reflecting class and economic interests (this would grossly underestimate the power of ideas). It is rather an independent power, itself sometimes influencing the class structure. It is the general influence of religious concepts everywhere, rather than changes in social structure, therefore, which gave this international society its special character.

## 6.5 The Age of Sovereignty (1648–1789)

The dominant elites of the age which followed were still more restricted in number and narrow in class basis. In an age of absolutism the control of foreign

39. "Religion was the binding force that held together the divergent interests of the different classes and provided them with an organization and a propaganda machine capable of forming the first genuinely national and international parties in modern European history . . . It was through religion that

policy was predominantly in the hands of a small class consisting of sovereigns themselves, assisted by an only marginally larger class of ministers and chief advisers.

In most countries the views of the sovereign ultimately prevailed on foreign affairs as on other questions. When, after the death of Mazarin, the chief officials asked Louis XIV to whom they should address themselves on policy from that point, his answer was simple: "A moi." From that time he took full personal control of his country's foreign policy, as of every other branch of government. So, too, the other great rulers of the age, William III in England, Frederick in Prussia, Maria Teresa in Austria, Catherine in Russia, personally guided and managed the foreign policies of their nations, often personally conducting correspondence with foreign sovereigns, ministers, and their own ambassadors abroad. It was *their* attitudes and ambitions which shaped the policy pursued by their states, and so dictated the whole character of the international society: Louis' passion for "la gloire" and for the expansion of France's frontiers, William's determination to resist French pretensions, Catherine's unscrupulous greed for territory, Frederick's ambition to acquire Silesia, and Maria Teresa's obsession with recovering it. Even more than in the age of dynasts (since they were less dependent on tradition or on powerful domestic forces), personal rulers imposed personal policies.

It is scarcely surprising, therefore, that sovereigns created an age of sovereignty. As in ancient China absolute rulers were concerned with promoting the power of the states they themselves ruled. The conduct of foreign affairs was as personal as all other policy. Louis XIV preferred to deal directly with other sovereigns, sending messages to his own representatives in foreign capitals, rather than dealing through their ambassadors in Paris. He personally directed, and sometimes personally worded, diplomatic correspondence. "Louis himself laid down his foreign policy after free discussion in the conseil d'en haut whose secrets no outsider could penetrate. The foreign secretary then worked out the details in daily consultation with the king, who frequently altered his minister's drafts."[40] William III wrote many despatches and memoranda personally and sometimes conducted interviews with foreign ambassadors and ministers without anyone else being present. Foreign offices remained very small, and the total number of individuals engaged in the shaping of policy was tiny. Louis XIV's foreign minister "had a competent staff of several first secretaries with a number of translators and clerks—his personal employees. It is unlikely that they exceeded 30 even after the establishment of a separate archival section. . . ."[41]

Royal ministers for the most part were engaged in executing policy, rather than

---

they could appeal to the lowest classes and the mob to vent the anger of their poverty and the despair of their unemployment in fanatical looting and in barbarous massacres. Social and economic discontent were fertile ground for recruitment by either side, and popular tyranny appeared both in Calvinist Ghent and in Catholic Paris." Ibid., 159.

40. Ibid., VI (1970): 177.

41. Ibid., 178.

in formulating it. A Colbert or a Pomponne was not a Richelieu or a Mazarin. To a considerable extent the great ministers of the day merely carried out the orders they received from their masters. The most they could do was to influence, by their advice, the form these orders took. The situation was only marginally different in the "constitutional" regimes of Britain and the Netherlands. In the seventeenth century English and Dutch rulers often exercised as much personal control of foreign policy as those elsewhere: "In effect William was his own foreign secretary, frequently negotiating with foreign ambassadors at home and penning the more important letters himself in the seclusion of his cabinet."[42] Only in the eighteenth century, in England, the Netherlands, and Switzerland, did elected ministers rather than royal appointees begin to carry greater weight: Heinsius in the Netherlands, Bolingbroke, Walpole, and Pitt in England exercised a personal control over foreign policy which no minister in an absolutist state was able to enjoy.

Insofar as officials acquired greater influence, it was often not so much through greater constitutional authority as through greater specialized knowledge and skills. The development of professional diplomatic services, with foreign offices at home to instruct them, instituted, for example, by Colbert in France (on the model of Venice) and widely imitated elsewhere, introduced a new element of expertise into the conduct of foreign affairs. But the diplomats themselves, as well as members of the foreign offices, were still primarily recruited from the ranks of the aristocracy (occasionally the upper bourgeoisie). Moreover, from the very fact of their appointment they were to a considerable extent dependent on royal favor. What the influence of officialdom brought, therefore, was not so much the divergent viewpoint of a totally different class as the sometimes more detached, better-informed, and more carefully thought-out calculation of state interests which a professional diplomatic establishment was able to present.

The councils of state and similar bodies, which often had a nominal constitutional role, were still narrower in class background, and equally closely tied to royal fortunes. Though a separate class, they would still promote the cause of sovereignty. But they might sometimes be able to bring to bear a somewhat different view of state interests then that of the sovereign himself. The emperor Leopold "made it a rule to abide by the decisions of the majority of his Council even when he disagreed with them."[43] So the use of such procedures could mobilize a diversity of views as a check on the purely personal vision of the monarch himself. But the sovereign did not necessarily listen to the advice he was given. The Venetian ambassador to the French court reported that "the king [Louis XIV] maintains the most impenetrable secrecy about affairs of state. The ministers attend Council meetings, but he confides his plans to them only when he has reflected at length upon them and has come to a definite decision." The attitude of most monarchs of the day to their councils was probably closer to that of Louis than to that of Leopold.

42. Ibid., 176–77.
43. Ibid., 177.

The nobility and other upper strata might in some cases have the opportunity, through the court, to exercise a marginal influence. But again the sovereign was under no obligation to listen. Louis XIV complained that all the French nobility on every occasion perpetually urged him to war, so as to find an opportunity to distinguish themselves there. Such promptings were probably quite without influence in most cases (Louis had no need to be persuaded to war). Except in Poland, and for a time in Sweden, this class was too powerless to exert any effective influence on policy.

How far wider opinion made itself felt varied from state to state as well as from one issue to another. It was no doubt greatest in the constitutional states, and was expressed there especially through parliament. It was not necessarily pacific in its influence. The nationalist fervor in the English parliament in 1739 (including the display of the famous Jenkins' ear) was at least in part responsible for precipitating the war of that name (and the fall of Walpole). But sometimes the pressure was the other way. The English parliament had some influence in causing the abandonment of the war with France against the United Provinces in 1674, and in the abandonment of the war with France in 1712–1713. In the Netherlands William of Orange and other leaders found themselves in conflict with the commercial classes, in parliament and elsewhere, who were increasingly reluctant to become involved in foreign conflict. In most countries, however, even the educated classes had little opportunity for making their voice effectively heard on questions of international policy. This was a matter primarily for kings and their ministers and a few specialized officials.

Among this limited group of sovereigns, the "family of kings," often themselves linked by ties of blood (in the late seventeenth century almost all of the chief royal families were related by marriage ties),[44] and their advisers, certain common understandings and assumptions developed. They shared, far more than their predecessors, a common European culture: French statesmen knew English philosophy, English knew French literature and court manners, German kings employed at their courts French literatteurs, and Russian sovereigns had German advisers and ministers. All inherited a common tradition of learning and belief, all shared in the same development of commerce and city life. They enjoyed a generally similar social structure, a similar system of landholding, and (with marginal exceptions) a similar political structure. Commerce, which was more international than ever before, promoted the exchange of ideas and life style as well as of goods. It was scarcely surprising that many felt that, sharing this common heritage, above all sharing the common rank and obligations of royalty, they could arrive at common understandings with each other to determine the great questions of the day, whether through civilized negotiations or, if necessary, equally civilized warfare. It is still less surprising that these understandings bolstered the power of sovereignty, for it was in strengthening that principle above all that they shared a common interest.

It is thus to some extent inescapable that, in an age of absolutism, the struc-

44. Ibid., 168.

ture of society and the nature of elites determined the character of the international society as a whole. But if the social structure had been different, would totally different foreign policies have been pursued, even within the historical context of the time? Such historical ifs are so unreal that it is impossible to answer them conclusively. If the structure of *all* societies had been different, it would have been a different age altogether—and the question becomes meaningless. But insofar as there is evidence, it seems to point the other way. The policies of the Netherlands, socially quite different from the rest of Europe, was scarcely distinguishable from that of other states. The policy of Britain during the Commonwealth, under a regime wholly distinct from those elsewhere, without a sovereign, was not significantly different: that government engaged in foreign war against the Dutch for dominance in the seas, and against Spain for the futile prize of a Flanders seaport, policies of a kind that might equally have been pursued under a royal government in the same age (indeed, essentially similar policies were pursued under Charles II for the next dozen years).[45] While, therefore, the social and political structure in the continent as a whole no doubt strongly influenced the foreign policies adopted, the structure of individual states appears to have been insignificant in its effect in this age as in other societies we have examined. In general, it was the assumptions and attitudes widespread throughout the society as a whole—in other words, the underlying ideology of the age—rather than the social structure of the individual members which determined the international policies pursued.

## 6.6 The Age of Nationalism (1789–1914)

In the nationalist age a new class emerged to dominance. The industrial revolution, and the political advances that succeeded it, in most countries for the first time brought the business classes, or at least a part of them, to power and international influence. The power of the king declined in most states. Control of foreign affairs dropped from the hands of the sovereign himself into those of his ministers and advisers. *Influence* on foreign affairs dropped to a still lower level: to parliaments, newspaper editors, merchants, and the educated everywhere. The dominant elite which controlled the international society, while still a small minority, became marginally less small than before.

The sovereigns still retain a powerful influence on foreign policy, in some cases (as in Russia or in the France of Napoleon III) the dominant influence. But in many others the role of the sovereign and that of his ministers now begins to be reversed. Instead of the ministers advising the sovereign, now, one might say, it is the sovereign who advises the minister. Day-to-day control is in the hands of the

45. It is true that Switzerland, under a different social and political system, increasingly isolated herself from the general rough and tumble in which other states were engaged, but this was the effect of her geographical isolation rather than of different social and political structure. Nor did it make her less concerned with the defense of sovereignty.

Ferry in France, were defeated on an issue of foreign policy. French parliamentary opinion was the vital factor in preventing France from joining Britain in joint action in Egypt in 1882. Thus the attitude of parliaments in the background was always an influence on those who made the decisions.

At least equally important was the influence of the press. The militancy of the German press stiffened and intensified the nationalism of the German government at the time of the Morocco crises in 1906 and 1911. The British press forced British governments to respond to the German naval challenge and to drop the idea of collaboration with Germany over the Baghdad railway in 1913. In other cases the fulminations of the press could be used to justify policies pursued on other grounds. On questions of foreign policy "the press assumed considerable importance. This press enjoyed a large measure of freedom but much of it was controlled by a variety of vested interests. Governments often exercised over it a substantial influence, and some of it was simply venal. The argument of domestic necessity, genuine or manufactured, became a tool in the arsenal of diplomacy."[49]

Opinion in the wider sense could also sometimes be of influence. When "public opinion" is spoken of at this time, it is of course the opinion of a relatively narrow group which is meant. The vast mass of the population probably had little opinion of any kind on most issues of foreign affairs. It is unlikely that they concerned themselves greatly about the Ems telegram, or the Kruger telegram, or the way the Turks treated the Bosnians in 1876. But if they did, their opinion was probably not known, far less heeded. When, therefore, it is said that public opinion became inflamed on such issues, it is primarily the opinion of intellectuals, parliamentarians, and publicists, in a word, middle-class opinion, that is meant. Few governments were under any clear political constraint to heed even this opinion, especially on matters of foreign policy. But most preferred to feel that they were at least in a general way acting in accordance with public wishes. The fact that Gladstone could fight an election campaign on the issue of the British government's support for the Turks in the Balkans is an indication not merely that public opinion could be roused on the question, but that it might, in his view, cast its vote to throw the Conservative government out on the issue. Even in the autocracies opinion, the fear of public disapproval or the hope of public acclaim, could act as a significant influence on occasion. Indeed, in some ways, where personal rule still prevailed, the importance of insuring that policies reflected popular opinions was even greater.[50]

Public opinion, in this wider sense, was generally more emotional and more nationalistic than that of the governments. Such sentiments as the violent British response to the Kruger telegram of 1895, the hysterical reaction to Mafeking, the passionate calls for war against Russia evoked in Britain by the smallest suspicion of Russian activity, even in areas close to her own border such as Afghanistan or

49. Albrecht-Carrié, *Diplomatic History,* p. 152.

50. Cf. Taylor, *Struggle for Mastery,* p. 229: "Though the Tsars were despots, they were always sensitive to the limited public opinion within their empire. . . . Constitutional governments can weather unpopularity; autocrats dread it."

the Straits, were sometimes an embarrassment to British governments. The reaction of French public opinion to Fashoda, or to the mild provocation of the Ems telegram, was difficult for French governments to restrain or ignore. Pan-Slav sentiment in Russia was frequently a factor stimulating Russian tsars to take a stronger line in the Balkans than they might otherwise have done, as in 1876, 1908, and 1914. And German public opinion certainly encouraged the already nationalistic mood of German leaders in the years before World War I. Very often it was national status, ''face'' rather than national interest, which was at stake. But it was on questions of face precisely that publics felt most strongly. However cautious and conciliatory were governments and their foreign offices, therefore, it was not always easy for them to resist such pressures. What Bismarck said of the Tsar Alexander III and his ministers had general validity for this age: ''The Emperor is himself well-intentioned. His ministers are prudent. But will they have the strength to resist the pressures of popular passions if they are once unchained?''

Often the influence was reciprocal. The leaders themselves, either deliberately or unwittingly, fanned and stimulated national sentiment. The loss of Alsace-Lorraine need not necessarily have been unforgettable to France: by imploring the French public to ''think of it always, speak of it never,'' Gambetta helped to make it so. In the same way Joseph Chamberlain in Britain, Theodore Roosevelt in the U.S., Bulow in Germany, Aehrenthal in Austria, would sometimes, for their own purposes, exacerbate rather than calm the hot passions of their own peoples.

Thus in this age, in somewhat more broadly based societies, governments were subject to pressures from a wider area of public opinion than in earlier times. And that public opinion was often more nationalistic in attitude than the rulers of earlier ages. But this was not primarily the *effect* of the structure of society. There was no special reason for the middle classes to be nationalistic—their commercial interests went the other way. It was the competitive and status-conscious character of the *international* society that influenced them. Within that environment all, sovereigns and bourgeois, statesmen and publics alike, were acutely sensitive to slights to national pride, resentful of threats to national honor, jealous of affronts to national dignity. It took little to arouse a strong wave of national emotion which could then influence governors as much as governed. Even if the dominant elites—cabinets and foreign ministers—wanted desperately to resist such pressures, they would sometimes have found it difficult to do so. Often subject to the same influences, they did not even want to resist. The wider environment of nationalism influenced their way of thought, their reactions to threats and crises, as much as those of their publics.

## 6.7 The Age of Ideology (1914–1974)

In the following age the character of the dominant elites changed yet again.

It was an era widely proclaimed as the ''century of the common man.'' Perhaps not every common man would have recognized the supremacy which that title implied. He felt himself often as helpless and incapable of influencing events as the common man in most other ages. And this applied even more to the field of foreign affairs than to most others.

Yet there were nonetheless substantial differences from the preceding age. One of these concerned the background from which political leadership was drawn. The characteristic figures of the age—a Hitler, a Bevin, a Truman, a Khrushchev, or a Mao—were essentially proletarian figures, wholly different in upbringing and outlook from the aristocratic or upper bourgeois leaders of the previous century. Their habits of thought and expression—the homely wisdom of a Bevin or the peasant proverbs of a Khrushchev—were different in kind from the formal language of diplomatic intercourse in the previous age. The characteristic attitudes of such leaders in the field of foreign affairs were often narrower and more parochial than those of their predecessors, but also often more hardheaded and realistic. Certainly they reflected more accurately the commonly held feelings of the mass of their fellow countrymen.

There were other changes of leadership which were perhaps even more important. Leaders were now primarily politicians rather than statesmen. In the previous age figures such as Bismarck, Gorchakov, and Aerenthal held office because they held the favor of the sovereign. They were to a considerable extent, whatever their constitutional position, independent of the twists and turns of party fortunes and maneuvers, often even of changes of government: Bismarck held office for nearly thirty years, through a succession of different Prussian and German governments. Even in Britain, where parliamentary institutions were strongly developed, figures such as Palmerston and Russell acquired political authority almost by birth, had permanent positions in parliament almost independent of party, and were not seriously threatened by parliamentary pressures. But in the succeeding age virtually every foreign minister and every head of government had influence on foreign affairs largely by virtue of being skillful politicians. Their continuance in office depended on their being able to maintain the confidence of parliament, or electors, or both. Even in totalitarian systems, such as the Soviet Union or China, political skill was one essential condition of maintaining ministerial power. Equally important, the unelected head of state who, in the age of Napoleon III, Alexander II, or the last Kaisers, had been a dominant influence, now counted for virtually nothing.

Politicians with such a background are inevitably often more concerned about political and ideological issues than about "national interests" in the old sense. Their training and experience has been bound up with such questions. The politician who has spent much of his time denouncing communists (or imperialists) at home may see himself as devoted to struggling against communists (or imperialists) abroad. The change in the experience and background of foreign policy decision makers thus reinforced the preoccupation of the public as a whole with ideology. And it accentuated the interrelatedness of internal and external affairs which derived from that preoccupation.

In an age of mass communications, moreover, and of deference to the common man, there is a new relationship between political leaders and the bulk of their populations. Not only must the leaders in this age, far more than the last, pay heed to the passions and prejudices believed to prevail among the people as a whole; those popular passions and prejudices may be *used* to mobilize the masses on the side of the leaders. So Hitler and Mussolini deliberately stirred up mass fervor or ideological antagonism against "barbarous Bolsheviks" or "decadent demo-crats" as a means of árousing their nations. Later campaigns, against communism in the U.S., against imperialism in the Soviet Union, against the superpowers in China, against neocolonialism in the third world, equally, in order to mobilize support, exploited prejudices believed to be held by the masses (yet also sought to create them). In pursuing their ideological goals government can gladly claim to be following the wishes of their publics; for they themselves have created those wishes.

But there is another change among the elites in this age the effect of which is sometimes contrary. Decision-making is increasingly institutionalized. Whoever is foreign minister or Communist Party leader will be surrounded by an army of committees, councils, advisers, and general bureaucracy, which will together severely limit their effective freedom of action. There is now virtually nobody, like a Napoleon III, or even a Palmerston, who can take foreign policy decisions virtually on his own authority alone. All decisions are in a sense collective, in that a large number of different people are involved. Even in authoritarian systems, collective leadership becomes the norm. This tends to make for a greater degree of caution and prudence in the conduct of foreign policy. Personal impulse, whim, anger, or caprice is toned down or eliminated by the sifting, processing, and restraining of advisers, colleagues, and institutions.

Nor is this all. All those involved in the decision-making process are, far more than in earlier ages, subject to a new kind of pressure. With the development of education, newspapers now reach almost every section of the population. With the rise in wealth, new media—cinema, radio, and television—bring an increased awareness of foreign affairs everywhere. These media, especially the press, become a powerful factor within the political system generally, influencing deci-sion makers. Whether or not they are representative of public opinion as a whole, they represent an important influence on the formation of foreign policy. Only in totalitarian states is this force largely without effect, since here the media are themselves in the hands of the authorities: public opinion can itself be manufac-tured. But in both cases the press projects and magnifies the prevailing concern with ideology, the prevailing hostility to political opponents.

Parliaments, too, though less than the press, become more powerful in most states. They at least debate, and sometimes effectively influence, foreign policy. Governments in general avoid a situation in which their policies are likely to be condemned by their own parliaments. Parliaments themselves, moreover, now elected on a system of universal suffrage in most countries, reflect a wider spectrum of views. Moreover, governments, even if indifferent to the views of parliament, cannot afford to be indifferent to the views of their electors, since their own continuance in office will depend on them. Though this influence is probably of less significance in the field of foreign affairs than in most others, even here it is difficult for governments deliberately to defy the widely held views of their publics.

Often more important than the pressure of mass opinion for the ear of government is that of particular powerful groups. So large industrial associations, such as the Comité des Forges or the Two Hundred Families in France, or powerful corporations, such as ITT or the big oil companies in the U.S., may be able to exert their influence for or against particular policies. So too, in every country, the military, working through the ministry of defense or the chiefs of staffs, or the intelligence establishment, such as the CIA, may enjoy special access, and so have a particularly powerful voice in the decisions reached. Often the more powerful of these groups *reinforce* the ideological prejudices of their governments. So governments are increasingly subject to new pressures of a particular kind, which often accentuate the general ideological competition.

In all ages statesmen have claimed to reflect or represent the opinions of their countrymen. But in this age there are more powerful mechanisms for making statesmen *conscious* of opinion, whether general or particular: the media, opinion polls, parliaments. This does not always serve as a restraint. On the contrary, opinion is often *less* peacefully inclined than governments themselves. Public opinion is sometimes more ideologically concerned, more emotionally aroused by a particular humiliation, grievance, or threat, than the better-informed and more sober-minded members of foreign office staffs (as in the U.S. during the McCarthy period). This too, therefore, may intensify the ideological content of foreign policy, especially at periods of extreme confrontation, as at the height of the cold war.

In general, therefore, in this age, the decisions of governments are affected by influences from a greater range of sources than in most other periods. Even in a totalitarian state opinions that are widely or deeply felt among the mass of population will have some influence on governments (though mainly because governments are subject to the same waves of opinions as their publics). Where ideological passions run high they may thus spur a government to slightly stronger action. But the influence of public opinion is marginal. Governments can be fairly confident that opinions on most questions are sufficiently uncertain, divided, or indifferent to allow them, the bureaucrats and ministers, effective freedom of action. Often they act in conformity with general feelings. But this is because they, the decision makers themselves, *share* the attitudes and motives generally prevailing, above all those relating to the dominant concern with ideology. Actions are influenced by ideology because ideological attitudes are everywhere dominant, not because a particular class or interest has come to control society.

There is indeed little evidence that in this age attitudes on ideology, and so on foreign policy, were significantly influenced by the character of elites. In the West union leaders are often as fervently anticommunist as businessmen and political leaders. In the East bureaucrats, managers, and technocrats accept the ruling orthodoxy as unquestioningly as proletariat and peasantry. New ideologies, emanating from Peking, Havana, or Dar-es-Salaam, find as willing adherents in one part of each population as another. Neither the type of ideological belief nor its intensity is significantly related to class background. This is true of foreign policy attitudes generally: archnationalists and archideologues, doves and hawks, are to be found impartially among the wealthy and the poor, the haves and the have-nots in the international society. Personality factors—the authoritarian and the liberal character traits, coercive or concessive attitudes—are probably more important than position in the social hierarchy. Fundamentally the elites within each state pursue policies which promote a particular ideology. But they do this because this is regarded as in the interest of their state, and indeed of the whole international society, not because it is the interest of the particular elite in power.

In the societies we have examined the characters of the elites determining policy have varied widely. They have varied in the *concentration* of power at the top from the almost total control of policy by individual rulers (in the ancient Chinese system, the age of dynasties, and the age of sovereignty), to domination by a powerful upper middle class (in ancient Greece and the age of nationalism), to influence divided among a variety of disparate elements (in the age of religions and the age of ideology).

It is difficult to establish any clear correlation between the dominance of a particular kind of elite and the character of an international society. Societies where individual rulers exercised dominant power, for example, have varied widely in the type of foreign policy pursued. Possibly concern for territory has been especially pronounced in such societies (compared, for example, to the situation in ancient Greece and during the age of ideology). But there is no indication that this was cause and effect: in the age of nationalism middle-class governments were as concerned with national glory and aggrandizement as absolute rulers. Still less is there any confirmation of the crude conclusion of Rousseau that if only one got rid of the sovereigns themselves a situation of peace among nations would be immediately established. Whatever the correlation between types of elites and types of international society, it is not as simple as this. Absolute rulers have had many different types of foreign ambition, varying from one age to another. That of the age of dynasties was quite different from that of the age of sovereignty. Conversely, international societies where power has been more widely shared have been equally varied in character. Middle-class societies may be somewhat more concerned with questions of ideology than others (for example, the society of ancient Greece and of recent times). But this is certainly not closely related to the political character of each state: the autocratic states of ancient Greece, or of modern times, have been as concerned with ideology as "democratic" states in which the middle class has had a predominant influence. Here too the international attitudes and policy of governments seem to derive rather from the character of the international society as a whole than from the character of each individual state. The nature of the elites, while significant, hardly seems to be the decisive factor.

The same conclusion seems to follow from comparing the attitudes *among* elites, or even among the population as a whole, within any given state. Attitudes and opinions of wholly different sections at any one time show remarkable resemblances, considering their divergence of interest in many foreign policy issues. Thus in the age of dynasties the common people often shared many of the same dynastic ambitions as their rulers, though they suffered most of the costs and gained few of the benefits from those policies. Nationalist ambitions and imperialist prides were indiscriminately shared among most sections of the population in the nineteenth century, with little distinction according to class origins. Anticommunist and antiimperialist sentiment today is relatively evenly spread among the populations of West and East respectively, depending more on personality factors than class interests.

Indeed, there is far more in common between the attitudes of *different* classes within the same age than between those of the *same* classes in different ages. Working people today will find little in common in their attitude to foreign policies with those of their predecessors in the age of dynasties or even the age of sovereignty; middle classes in the age of nationalism had wholly different attitudes from the middle classes in the age of religion. Within the same international society, on the other hand, all classes in all states share generally similar attitudes: the same concern with dynastic aims, with sovereignty, with nationalism, or with ideology. It is as though all are indoctrinated with the ideology that prevails in the society as a whole. In other words, attitudes on such questions seem to be dictated little by class interest or by domestic factors affecting one state alone, but very much by the international environment generally, affecting all states.

Within an entire society there is of course a relationship between the type of elite in power and the concern that dominates foreign policy. An age of dynasts creates an age of dynasticism, an age of sovereigns an age of sovereignty, and so on. But even this is not necessarily cause and effect. It is almost as reasonable to say that sovereigns exist because of the prevailing assumptions of the age of sovereignty as the reverse. Similarly, nationalism does not exist because nationalists have occupied the seats of power; on the contrary, prevailing elites are nationalist because all are nationalists everywhere (and elitist ministers are often less nationalist than their peoples). Elites in the age of ideology are not more ideological than everybody else; they *must* be ideological because this is the nature of their whole society.

Thus we must conclude that the basic ideology of an international society (in the sense here used) is not the result of the class structure or the character of the elites in individual member states. There is a relationship between them, just as there is between the dominating ideology within a primitive society and the social or political structure that exists there. The elites form part of a single integrated social whole, of which all the parts are connected. And the dominant elites inherit the common set of attitudes and aspirations which influences the society as a whole. They may vary marginally in their response to these influences, just as individuals vary in their response to the social pressures of a smaller society. But this is only marginal. In general it is the nature of the ideology which governs the elites, it would seem, not the nature of the elites which determines the ideology.

# Chapter 7.   Motives

In comparing different types of domestic society, one important distinguishing mark will clearly be the motives which activate its members. We frequently distinguish, for example, between those societies, whether ancient or modern, primitive or sophisticated, where motives are primarily cooperative or competitive; achievement-oriented or satisfaction-oriented; other-related or inner-related. Anthropologists sometimes distinguish among simpler societies according to whether motives within them are concerned primarily with status, with wealth or possessions, or with collective or individual activities and goals.

It is not necessarily important from the point of view of the sociologist, (as opposed to the psychologist), to know the source of these motives: whether they are deliberately instilled by parental and social teaching or acquired indirectly from the traditions which prevail within the society, whether they result from precept or example. The important point for the sociologist is the effect of the motives on behavior and social organization. Because certain motives have been widely instilled, members of the society will act in particular ways in relation to each other. And this in turn will determine the character of the society as a whole.

It is clear that the nature and structure of an international society will be equally affected by the motives that prevail among its members, that is, the nations within it. To take an obvious example, a society where the states are mainly peace-loving and satisfied will be different from one where they are warlike and aggressive in motivation; one where they are primarily concerned with rapid economic growth will be different from one where they are mainly concerned with dynastic ambitions or territorial gains; one where the governments are largely cooperative in their attitude to others is different from one where they are highly competitive. Just as the motives of individuals will determine their behavior in dealing with other individuals, so the motives of states determine their behavior in relation to other states, and so the character of the whole international society.

In speaking of the motives of states we are clearly guilty of some oversimplification. Only individual human beings are capable of motives in the normal sense. If we say that states have a particular type of motivation, what we really mean is

144

that the individuals who compose those states, above all those who determine their policies, are ruled by these motives.[1] Of course they may not all feel them in exactly the same way. But because the whole of a nation shares the same *situation* in relation to other nations, because they are affected in a similar way by influences coming from the international environment as a whole, they do in practice react in remarkably similar ways to the same stimuli. A threat to a nation's security, an insult to its honor, a challenge to its traditional status, will often be perceived in similar ways by members of the same nation and stimulate among them a collective response. The speeches of statesmen or the editorials of newspapers will arouse the same collective feelings among large sections of the population. In this way, motives which may originally have been those of only a relatively small elite become diffused among the population as a whole.

But if we are thus justified in speaking of the motives of entire states, can we be justified in assuming a similar set of motivations among different states of the same society? Here too the situation is not unlike that in domestic societies. Motives will vary considerably from individual to individual, both in Tibet and in the U.S.; some will be more ambitious, more self-seeking, or more public spirited than others. And yet there will be certain ways in which the motives of all individuals in Tibet are different from those of *all* individuals in the U.S. (and this will be even more true between different primitive societies, as between the Indians of the Northwest coast of America and those of the Pueblos of New Mexico). Similarly, among societies of states not all member nations will feel or behave in exactly the same way. But there may be fairly uniform *patterns* of feeling and behavior that will prevail among the members of the society as a whole. And these patterns may be entirely different from those characterizing other societies. As we have already seen, the states of ancient China and of ancient Greece felt and behaved in quite different ways from each other, but within each society there was a common pattern of expected behavior and feeling; the motives governing states in the dynastic age were quite different from those in the age of religions or in the age of sovereignty, but within each age states behaved and felt in similar ways. There were variations from state to state even in the same society. But these variations were less than those between the characteristic motives of different ages altogether.

In the pages that follow we shall seek to consider and compare the motives that were characteristic of individual international societies; to consider how they were related to the underlying ideologies governing those societies; and to examine how widespread and uniform they were within each state and among all states. On the basis of this comparison we shall seek to draw certain conclusions about the precise significance of this factor as an influence determining the character of an international society.

1. For a discussion of the sources of foreign policy motivations in recent times, see Evan Luard, *Conflict and Peace in the Modern International System* (Boston, 1968), chap. 1.

## 7.1 The Chinese Multistate System (771–221 B.C.)

Within the ancient Chinese society of states, the most important single motive was without doubt the search for territory. The history of the period itself shows this sufficiently clearly (see pp. 70–74 above). But this alone does not tell us enough. In examining motives we want to know *why* territory was demanded. Was it demanded for itself alone, or as a means to an end? And if the latter, what were those other ends?

In the early days it seems that the search for food was sometimes one underlying motive; wars were occasionally little more than grain raids.[2] This was true especially of the barbarian states and peoples, sometimes occupying less fertile areas on the periphery. It was not characteristic of the mature system, in which most of the states were usually self-sufficient in grain and could normally buy or borrow from other states in times of emergency. Another reason for seeking territory was (as in later societies) the desire to improve security. There are many accounts of one state attacking a smaller state to make it easier to defend itself from another larger one. In some cases the occupation of another state is mainly preventive: to forestall some similar action by another state. One reason Ch'u in the southwest enlarged its territory continually at the expense of its smaller neighbors was undoubtedly to enable it to promote its security more effectively against other large states, such as Chi'i and Chin. Chin conquered Yu in 655 to be able to pass through its territory to make war on Kuo, and in 632 it occupied Wei to enable it better to confront the threatening power of Ch'u. Lu persuaded Chin, the leader of the Chou league, that it was justified in absorbing small neighbors in order to promote the security of the league as a whole.[3]

Thus the desire to extend territory became in time an important motive in its own right. A minister of Chin declared in 579 that "the princes are full of covetous greed, indulge their ambitious desires without shrinking, and for a few feet of territory will destroy their people."[4] In some cases the motive was domination rather than the direct control of territory. The defeated state was brought to a situation of semifeudal subjection. Protectorates were established over defeated or enfeebled states. A whole range of different types of dominance could be secured by the conquest of territory.

More important in promoting the demand for territory was the desire to increase the fame and glory of the state's ruler. This is shown in many writings of Confucius and Mencius condemning rulers or their ministers for such ambitions, an indication that they were relatively common. We have already seen how the ruler of Chin bewailed to Mencius how he would be condemned by posterity for

2. R. L. Walker, *The Multi-State System in Ancient China* (Hamden, 1953), p. 44.
3. Ibid., p. 47.
4. J. Legge, *The Chinese Classics* I (Oxford, 1893), 337–39.

having lost territory to his rivals. National glory was of course not conceived only in terms of territory; Mencius describes how King Hwuy of Leang "loved warfare" for its own sake.[5] But the warfare which took place for the sake of territory served to promote patriotic pride, which then became an independent source of motivation.

> A great amount of patriotism grew out of the struggles which went on amongst the states in their efforts to maintain their existence; from their battles fought in the name of preservation; and their efforts to curb the extension of other states. Jealousies naturally were engendered and these in turn stimulated feelings of unity and reinforced the patriotism.[6]

In time the prestige of the *state* became a goal equally important with the glory of the ruler. The statesmen Yen-tzu of Ch'i is quoted as saying that the larger states cared only for prestige. Wu Ch'en, an ambassador of Chin, advised Wu to improve its defenses, saying: "Crafty men there are who think of enlarging boundaries for the advantage of their states: what state is there which has not such men. It is thus that there are so many large states. . . ."[7] The ability to conquer is, as elsewhere, identified with state prestige: when Chin had invaded Cheng in 563 but found that Ch'u, a much stronger state, was likely to come to Cheng's rescue, the ruler's advisers counselled withdrawal, because "if we fought and do not conquer, the other states will laugh at us." The popular Chinese classic work, "The Intrigues of the Warring States," belonging to the end of this period, records the various types of Machiavellian advice given to the rulers of various states by their counselors, designed to strengthen and promote their own state's power by weakening or even betraying other states (for example, by sending to an ally help suffieiently large to insure its attacker is destroyed, but sufficiently small and late to insure that the ally is weakened).

This cruder form of prestige, derived from conquest, merged into the more subtle Chinese concept of "face." There is a story that the famous Duke Huan of Ch'i was advised against an alliance he was contemplating with Chiang and Huang because he would not be in a position to defend them effectively against Ch'u, and would therefore lose face and reputation. The position of hegemon, or leader of the league, was regarded as an important source of prestige for a state, partly because it implied leadership and domination, and partly because it was associated with the perogatives of the Chou royal line; in either case it brought prestige for the state which held it. So equally did large armies, splendid hospitality, fine tombs, and other status symbols of the age.

In all societies there are complementary motives. In this case, for example, the territorial aspirations of the great promoted the desire of smaller states to protect

---

5. Cf. *The Book of Lord Shang,* trans. J. Duyvendak (London, 1928), III, 13: "Force produces strength, strength produces prestige, prestige produces virtue and so virtue has its origin in force."

6. Walker, *Multi-State System,* p. 36. See also *The Book of Lord Shang,* I, 3: "The means whereby a country is made prosperous is agriculture and war."

7. Legge, *Chinese Classics,* I, 39

their own independence. The ruler of T'ang, a small state situated between the two great powers of Ch'i and Ch'u, asked Mencius to which he should give his support; Mencius replied that to preserve his independence he should "dig deeper his moats and build higher his walls" and make sure that he retained the goodwill of his people, so avoiding dependence on either large power. The medium-sized states were insistent in demanding scrupulous respect for sovereignty. Sung determined to go to war against the powerful Ch'u, even though it knew it would be defeated, rather than submit to the indignity of allowing Ch'u's envoys to pass through the state without first securing permission. In other words, it fought for face, for the *principle* of independence even if independence itself might be lost in the process. The complex alliance policies of the smaller states were usually designed to preserve as much independence as possible for themselves, even if this meant frequent changes of alliance.[8]

Many of these motives were in themselves not significantly different from those which have been held within other international societies. The desire for independence, territory, domination, or prestige are motives that have been widely held among states in all societies. What distinguishes this one was rather the balance between them: dominance and power were *conceived* above all in terms of territorial possessions. Territory in itself appears to have been a more highly prized objective than in almost any subsequent society, perhaps because at the opening of the period there was territory that was unoccupied and easily possessed, and many very small states which could be relatively easily subdued. This established a pattern of relationships and expectations that were to characterize the age that followed. The competition for territory was mutually reinforcing since it encouraged the fear that, if a state did not itself swallow a weak neighbor, some more dangerous rival would do so. Nor were these basic motivations sufficiently modified by any accepted code of international conduct for the competition for territory to be significantly affected. As time went on, all came to share, in only marginally varying proportions, the ambitions, goals, and assumptions of state behavior which were widely shared within the society as a whole.

Motives in this society may originally have been partly influenced by the social structure: the demand for territory and other sources of prestige was partly the effect of the domination of the rulers over policy. But whatever their source they came to be part of the ideology governing the society as a whole, and so to be widely shared by others whose personal interest was quite different.

## 7.2 The Greek City-States (600–338 B.C.)

The principal motives influencing foreign policy among the Greek city-states followed naturally from the basic character of the society. Because it was above all

8. But Han Fei-tzu (*The Five Vermin*) pointed out how vain these efforts often were: "Chou deserted the side of Ch'in and joined the Vertical Alliance and within a year it had lost everything. Wey turned its back on Wei to join the Horizontal Alliance and in half a year was ruined."

a transnational society, motives were themselves transnational. Because distances were short and the inhabitants of different states mainly of the same race, culture, and language, with many close personal contacts, men were almost as concerned with events in other states as in those at home. Because politics was a universal concern, international motives were intensely political.

One major motive was the concern to see governments of a sympathetic ideology in power in neighboring states. In an age when political principles were passionately debated and strong views widely held, these inevitably deeply influenced foreign policies. The demand of Athens to make the Greek world safe for democracy, or of Sparta to establish oligarchies in the states in her own neighbourhood, were not mere verbal smokescreens. When Sparta intervened in the sixth century to secure the overthrow of tyrannies elsewhere, when Athens intervened to establish democratic governments in the fifth, when Sparta again sought to bring oligarchies to power in the early fourth century, this was, at least in part, from genuine conviction concerning desirable systems of government. Leaders who had gained power because of their belief in one political principle, classes who had acquired dominance through the application of that principle, inevitably wished to see it applied in other states as well.

Such motives were redoubled, however, by concern for state interests; the two motives reinforced each other. Athenians knew a democratic government would more likely be pro-Athenian, just as Spartans knew oligarchies were more likely to be pro-Spartan. Occasionally a difficult choice had to be made between the two motives. Epominondas, though himself a democrat, tried to convince the assembly of Thebes that the defeated Achaean cities were more likely to remain loyal to Thebes if allowed to retain their oligarchic governments. He was overruled by his more ideologically committed assembly, with the effect that subsequent revolutions brought oligarchies to power there which immediately reverted to Sparta. Among the client states too, the motives did not usually clash. A government belonging to a particular party automatically looked to the appropriate great power for support and protection, so that a kind of symbiotic relationship developed. In many cases a change in internal regime would automatically imply a change in external alliance. When Argos acquired an oligarchic government in 419, she abandoned the tradition of a century and allied herself with oligarchic Sparta; when a democratic government was restored shortly after, she once again reverted to her traditional alliance with Athens. When Arcadia split on political lines in 363, it was taken for granted that democratic Tegea would win support from Thebes and oligarchic Mantinea from Sparta.

But ideological sympathies had to be tempered by considerations of security and strategic interest. The small distances involved, and the wide disparities in power, made strategic motives of great importance. On these grounds alone most of the Peleponnesian states were usually allied with Sparta,[9] just as Euboea, Plataea, and most of the island states were usually allied with Athens. This

9. "Sparta now offered [in the Spartan league] security to her neighbors in return for security for herself. . . . Most of the Peleponnesian states welcomed the security which the new system seemed to offer." *Cambridge Ancient History*, V (1927): 72.

geographical solidarity could be modified, however, by the ideological factor: Mantinea, Elis, and later Arcardia, when they had democratic governments, transferred allegiance from Sparta to Athens. Geography could also be overruled by local rivalries. Plataea was allied with Athens rather than Thebes, Argos with Athens rather than Sparta, Aegina with Sparta rather than Athens, partly because of ideology but mainly because of long-term rivalries which divided them from their neighbors. The closer power was a greater threat than the farther.

Another complicating factor was racial differences. The people of every city were highly conscious of being Dorian or Ionian. When the Corinthian spokesman was seeking Sparta's support to protect Potidea, once Corinth's colony, against Athens at the beginning of the Peleponnesian war, an important part of his argument was that "they are Dorians and are being besieged by Ionians."[10] In Sicily Athens allied herself with the Ionian states against the Dorian. Hermocrates of Syracuse insisted that "the Dorians among us [i.e., in Sicily] are the enemies of the Athenians';[11] and even the Athenian representative to Syracuse accepted that "the Ionians are always the enemies of the Dorians."[12] Brasidas, encouraging the Peleponnesian troops before Amphipolis, reminds them that "you are Dorians about to fight with Ionians, whom you are in the habit of beating."[13] In the sixth century Argos followed a deliberate policy of Dorian domination. Sparta frequently intervened in central Greece to protect Doris, the home of the Dorian peoples from which she came. Sometimes the geographical and the racial sentiments were mixed, as when Gylippus, the Spartan leader in Sicily, declared that "it would be intolerable if Peleponnesians and Dorians could not feel certain of defeating and driving out these Ionians and islanders and rabble of all sorts."[14] However, racial solidarity was not a certain influence on action. Argos was usually allied with Athens and against Sparta despite her Dorian origin. Many of the Ionian states of the islands and Asia Minor eventually turned against Athens when Athenian imperialism became intolerable to them.

As in China, a particularly powerful motive counteracting ideological or racial affinity was the desire for independence. An alliance would often be formed against the dominant state of the age—Athens in the second half of the fifth century, Sparta and later Thebes in the first half of the fourth—to bring an end to the domination of that power. This motive also lay behind a number of the traditional rivalries between pairs of states. The bitter hostility between Argos and Sparta, between Aegina and Athens, between Plataea and Thebes, between Corcyra and Corinth, and between Elis and Arcadia, were the long-term results of the determination of the former in each case to remain independent of the latter. The effect was that, in most conflicts, whatever else occurred, these pairs were to be found on opposite sides. Determination to escape the domination of Athens and

10. Thucydides, *The Peloponnesian War*, I, 124.

11. Ibid., 124.

12. Ibid., VI, 82

13. Ibid., V, 9.

14. Ibid., VII, 5.

Sparta was one of the main reasons for medism (collaboration with the Persians). Thebes and Beoetia fought with the Persians against the other Greek states out of dislike of Athens, while Argos and Achaea stayed neutral out of dislike for Sparta. This common dislike of domination by the great powers was symbolized in the final defeat of Athens, Sparta, and Thebes by a coalition of smaller powers in the middle of the fourth century.

For the largest states within society a desire for national glory and domination was sometimes a significant motive. Thus Pericles is said to have told the Athenians: "The reason why Athens has the greatest name of all the world is because she has . . . spent more life and labor in warfare than any other state, thus winning the greatest power that has ever existed in history, such a power that will be remembered forever by posterity."[15] Similarly, according to Thucydides, the Athenian expedition to Sicily "looked more like a demonstration of the power and greatness of Athens than an expeditionary force setting out against the enemy. . . ." Alcibiades told the Spartans that the aim of Athens in that expedition was that "Athens would be the masters of the Hellenic World."[16] Conversely, the Syracusans felt "if they could beat the Athenians and their allies on land and sea, it would be an achievement which would make them famous throughout Hellas. . . ." This glorification of state power is accepted with cynicism. The Corinthian delegate, seeking to win Sparta's support against Athens, declared: "It has always been a rule that the weak shall be subject to the strong." This fatalistic acceptance of aggressiveness by the strong at the expense of the weak becomes a part of the assumptions and expectations, the general ideology of the age.[17]

In other cases *personal* ambition and the desire for glory and reputation were important factors in stimulating aggressive policies. Alcibiades is said to have spoken in favor of the Sicilian expedition because of "his desire to hold the command and his hopes that it will be through him that Sicily will be conquered. . . ."[18]

Finally, though they were perhaps not decisive, economic motives certainly played some part in influencing foreign policies. One of the main and acknowledged motives for Athenian imperialism, specifically mentioned by Pericles, was the economic advantage which Athens acquired from it. Part of the reason for the revolts against her, conversely, was the economic burden she imposed on her allies. Some conflicts arose out of competition for trade, for example, between Corinth and Corcyra, Athens and Aegina, Athens and Megara, and so on. And there were disputes over particular economic assets and resources, as between Tegea and Mantinea over water supplies, competition for the mines of Thasos, and the timber of Amphipolis.

15. Ibid., II, 63.

16. Ibid., VI, 90.

17. Hermocrates tells the Syracusans that the only reason wars occur is that "one side thinks that the profits to be won outweigh the risks to be incurred, and the other side is ready to face danger rather than to accept an immediate loss." Ibid., 58.

18. Ibid., 15.

The most striking feature in this society is the relative unimportance of territorial expansion as an aim, except in relatively marginal border regions. This is typical of ideological ages, and in this respect the society resembled the modern world more than any other international society yet known. Insofar as there were expansionary aims, these were related to the spreading of a political ideology or of regimes sympathetic with it; in other words, with indirect rather than direct control—another resemblance to the modern world. Influence and prestige depended on factors other than direct rule: Sparta for long was content to rest on the fame of her constitution and her military skills rather than on territorial possessions. Most of the smaller powers wanted nothing better than to be left in peace. The expansionary urges, therefore, which are always those which most give rise to conflict in any international society (since by definition they are competitive), were concentrated among a relatively small number of states, usually those with most power, and these took the form of a demand for colonies or satellites, not territory. This, however, together with the wish of others to resist such expansion, was sufficient to cause a state of almost ceaseless warfare.

## 7.3  The Age of Dynasties (1300–1559)

The motivations that influenced action in the international society in Europe between the fourteenth and sixteenth centuries were, inevitably, those of the kings and princes who largely controlled foreign policy; that is, they were dynastic motives. The overriding aim, not only of the rulers themselves but of their immediate entourage, even of many of their subjects, was the extension of the power and glory of the dynasty.

Dynastic success was to be measured in a very specific way: above all in the extent of territorial control. Feudal society placed a premium on landholding, which became the measure of the prestige of the rulers as of their noble followers. Real estate was valued for its own sake, and not (as in many other societies) for its instrumental value—increased security, economic resources, or political influence. Political *control* was scarcely desired at all. The aim of the dynasts was not to govern peoples in any direct way, nor to bring any noticeable change in their way of life; in most cases existing local authorities were allowed to continue in being. All that was required was to secure a nominal allegiance, at least acknowledgement of title.

> Nationality was still vague. Land was valued for the pleasures and profits of possession not for the language spoken in it. Nations were not to be satisfied with natural frontiers when such a conception did not yet exist. A monarch's hunger for land, which he shared with other landowners, did not depend on the consent of his country before it could be ratified.[19]

19. *New Cambridge Modern History*, I (1957): 261.

The importance of this motive is reflected, as in other societies, in the terms of peace treaties reached at the ends of wars. The demands imposed by the victors inevitably reflected their supreme aspirations. Thus the successive treaties negotiated during the Hundred Years' War were concerned above all with dynastic rights in Aquitaine, Normandy, above all in France itself. The successive treaties among France, Spain, and other countries during the Italian wars were concerned with dynastic rights in Naples, Milan, Burgundy, Savoy, and other countries (rights accorded or exchanged with no regard to nationality or popular wishes). Similarly, the settlements reached in the complex struggles among the kings of Bohemia, Hungary, Poland, and Austria concerned especially kingly rights within those countries.[20] Even the struggle between popes and emperors had changed from a basic struggle for authority between them, as between Innocent III and Henry IV, to a more limited contest for dynastic rights within particular areas, such as Hungary or the papal states.

A motive almost equally significant with the demand for territory was that for dynastic glory of other kinds. Rulers competed in extravagant display and conspicuous consumption. The building of vast royal palaces and the patronage of painters and sculptors were two expressions of this aim. Competitive displays, such as the Field of the Cloth of Gold, a form of royal potlach, was another. The pomp and ceremony within the courts, the sumptuous splendor shown in the equipment and reception of foreign embassies, the exchanges of gifts between rulers, the magnificent dowries of the princesses who were so freely bartered or assigned, reflected the same motive. Ambassadors were sent as much for representation as for negotiation. "Important negotiations or ceremonies always called for full-scale special embassies with several ambassadors, and, whenever a congregation of notables gave opportunity for competitive display, large and glittering retinues."[21] Such motives were not simply masks for some more general motive, such as 'power' or 'national interest.' Ceremony was valued for itself and as a source of glory. It was prestige rather than power that was at stake. And it was personal, not national, prestige that was involved here.

Dynastic interests were not purely personal. In some cases personal and dynastic ambitions reinforced each other. But the real aim was to advance the house, not the ruler himself. The agreements by which territorial settlements benefit the heirs but not the ruler himself, the system of *apanage* by which lords and titles are given away to sons, the rarity of wars of conquest except those based on dynastic claims, the surprising indifference to the exercise of power in the territories acquired, all point in this direction. It was the glory of the dynasty rather than of the prince which was the ultimate aim.

20. F. Pirenne describes how the Hapsburgs "prudently remained far from the line of battle, envisaging events whose importance they were capable of understanding solely from the dynastic standpoint, watching for an opportunity of appropriating the crowns of Bohemia and Hungary, the supreme ends of the equivocal intrigues of their ancestors." *A History of Europe from the Invasions to the Sixteenth Century* (London, 1939), p. 603.

21. G. Mattingly, *Renaissance Diplomacy* (London, 1955), p. 96

Other motives were promoted by the traditions of chivalry still current at this time. The desire to win honor and glory in military adventure abroad, for example, was widely held among the nobles and knights. War was thus not merely a means but to some extent an end in itself. The glory and romance which had been associated with the crusades spread by extension to almost any military adventure abroad. Moreover, liberally mixed with these sentiments of honor were considerations of personal interest, the chance of securing reputation and advancement, above all booty and other economic advantage, for many of the leading participants.

> The nobility had been educated for war and in peace was at a loss. . . . For financial and emotional reasons the knight longed for war and foreign adventure, and the wars of Italy were encouraged and prolonged by a nobility whose function at court had been taken over by professional administrators and whose estates were often incapable of supporting a large family. For the nonmercantile classes war offered the main chance of getting rich quickly by loot and ransom. And once war had started the same motives led to its continuing.[22]

Economic benefits extended to quite a low level of society. The Duke of Gloucester is said to have urged the resumption of the war in France in 1390 for the sake of "poor knights and squires and archers whose comforts and station in society depend upon war." For the king himself and his government, the economic gains from war were even more manifest. Apart from booty and ransom which indirectly benefited the whole country, huge payments could be obtained as the price of peace, such as the three million gold crowns obtained by England in the Treaty of Bretigny in 1360 and the successive payments, or protection money, demanded from France in the second half of the next century as the price of ceasing from war. The importance of this motive was blantantly shown in the war waged by Edward IV against France in 1474, which he agreed to call off almost as soon as it had begun in return for a generous financial settlement.

Another unique motive associated with the chivalric tradition was the concern for personal honor. Rulers and military leaders felt under an obligation to respond to a challenge or to live up to a claim, even when considerations of prudence or calculated self-interest would dictate otherwise. Froissart records how Edward III, when he found himself with his army by chance within two miles of the French king, felt obliged to give battle "for otherwise they could not depart saving their honor." The whole procedure of battle was often reminiscent of a tournament. On this occasion, for example, Edward sent his herald to the French king to declare: "Sire, the king of England is in the field and desireth to give battle, power against power," to which challenge the French king responded, naming the day for the battle, "the Friday next after."[23] In much the same way pairs of monarchs—Louis of Hungary and Johanna of Naples, John of Bohemia and Louis of Bavaria, Francois I and Charles V—felt themselves to be engaged in a personal duel for

22. *New Cambridge Modern History,* I (1957): 260.
23. Froissart, I, xl.

their own honor as much as that of their country. Personal insults from king to king could be of special importance and sometimes could provoke to war. Froissart records how the French king deliberately sent letters of defiance to the English king by a ''Breton varlet,'' rather than a more high-born messenger, as a calculated insult, and how this was one reason for the English king's determination to resume the war.

Equally striking and characteristic of this age was the *absence* of certain motives which have played a large part in other societies. Economic motivations of *states* (as against those of individuals) seem to have played little part in influencing wars, or even international relations generally. Edward III's alleged economic motive in starting the Hundred Years' War was certainly far less important than dynastic ambition. Strategic motives were of little significance; not only were no wars fought to obtain strategically important territory, but many were fought to obtain territories strategically almost indefensible. Political motives, the desire to spread a particular ideology or to stamp out another, were unknown. Even religious motives were not of great importance in international relations: the popes had little success in arousing support for crusades against the Turks; the Turks had Christian allies at times in the Balkans; while Christian kings employed Moslem troops, and a French Christian king had no compunction in allying himself formally with the Turks. The only exception was the bitter war against the Hussites in Bohemia, but this was a prelude to another age which was yet to come.

So again we see that the dominant motivations reflected the ''ideology'' of the society, in this case dynasticism. Perhaps the most striking feature of this age is the dominance of *personal* motivations. It was above all the aims and ambitions of individual rulers, for themselves and their houses, which determined behavior. Personal whims and impulses, such as those of Charles VIII and Francois I in relation to Italy, the sudden reversals of alliance by Henry VIII and by Maurice of Saxony during the same war, were often decisive. These personal ambitions related especially to the acquisition of territory and were guided by prevailing conceptions of rights of inheritance: territory was the *goal* which the dynastic *motive* instilled. They were ambitions that were widely shared within society.[24] But they were ambitions which, toward the end of the period, increasingly began to be modified and replaced by the aims related to quite different causes, as a new type of society, with a new ideology, emerged.

## 7.4 The Age of Religions (1559–1648)

In the age which ensued dominant motivations changed again. There was of course no sudden and clear-cut break, but a number of the traditional aims became

---

24. Cf. Pirrenne, *History of Europe,* pp. 420–21: ''[The Hundred Years' War] was a useless war, a needless war. . . It must be regarded merely as a war of prestige. And this precisely explains the passion with which the English people followed their kings to war.''

less significant. The ambition for territorial possessions, no matter how far removed from the homelands, and for marriages designed to achieve this, is less dominant. The demand for territory is now mainly for that at the frontiers of the state, like the areas on France's eastern border, so desired by Richelieu; the Baltic territories disputed among Sweden, Poland, and Russia; Scotland finally merged with England; and Portugal acquired for a time by Spain. The conception of the state as a continuous stretch of national territory, rather than a random assemblage of lands held by dynastic right, becomes more generally held. The chief exception is Spain, still holding territories in the Netherlands, eastern France, and Italy, as well as far further afield.

More important than this decline of traditional motivations was the rise of new ones, above all the almost universal preoccupation with religion. This dominant motive, the desire to promote or protect a particular religious faith against all rivals, was expressed in the first place on the domestic scene, as in the many religious civil wars of the period. But not only did these themselves often result finally in international conflict. They affected the foreign policy attitudes of the government concerned. For example, the threats posed to internal stability induced caution among rulers.

> From the 1550s onwards an acute awareness of all these various [internal] tensions and passions combined with a plain lack of money to restrain most rulers to modest ambitions in their foreign policies. . . . Well aware of how limited were the means for dealing with the growing strains and discontents within their own dominions, the last thing that most of them wanted to do was to add a large-scale foreign war to their burdens or to offer their foreign rivals any opportunity to send assistance to their own rebels.[25]

An important new motive, therefore, was the desire to avoid internal instability through excessive involvement abroad.

Against this, and often more powerful, was sympathy for coreligionists elsewhere. In a transnational society the desire to promote a particular religion was felt abroad as much as at home. Minorities abroad were often begging for intervention from elsewhere, and this demand was often supported by important groups at home. Intervention thus could scarcely be avoided. So even Elizabeth, James I, and the Lutheran princes of North Germany, though personally lukewarm, were ultimately obliged to involve themselves deeply in religious conflicts elsewhere. Many others felt a far greater commitment. Philip II felt himself to have a divine mission to preserve the Catholic faith and wipe out heresy. The Elector Palatine and Gustavus Adolphus of Sweden felt themselves to have a similar mission on the Protestant side. Priests and other religious leaders spurred the rulers to such action. And most of the conflicts of this period—Spain's three contemporary wars against the Netherlands, England, and in France, the Cologne war, the fighting between the Eastern empire and the Turks, the conflict over Cleves-Julich, above all the Thirty Years' War—stemmed partly or wholly from such motives.

25. *New Cambridge Modern History,* III (1968): 7.

As in other ideological ages these motives were rarely pure and never simple. What strengthened the position of one religious group abroad might also weaken an enemy, and vice versa. When England supported Protestants in France and the Netherlands, or when France and Scotland supported Catholics in Scotland and Ireland, they were promoting national as well as religious ends. Spanish support for the Catholics in France might insure the survival of a regime friendly to Spain, or even the succession of a Hapsburg king, as Spain herself proposed; French and English help for the Netherlands could preserve a Protestant ally in the Low Countries; imperial intervention in Cleves-Julich might preserve an essential element in Spain's communication system in friendly hands; Swedish intervention in the Thirty Years' War might establish a Swedish foothold in Pomerania and keep the Baltic as a Swedish lake. This did not mean that religious motivations were not genuine and sincere and the more important influence on conduct. It was simply that they were supplemented by other motives of other kinds. Few ministers and ambassadors

> had the strength of mind to follow consistently the austere logic of reasons of state. They and their sovereigns were not immune from the religious emotions which dominated their subjects. . . . The national rivalries of the great powers became entangled in the social, political and religious struggles within the different states and within the international patterns of religious loyalties.[26]

Religious sentiments also affected policy in a negative sense by *preventing* a state from taking action that national interests might otherwise have dictated. Thus Catholic France was not able to give Protestant Netherlands the support against Spain which France's national interests demanded. Protestant England could not intervene on Spain's side in the Thirty Years' War, though this would have been the logical course for a balancing power to take in the closing stages of that war. The Lutheran princes of Germany would not lift a finger to help the Calvinist cause in Bohemia, though they shared a common interest in resisting imperial pretensions there. Still less could Catholic states such as Bavaria make common cause with the Protestant states of Germany, though they shared a common interest in seeing Hapsburg power in Germany weakened.

Finally, there was another new motive typical of ideological ages. Religion injected a special intensity of fear and fervor into attitudes to foreign powers, something akin to paranoia. There was general apprehension of vast international conspiracies to undermine the established religious faith, as well as established political institutions, somewhat reminiscent of the mentality of McCarthyism in another ideological age. The Bishop of Winchester, in his funeral oration for Mary Tudor, spoke of the "wolves . . . coming out of Geneva and other places of Germany who have sent their books before, full of petulant doctrines, blasphemy and heresy to infect the people"[27] (just as cold warriors in the West were to warn of seditious propaganda being peddled from Moscow in a later ideological age). This fear was intensified, as in the modern age, by association of the hated doctrine with

26. Ibid., 336.
27. J. H. Elliot, *Europe Divided, 1559–1598* (London, 1968), p. 32

a foreign power already hated in itself: Englishmen hated Spain and Catholicism in the same breath; Spain, France and Calvinism. So a heretic would be seen as not only a heretic but a spy, a threat to the state as well as to morality.[28] This intensified fears and suspicions.

However, religious motives, though powerful, did not exclude all others. Strategic aims, for example, began to be a significant factor. These dictated the perpetual concern of Spain to retain the territories to the east of France, which gave her access from her Italian possessions to the Spanish Netherlands. They caused the Spanish acquisition of the *presidi,* the five ports on the Tuscan coast which enabled her to supply her forces in Italy and beyond without relying on the cooperation of Genoa for landing rights. They dictated the establishment of the fort of Fuentes by Spain, guarding the route from Italy to the domains of the other Hapsburgs in the Tyrol. Complementary strategic interests dictated French acquisition of the key position of Saluzzo, controlling the gateway from France into Italy, in 1600, her effort to end Catholic domination of the Valley of Valtellina on which Spain depended for her communications, and her determination to acquire Alsace. The strategic interests of both powers were heavily involved in the contest over Cleves-Julich in 1609–1614, since these territories occupied a key position on the Rhine. And they were a factor for both in the dispute over Mantua and Montferrat in 1626. England had strategic reasons for seeking to reduce Spanish dominance in the Low Countries and to destroy the Spanish sea power which made this possible.

Economic motives also, though rarely decisive, became more significant than before. Spain had a vital economic interest in defending the sea route to South America, from which she drew vital supplies of silver and gold, and the trading monopoly she claimed there. England had a contrary economic interest in challenging that monopoly. Venice had a powerful economic motive in maintaining her trading links with the East, even at the expense of accommodation with the Turks. Denmark had a powerful motive for maintaining control of the Baltic and the lucrative tolls which she exacted on shipping there; Sweden had an interest in breaking that control. Economic motives were sometimes important even in apparently religious disputes: One of the main reasons for the eventual entry of the German Lutheran states in the Thirty Years' War was their desire to maintain their hold on the rich churchlands which they had seized since 1555.

As always, there was an interaction among the different motives. National interests often had to be balanced against religious interests, for the pursuit of one might prejudice the other. Thus the English demand for French ports during the wars of religion in France promoted national interests but forfeited the support of French Protestants. Similarly, the Spanish proposal that a Hapsburg be made king of France after the murder of Henry III aroused even ardent Catholics in France against Spain. Philip II was prepared to offer financial assistance even to the Protestant Henry of Nevarre to promote Spain's national interests in the Netherlands. More often, however, wholehearted pursuit of religious aim sacrificed a

28. The mentality of McCarthyism was visible in other ways. Cardinal Alessandia wrote from Rome: "The most ardent defenders of justice have held that it is better to condemn an innocent man than to allow the inquisition to suffer any dimunition of its powers."

national interest. So Spain's determination to fight heresy wherever it might appear in the end enormously overextended her resources and brought about her ruin. Her determination to refuse toleration in the Netherlands at all costs condemned her to the loss of the northern provinces there. Religious fanaticism often distorted judgment[29] and so brought retribution later. It also led to the special intensity and cruelty of wars in this period, of which the Thirty Years' War is the supreme example. It was above all this dominance of the crusading spirit among the various motives governing foreign policy that gave this age its special character in the history of international society.

Can the importance of the religious motive be attributed to the changing social structure, to the type of elites in power? It is of course true that religious elements—priests, religious advisers, preachers—played a more important role in this age than in many earlier ones in shaping policy. But this was not cause so much as effect. It was not the power of Jesuits or Calvinists that brought an age of religious concern. It was an age of religious concern that brought Jesuits and Calvinists to power. Here again, therefore, it is the ideology rather than dominant elites that ultimately govern motives.

## 7.5 The Age of Sovereignty (1648–1789)

In the age that followed the motivations which counted were those of the monarchs who generally controlled foreign policy at the time. These monarchs were no longer dynasts, concerned above all about the number and extent of their personal possessions and the honor of their house, but sovereigns concerned above all about the interests and power of the state with which they became increasingly identified.

In some cases the motives of the state and that of its royal house were still closely associated. One motive that became of great importance was concern for prestige, typified above all by the preoccupation of Louis XIV with "la gloire." "Our primary objective," he wrote, "must always be the conservation of our glory and our authority, neither of which can be maintained absolutely without assiduous labor. . . ."[30] This was the principal motive which inspired Louis XIV during the whole of his reign. "He measured all the opportunities which offered themselves during more than 40 years in terms of their possible yield of glory. . . . Yet glory was to be won only by victories, and therefore by war. . . . He felt no scruple about declaring war, whenever a favorable opportunity occurred and he threw himself into it with a sort of joy."[31] And on his deathbed he admitted that he had perhaps "loved glory too much."

But Louis was no different in this aspiration from many of the other rulers of

29. Demonstrated when a Spanish deputy in the Cortes declared, "If we are defending God's cause, as we are, there is no reason to abandon it on the grounds of impossibility."

30. *Oeuvres de Louis XIV*, II (1667): 292.

31. *New Cambridge Modern History*, V (1961): 207.

Europe, who, in modeling themselves on his royal style, borrowed his ambitions as well. One typical manifestation of this competition for prestige were the perpetual disputes and conflicts over precedence and protocol (see p. 92 above). In 1660 the negotiations between France and Spain to end the long war between them had to be undertaken on an island exactly in the middle of a river in the Pyrenees, on the border between the two states, so as to avoid the need for either of them to lose face by negotiating on the territory of the other. After he had made use of an affray in London between members of the retinue of the French and Spanish ambassadors to compel Spain to apologize and accept henceforth French precedence in every court of Europe, this victory was greeted by Louis with the words, "I do not know whether since the beginning of the monarchy anything more glorious has ever occurred. . . . This has been for me a long and enduring subject of joy."[32] After a somewhat similar incident in Rome, when the wife of the French ambassador was insulted by the pope's guards, Louis seized Avignon and prepared to march on Rome until amends had been made; he later erected an oblisk in Rome to commemorate the diplomatic humiliation he had heaped on the Vatican. He demanded as part of the peace terms proposed to the Dutch in 1772 that every year a deputation from the United Provinces should come to France to present Louis with a gold medal bearing an inscription, thanking him personally for having consented not to rob them of their independence. In all these cases it was not only the honor of the monarch himself which had to be vindicated, but, almost as much, that of the nation with which he was identified. Ordinary citizens came to resent rebuffs to their monarch, which they saw as rebuffs to themselves as well.

A closely associated motive was the demand for an extension of national boundaries. The concern of French kings and statesmen to push the borders of France to the Rhine, or of Russia to extend its frontiers to the west and the south, of Austria to recover Hungary and Transylvania from the Turks, or of Prussia to acquire Silesia, expressed a widely felt aspiration. The desire was no longer for any territory, but especially for territory to round out the borders. But a similar aspiration was now felt, with increasing seapower, for acquisition of territories beyond the seas: North America, India, the West Indies, and the Pacific all became an arena for territorial competition among Britain, France, Spain, the Netherlands, and Portugal. Finally, in this age, the desire was now not simply for a nominal allegiance, but to secure in any territory acquired, at least in Europe, all the attributes of sovereignty, to rule and to govern as in the home state. So Alsace and Lorraine were incorporated into France, Scotland and Ireland into Britain, Hungary and Bohemia into Austria, Silesia into Prussia, and so on. Such territories were no longer mere colonies, but merged as integral parts of the state.

Another motive, in part personal but often becoming national as well, was the desire for revenge. When the Dutch prevented Louis from securing the victory he had hoped for in the War of Devolution, he swore publicly that he would teach them a lesson, and began to plan the war against them which he launched four years

32. Ibid., 9.

later. Albirone, chief minister in Spain after the War of Spanish Succession, devoted his policy for years to seeking revenge for the losses suffered by Spain in that war. Maria Teresa of Austria devoted herself for many years to avenging herself against Frederick the Great for his seizure of Silesia. Frederick the Great never forgot the betrayal he felt he had suffered from Britain during the Seven Years' War.

Because foreign policy was personally controlled, personal emotions of this kind remained of great importance. On many issues of this kind, princely and national interests coincided. A powerful army and military victories could bring glory and advantage to both equally. Thus motives of national security became more important than in any previous age. Most of the monarchs of the age devoted themselves to building up strong national armies to replace the polyglot mercenary forces which had played such a large part before. Louis' desire to advance the French frontier toward the Rhine and break the ring of Hapsburg territories which surrounded him, England's concern to prevent French domination of the Low Countries or to win naval stations abroad, the desire of Frederick the Great to establish a solid belt of territory for Prussia, were all of this kind. Increasingly territories were desired for their instrumental value as well as for themselves alone.

Economic motives also were sometimes important to sovereign and state alike. Commercial rivalries, for example between England and United Provinces, between France and United Provinces, between England and Spain, began to have a considerable impact on foreign policy. Peace treaties (always a reflection of motives) included provisions concerning trading rights as well as territories. William III was determined, during his two wars with France, not only to win trade concessions for both his two countries, but to damage the commercial interests of France (with whom he prohibited all trade for a time). Colbert was equally devoted to crushing Dutch competition, declaring ''so long as they are the masters of trade, their naval forces will continue to grow and to render them so powerful that they will be able to assume the role of arbiters of peace and war in Europe and to set limits to the King's plans.''[33] One of the prizes of the War of Spanish Succession most valued by Britain was the Asiento, the right to sell African slaves in Spanish colonies and the right to send an annual ship to trade with South America. Despite this change, in most cases commercial advantages were the happy side effects of conflict rather than their basic end.[34] Trade rivalry gave an *additional* reason for war, rarely the main one.

As always, there were vestiges of motives that had been dominant in earlier times. Dynastic aims, though rarely decisive, were sometimes a factor. The devastation of the Palatinate by Louis XIV, though primarily strategic, was partly the effect of the failure of his own claims to the territory through his sister-in-law.

33. Ibid., 214.

34. ''The upsurge in international economic activity did not signify that major political combinations were made, or wars fought, for economic motives. To those who decided the issues of war and peace or alliances, economic measures were instruments of policy never its aim.'' Ibid., VI (1970): 187.

Though Louis probably never hoped that his family would inherit all the Spanish possessions on the death of Charles II, he certainly hoped to use his dynastic claims to extend French power. In other words, dynasticism was now, rather than the basic aim and end of policy, one means that could be used, but now to extend *national* interests.[35] Religion too was less important than before. Rulers no longer cared enough about it to make wars over such matters. They did not always enforce their views even at home: When the elector Palatine was converted to Catholicism, he did not expect all his people to change their religion at the same time. But religion still mattered enough for Louis to ensure that the Catholic religion would be maintained in Maastrict when he gave it up after the Dutch war in 1678, and for him to offer 2 million livres to Charles II to convert him to Catholicism. It was, however, never now the cause of war, as it had been in the preceding age. Here too the assumptions of sovereignty prevailed. If territory was ruled by another sovereign, then it was accepted that it was his business what religion was tolerated.

In this as in so much else the assumptions of the prevailing ideology dictated the motivations that were widely held. Old aims were transmuted, new aims emerged. And these were the aims not only of the dominant elites. For the assumptions of sovereignty largely governed all who lived in that society, not simply the sovereigns themselves.

## 7.6 The Age of Nationalism (1789–1914)

In the age that followed, dominant motivations changed again. Attitudes to the outside world, conceptions of foreign policy, were now shaped above all by the prevailing ideology of nationalism. Most of the main objectives of governments, still more of their peoples, stemmed from this all-pervading aim: for national unity, national status, national power, in some cases national expansion, whether political, economic, or military. Where nations and states coincided, the motives of governments and peoples coincided too. But where, as in many cases, several nations shared the same state, or several states divided the same nation, the motives of governments and peoples often came into direct conflict with each other.

As we saw earlier (p. 96 above), there were three main forms of nationalism: explosive nationalism, arising from the demand of minority peoples to achieve independence from the state in which they existed previously; integrative nationalism, arising from the demand of scattered peoples to be united in a single state; and competitive nationalism, the urge of existing states to achieve greater status, power, or influence in relation to other states. In each of the first two cases, the motives of the peoples mainly involved inevitably conflicted with the motives of existing governments. Only when states had been made coterminous with

35. "It is misleading to speak of 'dynastic wars' in an age when princely matches were dictated primarily by reason of state." Ibid., 168.

nations were the objectives of governments likely to correspond to those of their peoples. So long as multinational states survived, there must always be some governments whose objectives were directly opposed to the national sentiments which so widely prevailed. Yet even these governments were motivated by nationalism of a sort. It was nationalism of a kind, for example, which in 1914 caused Austria-Hungary to declare war on the Slav nationalism which threatened its existence.

Territorial motives, in Europe at least, probably exerted less influence on governments than in any earlier time. Widespread adoption of the national principle set clear limits to national ambitions. The wars of the period did not mainly have territorial causes.[36] Even where existing empires distintegrated, as in the Balkans, the object (of Russia for example) was to create new nations there rather than to acquire large accretions of territory. Insofar as territory was demanded, it was no longer for its own sake but to secure the reunion of peoples felt to belong to the same nationality. Such wars ended in a map drawn more clearly on ethnic lines than ever before; this was largely accomplished before 1914 and almost completed by 1918. It was only in border territories where ethnic lines were not clearly drawn, such as Alsace-Lorraine or Macedonia, that territorial aims remained an important motivation. In general, all over Europe, most nations began to be satisfied with borders reflecting ethnic principles. This was a revolutionary change. The causes of war ceased, almost for the first time in history, to be primarily territorial, a fact which, apart from a brief reversion in the period between 1931 and 1939, has remained even more true of subsequent periods.

Outside Europe, on the other hand, territorial ambitions were larger than ever. There, just as the western hemisphere freed itself from colonialism, it was reimposed on Asia and Africa. At first sight one might say that conquest, which had become so much less attractive in Europe, was now merely displaced elsewhere. But the motives for colonial expansion were complex and territorial acquisition for its own sake was not the main aim, even here.[37] Often it was entered into with some reluctance, or on a temporary basis. Bismarck declared that he was never a man for colonies and that most of the advantages claimed for them were illusory. Disraeli thought that all colonies would shortly be freed once more and meanwhile were merely a millstone around the colonialists' necks. It was the flag which followed trade rather than the reverse. Often colonies were desired to prevent others from acquiring them rather than for their own sake. For some they were a kind of status symbol, but many important states never attempted to acquire overseas colonies at all: the Scandinavian countries, Russia, Austria-Hungary. In any case there was a sense that these remote and untamed areas of Africa and Asia were in a sense free, unoccupied, devoid of sovereignty, and so fair game for

36. The chief exception was the war of 1864 over Schlesburg-Holstein, but even this was demanded by Prussia and Austria for Germany rather than themselves. Other wars were for unification of existing territories or their independence: the acquisition of Alsace-Lorraine in 1871 was the result of the war, not its cause.

37. For an analysis of the motives see J. A. Gallagher and R. E. Robinson, *Africa and the Victorians* (London, 1961); D. K. Fieldhouse, *Economics and Empire, 1830–1916* (London, 1963).

whoever came to pick them up. They were a cause of competition but not of war among European states. But the fact of acquiring them tended to instill a sense of imperial pride in those more fortunate in the race, or of deprivation in those less so. In this sense, colonial competition may have served indirectly to intensify the nationalism which was already the dominating motive within the society.

More important than the desire for territory was the desire for *influence,* for a position of dominance in specific areas of special concern. Outside Europe this is reflected in the demand for "spheres of influence," as claimed by France in Morocco, by Italy in Ethiopia, by Germany in Southern Africa, by Britain and Russia in Persia, by Britain and France in Siam, and by nearly all the powers in different parts of China. In Europe it is seen in the competition between Russia and Austria for dominant influence in the Balkans, or the contest between Britain and Russia over the Straits, and between Britain and France in Belgium. That motive is seen also in the invention of the new status of "protectorate," a territory that is not formally a colony but effectively controlled by the protecting power, and of new types of semisovereignty, such as "suzerainty" (see p. 220 below). It is seen too in the acquisition in some cases of control over the finances of other states (as in Egypt and Tunis), or of their customs services (as in China and Turkey) and other ingenious new forms of domination.

Strategic motives, in a competitive age, become still more important. They are seen in the obsessive concern of Britain over the security of India, a motive which dominates her policies in a vast area of territory ranging from Morocco in the West to Tibet in the East. They are shown in Russian concern for influence in Persia, Bulgaria, and Manchuria, Austrian concern over Albania and the Sanjak of Novibazar, in French railway building in Belgium and German in Turkey. And they are shown even more obviously in the complex alliance policies of the powers from 1879 onward, with their reinsurance treaties and sometimes conflicting commitments, and in the arms competition of the immediate prewar years. The assessments of chiefs of staff begin to play a dominant role in the formation of foreign policy. And in crisis situations, as in 1914 especially, the role of the military in influencing policy becomes more important than in any earlier time.

Economic motives too play a larger role than before. This is seen most clearly perhaps outside Europe, and in competition for concessions and special trading positions. Though colonies may not have been acquired primarily for commercial purposes—certainly not those of Africa and southeast Asia, where strategic and status considerations were more important—they certainly had significant commercial *consequences:* the metropolitan power proceeded to establish trading positions favorable for itself, in some cases to reserve trade entirely to its own nationals. In noncolonial areas, such as China, economic motives stimulated the competition for spheres of influence, railway concessions, and similar facilities. And countries such as Britain and the U.S. favored an "open door" policy only because they believed their traders would fare still better without such carve-ups. But economic motives, though an influence on policy, were rarely a motive for war. There is not a single war of this period which can be said to have arisen mainly for economic reasons.

Finally, there began to emerge (an anticipation) new forms of ideological motivation. The prevalence of nationalism meant governments were obliged to adopt an attitude to the nationalism of others, especially to the national revolutions which threatened other states. To some extent attitudes were dictated by national interest: the multinational states had a built-in interest against national revolution and autocracies had one against political revolution. So there emerged, in the first thirty years after 1815, a fairly clear-cut confrontation between a Western bloc, Britain and France, relatively favorable to revolutions elsewhere and hostile to intervention against them, and an Eastern bloc which opposed such revolutions and was ready to intervene on occasion to prevent them. In most of the disputes that arose, over Naples, Latin America, Spain, Portugal, Greece, and elsewhere, normally the three Eastern powers stood for the status quo and the rights of the sovereign, however lacking in popular support, while Britain, and later France, stood for the revolutionary forces. This was reflected eventually even in the formation of clear-cut alliances endorsing each viewpoint: the Pact of Munchengratz of 1833, in which the three Eastern powers agreed to intervene anywhere in Europe to help a ruler defend himself and against the forces of liberalism and revolution; and the Quadruple Alliance of Britain, France, Spain, and Portugal, established in 1836, designed, in Palmerston's words, to "serve as a counterpoise to the Holy Alliance of the East."

Ideological motives of this kind, however, were not decisive in this age. They were relatively weak and always liable to revision in the light of more immediate national interests. If interests so dictated, the "liberal" governments could come down in support of the status quo, however disliked by the population, as when France intervened to support the ruler of Spain against his people, or Britain supported Austria in Italy in the 1820s, or Turkey against Mohammet Ali in 1839–1840. Conversely, even the counterrevolutionaries could sometimes be induced to accept revolution if this conformed with their national interests, as when Russia gave her support to the Greek revolution against Turkey. Especially in the second half of the century, national interests played a more important role than ideological prejudices in influencing motives. The paradox then emerged of Britain, previously the chief liberal, antiinterventionist power, as the staunch supporter of the status quo in the Ottoman Empire, while Russia, the archcounterrevolutionary, became the main supporter of revolutionary forces in that area. Moreover, traditional rivalries often weakened ideological solidarity. Between Britain and France differences, concerning Belgium and Italy for example, as well as memories of a century of war before, counted far more in the minds of statesmen than any consciousness of common ideological attitude. Between the conservative states local rivalries were even more significant: between Austria and Russia in the Balkans, between Prussia and Austria in Germany, and between Prussia and Russia whenever Bismarck was not in control of Prussian policy. So even here nationalist rivalries outweighed the ideological sympathies that were held in common.

Again the dominant ideology, nationalism, determined the dominant motives. It determined not only the form of the motives—national influence, national power, national unity, and so on—but the special *intensity* with which they were felt. Territorial ambition, for example (as for the recovery of Alsace-Lorraine), economic aims, strategic objectives, warfare itself, all acquired a new fervor and competitive quality which had been lacking in the preceding era. Even cultural aims had a nationalistic tinge, as in the "civilizing mission" of France to teach Africans and Asians the French language and literature, or British aims to make Indians into cultivated English gentlemen.

Yet nationalism was not equally shared. There were some nations, in Scandinavia, Spain, Portugal, the U.S. (before 1900), where it was not greatly felt. It was most powerful among the peoples deprived of nationhood, or among those who had only just acquired it. So the new Serbian state was not content with Serbia alone, it must liberate all Slavs, or at least all Serbs. The new Greece must acquire, by hook or by crook, all the territories in which Greek was spoken. The new Bulgaria must possess the Bulgars of Macedonia as well as of her own lands. And the new larger powers, Germany, Italy, and Japan, were even more demanding in their ambitions for greater status and influence.

But those ambitions were shared to some degree among all states of the age, for they were dictated by the surrounding international environment and the common attitudes and ambitions it instilled.

## 7.7  The Age of Ideology (1914–1974)

In the age that followed, dominant motivations changed again.

Some of the goals that had had a powerful influence in the previous age now counted for less. Colonial aspirations, which had remained an important factor in the years up to World War I, now declined. Already at the end of that war new colonial possessions had to be disguised under the euphemism "mandates," held in trust on behalf of the world community for a limited period. After World War II colonial ambitions had to be altogether renounced, and colonial empires in most cases rapidly, and even willingly, abandoned.

But even territorial ambitions of a more modest kind began to decline as an influence on policy. For a time, it is true, while the national principle remained imperfectly implemented in Europe, they continued to influence countries such as Germany and Hungary, to which its benefits had not been applied,[38] or nations such as Italy and Japan, which felt themselves frustrated in fulfilling the national ambitions of the previous era. But from 1945 onward territorial aims played no role at all in Europe (the most serious potential claims, those of Germany, were voluntarily renounced).[39] Elsewhere, though territorial disputes occurred—as

38. The chief exceptions to the application of self-determination in 1918 were made in the case of the German population in Czechoslovakia, the Saar, the Rhineland, and Danzig, in each case at the expense of Germany; and in the case of the Hungarian population left in Romania.

39. This may be compared to the situation after World War I when even the "good German" Stresemann made no secret that he sought to regain territories lost by Germany at Versailles in the East;

between China and India, China and the Soviet Union, Morocco and Algeria, and so on—these mainly concerned relatively marginal border areas where the line of demarcation was genuinely in doubt, not substantial territories such as had been contested in the previous age. In Africa, despite the illogicality of the inherited boundaries, they were explicitly acknowledged by all members of the O.A.U. Almost the only attempts at forcible territorial change were in divided countries, such as Korea and Vietnam, where the border was always intended to be temporary. In general, all over the world, with the increasingly clear-cut definition of boundaries, the demand for territory became a less important influence on action than in any previous era.

But these classical objectives were replaced by aims of another kind, more appropriate to an age of ideology: above all, the desire to see the accession to power of favored political forces in other states. The characteristic conflicts of the age are those undertaken entirely within the borders of a single state, yet often including large-scale intervention from outside, designed to determine the type of government to be established there: Greece, Korea, Lebanon, Yemen, and Vietnam, for example. For even if outright possession of territory no longer seemed so important as before, *control* over neighboring states became, with declining distance, more so than ever. The underlying motive was often negative rather than positive: to prevent the victory of forces seen as hostile, especially in strategically sensitive regions.

This is related to another important change concerning motivations. The majority of powers are, in practice if not in theory, status quo powers. "Revisionism" still exists to some extent between the wars, when territorial ambitions deriving from the previous settlement remain strong. But since 1945 even the most powerful states are willing to accept existing realities. They tolerate the ideological empires of their enemies. Conversely, they resist bitterly any attempt to encroach on their own, or to overturn any existing government which they favor. The demand for violent revolution in other states, as proclaimed at times by Russia, China, Cuba, and others, is mainly verbal rather than practical. Even these powers, except in a few cases such as the halfhearted and abortive attempts of Cuba in Latin America, or the reluctant involvement of Russia in Vietnam, are in general content to live with the political status quo. In other lands there is a readiness, as at the end of the age of religions, to apply a policy of *cujus regio ejus religio:* to allow the enemy creed to flourish in areas already controlled by the other side, and so to confine the ideological competition to the small number of remote or neutral regions. Even in such cases there is often a willingness to regard a genuinely neutral regime as preferable to the risks of an unrestrained struggle for supremacy.

---

after World War II Germany, far stronger and supported by many powerful allies, and deprived of far larger undoubtedly German areas, made no such claims. Similarly, Italy did not conceal its territorial ambitions between the wars. Mussolini declared in a public speech in 1927 that "we shall be in a position then . . . between 1935 and 1940 to make our will felt and to see our rights recognized," making clear that these included territorial rights. Members of the Italian chamber raised shouts of "Jibuti, Tunis, Corsica" in 1938 while the Italian press laid claims to Nice and Savoy. Such overt claims would have been unthinkable anywhere in Europe after 1945.

The result is that most civil wars end with the existing government maintained in power. Changes in the ideology of governments are rare; when they are attempted they are either forcibly reversed (as in Hungary, Czechoslovakia, Guatemala, Dominican Republic, and elsewhere), or at least such a reversion to the status quo is attempted (as in Cuba).

There is a third major change in motivations: the overriding importance of strategic considerations in influencing behavior. The reduction of distance, and the overwhelming power of the weapons available, has the effect that the defensive glacis required by each major power becomes far larger and wider than in previous times. Each of the major powers thus shows itself especially concerned to control events in the areas immediately adjacent to its own borders. Thus Soviet intervention takes place in East Europe, United States intervention in Central America and the Caribbean, Chinese in Korea and (in a limited form) in Indo-China. In more remote areas they are far more reluctant to intervene, so the U.S. does nothing in Hungary or Czechoslovakia, even to defend legitimate governments from attack; the Soviet Union is ready to withdraw from Cuba.[40] This determination to keep control of adjoining regions, together with reluctance to contemplate adventures in remote areas, again reflects the essentially defensive and status quo mentality of the major powers.

But as in ancient Greece and the age of religions, the fact that ideological ambitions are pursued with caution does not mean that they are not real. The desire to see the victory of favored political forces abroad and the conquest of hostile ones is genuine. It is not based only on national interests. Western statesmen and publics genuinely wish to see democratic systems of government established in East Europe, believing this would best promote the interests and reflect the wishes of the peoples there; communist states genuinely want to see communist systems established in the West believing this to be in conformity with the wave of history. As in the age of religion, there is a real belief that opposing viewpoints represent not merely divergences, but mortal errors which are morally wrong and must be defeated and overcome by every possible means. There is a sense that to compromise with such beliefs is sinful; that the battle is between forces of good and evil, so that any conciliation becomes a form of treachery. As in other ages of ideology, attitudes arise that border on paranoia: a terror of "communist conspiracies," "imperialist plots," "counterrevolutionary intrigues," thought to threaten and infect the fabric of society.[41] Ideological stereotypes replace national

40. U.S. activity in remote Vietnam is only an apparent contradiction, since this too is regarded, on whatever grounds, as essential to the defense of the U.S.

41. "So the Nazis had brought moral relief and reassurance to the German society by putting the blame for its failures on the Jews and by embarking on a course of extermination that would accordingly restore it to its former purity and invincibility. So . . . throughout the West, but especially in the U.S. men now accorded to the conspirators in the Kremlin the awe and the secret admiration that are the devil's due. Stalin was Satan, supreme in his craft and power, an adversary fit to grapple with the good lord himself, and perhaps to triumph. Just as witches were Satan's agents, their supernatural power being his power, so the sinister conspirators for whom the whole American society was now combed were the agents of Stalin, and his satanic court in Kremlin," L. J. Halle, *The Cold War As History* (London, 1967) p. 255.

stereotypes. Fear of communist expansion replaces that of German expansion, fear of imperialist aggression that of Japanese aggression.

These general fears are strongly reflected in foreign policies. They inspire the policies of "containment" designed to hem in and hold back the threatening forces. They inspire the desire for a "cordon sanitaire" in East Europe, which shall either keep communists from the West (as between the wars) or keep the West from communism (as after them). They inspire the policies of "peaceful coexistence" which may enable hostile ideologies to live safely at arms' length, without fear of contamination. Finally, they inspire the ideological crusades, the propaganda warfare waged on the radio, in international organizations, and by every other available means, which increasingly is substituted for the more lethal warfare of earlier ages.

Other aims are influenced by the prevailing ideological climate. The desire for military security is no longer for the national state alone but for the entire bloc; the U.S. continues to defend West Europe, though her own security is scarcely dependent on it. The desire for economic success is no longer for the nation alone, but for the entire bloc, to prove that one ideology is more successful than another in promoting growth. So the Soviet Union must assist East Europe, the U.S. West Europe economically as well as militarily. Even the desire for scientific or artistic progress is seen in this light: a desire to prove that the Western or communist world is superior in space exploration or in sporting or artistic achievement.

The prevailing motives, then, the desire to spread a particular political creed, the desire to insulate one's own nation or group from the corrupting influence of others, the desire for politically sympathetic governments in sensitive areas, here as elsewhere, reflect the dominant concern of the age: the preoccupation with ideology. But they are *conditioned* by other factors: those of an age of small distances and large weapons, which limit the conditions under which ideological aims can be safely pursued. Thus though each side genuinely desires the victory of its own creed in every part of the world, it is cautious in pursuing that aim. Its interest in an ideological victory in remote areas is sufficiently marginal, and consciousness of the dangers of involvement sufficiently great, to impose restraint. A similar caution is less necessary at home, and it is here the ideological battle is most vigorously pursued. In closely neighboring territories—East Europe, Latin America—it is almost as passionately fought. Everywhere else the dominant motivation is that of a crusade, but a crusade that is always carefully controlled—passionate but prudent.

Thus motives have varied widely from one society to another.

Indeed, one of the main distinguishing features between international societies has been the differing motives predominant within them. There is a wide variation between a society such as that of ancient China, in which the demand for territory was a powerful and all-dominant ambition, and that of ancient Greece, where it was rather *influence* in neighboring cities, for example through ideologically sympathetic factions, which was desired; between the dynastic age, where motives were largely concerned with dynastic success, and the age of religions, where motives were largely concerned with promoting particular religious beliefs; between an age of sovereignty, in which all states were concerned to protect their own sovereign rights and power, and one of ideology, where they are concerned with promoting a particular political creed. The character of the predominant motivation is perhaps the major feature distinguishing one age from another.

Is this tautological? Are the changing motives even *identical* with the ideology as a whole? There is clearly some relationship: It is because of dynastic aims that there is an age of dynasticism, because of religious aims that there is an age of religions, and so on. Yet it would be an oversimplification to see the dominant motive as identical with, or even the main component of, the ideology, the ethos or spirit of each age. For this would too narrowly restrict the essential significance of the ideology. In domestic systems the fact that a society is, say, a Christian society or a communist society will be reflected in the motives of its citizens toward each other. But it will not consist only in that fact. So, in an international society, the fact that it is dominated by a concern for religion or sovereignty will be reflected in the motives of states, but will not consist only in the fact. Here, too, the ideology consists in a wider set of attitudes and beliefs of which motives represent only one part, and imposes its own social structure and institutions.

There is another question: Do the motives of states derive entirely from the ideology which prevails there, or are they sometimes caused by other factors, such as the domestic environment? Some writers have laid considerable stress on the importance of domestic factors in determining foreign policy. If this were so, it would suggest that the motives of states within the same international society should vary widely according to the character of their own domestic systems. The evidence that we have looked at here, brief though it is, suggests the opposite. We have seen that nearly *all* the states in the age of dynasties exhibited dynastic ambitions, nearly all states in the age of ideology were affected by ideological aims, and so on. In other words, domestic factors are subsidiary: the motivations of states vary more widely from one international society to another than they do among the states within each particular society.

Indeed, one of the main conclusions of this survey is the wide difference between the motives held in different ages. This might suggest that motives themselves derive from the outer society rather than the inner state. Attitudes concerning relations between states seem to be instilled through intercourse, traditions, and knowledge of the expectation of others. The form they take may be modified by domestic factors, even by the character of the individual decision makers involved. But these are relatively weak in effect compared with the social pressures exerted by the society in general.

Nobody of course would maintain that domestic factors count for nothing in determining the motives of states. In the age of dynasties all to some extent shared dynastic aspirations, yet the form these took varied. The policy of Charles VIII was not the same as that of Henry VII; it was not even the same as that of his predecessor. The aims of Corvinus' Hungary were not the same as those of Casimir's Poland.

But these were all variations on the same spectrum. There were virtually no rulers who shared the religious aspirations of the age that followed; still less the motives of the subsequent ages of sovereignty, of nationalism and ideology. There were of course *degrees* of dynasticism. But all were dynastic to some extent. All borrowed the motives the social environment dictated.

In other words, just as individuals in smaller societies acquire their desires and ambitions from the society and environment in which they grow up, rather than from their innate character, so nations too acquire their aims and aspirations more from the social milieu in which they live, the social pressures to which they are subjected, than from the internal structure of each state, or the individual character of its leaders.

The form these social pressures take is determined by the character of the ideology as a whole. It is therefore to this ideology that we must look—rather than the internal character of states, or the power balance within a system—for the main factor determining the motives of states in any particular age.

# Chapter 8.  Means

International systems are distinguished not only by the dominant goals desired by their members, but by the *means* used to attain them. These may be almost as characteristic of a particular society as the goals themselves. Two international societies sharing the same dominant motive, such as the desire for territory, could be wholly different in character according to whether this was sought by military conquest, dynastic marriage, or diplomatic means. Two societies in which economic development was the most highly prized goal could differ radically according to whether this was sought by autarchic policies, international trade, or imperialism. Societies where dominance is a goal may vary widely according to whether it is sought by coercion or influence, military or economic power, and so on. It is thus important for us, in comparing different periods and systems, to examine the different means which have been used to attain the primary goals.

Obviously there must be a close relationship between means and motives. If territorial expansion is a dominant motive, armed conquest is likely to be a commonly chosen means (since nations will not normally concede territory unless compelled to do so). If dynastic ambitions are a dominant motive, dynastic marriage will be a commonly chosen means. In a more general sense, if ideological or religious (rather than national) aims are important, transnational means—assistance for minorities in another state, coups and countercoups, propaganda and counterpropaganda—will be more important than direct attacks against the frontiers of other states.

But means cannot necessarily be deduced automatically from motives. A domestic society may be dominated by the demand for status, but status may be attainable in many different ways in different types of society: so too with international societies. *Availability* of one means rather than another will obviously be important in determining choices among them. It is for this reason that the aim of ideological expansion or domination is pursued through preachers and pamphlets in the seventeenth century, but through radio, television, and the press in the twentieth. Again, conventions concerning what is socially permissible will change from one society to another: thus a demand for economic domination may be implemented through imperialism, direct occupation, and control of foreign colonies in one age, but by aid policies or the activities of multinational corporations

172

in another, when the earlier means are discredited. Finally, the same ends may be attained by quite different *kinds* of means: coercive or conciliatory.

So means may be chosen in consequence of prevailing motives on the one hand, and of availability and acceptability on the other. But once chosen they may *become* significant factors in their own right, influencing the character of each society. Once armed conquest is accepted as the normal means of acquiring territory within a society, it becomes quite different from one where dynastic marriage or internal subversion is regarded as the normal means for that purpose. A society in which economic domination is customarily won by trade is different from one where it is acquired by investment or the leadership of economic blocs, and both are different from those where it is acquired by conquest. Choices of this sort may therefore acquire an importance of their own in determining the nature of particular international societies.

Finally, what was originally conceived as a means may eventually become something like an end in itself. Thus armed power may be desired first as a means but may eventually become an end. Similarly, influence may be demanded first as a means toward security, peace, or wealth, but may eventually be regarded as an end in itself. This process too is one which will stamp a particular character onto a particular international society.

In this chapter, therefore, we shall seek to compare the means which have been commonly adopted as the instruments of policy in different international societies. We shall wish to consider why one means rather than another has been chosen to implement a particular goal and how the choice of means has affected the character of the society as a whole. We shall then seek to assess how far this can be regarded as an independent factor characterizing different societies of states.

## 8.1 The Chinese Multistate System (771–221 B.C.)

In all international societies of which we have knowledge, the ultimate means available to secure valued ends has been military power. The importance this may have in particular societies, however—how far it is actually used or at least threatened—will depend on a number of other factors, such as the distribution of military power, its costs, and the expectations, traditions, and norms influencing state conduct (in the same way, *within* states, while force is always ultimately available for attaining ends, its use within a political or social system will vary enormously from one to another). So it is not only the availability of a particular means but its prominence, its *saliency,* that will determine the character of a society.

Because in China territorial control was an important end and could usually be obtained only by conquest, military power was highly prized. So the *Book of Lord Shang* declared that "the means by which a country is made prosperous are agriculture and war. . . . If the country is strong and war is not waged . . . dismemberment will be inevitable.''[1] The same point was made by Han Fei-tzu more vividly:

> King Yen practiced benevolence and righteousness and the state of Hsu was wiped out. Tzu-king employed eloquence and wisdom and Lu lost territory. So it is obvious that benevolence, righteousness, eloquence and wisdom are not the means by which to maintain the state. Discard the benevolence of King Yen and put an end to Tzu-King's wisdom. Build up the might of Han and Lu until they can stand face to face with a state of a thousand chariots.[2]

The power of a state was usually reckoned by the number of chariots (occasionally the number of horses) it could call on: Chin is said to have had 4,900 chariots at one time. The chariot normally had a crew of four people, and was sent into battle surrounded by a phalanx of 50 to 80 foot soldiers armed with spears, halberds, swords, lances, knives, axes, and bows. The powerful states of Chin and Ch'u were said to have been able to put 100,000 men into the field on occasion. And toward the end of the period 400,000 men were said to have been killed in a single battle (though these figures are probably greatly exaggerated). There were also occasional naval engagements, especially among the coastal states of Wu, Yueh, and Ch'i, both on the sea and on the Yangtze River.[3]

With time the scale of military power grew. This was inevitable as the large states grew larger, with perpetual absorption of their smaller neighbors. Moreover, more was at stake with each war. Thus methods became more ruthless. By the Warring States period ''wars were no longer chivalrous duels between gentlemen. . . . Wars were fought in earnest to win. Armies became much stronger. . . . The principal reliance was placed on infantry and the proportion of chariots to infantry became relatively small.[4]

Assistance to rebel forces in another state was sometimes (as today) an attractive method. In 493, for example, Ch'i gave every possible support to a rebellion in Chin, its greatest rival. Such action was not uncommon. This was, strictly speaking, contrary to the rules of the system, but (again as today) convincing rationalizations would easily be found to justify it when necessary. Mencius, though not prepared to justify the intervention of one state (Ch'i) in another (Yen) at a time of civil war there, felt that intervention would have been justified if the people had wanted it (precisely the type of argument often used in recent times). In many cases intervening states sought to claim they were acting to restore the legal government after a revolution, or to dislodge an ''unjust'' ruler. Thus the rulers ''appreciated the value of supporting claimants to power in other states on even the

1. *The Book of Lord Shang,* trans. J. Duyvendak (London, 1928), I, 3–4.

2. Han Fei-tzu, *The Five Fermin.*

3. Industrial strength thus began to be an important resource. The weapons were originally mainly made of bronze, but when iron weapons came to be used, the larger states, which were able to develop the necessary technology, especially Ch'i and Ch'u, secured the advantage of more efficient armaments. The early strength of Ch'in was partly based on the industry it had built up, and later Ch'u hesitated to declare war on Chin because of the industrial strength the latter had established. R. L. Walker, *The Multi-State System in Ancient China,* (Hamden, 1953), p. 45.

4. H. G. Creel, *The Origins of State-Craft in China* (Chicago, 1970), pp. 274–75.

most tenuous grounds, and the use of satellite parties and puppet regimes was one of the most important strategies of state expansion (once more as today).[5]

Equally important as a means in such a society were alliances. Mencius quoted disapprovingly the ministers of his day who said, "We can form alliances with other states for our rulers, so we shall be successful in battle".[6] In a system of so many states it was inevitable that many, especially among the smaller, should group themselves together to resist the pretensions of the more powerful. Because states were small, alliances were large. The most important alliances, as we saw above, were the two great leagues, that of the Yellow River states, led first by Ch'i, and subsequently by Chin, and the more southerly Yangtsze states, grouped around Ch'u. Some of the states in the middle (near the Huai Valley), such as Cheng, Hsu, and Sung, would fluctuate from one side to another according to the balance of advantage. This was not a balance-of-power policy in the modern sense (in which the balancing power should ally itself with the weaker side), since the small state "often joined the power it thought would win, in order to avoid conquest and occupation."[7] Cheng, for example, is said to have transferred its favors quite arbitrarily "when it sensed the other power was on the rise, so that it would not have to suffer the ravages of an attack directed against it."[8]

On the other hand, a strong state such as Ch'in, on the periphery, pursued a genuine balance-of-power policy, allying itself with weaker states to attack any power in the ascendancy at the moment. Alliances were either long-term, as in the leagues, or ad hoc, and a great deal of the diplomatic activity of the period is concerned with securing the alliance of a particular state against another state. Chin, when on the point of defeat by Ch'u, sought an alliance with the remote southeastern state of Wu, trained its men in modern military techniques, and with this help defeated Ch'u. The effect was that Wu finally became the strongest state in the system, and for a period the leader of the Chou league. In a society where allies could be quite easily weaned away from one side to the other, means had to be found to maintain the solidarity of alliances. Thus, if an ally defected, its former allies felt justified in attacking it to bring it back to the fold, or even to extinguish it altogether. When Cheng, for example, transferred its allegiance from the northern alliance to the Ch'u camp in 642, the northern states made a concerted attack on it to win it back, an operation repeated by the same states for the same reason in 565.

A less coercive means employed to extend state power (as it was to be 2,000 years later in Europe) was that of dynastic marriage. Though this did not normally bring with it, as in Europe, automatic transfer of territory or inheritance, it was a widely used method of securing allies. The kingdom of Lu, for example, made dynastic marriages with Ch'i, her powerful neighbor, in 672, 623, and 604, and these were supplemented with similar marriages to the ruling families of Ch'u and

5. Walker, *Multi-State System,* p. 86.
6. *The Works of Mencius,* VI (Part II), IX, 2.
7. Walker, *Multi-State System,* p. 51.
8. Ibid.

Chin. Such marriages could provide a reason for alliance and friendship. Some-times claims to the thrones of other states could be based on a child born to a princess who had been married to a son of another ruler. Support for pretenders might be used as a means of expanding state power, as in sixteenth- and seventeenth-century Europe. "The rulers of the Ch'un-chiu period appreciated the political value of supporting claimants to power in other states on even the most tenuous grounds. . . . In some cases indirect support to the claimant was sufficient, but more often a fostered civil war was combined with invasion."[9]

All of these means could be supplemented by the least coercive method: diplomatic activity. There was, as we shall see later (p. 231 below), a highly developed system of diplomatic intercourse. Because of the large distances be-tween the states, however (in terms of traveling time), and because permanent envoys were not accredited to other rulers, this was employed only for major objectives: the conclusion of alliance or marriages, state celebrations, and similar purposes. Because economic relations between the states were relatively limited, the scope for trade treaties or economic pressures and inducements as a means of promoting state interests was reduced.

Thus the means employed reflected the motives that were dominant, and so indirectly the ideology. Other factors, communications and technology, affected the choice (the former stimulating increasing use of diplomatic contacts and more wide-ranging military campaigns). For each state it was influenced by size and military strength. But the ultimate end desired was the decisive factor. Where territory, as here, is the end most widely coveted, means are inevitably mainly warlike, since territory is almost never voluntarily relinquished. Diplomacy had a significant role to play, but force was usually the ultimate instrument of policy.

## 8.2 The Greek City-States (600–332 B.C.)

With its bipolar structure and overwhelming concern with ideology, quite a different set of means was adopted in the ancient Greek society.

Because distances were small and the units numerous and mainly weak, defense could often, as in China, be secured only through alliances. A considera-ble proportion of the cities were thus mobilized in one or the other of the two great alliances. The Athenian alliance alone is said to have had over 100 members in about 450, while the Spartan league had around 40 members. For the superpower, such allies could be a source of manpower, financial resources, ships, and strategic positions. The Spartan king, Archidamus, at the beginning of the Peleponnesian war, is said to have recommended to his people: "We should be making our own preparations by winning over new allies, both among Hellenes and among for-eigners, from any quarter in fact where we can increase our naval and financial

9. Ibid., p. 86.

resources."[10] A little later both Athens and Sparta "tried to ally themselves with other Hellenic states who were not yet committed to either side."[11] Persia, the most powerful state of all, was a particularly valuable ally and was often ready to throw her weight in the balance with one of the major powers. At the time of the peace of Nicias, Argos and Sparta competed together to secure the alliance of Corinth, just as Athens and Syracuse later sent rival delegations to win the support of Camarina in Sicily.

The importance of allies in a society of so many members meant that the capacity to hold together an alliance and reach generally acceptable decisions became of special urgency. The Athenians are said by Thucydides to have felt considerable confidence because their enemies, the Peleponnesians, "have no central deliberative authority to produce quick decisive action. They all have equal votes . . . and every one of them is mainly concerned with its own interests."[12] The Spartan system, by which both she herself, and her allies voting together, had to agree to any action proposed, was supposed to minimize friction, but could undoubtedly lead to delays and hesitation. Though the system in the Delian alliance was in theory similar, in practice Athens was often able to impose her will on other members more decisively. As the Mytileneans complained to Sparta: "Because of the multiple voting system, the allies were incapable of uniting themselves in defense and so they all became enslaved except for us and Chios. . . . It was more through terror than through friendship that we were held together in a common alliance."[13] Coercion, however, proved an ineffective way of holding an alliance together permanently, and the defection of her allies was one of the reasons for Athens' ultimate defeat.

But there were other means which, in a transnational society, were also of great value, especially to superpowers. Assistance to rebels to seize power in another state was encouraged by the existence of ideological minorities almost everywhere. This could be an important means of winning over the ally of an enemy, or converting a neutral. In Megara, a crucial state controlling the isthmus, Corinth and Athens supported rival factions in the Peleponnesian War, each of which obtained power at different times. In Corcyra, an equally important state in western Greece, with its powerful navy and control of the western approaches, the same two states again supported rival factions. While the factions supported were usually of the same political complexion as the helper, this was not invariably so: Thebes, though herself then oligarchic, helped the democrats to return to power in Athens in 403 because her state interests demanded this.

A particularly powerful and widely favored means, in such a society was support for rebels or potential rebels in time of war. The colonies of another state were always fair game for this kind of activity. Athens gave support to three

10. Thucydides, *The Peloponnesian War,* I, 81.

11. Ibid., II, 7.

12. Ibid., I, 141.

13. Ibid., III, 11–12. Cleon advocated the slaughter of all the men of Mytilene after the revolt there in order to deter other cities of Athens from revolting.

rebellious allies of Corinth at the opening of the Peleponnesian War. In return, the Corinthian delegate to the congress at Sparta recommended that "we can foster revolts among the allies of Athens". The subject peoples of another state could prove especially useful material. Athens devoted considerable resources to inciting the helots of Sparta to revolt in the Peleponnesian War, deliberately retaining Pylos in her hands during the short-lived peace of Nicias because of its potential value as a focus for supporting guerrilla action by the helots. Sparta intrigued with the oligarchs of Athens in the early years of the war, as did Athens with the democrats of Thebes, and Thebes with the oligarchs of Plataea. Slaves were, of course, particularly favorable material for disaffection. During the fighting at Corcyra, "each side sent out to the country districts in an attempt to win the support of the slaves by offering them their freedom." Similarly, after the Spartans occupied an important town in Attica, "more than 20,000 slaves, the majority of whom were skilled workmen, deserted."[14]

A related activity was the use of emigrés from foreign states. The Persians tried to make use of Alcibiades to help them against Athens, and he did give his support to an oligarchic revolution there. Persia sent Greek emigrés to the Ionian states in the early sixth century to encourage them to medise. Puppet rulers might be installed in conquered territories: Peisistratus, the Athenian tyrant, established friendly regimes in Naxos and Samos, and placed his own son in Sigeum, for this purpose. The Persians established puppet regimes for a period in Asia Minor, the islands, and even in part of the mainland.

In such a society, ideology could be used as a means as well as an end. "In going to war, Athens did not count only on her naval and military resources. Her democracy was a weapon of political warfare, capable of forming a bond of common interest with other states."[15] Athens deliberately spread democratic regimes in Boeotia which, so long as they lasted, usually supported alliance with Athens. Sparta used her reputation as the leader of the oligarchic states to similar effect in the years after 404: "In the liberated states there was a natural swing towards an oligarchical form of government, prompted partly by antipathy to the pro-Athenian democrats, partly by the knowledge that Lysander favored such governments."[16]

Ideological warfare, as in the age of religions and more recent times, was peculiarly ruthless in its methods. Members of a defeated faction, as in Corcyra and Plataea, were shown no mercy by the external power which intervened. As Thucydides put it:

> Fanatical enthusiasm was the mark of a real man, and to plot against an enemy behind his back was perfectly legitimate self-defense. These parties were not formed to enjoy the benefits of the established laws but to acquire power by overthrowing the existing regime. . . . If pacts of mutual security were made they were entered into by the two

14. Ibid., 27.
15. N. G. L. Hammond, *A History of Greece to 233* B.C. (London, 1967), p. 298.
16. Ibid., p. 422.

parties only in order to meet some temporary difficulty and remained in force only so long as there was no other weapon available. When the chance came, the one who first seized it, boldly catching his enemy off his guard, enjoyed a revenge that was almost sweeter from having been taken, not openly, but because of a breach of faith. . . . Love of power, operating through greed and through personal ambition, was the cause of all these evils.[17]

In a transnational world, the ambitions of factions and parties were now as important as those of governments in determining the means employed. The more conciliatory means, such as diplomacy, operated mainly between ideological allies only.

Economic means were sometimes significant. Measures affecting trade could be used to promote one's own commerce and damage that of one's enemies: One of the many causes of the Peleponnesian War was the Megara decree, by which in 433 Athens sought to exclude the goods of Megara from all the ports of her empire and from the markets of Athens itself, imposed as a punishment for sheltering escaped Athenian slaves and cultivating land which Athens claimed did not belong to Megara. In a more direct way economic strength was a source of power. Archidamus, the Spartan king, pointed out that "war is not so much a matter of armaments as of the money which makes armaments effective. . . ."[18] Pericles, seeking to prove the capacity of Athens to defeat Sparta, pointed to the poverty of the Peleponnesian states, which "have no financial resources, either as individuals or as states, and have no experience . . . of any fighting that lasts a long time, since the wars they fight among themselves are necessarily short because of their poverty."[19] Athenian wealth was recognized as an important source of her military power. Pericles argued that "the strength of Athens came from the money paid in tribute by her allies."[20] This enabled her relatively quickly to build and fit out ships, to purchase arms, and to pay her hoplites.

In such an age, moreover, since state loyalties were weak, mercenaries could be hired or subventions made to friendly cities. When the Corinthian spokesman was urging war against Athens and Sparta, he pointed out that if they borrowed money from the funds of the temples they "would be able to attract the foreign sailors in the Athenian navy by offering high rates of pay. For the power of Athens rests in mercenaries rather than her own citizens."[21]

But even in this ideological society military action by the state was the ultimate means available for promoting ends. The state remained the basic political unit and state power the basic political end. No state hesitated to use military force when necessary to protect its interests, and used it sometimes with great brutality. There was in general a high regard for military power and a cynical recognition of the

17. Thucydides, III, 82.
18. Ibid., I, 83.
19. Ibid., 141.
20. Ibid., II, 12.
21. Ibid., I, 121.

advantages it could procure. It was not only the demagogues and militants, such as Cleon and Alcibiades, who argued that the Athenian empire could be maintained only by brute force. Such views were widespread. The Athenian spokesman, sent to coerce Melos into accepting Athenian rule, declared: "You know as well as we do . . . that in practice the strong do what they have the power to do and the weak accept what they have to accept. . . . Our opinion of the gods and our knowledge of man lead us to conclude that it is a general and necessary law of nature to rule wherever one can. We are merely acting in accordance with it."[22] It is thus perhaps scarcely surprising that, when the Melians finally surrendered unconditionally, the Athenians put these principles into practice by putting to death all the men of military age whom they took, and sold the women and children into slavery.

This punishment, the killing of all able-bodied men and the enslavement of women and children, was a recognized penalty enacted by one city against another. The killing of prisoners was not uncommon: Athens slew about a thousand Lesbians held after the revolt of Mytilene. Even ambassadors were sometimes put to death, contrary to Greek law: Thucydides recounts how the soldiers of Athens persuaded the ruler of Thrace to hand over to him an embassy from the Peleponnesian cities and "without giving them a trial or waiting to hear what they had to say in defense put them to death and threw their bodies into a pit."[23] Even Spartan commanders on occasion put prisoners to death, for example, those taken at Plataea.

Here we see a society in which, because political rather than military expansion was the aim, *political* means—the establishment of politically sympathetic governments rather than military control, the organizing or assistance of coups in other states—were the favorite means employed. The means used inevitably reflected the dominant spirit of the society. Because the ruling elites were highly political, ideology was used as an important means (as well as justification) for changing governments elsewhere. Because there were politically dissident elements in the populations of other states, subversion became a favored method. Because commercial contacts were widespread and commercial forces internally powerful, economic means, such as the boycott, the tariff, or the monopoly, also had a part to play. All of these were typical means within an ideological society. They represented a significant variation on the traditional diplomatic and military means almost exclusively employed in the contemporary Chinese society.

# 8.3 The Age of Dynasties (1300–1559)

The foreign policy instruments adopted in the later middle ages were different again. They too reflected the character of the society as a whole, especially the

22. Ibid., V, 89–107.
23. Ibid., II, 67.

motives of the elites then dominant. These motives, as we have seen, were largely dynastic.

Perhaps the most widely adopted of all the means used was the dynastic marriage. Territory, which was the ultimate objective of dynasts, could be acquired more simply and with less expense through a well-judged marriage contract than by any other means. Considerable ingenuity and patience were shown in the search for these. A well-endowed daughter, such as Mary of Burgundy or Bona of France, would be hawked around Europe to the highest bidder (Mary was betrothed seven times to different suitors before finally landing Maximilian of Austria). She could be transferred from one husband to another if the first one inconsiderately died, as Catherine of Aragon was transferred from one son of Henry VII to another; or from one betrothed to another, like Henry's sister Mary, transferred from Charles V, king of Spain, to Louis XII, king of France; or the unfortunate Portuguese Princess Beatrice, betrothed in 1382, to the prince of Castile, who found herself before the end of that year married instead to his father, the king, who found her too good to waste on his son. Rulers would abandon one princess when another more attractive heritage appeared, as Charles VIII of France abandoned the Burgundian princess to whom he had been betrothed since childhood for the heiress of Brittany (who had to be compelled by force to accept him). Or a ruler could be compelled to marry by duress, as Francois I, held a captive, was made to agree to marry the Queen of Portugal, the sister of his conqueror, as a condition of his release. An heiress might even be forced to divorce one husband and to marry another to bring him her territories, as Lewis of Bavaria divorced Margaret of Maultasch and her lands from her husband to marry them to his son.

Princesses were bought and sold: Galeazzo Visconti, for example, paid 600,000 gold florins for a French princess. They were cast from one husband to another, as when Anne Neville, heiress of the greatest house in England, was married first to the Lancastrian heir to the throne and, after the change of regime and the killing of her husband, taken over by the Yorkist heir, who had brought about the former's death (only to be cast off in turn by him so he could marry his own niece, a still more valuable heiress). Wives were abandoned for the sake of a further inheritance, as when Louis X of France got rid of his first wife to marry a Hungarian princess in 1315. The choice of a husband was often denied to an heiress, even when her father had died, as when the people of Ghent decided who Mary of Burgundy should marry, or when the Poles elected Hedwig, the daughter of Charles IV, as their queen on condition that they chose her husband. Even men had to renounce choice: the duke of Orleans agreed, under the treaty of Crespi, to accept a wife chosen for him by Charles V (provided only it was either the latter's daughter or niece). Everywhere it was accepted that the marriage of a member of the royal house was an affair of state policy, requiring great care and consideration and far too important to be left to the choice of the individual concerned.[24]

24. It was a corollary that sometimes an agreement *not* to make certain marriages could be a condition of a peace treaty, as in the Treaty of Barcelona in 1493 in which Charles VIII persuaded Ferdinand and Isabella to agree not to marry their children to the Hapsburg, Tudor or Naples royal family.

In such a system dynastic marriage had another importance. Even if it did not bring territory, it might bring alliance. Sometimes it was expected to *cause* an alliance: When England and France were competing for the support of Flanders in the 1330s the French king sought to clinch the matter by offering his brother to the Count of Flanders' daughter. The two warring houses of Luxembourg and Hapsburg tried to secure peace between them by a treaty of mutual inheritance. The marriage of Margaret of Anjou to Henry VI while their two countries were still at war was a deliberate move of the peace party in England to bring the war to an end. In other cases a marriage was designed to *seal* an alliance: Catherine of Aragon's successive marriages to English princes were designed for this purpose. Henry VIII's sister Mary was transferred from the king of Spain to the king of France according to the shifts in Henry's alliance policy. Nor were the infidel Turks excluded from such arrangements: the Emperor Manuel gave his highly Christian niece as a wife for the Sultan Suleiman to win his friendship. Even the bitterest enemies, such as the royal houses of Spain and France, in the intervals of fighting each other, would conclude marriage agreements as a symbol of peaceful intentions; almost every truce in that long struggle was marked by a new betrothal. And the Treaty of Cateau-Cambrésis at the end of the period sought to bring seventy years of conflict to a close, like the finale of a contemporary play, by a double wedding, in which Philip, the Spanish king, was to marry the thirteen-year old French princess (previously destined for his son) and the French king's sister was to marry the king of Savoy.

Another important means inevitably employed in a dynastic age was support for pretenders elsewhere. In such a society a simple means of hurting an opponent was by helping a rival claimant to dethrone him. If successful, this could procure a friendly and compliant ruler in place of a hostile one. If unsuccessful it might in any case preoccupy a rival with domestic conflict. Any claimant who chose to set himself up, on good grounds or bad, as a pretender could thus usually command some foreign support. The English pretender, Perkin Warbeck, was given aid by Spain, France, and Burgundy. In the Hundred Years' War England supported the pretender, Edward Balliol, against France's ally, Scotland, as well as pretenders in Artois and Brittany, while France helped the Welsh rebel, Glyn Dwr. Thus domestic conflicts could be made international.

But equally often (as in the modern system) international conflicts influenced domestic quarrels. Outside powers supported rival contenders and factions. In Castile during the Hundred Years' War England supported Pedro the Cruel on the grounds of his legitimacy, while France supported Henry of Trastamara as being more popular with the people (compare the grounds put forward in modern times by the two outside powers in Vietnam and elsewhere). Charles V gave his support to a pretender to the Danish throne and so forfeited Denmark's alliance, and by assisting a peasant revolt in Sweden caused Sweden to go over to his enemies. Sometimes support was given not to individual claimants but to rebellious provinces or neighbors: France supported an independent Navarre against Spain, while Spain supported an independent Brittany against France; England supported nationalist movements in Flanders, Burgundy, and Brittany against France, while France supported Scottish and Welsh nationalists against England. Even the popes on occasion stimulated revolts, as in the papal states in the 1350s, or in Naples at other times, to help restore their own influence. In consequence, to counter this trend and restore security for monarchs, nonintervention pacts were sometimes concluded, as in the Treaty of Étaples in 1492, under which French and English kings agreed to refrain from supporting rebel causes in the territory of the other.

Conversely, among small powers, the calling-in of great powers might be a vitally important means of promoting their own interests. The rulers of Italy at this time were perpetually tempted to boost their own position by seeking support from France, Spain, or even Germany, with which many had dynastic links. There was thus never "a decade in which some Italian power was not intriguing to call in a foreigner in order to gain for itself some local advantage."[25] Genoa and Milan called for French assistance, while the Spanish dynasty in Naples necessarily looked more often to Spain. Small powers such as Flanders, Burgundy, and Savoy could only maintain themselves by recourse to a flexible alliance policy of this kind, calling in one power against the main threat to their independence. So the disaffected nobles of Naples could encourage the remote dynastic claims of Charles VIII of France to that city for their own domestic purposes.

Economic means, like economic motives, were not common in this age. By cutting off the wool trade to Flanders in 1336, Edward III sought to compel Flanders to join him against France. France and Castile together used a blockade against England in the same war. But in general, since trade itself was small in volume, economic sanctions were relatively little used. On the other hand, the availability to the rulers of adequate financial resources for waging war was an essential condition of an effective foreign policy, and this meant wealth immediately available to the king, not simply potential resources. Money was required to equip fleets and armies, to pay mercenaries, or even to buy peace. It is not surprising that the French writer Robert de Balsac concluded that "success in war depends on having enough money to provide whatever the enterprise needs."[26]

Even military means were affected by the dynastic character of the age. Machiavelli believed that "a prince ought to have no other aim in thought, nor select anything else for his study, than war and its rules and discipline."[27] But the lack of national sentiment made it necessary for kings to rely either on feudal levies or on mercenary troops, who fought for money, rather than on citizens fighting on patriotic grounds. The "free companies" in France during the Hundred Years' War fought for whoever would hire them, alternately supporting the French and the English. German troops, taken originally by German emperors to Italy,

25. G. Mattingly, *Renaissance Diplomacy* (London, 1955), p. 57.

26. Quoted in the *New Cambridge Modern History,* I (1957): 176. "Apart from a minimum of internal stability, the prerequisites of war were money—of which the powers, apart from the empire, had enough—and troops." Ibid., p. 263.

27. Machiavelli, *The Prince,* Ch. XIII.

subsequently sold themselves to whatever city would hire them. Later, Italian troops were hired on a similar basis, passing successively into the service of different cities while their leaders, the condottieri, were equally devoid of fixed loyalties, often non-Italian even, selling themselves to the highest bidders. Swiss troops, though renowned as the toughest in Europe, sometimes embarrassed their employers by suddenly deserting to the other side: abandoning the French in 1512, for example, when they decided they were not being paid enough, and so bringing about the expulsion of French forces from Milanese territory, while on another occasion they suddenly deserted Ludovico of Milan because they did not wish to fight against the Swiss troops employed by his enemy. Against these drawbacks, mercenary forces were usually professionally more competent than local ones and left the citizens free for more profitable activities: "It was cheaper to be heavily taxed for the maintenance of a hired force than to leave the shop or the counting-house for a protracted campaign."[28]

Another new means for promoting state interests developed at this time was the art of diplomacy. Sometimes the methods used could be somewhat crude; diplomats were frequently caught out in bribery, spying, and even attempted assassination. These activities were undertaken not so much for state or government as for the ruler personally. There were few activities to which the faithful diplomat would not stoop for this end.[29]

> The diplomats of the 16th and 17th century . . . bribed courtiers; they stimulated and financed rebellions; they encouraged opposition parties; they intervened in the most subversive ways in the internal affairs of the countries to which they were accredited; they lied, they spied, they stole. An ambassador of those days regarded himself as an honorable spy. He was sincerely convinced that private morality was a thing apart from public morality. . . .[30]

Nonetheless, diplomacy in this wide sense—activity at foreign courts—became an important instrument of foreign policy. In the words of the Italian writer, Barbaro, describing the new diplomatic revolution: "The first duty of an ambassador is exactly the same as that of any other servant of the government, that is to do, say, advise and think whatever may best serve the preservation and aggrandizement of his own state."[31]

Here the means employed reflected not only motives but the kind of elite in power: absolute monarchs dealing directly with other rulers and their courts, themselves also totally controlling policy. Because power was concentrated, to *bribe* a minister or murder a ruler could secure, relatively simply, the change desired in another state's policy. Ruling elites at this time thus showed considera-

28. Sir. R. Lodge, *The Close of the Middle Ages* (London, 1957), p. 150.

29. "The aim of a diplomat was moreover to outwit, to deceive without being deceived—an aim formulated by Commynes from the behavior of Louis XI, who not only boasted of the useful lies he had told but preferred to use occasional ambassadors on the grounds that the promises of one might be disowned by the next." *New Cambridge Modern History,* I (1957): 273.

30. H. Nicolson, *Diplomacy* (London, 1938), p. 20.

31. Quoted in Mattingly, *Renaissance Diplomacy,* p. 103.

ble cynicism and brutality in the methods employed. A Gresham's law existed by which bad means drove out good. In Machiavelli's words:

> The experience of our time shows those princes to have done great things who have had little regard for good faith, and have been able by astuteness to confuse men's minds and have ultimately overcome those who have made loyalty their foundation. . . . Therefore, a prudent ruler ought not to keep faith when by so doing it would be against his interest and when the reasons which made him bind himself no longer exist. If men were all good this precept would not be a good one, but as they are bad and will not keep faith with you, so you are not bound to keep faith with them.[32]

The French king, Louis XI, boasted of the skillful lies he had told for diplomatic reasons. One of the famous foreign policy advisers of the time, Commynes, was in the pay of both the French and the Florentine governments and was paid by the latter to alter the policy of the former. Even the assassination of foreign rulers or rival contenders was not unknown or even uncommon, especially in Italy; Johanna of Naples is even thought to have murdered her husband to rid herself of his embarrassing claims to her own throne.

Here too, therefore, the means employed reflected the general character of the age. The dynastic marriage, the dynastic claim, the dynastic agreement, played a far larger role than in other societies. Among military methods, widespread use of mercenary forces and feudal levies reflected the structure of a society in which national loyalties were still weak. The more conciliatory means, bargaining and diplomacy, were not much in evidence. Bad faith, conspiracy, and assassination were tolerated for dynastic ends, for the sake of the prince and his house. The character of the ruler, more often than anything else, determined the success of his dynasty and his nation. Nearly all the means employed, from diplomacy to military force, were under the personal control of the ruler; even at the end of the period Francois I and Charles V were leading their own troops in battle.

Not only the choice of means but the effectiveness with which they were used therefore depended here more than in most societies on the individual rulers themselves. It was neither the political structure nor the motives of the leaders which alone dictated the means. Authoritarian rulers existed earlier, in the ancient Chinese society, and again in the age of sovereigns two centuries later; their motives, the extension of personal and state authority, were not dissimilar. But the means they employed were quite different. For these stemmed from the dynastic character of the society as a whole and the assumptions and attitudes this created.

## 8.4 The Age of Religions (1599–1648)

In the age of religions, the means employed inevitably changed again. In an era when many of the most important objectives of the dominating elites concerned the

32. Machiavelli, *The Prince,* Ch. 18.

defense or promotion of particular religious beliefs, new and more appropriate means had to be devised.

One means of this kind, which had played little part in the preceding international society but became of increasing importance, was the use of propaganda. Where the struggle was between religious creeds as much as between nations, this obviously must (as in the modern ideological age) play a substantial role. Though governments themselves did not usually have the means or the resources to undertake such propaganda, they could give their support and encouragement to those organizations which were responsible for it. For example, the Jesuits, among the Catholics, were accorded a semiofficial position in a number of states and played a major role in reviving the Catholic faith, and bringing back Protestant heretics. Emperor Ferdinand II, himself educated by Jesuit teachers, gave them full authority to preach and to convert in the areas which he reconquered in Bohemia, Austria, and Hungary, a task which they undertook with the greatest fervor and efficiency (a single priest claimed to have made 6,000 converts). Spain made equally widespread use of the Jesuits to proclaim the cause not only of her religion but of Spain herself; indeed, they were often seen as the agents for Spain. "Wherever Spain triumphed, the Jesuits followed; wherever the Jesuits were admitted, a pro-Spanish party was created."[33] In a sense the whole counterreformation represented a huge, jointly organized propaganda campaign.

On the Protestant side, the Calvinist preachers made equally skillful use of propaganda, which equally often promoted state interests as well as those of their religion. They were as implacable in their opposition to Spain as the Jesuits were in her support. Both in the Netherlands, in the 1570s and 1580s, and in Bohemia in 1618–1620, a massive propaganda war was undertaken in which huge numbers of pamphlets were produced and widely distributed. In the latter about 1,800 different pamphlets were said to have been produced in 1618 alone.[34]

In some cases these ideological means were negative in aim rather than positive, designed to *prevent* a rival view from being expressed. Persecution was then the means adopted. This was the method employed in its most brutal and fanatical form by the Inquisition. But it was also employed by Elizabeth in persecuting Catholic preachers and by Philip II in supressing Protestantism in Spain, and in oppressing, and finally expelling, the Moriscoes.

Another means characteristic of an ideological age (and again the modern age is a close parallel) was external assistance to coreligionists elsewhere. This was an instrument of policy employed by virtually every government. In the previous dynastic age, almost the only internal force of which an outside government could make use to promote its own cause was the dynastic pretender; and his adherents were not always large in number. But in a religious age there were often substantial minorities in other states, many of whom might be prepared to support, or even welcome, external intervention, and who therefore represented potential fifth

33. *New Cambridge Modern History,* IV (1970): 270.

34. D. Ogg, *Europe in the 17th Century* (London, 1925), p. 120.

columns. So England was able to find supporters among the Protestants of France during the early years of the wars of religion there and in 1628–1629, and was prepared to finance intervention from the Palatinate in 1574. Conversely, France under the Guises supported Scottish Catholics and plotted to put their niece, the Scottish queen, on the throne of England. England supported the Protestants of the Netherlands against Catholic Spain, while Spain supported the Catholics in England and Ireland against the Protestant queen of England. The Elector Palatine gave military support to his coreligionists in Bohemia, while the ruler of Bavaria gave equally fervent support to the Catholics.

> The governments of the later 16th century could almost always expect to find friends, even perhaps armed allies, within their enemy's camp, which the previous generation had found only upon rare occasions. The fostering of "fifth columns," the underhand helping of rebels, thus became regular and recognized instruments of later 16th century statecraft. They were instruments resorted to all the more readily because it was so easy for one government to give help to rebels against another unofficially and without committing any overt act of war. Yet they were dangerous instruments precisely because the line between underhand help to rebels and open war between governments was so blurred and uncertain that even the most cautious and skillful statesmen could easily overstep it unintentionally.[35]

In other words, these were cold war means typical of an ideological age (the passage above could be applied virtually unchanged to the modern world). And as in recent times too, it was not always the outside government which incited the rebels. In most cases the *origin* of the conflict was internal, and it was the rebels themselves who implored, often in vain (like William of Orange to England and France, or the Elector Palatine to England in the next century), for more active assistance from abroad.

One form which such assistance might take (again, as more recently) was the dispatch of "volunteers," acting nominally on their own behalf rather than that of their government. This is always a means likely to be employed in an age of ideology, since in such times *personal* motivation to assist is often more powerful than that of governments, while the government permitting such action may be saved both the embarrassment and the expense of full-scale intervention. Thus Elizabeth encouraged Englishmen to fight as volunteers for the Protestant cause in the Low Countries, and allowed English ships to attack Spanish ships sailing there, without needing to risk a declaration of war. Similarly, English "privateers," freebooting fighting ships, harried and attacked Spanish ships traveling to South America without the disagreeable necessity of a formal declaration of war by the government. English regiments stayed semiofficially in the Netherlands fighting for the Dutch, long after England had made peace with Spain in 1604. Catherine de Medici, who was inhibited on religious grounds from full-scale support for the Netherlands against Spain, was nonetheless prepared to allow Protestant volunteers to fight there. In the Thirty Years' War volunteers from the Netherlands and

35. *New Cambridge Modern History,* III (1968): 7.

England fought on behalf of the German Protestants, while Catholic soldiers of fortune enlisted in the army of Wallenstein.

Financial assistance might also be given to such a cause. Elizabeth financed military intervention in the Netherlands by the Elector Palatine, just as France later financed the armies of Gustav Adolfus. In other words, just the same kind of ambiguous commitments were made to ideological allies, involving external support without a declaration of war, as in more recent times.

However, "war underhand" could be still more underhand. Plots and intrigues designed to overthrow a foreign government could be hatched in conjunction with supporters in the other state. Throughout this period conspiracies in which foreign powers were engaged were uncovered with monotonous regularity. Ambassadors were widely employed for this purpose. Assassination as an instrument of policy was more widely employed than in any other age in history. Both the Jesuits and the Calvinists in some of their writings seemed to give tacit support to such an undertaking, if religious necessity demanded it. The Spanish government offered 25,000 crowns and a title of nobility for anybody who would assassinate William of Orange. Never have so many prominent figures lost their lives as a result of assassination: in France two kings (Henry III and Henry IV) and the Queen of Navarre (probably), the four chief leaders of the religious parties (three dukes de Guise and Coligny), not to speak of several thousand Protestants murdered at St. Bartholomew; in the Netherlands, William of Orange; in Scotland, Cardinal Beaton, Rizzi, Darnley, and Moray; in Germany, Wallenstein; in Spain, Don Carlos; and so on.[36]

Even the traditional means were transformed in the religious environment. The alliance now becomes typically the religious alliance. Though there were still occasional alliances across the ideological barrier—such as that between Venice and the Netherlands in 1618 and between France and Sweden in 1631—these were rare. The most typical product of this age was the religious leagues. Among these were the Unions of Arras and Utrecht among the Catholic and Protestant states of the Netherlands; the alliance of Catholic states said to have been planned between France and Spain in 1564–1565; the alliance of Protestant or semi-Protestant states (including France) planned by William of Orange; the Evangelical Union set up among the Protestant states of Germany in 1608, subsequently linked with England and the Netherlands; and the Catholic League established there in 1609 and equally clearly linked with the emperor. Gustav Adolfus of Sweden wanted the formation of a still wider league of Protestant states in 1624, and James I supported a congress of Protestant states at the Hague at that time. Formal alliances were sometimes made with Protestant groups which were not sovereign states, such as that between Elizabeth and the French Protestants in the Treaty of Hampton Court, and that between Philip II of Spain and the Ligue in France in 1584. Such alliances and leagues were the equivalent of the ideological blocs of modern times, and they

36. If executions are included, the names of Egmont and Hoorn in the Netherlands, Mary Queen of Scots and Charles I in England, members of the French aristocracy executed by Richelieu, and many others would need to be included.

were similar too in that they were somewhat more stable than the purely opportunistic alliances, not based on common beliefs, of the subsequent age, since
ideological viewpoints did not change so quickly as *raisons d' état*.

Another traditional means, dynastic marriage, also took new forms. Dynastic
marriages might still be arranged between states of the *same* religion (even between the archrivals, Bourbons and Hapsburgs, as in 1611 and 1660), but they
could not easily be arranged between opposing religions. For the moment the
Catholic houses of south Europe rarely sought such matches with the Protestant
houses of the north. And when James I sought to defy such prejudices by seeking a
wife for his son in Spain, the project eventually broke down on the religious
prejudices of both sides. *Within* the same religion marriages were now expected to
secure religious alliances: The marriage between James I's daughter Elizabeth and
the Elector Palatine was expected (wrongly) to commit James I firmly to the
Protestant cause in Germany. But a marriage could also perform totally different
functions. It might be offered as a way of *changing* the religion of another
sovereign, and so of all his population, as when Philip II offered marriage to
Elizabeth on condition that she became a Catholic. And it might be used to
*reconcile* religions (just as it had been used before to reconcile conflicting nations),
as when Catherine de Medici arranged a marriage between the Protestant Henry of
Navarre and her Catholic daughter.

War remained, as ever, the ultimate resort. But even this was used, in this age,
primarily for religious ends. Though at first sight an inappropriate means for this
purpose if the object were convincing or converting, it sometimes could secure its
object. Even though the original issue concerned other questions—control of
church property, recognition of local autonomy, the imperial constitution, succession rights, the right of private or public worship—often conversion came, as in
Austria and Bohemia, after the event, by means little short of coercion. Men did
not consciously fight to compel others to believe. But they knew that in practice
victory sometimes secured that result.

The means employed in this age were thus those of a transnational society.
Motives were concerned not with the transfer of territory, resources, or values
from one state to another, but with changing the *internal* situation in another state,
especially the religion generally practiced there: So appropriate means had to be
found. Fortunately not only ends are transnational but capacities too. Thus each
state can expect to find allies within the territories of another who may assist it in its
own ends in return for assistance to them in theirs, or mercenary forces of loose
allegiance who can be easily engaged. The appropriate means are often manipula-
tive, designed to *influence* events elsewhere, rather than coercive, designed to
extract direct concessions: propaganda, subversion, aid and financial assistance,
assassination, and intrigue, rather than the seizing of territory from other states or
unprovoked assault.

Yet it cannot be said that the means result here *directly* from the motivations.
Religious conversion could have been sought by peaceful propaganda and indoctrination alone, or exclusively by the war underhand. That full-scale war was also

often employed resulted from the expectations and overall character of the age: in other words, its ideology. The tradition of kingly rights was still such that the overthrow of one ruler (as attempted by Spain in her "great enterprise" against England, as achieved by Austria against Bohemia) could transform the beliefs of his peoples. On the other hand, the rulers themselves and their governments were influenced by the changing pattern of their subjects' beliefs. So means reflected a complex structure of attitudes and ideas. As always, it is the balance among them which counts. And the balance among the means used is here quite different from the age before and the age after. It is a balance not even approached again until another, in many ways similar, society was to emerge 350 years later.

## 8.5  The Age of Sovereignty (1648–1789)

In the period that followed the dominant aim was the strengthening of the state, externally as well as internally, and the enhancement of its prestige. It was the means which might best serve those purposes which became most attractive to governments.

One important means of achieving these ends was through force of arms. More than in most ages warfare was acknowledged as a *legitimate* instrument of state policy. Thus, almost every state of Europe now began to maintain standing armies to replace the mercenary forces of the previous age. It was through French military power that Louis XIV extended France's frontiers and exalted her prestige in Europe. It was Austrian power which Emperor Charles VI was advised by his ministers to strengthen when he was seeking to persuade the other rulers of Europe to recognize his daughter's inheritance to his territories. And it was Frederick the Great's military power which in the event prevented Maria Terese from obtaining part of that inheritance. It was taken for granted that major issues would be resolved by force of arms.

But, as we saw, state aims were generally limited—not to overthrow monarchs elsewhere or to conquer whole countries, but to secure relatively marginal border regions. Thus the means employed even collectively, were also limited. Armies were smaller than in both the preceding and succeeding ages. They were professional rather than conscript. The mass of the civilian population were little involved in warfare. Loss of life was fairly small. A war of maneuver, with many sieges, fought for a few key fortresses, with a close season during the winter when operations were abandoned, replaced the large-scale set battles, involving huge armies, of the wars of religions. These generally more civilized methods of warfare reflected the moderation in aims inherent in the system.[37] But the very fact that warfare was less destructive also meant that it could be resorted to more

---

37. See p. 245 below. See also E. V. Gulick, *Europe's Classical Balance of Power* (Ithaca, 1955), pp. 172–77.

readily. Though each war was less long and less costly than in previous ages, in frequency there were more in this period than in any other of European history.

The use of alliances was also transformed by this new environment. Since ideological considerations now counted for little, there was no stability or permanence in the alliances made. They were essentially short-term practical arrangements to suit the convenience of each sovereign, which could be modified and abandoned at very short notice. So in the second half of the seventeenth century England fought sometimes with the French against the Dutch, and sometimes with the Dutch against the French. Spain in the years after 1714 swung rapidly between alliance with France and with Austria. Within a short space of time in midcentury, France fluctuated among Austria, England, and Prussia, Austria among France, Prussia, and Russia. Sweden, Denmark, Poland, and Russia entered into changing agreements with each other to fight their main rivals of the moment. The most spectacular general post occurred in the famous diplomatic revolution of 1755–1756 when the main alliances totally changed about, so that though the two chief rivalries, between England and France and between Prussia and Austria, remained constant, each state found itself fighting with a different partner against its main enemy.

A new means now commonly employed was the *secret agreement*. In a world controlled by sovereign princes, wielding absolute authority and dealing with similar princes elsewhere, such agreements could be relatively easily concluded and easily kept secret from the world. By such arrangements deals would be arranged to suit their mutual convenience. They might relate to alliances in war, such as that between England and France in 1667, in which France agreed that the French fleet would not help the Dutch against England, if England in turn did not prevent the impending French invasion of the Spanish Netherlands. Sometimes they referred to the disposition of territories, for example on the death of the existing ruler, as in the Partition Treaty between Louis and the emperor in the following year. Sometimes they were merely the settlements of a war, reached by one party to an alliance without consultation with its allies, like Britain's private settlement with France in 1712 or Prussia's with Austria in 1745, or the separate peace which France tried to reach with Britain in 1761. It was indeed entirely normal in this age for each member of an alliance to seek peace terms with its enemies independently of its allies. Since the fundamental conflict was one of all against all (rather than of competition between close-knit groups, as in the ages of religion and of ideology), it was taken for granted that each would seek to make the best arrangement for itself, even if this meant abandonment of allies.

The conclusion of such agreements and alliances, secret or otherwise, did not prevent their frequent violation within a year or two of their having been reached. Another feature of this age was the widespread *unscrupulousness* of the means employed. *Raison d' état* came to be the rationalization used to justify flagrant disregard for normal standards of honor. Frederick the Great, having explicitly given his assent to the Pragmatic Sanctions, was not inhibited from invading Silesia in direct violation of that agreement as soon as Emperor Charles VI was dead. Britain had no hesitation in abandoning her allies in 1712, in clear disregard of her undertakings, and reaching a settlement with France to suit her interests. Tsar Peter III in 1762 had equally little scruple in abandoning the allies with whom his country had been fighting for the past six years to ally himself instead with the nation they had mainly been opposing, nor in offering a part of his army to be used against his recent cobelligerent, Austria—consistency was not regarded as important in this age. The opportunistic alliance replaces the religious alliance.[38]

Another form of unscrupulousless was the use of *intimidation:* the threat of force by large powers against small to induce them to induce them to change their policy. So France virtually forced Savoy and Genoa to send troops to fight for her in the 1670s; she laid waste the Palatinate without warning or any due cause; she besieged Luxembourg; she employed the dubious method of *chambres de réunion* to provide a legal fig leaf for the annexation of the towns of Alsace. Spain, under Alberoni, sought to secure the return of Sardinia and other territories, first by bluster, and ultimately by force. Bribery was almost universally used to secure state ends.

> Pensions and gratifications to foreign statesmen were intended, as a rule, . . . to build up a party and influence policy. . . . In most instances the lesser princes at least surmised that their ministers were receiving pensions from a foreign power. . . . For that matter many a prince relied on foreign subsistence himself. . . . Among the lesser princes only Charles XI of Sweden openly tried to defy this fact of political life: for most of the others, the question was not whether to receive financial aid but from whom to receive it. It was a question usually resolved . . . in accordance with their political interests.[39]

Economic means were increasingly used for state ends. One frequently employed was the attempt to hamper and damage the trade of other states. William III in 1689 sought to damage France by cutting off her trade, not only with his own allies, but with neutrals as well. Louis XIV played on the commercial rivalry of the Dutch and the English to dissuade them from alliance against himself. He imposed tariffs against the Dutch in 1688 and 1701, not so much to protect French industry as to damage that of the Dutch and to stir up feelings against the government there. In 1701 France offered the Danes commercial inducements to persuade them not to join her enemies. Blockades were customarily used by sea powers as a means of making war, and in the eighteenth century the unheralded attacks of English privateers on neutral shipping were a perpetual source of resentment in Europe.

Finally *propaganda* began to be used as a deliberate instrument of state policy (as opposed to that of religious sects). Even before this age began Richelieu had employed teams of writers to explain and defend his policies toward other states. In the time of Louis XIV "several propagandists were attached to the ministry, partly

---

38. Diplomacy was therefore equally unscrupulous. "Not only did diplomatists in those days pay large bribes to court functionaries, not only did they wrangle interminably over precedence and status, not only did they steal official documents, but they strove by every means in their power to win the support of the reigning favorite or, if that were impossible, to secure his or her replacement by some successor more amenable to their influence." Nicolson, *Diplomacy,* p. 61.

39. *New Cambridge Modern History,* VI (1970): 183.

to combat hostile publications: as in England there was increased awareness of public opinion as an instrument of foreign policy."[40] Nonetheless, "although pamphleteers were never more numerous than during this reign, they served above all his [Louis'] enemies. The Dutch presses in particular flooded Europe with libels directed against French policy."[41] Toward the end of Louis' reign in particular, "when disappointments and reverses multiplied and the financial reserves were exhausted, the role of money diminished and that of propaganda by the printed word grew steadily in importance."[42]

The means used in this age, therefore, reflected the assumptions and expectations of an age of sovereignty. They were means characteristic of a cellular society (one with strong barriers between one state and the next) where transnational factors therefore played little part. Warfare was generally regarded as the most normal means of promoting state ends, but it was usually limited warfare for limited ends. Diplomacy, alliances, secret understandings, all had their part to play. And since state power now depended partly on economic relationships, economic threats and inducements represented a new addition to the range of instruments. Whatever means were adopted, since there were few clearly recognized rules, unscrupulousness in their use was not uncommon, and not necessarily even against the rules. The means of Realpolitik began to be developed.

## 8.6 The Age of Nationalism (1789–1914)

The means pursued in the age of nationalism again reflected the changed character of a new age.

The ultimate weapon available was still armed power. To win nationhood for Greece, Egypt, Bulgaria, and other new states, to win national unity for Italy and Germany, to win national glory for every major power in their competition with each other, it was armed force that was mainly needed. Nationalism implied above all competition. And it was assumed everywhere that in the final resort the competition might need to be resolved by force of arms. When Bismarck declared that it was not by speeches and resolutions but by blood and iron that the great issues of the day would be decided, when his fellow countryman, Clausewitz, declared that war was merely the continuation of policy by other means, they only expressed, in somewhat cruder terms, what most statesmen of the day secretly believed.

But force was used, if at all, in a different way: not for suddenly conceived military adventures, with a new ally each time, but for a planned program of national advancement. Disraeli recounted his astonishment at hearing Bismarck,

40. Ibid., 178.
41. Ibid., V (1961): 208.
42. Ibid.

not long after he became chancellor, outline in some detail his plans for a forthcoming series of wars against Denmark, Austria, and France; which duly followed in the succeeding years. Cavour planned in cold blood, in secret conclave with Napoleon III in July 1858, the war which was to win Italian unity from Austria in the following year. Japan launched successive onslaughts on China and Russia, without the formality of a declaration of war or even any serious pretext, to assert her birth as a modern nation. Serbia and Bulgaria in turn launched onslaughts on the other in 1885 and 1913 without any real provocation other than mutual jealousy and growing nationalism. Sometimes nationalism provoked the use of force by reaction: Austria in 1914 determined to have her war to stamp out Slav nationalism and refused to be deterred even when Serbia gave way to almost every demand she made. Though war was less frequent, on occasion military assaults as brazen as any of previous ages were still used as the means of satisfying the all-consuming drives of nationalism.

Even now, limited war was still usually the instrument employed. Apart from the two great holocausts which began and ended the period, every war was fought for a relatively restricted objective and involved only two or three powers. Nationalism dictated its own limitations. Concessions claimed from the defeated powers were nearly always relatively modest: Prussia and Austria took no ethnically Danish territory in 1864; Prussia took no Austrian territory at all in 1866. After the Crimean War the victorious Western powers did not demand territorial acquisitions from Russia. Napoleon III, alarmed at his own success against Austria, insisted on handing back to her half of what he had already won. In most cases only sufficient force was used to attain essential national objectives.

Another means characteristic of the age was the *ultimatum*. This might be used as a threat, itself sufficient to secure the concessions demanded, or it could be used simply as a provocation, equivalent to throwing down the gauntlet, in expectation of a refusal which would provide the justification for war. This was probably the case with the ultimatum issued by Japan against Russia in 1904, when she did not await the Russian reply before attacking; and it was certainly the case with the Italian ultimatum to Turkey in 1911, when the latter country was not even given time to reply if she wished to do so. Sometimes the threat was *private*, as when France threatened Austria in 1866 that, if she was not awarded Venetia, she might join Prussia against Austria.

Similar in effect was the *demonstration,* often by naval forces, which was equally popular among certain powers. It was used often by Britain against Russia, usually by sending a fleet to Bezika Bay; it was used by Britain and France against Egypt in 1882; by Britain and Germany against Venezuela in 1902 (to insure the settlement of a debt); and it was even used by the powers collectively, or by one or two nations on behalf of the powers, especially in the Balkans or against China (see p. 000 below). Both the ultimatum and the demonstration were methods of singular crudity, the equivalent of the gunman's stickup. Though there was somewhat greater concern for appearances than in earlier ages (shown, for example, in the desire to provoke others to war rather than declare it [see p. 302]), the age of nationalism had little more compunction than its predecessor about the methods it employed.

A modified form of ultimatum was the act of *mobilization* (again typical of this period alone). It resulted from changes in military technology: the adoption of conscript armies, the believed importance of the first battle, the use of large numbers in land warfare, and the necessity of speed in their deployment. Since wars were sometimes finished in a matter of weeks (the 1866 war between Prussia and Austria was over in three weeks, and most of the fighting in 1870 in little more), it was essential to be able to put armies in the field in the shortest possible space of time. As a weapon for persuasion, however, mobilization often had the opposite effect to that intended. Instead of a threat that a power *might* make war, it was taken as a sign that it *would* do so. It thus only precipitated countermobilization or even attack by the other side. In both cases a complicated series of operations was set in motion which was almost impossible to halt, since any slowing down of the process could lead to a serious military disadvantage. A race would begin in which every participant, while not necessarily desiring war itself, might feel the necessity to act first to prevent a certain victory for the other party—a danger which was conclusively demonstrated in 1914.

Another means promoted by an age of nationalism was *intervention* in neighboring states. This might be necessary to assist a national revolution, as in the intervention of Russia on behalf of Greece in 1829 and of Serbia in 1877. Or it might be required to *prevent* national revolutions, as in the intervention of Russia in Hungary in 1849 or of Austria on many occasions in Italy. Or intervention, while justified on the grounds of restoring "law and order," might be designed to promote national interests in a sensitive area, as was British intervention in Egypt in 1882 or French in Morocco in 1910. Or intervention might take place to counter the believed activities of rival powers, like British and Russian intervention in Persia and China, or that of Austria and Russia in the Balkans. In a society in which half a dozen powers were of overwhelming strength in relation to the rest, and most of the others in a situation of helpless weakness, it was sometimes convenient that the competition of the former was fought out in the territory of the latter.

Somewhat less coercive were the purely political means by which this competition could be conducted. A perpetual struggle took place for *influence* by the greater states over the lesser. We have seen how new types of relationship—the protectorate, the sphere of influence, the client state—were developed to assist the larger powers in this competition (p. 220). Political agents, advisers, and military attaches supplemented the normal diplomatic staff in achieving this objective. Even the consular system was adapted to the purpose: Russia had large numbers of consulates in remote parts of the Balkans, where they had a minor role to play in stamping passports or protecting traders, while Britain had "consulates" in Chinese Turkeston and other areas where there were no British subjects whatever, but acute concern to watch for Russian infiltration toward India. In other cases consulates were overtly military in purpose: under the Treaty of Paris, Britain and France obtained the right to place consulates in the Black Sea ports to supervise

Russian disarmament and demilitarization in that sea, and in 1878 Britain obtained the right to establish "military consuls" in Anatolia to enable her to fulfill the guarantee she then gave to Turkey (they were withdrawn by Gladstone in 1881). Similarly, railway concessions, leases and settlements, and positions of commercial, or financial preeminence could be used to promote purposes that were political and strategic as much as purely commercial.

The alliance system was also transformed. In the early part of the period alliances remained, as they had been in the previous century, essentially temporary arrangements for mutual convenience which perpetually shifted according to circumstances. This remained the situation until 1871. Between 1866 and 1870, for example, France tried for an understanding with every other great power in turn, and failed with all of them. Because almost every power had differences with every other in one part of Europe or another, even temporary alliances were difficult to arrange in this period. But after the Franco-Prussian war more stable groupings began to emerge. Now Germany and France were inevitably ranged on opposite sides, while Germany and Austria, their differences concluded, were likely to be together. Eventually Russia and France came together, and Britain, through fear of Germany, finally sank her traditional hostility to each to join them. So the opportunistic alliance was replaced by the long-term national alliance. The terms of the alliances were often secret; they were complicated and always highly qualified. But even where there was no clear-cut commitment at all (as in the case of Britain's arrangements), they created a relatively distinct alignment within the society, of a permanence which had never previously existed. Their importance was symbolic rather than literal: in July 1914 virtually none of the powers of Europe were committed, under the precise terms of their alliances, to go to war in the circumstances that arose, but they were under a strong moral and political obligation to support those with whom they had associated themselves. Here again the emotions of nationalism affected the means employed. Rivalries between particular nations—between France and Germany, Russia and Austria, Germany and Britain—provided an emotional basis for a commitment which was often more important than the terms of the alliances themselves. Germany did not have to support Austria; she wanted to. Russia did not have to support Serbia; she wanted to. In such a society a crisis becomes not a threat but an opportunity.

Another means emerging was the *purchase* of substantial areas of territory, a practice distinctive to this society. The purchase of Louisiana from France by the U.S. in 1803, followed by that of Florida from Spain in 1819 and that of Alaska from Russia in 1867, are examples. In 1867 France attempted to purchase Luxembourg from the Netherlands but was prevented by Prussian objections. While the motive involved, territorial acquisition, was common in earlier ages, the means were adapted to the prevailing commercial culture of the age. Even here the national principle was at work, in that the purchases were usually for the purpose of territorial consolidation rather than random aggrandizement.

So here too the means employed reflected the preoccupations of the age. They were those appropriate for promoting the political, strategic, and commercial purposes and interests of national states rather than of individual rulers. Sometimes this could be done by mutual accommodation, in the new institutions devised for this purpose (pp. 329–334 below). But because nationalism was by its very nature highly competitive, those means were often ruthless and brutal. Nationalism became not merely an incentive, but a justification for such brutality—the glory and honor of the nation became adequate cause for calling on millions to sacrifice their lives. And the power of nationalism was such that, in such a cause, those millions were often only too glad to do so.

## 8.7 The Age of Ideology (1914–1974)

The means appropriate to a society concerned primarily with political ideology were inevitably different. Since the main object was no longer territorial conquest but ideological expansion, victory for a political belief rather than for a nation, new strategies and techniques had to be evolved.

The clearest change is the increasing recourse to indirect, rather than direct, methods of winning control or influence in other countries. The declining concern for territory, increasing concern for hearts and minds, the higher costs of full-scale warfare, meant that more subtle methods must now replace the old-fashioned war of conquest. So the organization of coups in foreign countries, assistance to one faction in a civil war, aid to revolutionary forces, subversion of every kind, become the typical means employed. This gives birth to new instruments, more appropriate to such aims: the CIA, the Comintern, international political organizations, "fronts," propaganda machines. The "fifth column," the organized party loyal to a foreign state and its beliefs and acting to promote the interests of that state, is perhaps the most typical manifestation of this trend.

External intervention in civil war is seen over and over again: in the Russian civil war, perhaps the most important ideological contest of the age, in the Spanish, Greek, Lebanese, Yemen, Nigerian, and the three Indo-China civil wars. The assistance given may take the form of supplying arms (as in Nigeria); providing sanctuary for guerrillas (as in Greece); sending "volunteers" (as in Korea and the Congo); or "advisers" (as in Vietnam); or even large-scale military forces (as in the Russian civil war, or as used by Egypt in Yemen). Coups inspired or supported from outside are seen in Czechoslovakia, Guatemala, Laos (several times), South Vietnam, the Congo, and other places. All these show how easily an external power can win or regain domination in another country, at little cost to itself and with small visible involvement. Conversely, emphasis on counterinsurgency, training and equipment of police and internal security forces, and large-scale economic aid, demonstrates changes in defensive strategy in an era of civil war.

Because indirect methods of this kind may often secure the type of influence or control that is mainly desired, outright annexation of territory becomes rare (except in a special case such as the Middle East). Setting up puppet governments becomes a simpler and more acceptable method of winning control. The pattern for these is set by the governments established by Japan, first in Manchuria, then in China, Indonesia, and other conquered territories, and by Germany, first in Slovakia and later in other parts of Europe. After 1945 the regimes of Eastern Europe, largely installed by the Soviet Union and subsequently extensively purged by her, have little greater independence from their patron. In Central America a somewhat looser control is maintained. Although the governments retain a general freedom in their internal affairs, in foreign policy they must conform with certain known conditions: They may not, for example, purchase arms from communist countries, as the government of Guatemala found in 1954.

An extension of the use of dependent governments of this kind is the proclamation of "doctrines": the Truman, Eisenhower, and Brezhnev doctrines are all designed as a means of preventing the establishment of governments of hostile ideology in areas of strategic concern to a major power. Policies of "containment" are designed to impose a political barricade against hostile ideologies, just as the "cordon sanitaire" was designed to do between the wars.[43] In an ideological age the means of defense, as well as of attack, need to be changed.

The time-honored means of the alliance now becomes largely ideological in aim and composition. Thus, between the wars, Germany, Italy, and Japan, whose only genuine common interest is their opposition to communism, are able to come together in the anti-Comintern Pact. Conversely, the Soviet Union and the Western powers, who have an overriding common interest in a common front against Germany, are *unable* in 1938–1939 to reach an alliance because of mutual ideological suspicions. In the postwar world alliances are formed even more clearly on an ideological basis. Ideological fears and sympathies dictate the formation and composition of the Atlantic and Warsaw pacts. Almost every state begins to be drawn into such groupings. While in the interwar period there remained a number of mavericks in Europe—Poland, Italy, the Little Entente countries, and others who might equally well link themselves with any major power—after World War II virtually the whole of Europe is firmly aligned in one of the major blocs according to their political viewpoint. Indeed, in the 1950s most of the states of the world are associated directly or indirectly with the Western or communist powers. Even regional organizations, such as the OAS or the Council of Europe, become linked implicitly or explicitly with a particular type of political belief.

A major feature of the age is reliance on limited means. This reflects greater awareness of the dangers of unlimited war, together with a widespread willingness to accept the territorial status quo. Thus, apart from the two world wars, all the conflicts of the age are restricted, both in weapons employed and in geographical

43. "Containment" is in a sense the mirror image of the concept of "capitalist encirclement": each describes the same phenomenon in essentially subjective terms. The former presupposes that the object contained is itself dynamic and expanding and so must be held in; the latter assumes it is passive and peaceful, and that the surrounding forces are themselves the major threat to stability.

areas covered. Most are deliberately confined to the borders of a single state. In Korea and Indo-China, for example, there is explicit restriction of this kind, despite the large-scale involvement of external powers. Wars are also limited in the caliber of weapons employed. There exist in this age, for the first time, an entire range of weapons—not only nuclear weapons, but strategic missiles, gas, bacteriological weapons, lasers, and others—which are considered too powerful and dangerous to use. Thus in practice it is now the balance of *conventional* forces on the spot which determines events, as shown, for example, in Cuba and Vietnam.

A means particularly appropriate to an age of ideological conflict is the use of propaganda. Foreign radio broadcasts, embassy press sections, news releases, and news management, among other means, are used to promote particular beliefs and to counter those of others, both at home and abroad. In some countries ministries of propaganda are even established. Governments become almost as concerned about verbal conflicts of this kind as they have traditionally been with military struggles. Diplomacy becomes as closely involved with winning friends and influencing people as with the traditional tasks of negotiating with foreign governments. Negotiation, indeed, as in the age of religions, becomes difficult or impossible at the height of the ideological conflict because of mutual distrust and lack of communication. Thus the U.S. had no diplomatic contacts with the Soviet Union for sixteen years, or with Communist China for twenty-three years, after new governments were established there. During the 1950s proposals for summit meetings, or for negotiations with the Soviet Union on the Middle East, are widely regarded as a form of treachery. In many cases governments are more concerned with speaking over the heads of other governments to populations all over the world than they are with meaningful dialogue in intergovernmental conferences.

Again, therefore, new means arise, more appropriate to the currently adopted ends. Some of these are influenced by the special technological and social conditions of the age—mass communications, the establishment of international political movements and organizations, the increased power of new weapons. Together these lead to a lesser reliance on purely coercive means, greater resort to persuasion and negotiation. Others arise because this is an ideological age and the means resemble those used in earlier ideological ages: propaganda, the organization of coups abroad, intervention in civil wars, establishment of ideological alliances, and so on. Once again, even more than technical advance, it is the underlying character of the age which determines the character of the means employed.

In general, a wide variety of means were employed in these various international societies.

To some extent the variations followed automatically from changes of other kinds. Developments in technology, for instance, altered the *available* means. Thus the development of radio, television, and other means of communication has made propaganda a far more easily applied technique in modern times than it ever was before. Sometimes social changes have brought shifts in the balance of means employed. The development of a commercial society and the doctrines of mercantilism, for example, encouraged the idea of purchasing territory for cash and the demand for indemnity as the peantly for losing a war.

In other cases, as we saw, changes in *motivation* automatically brought changes in the instruments chosen: for example, the goals of the age of dynasties dictated the use of a dynastic marriage or the inheritance pact, means which played little part in most other societies. The aims of idoloogical ages have dictated greater emphasis on conversion and propaganda and on efforts to bring about internal changes, such as a change of government or ruler, rather than territorial change.

But there may be a change of means without any change of goal. Quite often alternative means are available to pursue similar ends. Thus national status may be sought by the building of palaces in an age of sovereigns, by the building of armies and navies in the age of nationalism, and by the building of space vehicles and better football teams in the modern age. Here the end is the same, but the means reflect differing attitudes and values within each society. In each case the means chosen will, however, in turn influence the character and image of the society.

Again what may originally be desired as a means (such as armed power) may, as we saw, eventually be desired as an end in itself. Decision makers themselves may not be clear in which capacity it is sought—a large army appears first a means of defense and becomes almost an objective in itself (Germany before 1914 and Iran today). In other words we find here, as in smaller societies, that means and ends interact with each other in a complex way. Both represent parts of the social fabric as a whole; both help to make up the special feel, texture, and character of a particular society. Just as the institutions of religion, marriage, or tribe may have quite a different form in different types of domestic society, and perhaps perform quite different functions, so in different international societies such means as the alliance, diplomacy, or war may perform a different social role according to the general configuration and spirit of the age.

Even in the same society, *some* alternative means are available for obtaining essentially similar aims; for example, warlike or peaceful, intrigue or bluster, negotiation or coercion, manipulation or deceit. The choice made by one state will often depend on that commonly made by others; in other words, on the character and example of the age as a whole. The choice of means, like that of motives, therefore depends to a considerable extent on the expectations and values of the society in which the choice is made: that is, on the nature of the underlying ideology.

# Chapter 9.  Stratification

One of the factors which sociologists have been most concerned to study in examining domestic societies has been the system of stratification, or class structure, established within them: the hierarchies of authority, wealth, or status established, and the way these are maintained. In examining international societies, similarly, it is useful to look at the different types of stratification among states that have been maintained in different ages.

An international society is of course much smaller in the total number of its members (states) than domestic societies in the number of their members (individuals). But similar tendencies occur. In each case certain members may become more powerful, wealthy, influential than others. Groups of privileged and underprivileged will arise within them. Such groups are not necessarily "classes" in the sense of being linked by a clear common interest against the rest. The powerful within states, as between them, may be in rivalry with each other more than they are with the less powerful. They may each form their own group of supporters from among less powerful adherents, who may secure protection or other benefits in return for their support. In this case the links may be vertical, as in a feudal society, rather than lateral, as in modern states (between all those of a similar economic level).

Sociologists, in discussing domestic societies, compare different types of stratification. If there are large disparities in wealth and way of life between different sections of the community we may call it a highly stratified society. Similarly, in international societies there may be very large absolute differences between the extremes of power (as in the modern world between superpowers and ministates); in other types of society all may be relatively equal in power and influence. Among international societies this contrast may be seen in ancient China and ancient Greece in their early days. Again, in domestic societies stratification may be abrupt rather than extreme; there may be a number of sharply defined classes, perhaps enjoying quite different status, even though the differences in wealth or way of life may not necessarily be very great (as under the caste system in India). Again, something similar is at least theoretically possible in international societies, where there may be clear distinctions between the "powers" and the rest, between nuclear and nonnuclear powers, permanent and nonpermanent members of the Security Council, whether or not absolute differences in power are great.

But perhaps more important than these differences in degree of stratification are differences in type. Domestic societies may vary greatly in the way status is measured: for example, in the number of cattle owned, or the number of blankets burnt, in wealth or in power, in birth or profession, artistic achievement or sporting ability, in beauty of person or beauty of character. International societies may vary in the same way. There are some ages (indeed, the majority) in which success in war is seen as the chief mark of status: "great power" has usually referred to those who could defeat others in armed combat (so, Turkey and China in the nineteenth century, though large in numbers, were not great powers). There are other eras, such as the modern age, in which economic success, a high standard of living or a high growth rate are seen as equally important (so Japan acquires high status with little military power). There are others, as in ancient Greece, in which the artistic achievement of a state was of some significance (so Sparta might defeat Athens in the Peloponnesian war, but it could not boast the sculptors, writers, and philosophers who won prestige for Athens).

It is evident that there must be some relationship between underlying ideology and the nature of status. In a dynastic society dynastic success will bring status almost by definition; in a territorial age, such as ancient China, acquisition of territory equally will bring prestige. But the relationship is not always simple. For example, in an age of ideology a nation that is ideologically successful, in the sense of spreading its own ideology among other states, may win status among those who share that ideology (as Spain did among Catholics in the early seventeenth century, or the Soviet Union among communists today), but may be reviled among those who uphold the opposite ideology. In such situations the nations which enjoy status in one part of the society may enjoy obloquy in another.

In international societies, moreover, status is usually less explicit than in domestic society. There are no formal ranks—such as the ranks of the nobility—which explicitly mark out those who enjoy status. It is easy to distinguish a large power from a small power, or a militarily successful one from one that is defeated. But it is not necessarily easy to say exactly who enjoys status in any other sense within each society. If capacity to conquer is the test, how shall one judge the state that never makes war? What is the status of Switzerland, for example, in the nineteenth century, or of Sweden today? Moreover, a country may win status in one field but not in another: A nation that scores well in terms of military power may score badly in terms of general civilization or culture (like the Ottoman Empire in the age of dynasties); a nation may perform well in terms of culture or standard of living, but poorly in warfare (China in the nineteenth century). In other words, there may be different types of status which can exist side by side in the same society.

We shall seek in this chapter to explore the various forms of status and of stratification which have prevailed in different international societies of the past. And we shall seek, then, to consider their relationship to the underlying ideology of the age.

# 9.1 The Chinese Multistate System (771–221 B.C.)

The Chinese multistate system, because of the very large numbers of member states in the early years and the wide disparities in size among them, was highly inegalitarian in structure.

Mencius makes distinctions in status among the states according to the number of li (leagues) they controlled, in other words, their area (this was, of course, a somewhat inaccurate measure of their power). He reckoned states of 100 li square to be big powers, those of 70 li square to be middle-sized states, and those of less than 50 li to be scarcely states at all, but in most cases dependencies.[1] This was a highly theoretical schema and Mencius himself admitted he was referring to the past rather than to the structure of states existing in his own age. But it gives some indication of the varieties in size and power among members of that society. This remained characteristic of it almost to the end.

A few of the medium states, such as Lu, Sung, and the three portions into which Chin was ultimately split, managed to retain their independence until a comparatively late stage, whether as a result of natural strength, skillful diplomacy, geographical remoteness (as in the case of Yen), or other reasons. But in general the smaller states were progressively swallowed by the larger. This in a sense brought an increasing *equalization* of power by the elimination of the very small. The seven states remaining in the Warring States period were able to compete on relatively equal terms for a century and a half. It was only in the last ten years of the period that the last six states were finally gobbled up and the member-states reduced to one (in other words the society ceased to exist).

At the head of the structure were usually three or four very powerful states largely dominating the system. The only two which retained this position from the beginning to the end were Ch'i and Ch'u. Ch'in in the west, the ultimate conqueror of all, only emerged as a great power in about the sixth century; Wu and Yueh in the southeast attained prominence for a relatively brief period between 522 and 450. Chin in the northwest was the leading state of all between 640 and 510, though it was in almost perpetual conflict during this time either with Ch'u or Ch'i. None of these powers were seeking, for the most of this time, conquest of all other states; the permanent occupation and administration of the entire area would have been, at any time before the Ch'in conquest, an extremely difficult task, probably beyond the capacities of any state. They did seek dominance in their own areas, and so they came perpetually into conflict in the marginal regions, especially the upper reaches of the Hwai Valley, where their domains came into contact. These then were the great magnates of the society.

Below these there was a larger number, perhaps a dozen or so, medium-sized states for whose allegiance and alliance the larger states often competed. These included Wei, Ts'ao, Ts'ai, Sung, Ch'en, Lu, Shi, Cheng, T'ang, Yu, Kuo,

---

1. *The Works of Mencius*, V, II, 4.

Liang, Sui, and Yen. The alliance policies of these states were sometimes determined by their geographical position: those in the sphere of indluence of Ch'u and
Ch'i were usually likely to ally themselves with those states. Nonetheless, the
middle-sized states showed themselves in many ways resentful of the dominance
enjoyed by the magnates, and in some cases acted to counteract this. They were
particularly jealous of their own independence. The "states of secondary magni-
tude ... insisted on certain sovereign rights and especially in the Chou area
tolerated little interference by the great powers in their relations with each other."[2]

There was another hierarchy of states that was independent of levels of power.
Originally states were graded according to the rank of their ruler: duke, marquis,
earl, viscount, or baron. This was the order in which in the early days they enjoyed
precedence at conferences and similar occasions. Among the Chou states, Lu and
Wei secured a special status because of the descent of their princes from the royal
Chou house, and could use it to their advantage in relation to other states. But from
about 680 onward states were ranked at conferences only according to their power
position, the larger and more important having precedence. From this order it
becomes possible to obtain a fairly clear idea of the status accorded to different
states. In some cases the smaller states became so dependent that they were not
acknowledged as equals by the others: At the big conference among most of the
states held in 546, Chu and Tang, which were then dependencies of Ch'i and Sung
respectively, were not even permitted to sign the treaty.

There were other distinctions which were important. The genuinely Chinese
states felt a considerable cultural superiority to the barbarian and semi barbarian
states on the periphery. Some of the latter became relatively quickly assimilated
and fully accepted as members of the system; for example, Chin was not one of the
early Chou states, but eventually led the northern league. Ch'u, living far further to
the south and probably with a smaller admixture of Chinese culture and Chinese
blood, remained a more alien power, as did Wu, Yueh, and Ch'in for the same
reason. Beyond these states were the genuinely barbarian, often nomadic peoples,
such as the Ti, Jung, Yi, and Hui.

The supreme mark of status for any of the states was to become hegemon (pa).
This was a position occupied in turn by Ch'i, Sung, Chin, Wu, and other states.
Because the hegemon assumed some of the perogatives of the Chou monarchy, it
acquired some of the status and dignity associated with that monarchy.[3] The
hegemon was able to convoke meetings of the league, direct most of its policies,
secure tribute, and became known as the President of Covenants. The hegemon
"arrogated to himself in practice nearly all the powers and functions of the king.
He repelled invasions and directed punitive expeditions, acted as arbiter of differences between feudal rulers, punished those who disobeyed the orders and re-

2. R. L. Walker, *The Multi-State System in Ancient China* (Hamden, 1953), p. 38.

3. The system was described by Legge as "the system of one such state taking the lead and direction
of all the others and exercising really royal functions throughout the kingdom, while yet there was a
profession of loyal attachment to the House of Chou" (J. Legge, *The Chinese Classics*, V [Oxford,
1893], 114). As he points out, Ch'i and Chin were "fully acknowledged as directors and controllers of
the states generally by the court of Chou."

ceived the revenues which had formerly gone to the king."[4] Leadership "was exercised by a mixture of the authority of the ancient royal titles and the fear of the armed force that could be used against allies who defected."[5] Ch'u also held a certain prestige as leader of her own alliance in the south, though in this case leadership was not associated with the ancient dignity of the Chou royal title and the relationship of the smaller states was one of more immediate subjection. In this society, then, there was a form of leadership much more *explicit* than in many other international societies—more so than that exercised by superpowers today, for example.

These forms of political status were, as in other ages, associated with economic advantages or liabilities. The dominance of the hegemon was expressed in demands for tribute. This was not usually directly exploitative in character. Tribute was the result and not the cause of domination; it was desired largely for symbolic purposes. Nonetheless it could represent a considerable hardship for smaller states, many of which had to pay tribute both to the Chou kings and to the hegemon of the day, and occasionally to some other dominant powers as well.[6] In the *Ts'o Ch'uan,* Tz'e ch'an of Ch'ing complains that

> formerly the sons of heaven regulated the amount of contributions according to the rank of the state. Ch'ing ranks as the territory of an earl or a baron, and yet its contribution is now on the scale of a duke or a marquis. There is no regular rule for what we have to pay, and when a small state fails in rendering what is required, it is held to be an offender. When our contributions and offerings have no limit set to them we have only to wait for our ruin.[7]

Finally, at the foot of the pyramid, there were many small states, usually in various forms of dependence. There were the so-called attached or dependent states (Fu'yung), usually fairly small in size (Mencius said they were originally less than 50 li). The ruler would not have direct access to the Chou court (for what that was worth) and they had virtually no independent conduct of foreign affairs. Next, there were colonies (shu) that were directly ruled by the conquering state, but not assimilated to their own territory. A still lower order were the states which had been totally conquered and "extinguished." Even these sometimes retained some degree of administrative autonomy, or at least retained their names as provinces of the larger state. Finally there were the extinguished states which had lost any kind of independent identity at all.[8]

This was a society, therefore, in which there was, for much of the time, a very wide spectrum of power between the largest and the smallest. Differences of status

4. H. G. Creel, *The Birth of China* (London, 1936), p. 244.

5. J. Legge, *Chinese Classics,* V, 116.

6. Ibid., 116.

7. *Ts'o Ch'uan,* XIII, V, 6.

8. The barbarian peoples were also sometimes brought into various kinds of subjection. It is known that the Huei and the Yi sometimes paid tribute to the Chou king. There are references to "revolting" barbarian tribes, which suggest that they were sometimes more directly ruled, for example, by a Chinese governor with his own armed forces.

were expressed in certain overt forms, such as in the rules of precedence at conferences. There are frequent references to the relative power of states, as expressed in the extent of their territory or the numbers of their chariots or horses. These reveal a keen awareness of the divergences in power and authority of the different states or rulers and strong mutual competition for status. The sharp consciousness of hierarchy within states was thus reflected at the international level. No wonder that Duke Wan of T'ang said to Mencius, "T'ang is only a small kingdom; I do my utmost to serve the larger kingdoms on either side of it, but we cannot escape suffering from them."[9] The force at the disposal of the large states ultimately became the determinant of the positions held by states. Status was increasingly measured in terms of the power attributed to each.

## 9.2 The Greek City-States (600–338 B.C.)

The Greek international society was also clearly stratified. It, too, had its great magnates, Sparta, Athens, Thebes, above all Persia; its middle class, Corinth, Argos, Corcyra, Thessaly, and Syracuse; and its common people, the very many small, weak cities of the mainland, Ionia, and Sicily, which remained always dependent on the goodwill and support of the major powers.

The most dominant force of all, though only marginally a member of the society, was Persia. The Persian king and his satraps sought to assert this predominance by demanding a clear-cut act of submission of the Greek states, especially in Asia Minor. The symbolic act of deference demanded was the traditional ceremony of presenting earth and water. Successive peace terms were designed to secure recognition of Persian hegemony in Asia Minor, as in the agreement negotiated with Sparta in the Peleponnesian War, and in the King's Peace of 386. There were only relatively brief periods during the fifth and fourth centuries when first Athens and later Sparta seriously resisted this claim. The name widely accorded to the Persian king, the Great King, as well as the widespread practice of "medism" (acceptance of Persian sovereignty), and the readiness of even Athens and Sparta to seek the Persian alliance where possible, is an indication of the dominant place widely accorded to Persia within the society.

Among the Greek states the considerable dominance of Sparta and Athens was more immediate and was marked in a number of ways. The position of hegemony they enjoyed within their two alliances was not unlike that enjoyed by league leaders within the Chinese system. In those alliances they called the meetings and proposed the actions. Since their assent to a decision had to be given separately from that of the other members, their judgment was given equal weight with that of all the others together (which decided by majority vote). They normally enjoyed supreme command in the field. And in practice they came, at least in the case of

9. *Mencius,* I(Part II), XV, 1.

Athens, to demand a more sweeping submission—no ally was free to pursue a policy unacceptable to her. When Phasos refused to concede to her a share in her possessions in the Thracian coast in 455, Athens reduced her by force, compelled her to join the league, and made her surrender her fleet and give up her mainland possessions to Athens. When Samos refused to accept Athenian arbitration in 439, she was treated in similar fashion. Mytilene and Melos were forced into total subjection in the same way during the Peleponnesian War. Though Sparta did not treat her allies in quite such dictatorial fashion, she too demanded a considerable degree of compliance among the Peleponnesian states, and struck repeated blows at her most powerful neighbor, Argos, which refused to join her alliance. In general, therefore, the middle-sized and small states were expected to show to the superpowers at best deference, and at worst submission.

*Between* Athens and Sparta there was also a struggle for precedence and for leadership of the Greeks generally. Thucydides declared that Sparta's preeminence was generally acknowledged before the Persian War, but came to be contested by Athens after that war, and that it was the dominance Athens came to enjoy by the middle of the century that provoked Sparta to join in war against her. Here too there was a symbolic sign of preeminence: the right to consult first the Delphic oracle. This was demanded and taken by each great power in turn as it secured dominance and acquired control of Delphi: by Athens in 451, Sparta in 449, Athens in 447, Sparta in 404, and Thebes in 361. More subtle forms of symbolism were found. Just as Sparta had sought to show her right to leadership of the Peleponnesian states by acquiring the sacred relics of Orestes, so Athens sought to acquire divine authority for her hegemony by claiming the bones of Theseus, said to have been discovered at Scyros. These were the typical forms of status competition, comparable to competitive palace-building in the eighteenth century, competitive colonialism in the nineteenth, or competitive space programs in the twentieth. Certainly in the minds of ordinary Greeks there was no doubt that Athens and Sparta were engaged in a competition to be the acknowledged top dog of Greece.

The middle-sized powers, though they needed to be circumspect in their relations with the superpowers, often exercised a domination of their own in relation to smaller states. In some cases this consisted in a dominion of the area surrounding their own cities. Thebes made herself in this way the center and dominant force within the Boeotian federation. Argos controlled Argolis, and occasionally had to reassert her power there; Syracuse eventually dominated Sicily. In other cases middle-sized powers extended their influence through their colonies: Chalcis, Corinth, Argos, Athens, and other states won not only prestige but political influence through their settlements in other remote parts of the Greek world, even when those colonies had made themselves to a large extent independent. So colonialism, here as in Europe 2,000 years later, was partly a means of winning status.

Finally, there were many very small states which were always under the domination of those larger than themselves, and therefore required to conduct their foreign policy with considerable skill if they were to retain any independence at all. In some cases these small states would find it advantageous to seek the support of a distant superpower against a neighboring major power. Being more distant, the former were less likely to be a major constraint on their own policy. Thus Plataea welcomed Athenian help against Thebes, just as Mycenaea welcomed Spartan help against Argos and Tegea sought the aid of more distant Argos against Sparta. Megara skillfully used its strategic position to balance Athens and Corinth against each other. Occasionally painful conflicts of loyalty arose, as when in 431 Potidea had to try to balance allegiance to its mother country, Corinth, against allegiance to its league leader, Athens, and when Corcyra at about the same time had to decide between Corinth as a mother country and as a commercial rival.

Domination often took economic as well as political form. Athens in particular used her military supremacy to obtain trade preferences or monopolies. She secured tribute, reparations, rents, and spoils of war. These exactions aroused considerable resentment. Thucydides records that "the Athenians insisted on obligations being exactly met, and made themselves unpopular by bringing the severest pressure to bear on their allies, who were not used to making sacrifices and did not want to make them."[10] The argument, used by Pericles, that such tribute was payment for protection provided by Athens against common enemies was not one that appealed much to the states which paid it, any more than did the similar argument used by colonial powers over the last century. One of the reasons given by Thucydides for the determination of many Athenians to pursue the Peleponnesian War to the bitter end, after the great disaster in Sicily, was reluctance to lose the economic advantages of the tribute.

Domination could also bring trade benefits, preferences, or even monopolies. Moreover, once a powerful trading position had been built up, something like an economic stranglehold could be used to win political advantages by applying boycotts or embargoes. The decree issued by Athens in 443 against Megara was precisely such an attempt to make use of economic pressures for political purposes. These material benefits however had to be weighed against the loss of prestige and good name which such methods incurred.

Thus stratification of a number of kinds—military, political, economic— became more pronounced among the Greek states as time went on. But here, more than in China, factors other than military power were used as a measure of status. Cultural differences were important. Many compared the superb cultural achievements of Athens in the fields of philosophy, drama, sculpture, and fine buildings with the cultural impoverishment of Sparta. As in the modern international society, economic differences were highly significant. Not only did many admire the high standard of living achieved in Athens, Corinth, and other wealthy cities, but from these differences in other spheres, such as the military and the cultural, largely followed. The glory which Athens achieved, both in the eyes of her contemporaries and of history, despite the brutal imperialism of her external

10. Thucydides, *The Peloponnesian War*, I, 98.

policies, was ultimately the effect of the success of her merchant class in establishing her prosperity. Above all ideology here affected status: an oligarchic state such as Sparta might rank high among the oligarchic states, yet be reviled by democrats.

This then was a complex class structure evolving in a complex society, where external, non-Greek powers always held a powerful but peripheral role. The ideological character of the society influenced the nature of all relationships. Athens and Sparta acquired their prestige partly as the leaders of the democratic and oligarchic forces respectively. Thus the respect in which they were held by others (like that of ideological superpowers today) varied according to the ideology of those other states. Yet in the final resort the respect in which such powers were held depended not only on the force of which they could dispose but the use to which it was put: Athens won power but not respect from her dominance in the second half of the fifth century, while Sparta at that time enjoyed both. At the beginning of the fourth century their roles were reversed and Sparta in turn forfeited the respect of public opinion by her abuse of power.

Thus status depended on a complex of factors. But ideology here affected and marginally modified the effect of a stratification determined ultimately by power.

## 9.3 The Age of Dynasties (1300–1559)

The class system established in the international society of Europe from the fourteenth to sixteenth centuries reflected a wholly different world view. Status here, reflecting the ideology of the age, depended above all on dynastic glory.

This glory could be measured in a number of ways. In a crude sense it could be measured by the number of territories and peoples ruled. The intensive competition engaged in for new dominions is itself perhaps the clearest evidence of the importance of this as a status symbol. The delight of kings in styling themselves as rulers of long lists of territories reveals the same concern. Glory was measured to some extent in the sumptuousness and extravagance of royal display, the size of palaces, and the style of entertainment of guests. It was widely judged, especially in popular estimation, by success at arms: England rose highly in the eyes of Europe from her successes at Crecy, Poitiers, and Agincourt, and again briefly from the capture of Tournai a century later, but she lost face heavily from her humiliating eviction from France in 1450 and her failures in the wars of the 1540s. Francois I won huge renown at Marignano, and lost it again at Pavia ten years later. It was the success of his troops, as much as the size of his empire, which brought renown to Charles V's Spain. And so on.

The strength of a dynasty abroad also depended partly on its strength at home. Relative power depended during much of this age not so much on resources or population as on dynasty's success in securing order and centralizing power in its own hands.[11] The fact that for nearly a hundred years England was able to succeed militarily against France, despite being weaker in resources and having only a third of the population, resulted largely from this strength. When, in the second half of the sixteenth century, the French monarchy became stronger at home and the English monarchy was beset by civil conflict, the roles were reversed. When toward the end of that century Spain finally achieved unity and her kings total domination over the nobility there, she began to acquire greatness abroad as well. In central Europe as well, the relative power of the rulers depended on their successes in overcoming their own magnates at home: Bohemia was powerful when Charles IV succeeded in subduing the great landlords who had previously challenged central rule, but weak in the next century when the country was wracked by internal disputes. Poland was powerful in the early fifteenth century when the boyars were subdued, but weakened a century later when they regained their strength. And clearly the weakest countries of all internationally were those where there was never any central dynastic power, such as Germany and Italy.

Additionally, in an age when territories and peoples could be added together, however distant or disparate, by the exchange of a ring, fluctuations in the power of states depended on success in the marriage stakes. Thus in central Europe the House of Luxembourg expanded the prestige of Bohemia by marrying Hungary in 1372, as Poland did by marrying Lithuania at the same time. The dukes of Bulgaria married their way to an empire in the fourteenth century, as the dukes of Burgundy did in the fifteenth. The most spectacular example of all was that of the Hapsburgs, who, largely by judicious marriage, won themselves the mightiest empire of all and the role of superpower in Europe.

But beneath this surface hierarchy based on size of territory there lurked another, based on the more intangible relationships of a previous age. A special status still attached to pope and emperor, for example, even though they possessed no military power to match. Their authority was still invoked, for example, by Italian rulers seeking *legitimation* for their claim to Italian cities, or German cities and princes in their contests with each other. Feudal relationships still played a residual role in assigning rights, even while their substance was being overturned. English kings were prepared to pay homage for their territories in France even up to the moment when they began to claim the crown itself. One of the most spectacular examples of the power of these relationships is that given by Froissart of the Earl of Namur who, because Edward III had been made vicar-general of the empire, would support his claims against France while he was in imperial territory, but "as soon as they entered into the realm of France, he would forsake him and go and serve the French king who had retained him."[12]

These different factors led to a highly unstable class structure. The dynastic principle had the effect that a state could be suddenly translated from a relatively

11. "It was no mere chance that both north and south of the Pyrenees the reconquest of national territory was the prelude to a forward foreign policy." C. N. Petrie, *Earlier Diplomatic History, 1492–1713* (London, 1949), p. 4.

12. Froissart, *Chronicles*, I, xxxviii.

humble to a very exalted status, according to the hazards of the marriage market. If Mary of Burgundy had been married to the French dauphin, as once was planned, rather than to Maximilian, the balance of power throughout the society in the succeeding century would have been totally different. If Mary Tudor had lived and produced children to the King of Spain, the history not only of England and Spain but of Europe might have been transformed. If Charles V had not decided to divide his territories with his brother, the whole future of Europe could have been different. International history—and the distribution of status—could thus be determined by the hazards of marriage, birth, or death in a way possible in almost no other age. The chances of an imperial election could transform the fortunes of a family. Finally, international status could be totally changed, regardless of the real resources of a territory, according to the character and military skills of the dynasts, as Milan was raised in status by the Viscontis, or Florence under the Medicis, Hungary under Matthias Corvinus, and Poland under Jagello. For these reasons there was greater social mobility (for states) here than in any other society.

The dynastic principle also leads inevitably to a highly *unequal* class structure. For the size and power of states in this society is not limited by the number of peoples of the same race or language, nor by geographical features. There was virtually no limit to the size of the territories or the numbers of peoples who could be put together by the appropriate marriage policy. The units might vary in size from huge unwieldy conglomerates, spanning two hemispheres and innumerable peoples, such as Charles V's Spain, to the tiny ministates and cities of Germany and Italy. Between these two extremes, in descending order came the kingdoms of France, England, Poland, Lithuania, Hungary, and Bohemia, to a number of smaller states playing a more marginal role, such as Portugal, Denmark, Norway, Venice, Milan, Brandenburg, and Burgundy. There were the semistates, such as the papacy, the two empires, the Hanseatic League, and the Teutonic Knights, which still had vestiges of power and influence but an ambiguous status. And finally, lurking always at the borders of the society and occasionally launching devastating forays within it, in the Balkans, Austria, and even Poland, was the most powerful force of all, the Ottoman Turks, exerting a menace that was never far distant from people's minds, yet against which there was rarely effective joint action.

This stratification was in some ways less *explicit* than in either the Chinese or the Greek systems. There was no acknowledged system of hegemony, no long-term alliances giving rights of overlordship. At the same time there was no such clear-cut conception of sovereignty as was to emerge two or three centuries later, and which would reduce dominance and *increase* the independence even of small states. There was simply a mutual competition for territory and prestige, resulting in huge disparities in power and size.

If any consistent long-term trend is discernible, it is perhaps the constant extension in the power of the great at the expense of the weak. The dynastic principle that ruled the age partly dictated this: many states were simply married out of existence. Entities that had been largely independent units in the early part of the period—Flanders, Brittany, Provence, Navarre, Castile, even Portugal for a time—were absorbed in this way by larger national units. In other cases the same process occurred as a result of the contest for dynastic *expansion:* Competition between the great powers swallowed up the smaller. Not only were the small cities in Italy absorbed by the larger ones, but by the end of the period many of the latter—Naples, Milan, Genoa, like Burgundy, the Low Countries, and Savoy beyond the Alps—had been obliterated from the map. In the east the emerging nations of Serbia, Wallachia, and Bulgaria were absorbed by the expansion of Turkish power. Since there was no restraint on the destruction of states, such as emerged later, and since territories however diverse could be simply added together, there were continuous absorptions. So the strong got stronger and the weak got weaker. An essentially competitive class structure, where aggrandizement was the dominant goal, led, almost inevitably, to an increasing concentration of power among the victors, the most successful dynasts.

## 9.4 The Age of Religions (1559–1648)

The system of stratification changed again during the age of religions between 1559 and 1648. Nations were now mentally classified, and their status judged, on a wholly new basis: how they stood in the new religious confrontation that was coming to divide the world.

To religious eyes Spain was seen, for example, not simply as a superpower of predominant strength and huge possessions, but as the protagonist of a faith, the leader of the counterreformation, seeking to stamp out the new Protestant heresy which threatened the Catholic cause, and was revered or reviled accordingly. Sweden was seen not simply as a suddenly emerging military power, but as the savior and supporter of the reformed faith against the forces threatening it. Conversely, the nations which stood aside in that conflict, such as Saxony and Brandenburg in the early years of the Thirty Years' War, or England, with their halfhearted and ineffective support for the Protestant cause, saw their prestige decline in consequence. Conceptions of the sovereign as ''defender of the faith'' or ''most Catholic majesty'' created a new image and standard for judging both nations and their rulers. It was not a country's strength alone but its ideological steadfastness, its reliability in the cause of ''truth'' against error, that lent it status in the eyes of contemporaries.

Naturally, behind this new set of standards the older hierarchy, based on power and possessions, still persisted. Indeed, the two interacted. A nation's strength in the traditional sense gave it added prestige in its support for the favored cause. It was because of Spain's success in arms, as much as because of its sovereign's devotion, that she became the leader of the Catholic cause. It was because of Sweden's meteoric rise to power that she could be seen as the champion of the reformed faith.

There were now two main superpowers of a wholly different order of strength from the rest: Spain and France. But the relative positions of the two altered radically as the period progressed. At its beginning Spain, clearly the victor in the seventy-year struggle for Italy, was unquestionably the leading power of Europe. Even the reverses of the following forty years—the loss of the United Provinces, the defeat of the English enterprise, and the inconclusive intervention in France—though they humiliated her, did not seriously weaken her. She retained her hold on the Spanish Netherlands, on the richest cities of Italy, on Franche-Comté, on Alsace (which she took over from her fellow Hapsburg), together almost totally enclosing France, in addition to the vast overseas empire from which she secured much of her wealth. Even in the early years of the Thirty Years' War Spanish forces continued to demonstrate their unique military skills. But the successive calamities of the last decade of that war, the loss of Portugal, the revolutions in Catalonia, Andalusia, and Naples, severe military defeats at the hands of France, above all progressive financial exhaustion, brought about a dramatic decline in her power and prestige by 1648. France, on the other hand, which at the beginning of the period was crippled for thirty years by a ruinous civil conflict, reached at its end a never previously attained peak of power. After the considerable achievement of Henry IV and Sully in restoring religious harmony and economic prosperity, the powerful statesmenship of Richelieu brought the reestablishment of strong central government and successive victories against her Hapsburg enemies. Thus by 1648 France had become as unquestionably the supreme state of Europe as Spain had been ninety years before.

Below this upper stratum there was a second layer of medium powers. Greatest in terms of territorial possessions and status was the empire, now firmly secured to the other house of Hapsburg, based mainly in Austria, but in practice also joining the crowns of Bohemia and Hungary which, though nominally still elective, she had made virtually hereditary. But the defeats she suffered in the Thirty Years' War, and the effective collapse of imperial power in Germany at its close, fatally weakened her pretensions, and reduced her to a power of merely middle rank. England, though strengthened by the centralizing authority of the Tudors, the absorption of Scotland, and her growing sea power, remained in Europe a muted force. While she contributed significantly, through her harrying of Spain at sea, to the decline of Spanish power, her interventions on the European continent were few and uniformly unsuccessful. Against this a number of new middle powers emerged, if only briefly, to play a significant role on the world scene. Sweden and Poland enjoyed a brilliant expansion of power and territory, each acquiring substantial empires, in the Baltic and East Europe respectively, in the period 1590–1660 (which was only to be followed in each case by a dramatic reversal of fortune, mainly at the hands of Russia, in the following sixty years). Sweden in particular, during her period of success, played a dominant role in the affairs of Europe. The United Provinces, through commercial enterprise as much as through successful military defiance of Spain, established itself as a significant European power with a growing overseas empire. Russia, after a period of total collapse at the beginning of the seventeenth century, later began to reemerge, though she still played a relatively small role in the main arena of European politics. Portugal, though extinguished between 1580 and 1640, recovered with her independence a substantial overseas empire. Even Denmark, though increasingly overborne by Sweden, remained a significant power. In Germany, Bavaria was the most significant military force. But Brandenburg and Saxony, though playing an inglorious role in the Thirty Years' War, were also developing into significant powers. Finally, in the south, Savoy and Venice were beginning, with increasing effect, to defy the all-pervasive power of Spain in Italy. Altogether there were now a larger number of significant European powers than in any previous European society.

Below this stratum again was another layer of very small states, of little serious consequence in the consideration of statesmen: the remaining independent states of Italy, such as Tuscany, Genoa, Mantua, Ferrara, and Urbano; Lorraine, Transylvania, and other semisovereign entities; as well as the 350 mini-states of Germany. Outside the European system proper there still lurked the menacing power of Turkey. Still the dominant force in the Mediterranean at the beginning of the period, her failure to take Malta in 1565, followed by the crushing defeat at Lepanto in 1571, had left her increasingly a land power, still capable of dramatic victories, as she was to show again even a century later, but now beginning the slow process of decline which was to continue for the next 300 years.

Paradoxically in this religious age, the power and status of the two forces most closely associated with religion, the pope and the emperor, declined further than ever, even in the Catholic world. The net result of the Thirty Years' War was a clear diminution in the authority exercised by the emperor in Germany (though his power in his own domain was reinforced). The popes too, after a period of increased influence under unusually devout pontiffs at the time of the counter-reformation, found their voices heeded less and less in the period that followed. When they refused to accept the terms of the Peace of Westphalia, their protests were totally ignored, and their effective influence on world history virtually ceased from this point. Though religious issues were the dominating ones, it was secular power alone which resolved them.

There were, however. measures of status other than military power which now began to count for something. One was economic prosperity. The rapid economic growth of the United Provinces within fifty years of achieving independence, helped to win it recognition as a serious European power. English travelers who marveled at the prosperity of Germany before the Thirty Years' War were not, like their predecessors a century or two before, eyeing rich lands to plunder, but expressing respect for the industry and skill which had built up these prosperous cities and countryside. Administrative competence and a stable regime won esteem elsewhere: the efficient administration built up in Piedmont by its autocratic ruler was generally admired, while Spain's successive bankruptcies and continued indebtedness did much to undermine the respect her huge empire might otherwise have won for her. Cultural achievements counted, and these did something to win for Italy the respect her political condition forfeited. Even political maturity won plaudits in some quarters: There were many elsewhere in Europe who envied the power acquired by Parliament in England, demonstrated in the most dramatic way at the close of this period, when it proceeded to try, and execute, its sovereign.

This then was a new system of stratification from that of the age before. Respect was now increasingly accorded not to the dynasty but to the regime. And it was bestowed sometimes for causes other than military successes. The conventional stratification in terms of size and power was perpetually balanced, in the mind of the age, with a new classification in terms of religion. However great its prosperity and strength, a nation could not be respected if it represented heresy, schism, and the forces of darkness. This meant that, for a time, as in ancient Greece, there was no longer any *common* standard of measurement of a state's greatness. Spain's role as leader of the Catholic powers, which won her the veneration of some, for others made her the leader of the powers of evil. Sweden's position as the Protestant savior condemned her to the execration of the Catholic peoples. Europe was ranged into rival camps. And military strength, though important as always, was now no longer the first attribute remembered in classifying nations. Once again it was the general character of the society, in a word its ideology, that determined the kind of class structure established.

## 9.5 The Age of Sovereignty (1648–1789)

The class structure which developed in the succeeding period differed in a number of ways.

There was greater consciousness of relative status, both among sovereigns themselves and their subjects, than ever before. New ways of *measuring* status— for example, in terms of diplomatic precedence, the dipping of flags at sea, the relative splendor of courts— stimulated competition in this field. There were, as we saw earlier (p. 92), a whole series of diplomatic incidents over such matters. At least two wars, the first Anglo-Dutch war and the War of Jenkin's Ear, were at least partly caused by disputes over status of this kind. This led in turn to a strict ranking of states and a hierarchical structure:

> There was a general consensus that the states of Europe were not all equal in rank, though they might be in point of sovereignty. Republics, besides dukes and other inferior princes, willingly conceded the superior status of the "crowned heads", and Catholic sovereigns recognized a certain preeminence in the pope. Beyond this there was much quarreling over precedence, for the contestants could neither find common ground for classifying the sovereigns, nor agree upon the merits of each claim. Thus the emperor would barely concede the title of "majesty" to the king of France, while Louis sought to justify on many grounds his profession to be at least the equal of the Holy Roman Emperor. . . . The great states, even the lowliest baronry of the empire, quarreled over rank.[13]

13. *New Cambridge Modern History,* VI (1970): 169–70.

Some kind of pecking order inevitably emerged. At the beginning of the period France was beyond question the leading power of Europe, whose preeminence was widely recognized. Her power was, however, substantially weakened from the end of the seventeenth century onward, both by defeats in war and by internal decay. Conversely, the power of Britain, Prussia, and Russia rose dramatically. Britain won supremacy at sea, two clear-cut victories over France, and a large empire abroad; Prussia secured a substantial expansion of territory, and was the only power to be successful in both the great conflicts of the mid-eighteenth century; Russia overcame Sweden, Poland, and Turkey in turn, and established the beginnings of her huge empire. Austria, though apparently weakened in 1648, won spectacular victories in the first two decades of the next century before seeing her power diminish again in later years. Spain continued her progressive decline, yet remained a significant power which, under a determined queen, showed at least its capacity for nuisance in the years between 1714 and 1748. Even Sweden, Denmark, and Poland were still regarded as great powers at the beginning of the period, though the status of all was severely weakened by the defeats they suffered at the beginning of the eighteenth century. Similarly, United Provinces, still a significant power at the beginning of the period, sank to second-class status before its end. Turkey continued her gradual decline, but remained a serious military menace even in the middle of the eighteenth century. The effect of all this was an unusually evenly balanced society, with eight or ten states each of which represented significant powers at some time during the period. Beneath this upper rank was a lower tier of much smaller states, especially in Germany and Italy, of which the most important were perhaps Sardinia-Savoy, Bavaria, and Saxony.

Prestige, however, was no longer measured exclusively in terms of military strength. Pride was taken in a society's culture and civilization as well as its power. France won status as much through her artistic achievements, her great writers and thinkers, and the finery of her court and palaces, as through military conquests. The political system and political philosophers of Britain won her as much prestige as her overseas possessions. The governmental and cultural reforms of Peter the Great and Catherine, as much as their military successes, won Russia's acceptance as a member of the European family. Prussian administrative advances added almost as greatly to her reputation and success as the conquest of territory. Conversely, Spain sank almost as much because of the decline in her cultural achievement as of her military power. Turkey, even though she remained a significant military power, was not a member of European society in the eyes of most contemporaries because she lacked the marks of "civilization."

Imitation was the surest evidence of the valuations widely held. The German princelings who sought to ape the manners, and even the architecture, of Versailles showed only too clearly which model represented distinction in their eyes. In the late seventeenth century

> the leading role of France was not only marked in the political and military fields, but extended into those of literature, thought, art, education, manners and fashion. . . . French increasingly became the language of polite society, of the educated, and of the upper classes in many parts of Europe. . . . French fashions became dominant in dress

and hairstyles, in cooking and gardening, in furniture and in interior decorations, as far as the wealthy and upper classes were concerned.[14]

In the next century the imitation of Prussian military organization or of English political ideas indicated equally clearly where preeminence was held to lie in these fields. With increasing ease of communication and a common European culture, transnational influences of this kind became more important than in any previous international society.

So the scale of measurement by which status was judged changed once more. With the decline in religious fervor, a country's position in the great ideological division of the previous age no longer colored the regard in which it was held. The dynastic considerations which had influenced attitudes still earlier were also of little account (though one of the grounds on which Louis XIV claimed preeminence in Europe was that his was the oldest hereditary crown in Christendom). It was now a state's capacities and performance in the new contest of sovereignty— in its military successes, the splendor of its capital, its palaces and buildings, its economic prosperity, the richness of its commerce, in a word its glory—which above all determined where a nation lay in the scale of public estimation. This was still another form of stratification, and again it was determined by the prevailing character of the society as a whole.

## 9.6 The Age of Nationalism (1789–1914)

The system of stratification in the age that followed was established at the Congress of Vienna. At that Congress, though many nations had taken part in the twenty-year conflict just concluded, a special role in determining the terms was accorded to the five largest powers—Britain, Russia, Prussia, Austria, and France. That preeminence was reinforced in the provisions of the Treaty of Chaumont of 1814, by which the four major victors agreed to meet together regularly to consider the affairs of the Continent. In other words, a kind of directory to run Europe was established, to which in 1818 France, too, was admitted. Spain, Portugal, United Provinces, Sweden, and Denmark, all of which had been great powers at the beginning of the previous era (though Portugal was even then rapidly declining), were now relegated to a secondary role. In accepting this fact they implicitly acknowledged the preeminence of the five. The authority of the "Concert" was widely acknowledged. Its members were known as "the powers," unquestionably higher in status and prestige than the other nations of Europe. They were to exercise a role as elders, umpires, regulators, throughout the century that followed. Only much later, toward the end of the century, was a sixth power, Italy, accorded a semiequal status among these "powers."[15]

The Treaty of Vienna also did something to clarify the class structure at the

14. Ibid., V (1961): 4.
15. Turkey, though nominally admitted to the Concert in 1856, was never regarded as an equal.

bottom end of the scale. The innumerable princely and ecclesiastical states of Germany were consolidated and reduced to thirty nine. The curious anomalous entity known as the Holy Roman Empire was finally abolished, only half replaced by the German Bund. One or two small states, Norway and Sweden, Holland and Belgium, were merged temporarily, which again marginally increased the size and power of states at the bottom end. The secondary role of these smaller states was clearly acknowledged. For the first time an international society that was clearly and explicitly divided into two distinct classes was established. While in every international society there had been differences in size and power, often of even greater dimension, this had nearly always been on a graduated scale, so that it was not easy to say exactly where the division between one stratum and another came. In the nationalist society the division was more clearly marked, and indeed acknowledged, not only by the larger but the smaller powers as well (as in a domestic society where variations of class are defined by differences of caste or title).

Thus the "powers" were not now a vague category of marginally stronger states. They had a specific role and function to play within the society. They were the members who came together at regular intervals, usually every two or three years for most of the period, to deliberate together and decide the affairs of the continent, including many issues that were of primary concern to other and smaller nations. Those smaller nations were often not permitted themselves to participate even if directly interested: Sardinia, for example, though she had participated in the Crimean War on the side of Britain and France, was not allowed to take part in the Congress of Paris on the same footing as Austria, even though Austria had remained neutral. Again, when Sardinia demanded that she be treated on an equal basis with Austria at the conference on Italy proposed in 1859, this was rejected by Austria out of hand. As in smaller societies, therefore, there were definite prerogatives associated with membership of a particular class, and these were not willingly shared with others held to be of lower status.

This class structure did not remain immutable. There were some promotions from the lower level to the first. In a formal sense Turkey was invited to be a member of the Concert of Europe of 1856, though in practice her power continued to decline and she never effectively functioned as one of the "powers." Italy, after 1860, did begin to do so; she was invited to take part in the London Conference on Luxembourg in 1867, largely as a reward for being on the winning side in the Austro-Prussian war (even though she herself had been disastrously defeated in that war). The U.S., which had far outstripped all the European nations economically, and so potentially militarily, before the end of the nineteenth century, remained too remote and disinterested to play a significant role, though she participated in the Algeciras Conference in 1906 on much the same terms as the other big powers. Finally, in effect if not in theory, Japan from the time of her defeat of Russia in 1905 came to be regarded as a great power, though she was too distant to act in that role. "The powers" were thus measured by function rather than capacity. They were the larger *European* powers which took part regularly in the directorate: for this was an international society largely directed and run from a headquarters in Europe.

*Among* the great powers there was no such evident preeminence as had distinguished Spain and France from the rest in the two preceding eras, but there was nonetheless some disparity. Throughout the period there was a continuing decline in the power of Austria, which, having been four times conquered by Napoleon, was again defeated three times in the following century (each time in wars which she herself, at least formally, initiated). There was a more marginal but steady decline in France's power, from the upsurge of the Napoleonic era to the disastrous defeat of 1870. Britain and Russia both moved upward during the first part of the period, and perhaps slightly down again in the second: just as Spain's century of preeminence ended in the mid-seventeenth century and France's in the mid-eighteenth century, Britain's ended in the middle of the nineteenth century, when Germany's rise began. Indeed, by far the most significant change was the emergence after 1870 of a united Germany, which became unquestionably the strongest power of the continent and an increasing threat to the traditional equilibrium.[16]

The military preeminence France had shown in the Napoleonic Wars was taken over by Germany at least from 1870 onward. Russia had the largest land forces, but these lost much of their prestige in the Crimean War, in the War of 1877–1878 and above all in the Russo-Japanese War. Austria and Italy also had little to show in the way of military success, though the former remained potentially powerful. Britain's land forces were small and poorly trained, but her supremacy at sea was unchallenged, and until 1914 she continued to maintain there a two-power standard—that is, a naval strength equal to that of any two other powers. In economic power in Europe, Germany took over the lead from Britain before 1900. But the shape of the future was indicated by the fact that by the beginning of the twentieth century Russian and U.S. industrial production was increasing much faster than that of any other country.

There was a huge disparity between the power available to any of these larger nations and that available to the rest of the countries of Europe. The latter were therefore obliged to show considerable deference to the great powers which disposed of the affairs of the Continent. Still more dramatic was the difference in the power available to the great European powers and that which existed outside Europe, in Asia, Africa, and Latin America. For this determined the international system established in that wider region where most countries had to adopt a subordinate role.

New ways were devised by which dominance was established by European powers in these areas, short of outright conquest and colonization. One was the

16. In population Russia remained easily the largest throughout the period, though since her average level of education and standard of living was low, this was little indication of potential strength. Of the rest, at the beginning of the period France had the largest population, followed by Austria. By 1900, with the unification of Germany and the higher birthrate of the other powers, this order had been completely changed to Germany–Austria–Britian–France, with Italy still in the rear.

device of the "protectorate" according a considerable degree of control to an external power; it was used by France in Tunis and Morocco, and by Britain in Brunei, Aden, and parts of southern Africa. The "sphere of influence" was invented, under which European powers accorded each other a dominant position in particular regions outside Europe, regardless of the views or wishes of the local peoples and rulers; such arrangements were made between Britain and Russia in Persia, between Britain and France in Siam, between Britain and Germany in New Guinea and the Pacific, and in many other areas. The control of foreign policy of another state was sometimes taken over, an overlordship enjoyed by Austria in Serbia for twenty years from 1878 and by Britain in Afghanistan for a time. The concept of "suzerainty" was used, under which the figment of authority was retained by one state, the "suzerain," while the reality of power was taken by another, as from Turkey by Britain in Cyrpus, from Turkey by Greece in Crete, from China by Britain in Tibet, and so on. Leases were demanded and given in strategic areas or commercially favorable sites, as almost all the powers obtained in China. Sometimes the relationship was still more undefined, as when a large state was able to offer to a small one "authoratative advice," as Lord Rosebery delicately described it. This was roughly the situation of Britain in Nepal and in the princely states of India (where she enjoyed "paramountcy," another vague term legitimizing imperialist power), or of Russia in Bulgaria in the later part of the nineteenth century, and of the U.S. eventually in Cuba and Central America; in other words, the relationship of a rich and powerful protector to a client state.

Through such devices the European powers managed the affairs of the smaller ones in many parts of the world, even distributing to each other facilities which did not belong to them. So Bismarck generously told Britain, "Take Egypt"; and so all the powers in turn gave Italy carte blanche to take Tripoli. Britain generously gave France permission in their agreement of 1904 to "preserve order in Morocco" and to "provide assistance for all administrative, economic, financial, and military reforms which it may require," entirely without reference to the views of the Moroccan ruler, still less of his people. So, too, Russia, Britain, and other powers discussed in considerable detail a possible partition of the Ottoman empire, and Germany and Britain decided how to divide up another nation's colonies (Portugal's Southern African possessions), equally without reference either to the government or the people concerned.

Among the great powers these colonies were themselves a mark and measure of status. Though they might have been *acquired,* as the British colonies are said to have been, in a fit of absence of mind and without deliberate plan, once possessed they became a source both of pride and of envy. Nations left behind in the race for them, such as Germany, Italy, and Japan, felt deprived and aggrieved, and so sought to make up the lost ground. Germany's call for a place in the sun was a demand for the prestige, rather than the territory or resources, derived from colonialism.

In an increasingly commercial society dominance was also sometimes secured by commercial or financial means. In China foreign powers, complaining of the high and arbitrary rate of duties imposed by the Chinese government, secured full control of the customs, placed them under a Western official, and set a maximum duty of 5 percent (far lower than most Western tariffs). The chaotic state of Turkey's finances provided justification for ever-increasing control of the Ottoman revenues by Western countries; in return for a series of loans made between 1854 and 1875 they obtained a prior claim on a considerable proportion of the tax receipts, taking for this purpose, in turn, the Egyptian tribute, the Syrian customs duties, the Constantinople customs duties and octroi, tobacco, salt, stamp, and license duties, the "sheep-tax of Rumelia and the archipelagoes," the produce of the mines of Tokat, and finally the "general revenues, present and future of Turkey."[17] The Caisse de la Dette established by the Western powers in Egypt gradually took over control of the railways, the telegraphs, and the harbor of Alexandria; by 1880 40 percent of all Egypt's revenues went to pay off the national debt, and she had been made to sell off her 15 percent share of the Suez Canal, so that until 1936 she obtained no revenue at all from her most important single asset. In Persia, Britain and Russia in turn gave large loans, and in return received virtually complete control over the customs revenues. In this way not only did weaker countries increasingly forfeit important sections of their revenues, but whole areas of economic policy were taken out of their control altogether and assumed by the powerful oligarchy which financed them.

In other cases dominance was sought by outright gifts and subventions. The government of India (i.e., Britain) made extensive gifts to the Amir of Afghanistan to ensure his favor (200,000 pounds a year from 1857 to 1863 and smaller sums for most of the rest of the century), an expenditure that would scarcely have been undertaken if it was not thought to procure effective influence. Governments competed with each other for the right to give loans to those in need; for example, Russia, France, Britain, and Germany all competed bitterly for the privilege of making a loan to China to enable her to pay her indemnity to Japan in 1895. Though the motive in such cases was partly that of the usurer, it was also to place the receiving government in a dependent position in which it was more likely to listen to advice. Competition for railway building was another expression of the desire for economic dominance: like the making of loans, this could provide not only commercial benefit but political and strategic advantages as well.[18] Chartered companies were used, as in India, East Africa, Nigeria, the Congo, and other places, to win not only important economic benefits but sometimes considerable political influence as well.

17. *New Cambridge Modern History,* XI (1962): 328.

18. In China all the powers competed for railway contracts but were particularly concerned to obtain these in their own sphere of influence, where their strategic value was greatest, and so left China with railways of differing types, even differing gauges. The concern of Austria to build the railway to Constantinople and of Germany to build that to Baghdad was certainly as much political as economic, as was the apprehension that these plans caused among other powers. One of the more unusual agreements was in Persia, where Russia and Britain each satisfied each other by agreeing *not* to build railways in their own spheres. This pleased Russia because she had no money to build railways anyway, and it pleased Britain because it kept Russia further away from India. Whether it pleased Persia is not recorded.

Often domination in one area was linked to the demand for domination elsewhere. Increasingly territory might be required not for itself but because of its strategic significance in relation to other territories. The scramble for Africa took place more to prevent control by others than to win the territories acquired for their own sake. Britain and France were concerned with the protection of existing possessions in North and South Africa, rather than with the value to be gained from the black African territories they took. An almost infinite chain of strategic relationships was sometimes established. For Britain, the defense of India made necessary (among many other things) control of the Suez Canal; this in turn demanded control of Egypt; this required control of the Sudan; these together made necessary control of Mombasa; and that eventually entailed control of Uganda and Kenya.[19] Similarly, France wanted Algiers to protect her position in the Mediterranean, Tunis and Morocco to protect Algiers, and the French Sahara and West Africa to protect them all. So gradually the means were converted into ends in themselves.

In all these ways in this society new ways of institutionalizing dominance were found. The conceptions of sovereignty established in the previous age were modified to allow dominance in some areas to be exercised by outside powers. These new institutions for exerting influence, the protectorate, the control of foreign policy, suzerainty, the control of financial or customs administrations, were inventions which reflected the structure of this society—one in which a small number of great powers, engaged in intense nationalistic rivalry, sought to adjust and modify traditional conventions to suit the interests of their mutual competition.

There was another way in which nationalism influenced the competition for status. Status was now conceived in national and not personal terms. Instead of Henry VIII and Francois I personally vying in conspicuous consumption at the field of the cloth of gold, or Louis XIV and Frederick the Great competing in the rival splendors of Versailles and Sans Souci, it is competition in *national* power and glory which now takes place. The naval race between Germany and Britain is a national contest, engaged in as much for symbolic glory as for national security. The competition for colonies, as between Italy and France in North Africa, or Britain and France in Southeast Asia, reflects the same national competition for status-symbols. Most of the crises of the day, Fashoda, Algeciras, Bosnia-Herzegovina, Agadir, not to speak of Sarajevo, the issues on which wars were or might be fought, all involved contests for status more than for real and tangible assets; it was precisely this which gave them their danger. While the great powers could usually reach an accommodation if it was only a question of sharing out colonies or spheres of influence, agreement was less easy to achieve when it was

19. One effect of this was to *increase* Britain's vulnerability to threats at any point. If Germany threatened to withdraw support for her position in Egypt, Britain was obliged to make substantial concessions elsewhere. If Russia began to threaten Afghanistan, Britain had to cease all military activity elsewhere. Tsar Nicholas II boasted in 1900 that he had only to order the mobilization of Russian forces in Turkestan to immobilize British policy all over the world.

the competition for national prestige which was basically involved, as 1866, 1870, and 1914 all dramatically demonstrated.

This then was a complex hierarchy, with a widespread network of relationships, military, political, economic, and cultural, each mutually reinforcing each other. Five or six powers enjoyed a clear-cut and acknowledged supremacy, above all in their capacity to order many of the issues of the day. Among these powers there was a continual struggle for influence, territory, military success, and above all status. But they themselves as a group enjoyed a position of considerable dominance over most of the rest, in Europe and to an even greater degree overseas. On the basis of their superiority of power they were able to obtain economic, political, and military positions which were highly favorable to themselves. The dominant ideology of nationalism intensified, sometimes even created, the competition for status. The small as much as the great struggled for national identity, national glory, and national greatness. Economic, political, and cultural achievement had their part to play in securing prestige. But because the possibility of war was never far from people's minds, even through the long years of peace, the prime measure of status used was still that of military strength.

## 9.7 The Age of Ideology (1914–1974)

The following age saw the emergence of a completely new power structure. Of the five major powers of the previous age one (Austria) declines to insignificance; three (Germany, France, and Britain) slowly, after a brief revival of German power, sink to the level of second-class powers: only Russia, with its far larger population, remains a world power of the first rank. Rivalling, and indeed surpassing, her stands the U.S., which, though for long potentially the strongest, had previously stood only on the fringes of world politics. For much of the period these two powers stand alone, the acknowledged superpowers. Toward its end they begin to be approached in their eminence by two oriental powers, considered until not long before to be far less considerable: Japan approaching them in industrial strength, and China approaching them in strategic power and ideological influence, and far surpassing them in population. Finally, the nations of West Europe, though individually considerably weaker, now begin to attain a kind of unity, at least in economic affairs and to some extent in foreign policy, and so begin to represent a fifth center of power, potentially at least equal in weight to any of these.

This concentration of power at the top, first between two, eventually among five superpowers, is accompanied by a corresponding dispersion of power at the bottom. The total membership of the world community is hugely increased, now approaching 150 states. This is partly because all parts of the world are now included in a single world society, so that the nations of Latin America, for example, for the first time become absorbed within it. It is partly because a large number of nations are created in the process of decolonization, beginning in

Europe and the Middle East after World War I and continuing on a much greater scale in Africa and Asia after World War II. A large number of these new nations are, in terms of resources and economic development, small and weak. In consequence the great majority of the members of the international society are now powers of the third rank, having populations of under 5 million and income below 300 dollars a head. A highly unequal social structure is thus established.

There was thus a further disequalization among states. While in the eighteenth century the effective international community had consisted of a dozen or so nations, none of them wholly disproportionate in power to each other, while in the nineteenth century half a dozen states of the first rank were surrounded by twenty or thirty lesser powers, there are now only two genuine superpowers and eight or ten other powers of major strength, with the rest almost negligible in comparison. Thus, though lip service continues to be paid to the concept of "sovereign equality," it now bears less relation than ever to the realities of the world.

There are a number of reasons why inequalities increase all the time. The technical level and economic power necessary to manufacture the most advanced weapons, such as nuclear warheads, strategic missiles, satellites, nuclear submarines, radionics, supersonic aircraft, and so on, are beyond virtually all nations but the superpowers themselves. The widening economic gap, which continues until almost the end of the period, thus creates a widening military gap to match. This exists not only between the middle and small powers, many of which (for example, in Africa and Central America) have virtually no resources to spend on their armed forces, but between the superpowers and the middle powers as well. The system of stratification now begins once more to recall that of ancient Greece: a large number of members, mainly very small, with a concentration of power among the two or three largest.

The dominance of the great powers is shown in new ways. It is institutionalized in the system of "permanent membership," first in the League Council and then in the UN Security Council. In the latter case this privilege carries with it the important right of veto through which they can protect their own interests. Much of the important negotiation and decision making, from the Versailles conference to the SALT talks, is mainly confined to the largest powers of all. "Superpower politics," the dialogue between the bloc leaders, becomes a key feature of international relationships, settling the affairs of the whole world—the Middle East and Southeast Asia as much as Europe.

This ideological hegemony is increasingly resented by smaller powers. It is consciously resisted by China and even, to a lesser extent, by Japan and West Europe. But the increasing distance between the superpowers and the rest is matched by another lineup, possibly of even greater significance for the future. In many international organizations and in discussions of other kinds, the main confrontation now is often between the rich countries and the poor. New organizations, such as OECD and UNCTAD, IEA and OPEC, are set up to represent the interests of each. So the increasing inequality in the wealth and power of states is reflected, between states as within them, in new types of political organizations.

The division between rich and poor threatens to become the major political division in the age to come.

The ideological character of the age is reflected in this social structure. One of the chief roles of the superpowers is as leaders of the great ideological blocs. In this role they are expected to give ideological as well as military leadership: They are the sources of militant crusading programs used to inspire the two great alliances, and seek to mobilize and stir up their weaker allies to similar ardor. Often they speak for their bloc as a whole in ideological confrontations. Ideological fervor, or a distinct ideological viewpoint, is sometimes even the means of securing a position as bloc leader. So China, for example, though still limited in military strength, seeks to make herself the leader of a new group, opposed to both the two main superpowers and representing the interests of less developed nations, on the basis of her political creed. Conversely, the nation having no clear ideological role, such as India, or representing an unpopular ideology, such as Brazil, may exercise little influence elsewhere.

There is another change in the social structure in this era. With a decline in overt military relationships, new forms of dominance and dependence emerge. Colonialism of the old kind is abandoned; even the modified forms developed in the previous century (protectorates, suzerainty, acknowledged spheres of influence, and so on) now disappear, though mandates and ''trust territories'' represent a vestigial form of them. Now wholly new ways of securing influence and dominance are found. Ideological dominance keeps entire areas, such as East Europe and Central America, in a form of purdah, within which no state may be defiled by the opposing ideology. The supply of arms is used as a means to establish a considerable degree of dependence. Economic aid and technical assistance, though not given for this purpose alone, have a similar effect. Still more insidious (though also more tenuous as a form of influence) is the development of a network of financial and economic ties by which the great companies of the richer countries, national or multinational, begin to acquire a dominant influence within the economies of poorer ones. The poor countries are thus faced with an agonizing choice:either they must forgo the technological and managerial benefits which usually foreign capital alone can supply, or they see much of their economy falling into increasing dependence on the richer states and their large companies. This relationship intensifies the resentment between poor countries and rich which the unequal power structure already generates.

Status is no longer associated exclusively with degrees of military power. Other factors began to become the means of winning respect: economic development, technical or scientific attainment, cultural level, political development, even sporting achievement, all play their part. Military power may be feared, but it is not necessarily always respected. Successful space flights, a pollution-free environment, or a generous aid record may do as much to win high regard, in many eyes, as extensive stocks of nuclear warheads.

Once again, therefore, a new type of society breeds a new class structure. The changes in stratification are a result of a number of factors—increasing divergences in economic and technical capacity, decolonization, a decline in respect for military power, the birth or growth of new states. But others derive from the special importance of ideology within society. The way a state is seen depends on the type of policy it pursues as much as on crude power alone. Leadership positions, dependence or dominance, respect or contempt, depend now, as in no previous age, on the ideological complexion of governments as much as on anything. So the Soviet Union, South Africa, and Spain are not accorded the status which their power alone might command; while Sweden, Canada, and Tanzania enjoy a status far higher than their power rating could earn them. As coercion declines as an element in the normal foreign policy of states, the capacity to coerce alone becomes a less significant factor in determining status.

A number of quite different types of class structure can be observed in the different international societies that we have been examining. They have ranged from formal systems of hegemony by a single state in at least a part of the society, as seen in ancient China and in ancient Greece; to the dominance of a single superpower, superior in strength to all the rest, as enjoyed by Spain in the age of religion or by France at the beginning of the following age; the ascendancy of two or three superpowers, as in recent times; a directorate of five or six powers largely controlling the affairs of the rest, as in the age of nationalism; and an age in which there were about a dozen powers of relatively equal power, as in the eighteenth century. At the other end, the numbers of rank and file members have varied from over a thousand members, as in ancient China in early times; hundreds of states, varying from the very large to tiny cities and bishoprics, in the age of dynasties; two or three hundred city-states, as in ancient Greece; 140 states of widely varying size in the modern age; to only twenty of thirty significant members in the age of nationalism. These bare statistics, however, do not tell us the whole story. The *degree* of dominance enjoyed by the states that are powerful, and the ways in which their dominance has been enforced or otherwise expressed, have varied widely from one society to another.

All the societies we have looked at represent forms of oligarchy. There has never been a genuinely ''democratic'' international society in which stratification was slight and dominance limited. There have always been great powers and small, and the former have always demanded a degree of dependence from the latter. Perhaps that which came closest to being democratic has been the modern age, where overt military attack has declined and even overt intervention, though practiced, is widely condemned. Very small powers today probably enjoy a greater degree of effective freedom of action, *politically* at least, than at any earlier time. It is now rather economic dependence, such as is secured through aid and investment or the presence of large foreign companies, which replaces the more obvious political dependence of earlier times. Against this the development of international institutions gives small countries at least a voice, and so a marginal influence, in the discussion of major issues, which they have not usually had in earlier times and even a forum for bargaining on economic matters. Just as internally most societies have become a little more democratic with time, more willing to heed the views of the mass of the population, so perhaps a somewhat similar development takes place in international societies.

It is not easy to trace any correlation between a particular system of stratification and a particular "ideology." At first sight the ideological ages, where direct aggression by one state against another is somewhat less common, might be expected to be less stratified. It is true that in ancient Greece, in modern times, and to some extent in the age of religions, governments had to rely more on the less certain control obtained by indirect methods (subversion, assistance to revolutions or particular factions in other states, and so on). The political allegiance of allies in such a system, depending partly on conviction, has been somewhat unreliable: Athens could not prevent Argos from defecting for a time, Spain could not secure the allegiance of France or England despite large-scale intervention there, Chile, Cuba, Yugoslavia could in modern times leave the camp to which they were previously attached, despite efforts to prevent this. But in practice superpowers even in such ages have usually been able to win for themselves an influence that was relatively secure: Athens and Sparta could intervene to reclaim errant cities, Spain could acquire control of most of Italy, and the emperor restore his power in Bohemia, without difficulty; Hungary and Czechoslovakia, Guatamala and the Dominican Republic could be subdued by neighboring super-powers. So in general the great powers are no less dominant in the ideological societies than in others. Indeed, it is precisely in such ages that the role of superpowers often becomes most important. Conversely, in nonideological ages, such as the age of sovereignty, despite the unscrupulousness of the methods used, a relatively equal social system may be established through the maneuvering and bargaining of each member state acting for its own interests (as in the eighteenth century, for example).

But there is some relationship between the type of class structure and the ideology. A society marked especially by an ideology of territorial ambition, such as that of ancient China, for example, cannot fail to become one in which the powerful become more powerful and the weak are in time eliminated. Similarly, an age of dynastic ambition must also lead to a progressive extension of the territories of those powers which are dynastically successful. A society of ideological conquest, on the other hand, especially where there are two or three superpowers leading individual blocs, as in ancient Greece and in modern times, may lead to a high concentration of apparent influence among bloc leaders but unpredictable real power for those dominant states. So Spain in the age of religions, the U.S. and the Soviet Union today, though unmistakably superpowers, wield an ambiguous and widely challenged influence, sometimes undermined by overextension of their power. An age of nationalism, on the other hand, may lead to the breakup of old established empires and the creation of new and small states based on the national principle; in this way the class structure is superficially democratized.

Thus the social structure established is partly an effect rather than a cause: the outcome of the basic ideology of the society and the type of conduct it induces. We have seen in this chapter the different kinds of class structure created by different "ideologies." It is not of course the balance of *power* that will be affected by the ideology. The number of very large powers or of very small, for example, in any particular society will depend largely on the hazards of history. But the *effect* of this, the degree of dominance which results, the type of status which is valued, the different ways of winning or keeping status, these will depend on the nature of the ideology that prevails. Thus the distribution of power in itself is not the decisive factor which determines the character of the society as a whole; a bipolar structure, for example, will be wholly different in effect in an ideological and in a dynastic society. On the contrary, it is the character of the society which will determine the *effect* the power balance has on relations between states.

Stratification is thus one of the elements which gives a society its special character. But no such factor can be taken in isolation. The society hangs together as an integral entity. Status may be won by many different means in different types of societies according to their ideology. In very few does it depend on brute power alone.

# 10. Structure

Whatever the dominant elites, whatever the chief motives and means, whatever the class system established, every society seeks to establish an organized framework of relationships among its members. It is thus necessary, next, to examine the different structures that have been evolved in historical international societies, and to investigate how they have varied.

Here too there is an analogy with domestic societies, though there are also obvious differences which must be kept in mind. International societies are in general (though our own is a possible exception) far looser, less integrated than domestic societies. Contact between the members in some cases (as in ancient China) may be only sporadic. Relationships are not highly organized. Yet in every case there does exist some regular system for communication (they would not otherwise be societies). And this normally leads to relatively well-established patterns of behavior among the members: an embryonic system for regulating relations.

We are concerned here, of course, with communication among states, not individuals. Individuals may, within any international society, undertake extensive contacts with individuals in other states for commercial, touristic, or social reasons. But these only affect the structure of the society, in the sense we are here concerned with, insofar as they alter the relationships between the states as a whole. Sporadic visits by businessmen or tourists will normally have little effect on the general pattern of relationships between states. Only where extensive business travel leads to the establishment of large-scale commercial links, or to the signing of formal trade agreements, or to the domination of large parts of a foreign economy by foreign businesses, will the structure of the society change. It is in general here not personal but intergovernmental relations with which we are concerned.

One such relationship affecting the structure which will clearly be important to us is the alliance. An alliance may seem to be a private agreement between two states, but it will also affect the way other states approach them and behave toward them. It may cause the establishment of counteralliances designed to resist it. And where, as sometimes occurs, virtually the whole membership of a society is recruited to one alliance or another, the whole structure of the society and the

229

whole character of its relationship are affected. The balance among these alliances may act as a regulating mechanism, even as a means of keeping order. So the system of alliances is one of the features determining the structure of a society.

But usually there is a more elaborate regulating mechanism. Sometimes, instead of fixed alliances of this kind, alliances may be relatively short-lived and opportunistic. This situation may develop into one where a convention emerges that alliances will be formed always against the main threat to the peace at any one time, especially against the most powerful state of the age. This is what occurred at the end of the seventeenth century in Europe and led to the establishment of the so-called "balance of power" system (p. 245ff below). Insofar as this device is systematically practiced it represents an attempt to create a self-balancing structure, so that no single state, or group of states, will be in a position to dominate it.

Another practice which will modify the general social structure is the establishment of "spheres of influence" by those states powerful enough to do so. This again can be seen as a means of securing equilibrium, by assuring the security of large states at the expense of the small. For the essence of the system is not simply that one great power seeks to exercise domination among a group of states around it, but that the right to exercise this influence is accepted and *recognized* by other great powers. The effect is that the interests of small states are largely subordinated to those of the great states. Once again a different structure is formed within the society.

Clearly, certain types of "ideology" among societies will favor particular social structures. In an age of religions or ideology, large-scale alliances joining those who share the same belief are likely to be formed. This happened among the ancient Greek states, in the age of religions, and in the recent ideological age. An age of sovereignty, on the other hand, is likely to be one where states are concerned to maintain their own independence, and will engage in alliances only for short-term and opportunistic reasons; alliances then are likely to be smaller in size. But the structure will depend on things other than the ideology alone; for example, the power relationships that prevail. In a society where there are two superpowers (as in the age of ideology) the structure will be different from one where there are five large states of equal power (as in the age of nationalism). Yet we shall see that ideology is the most basic factor, for it modifies the effect power relationships might otherwise have.

There will therefore be a number of different factors affecting the types of social structure established. And one of our tasks in this chapter will be to determine what these are and how they are interrelated.

## 10.1 The Chinese Multistate System (771–221 B.C.)

One of the most fundamental devices, adopted in some form in almost every society we shall examine, is a system of diplomatic relations. Within the Chinese multistate society official contacts among the states increased rapidly as time went on. An elaborate system for the conduct of interstate relations developed. The increase in contacts can be reasonably well quantified from the records of Lu contained in the Spring and Autumn Annals. Between 720 and 701 the diplomatic missions of Lu covered 780 miles; sixty years later, between 660 and 641, this had increased to 1,650 miles; and between 540 and 521 the number had increased to 6,360 miles. During the same period the number of missions had doubled.

There were five main types of diplomatic visit.[1] There was the Ch'au, a state visit by one ruler to another; the Hui, a meeting or conference, usually of officials or nobles; the P'in, a mission of friendly enquiry; the Shih, an embassy sent for a ceremonial purpose, or with a special message occasionally involving a prolonged stay; and the Shao, hunting parties used for the conduct of business as well as pleasure. In other cases communication was by diplomatic note: a relatively junior official would transmit a note or message usually from one prime minister (hsiang) to another. Special missions were undertaken by hsing-jen, or messengers; these were usually high-ranking government officials given a temporary commission to try to resolve some current issue of international relations (comparable to the "troubleshooters" used by some governments in the modern system for similar purposes). There do not seem to have been permanent embassies attached from one state to another, but the frequency of visits made the system little different.[2] Certainly there existed a state of "diplomatic relations," which were sometimes formally broken off, for example before declaring war.

But over and above a means of contact, a regulatory mechanism for governing relations within the society was evolved. In this society, more than in most others, ceremonial played an important role. There were formal rules laying down the ceremonies required for the reception of a mission from another state. These included the way the visiting mission was to be housed, the meals to be given them, and the type and number of dishes to be served at each meal. There were (as today) exact rules relating to the presentation of credentials (Chieh) by the ambassador or emissary to the ruler. Ceremonies had to be arranged exactly in accordance with the rank of the visiting official, who must not only refuse a lower treatment, but be scrupulous in turning down honors to which he was not entitled. The making of the correct speeches, including the quotation of suitable verses, was an important part of diplomatic etiquette. There was some competition in lavishness of hospitality. Large-scale hospitality was taken as an indication that the state was in good order, while a failure in this respect could cause loss of face and might even lead to an invasion.[3] A considerable proportion of the visits were to celebrate a marriage, a funeral, or a ruler's accession. Missions of condolence were sent when a foreign

1. There were also certain types of visit, not here described, connected with the Chou royal ritual. "Not only was there an interchange of friendly missions among the princes themselves but also between them and the king. Indeed the king was supposed to send annually to every one of them to inquire about their welfare." J. Legge, *The Chinese Classics* (Oxford, 1893), V, 233.

2. R. L. Walker, *The Multi-State System in Ancient China* (Hamden, 1953), p. 78: "Although there were no permanent legations maintained in Ch'un Ch'iu times, the frequency of diplomatic intercourse, even from the earliest years, provided almost the equivalent."

3. Ibid., pp. 77–78. Failure of a small state to send a mission at a specified time, regarded virtually as an act of tribute, could also lead to invasion by the larger state.

state was suffering from drought, flood, or famine. Usually a visit in one direction would require a return.

As time went on the role of ceremony declined. "The rules of propriety gave place to the way of the world. Great states gave up these visits altogether and small ones observed them by constraint, not willingly."[4] Diplomatic visits were increasingly for business purposes: to conclude an alliance, to negotiate an agreement, to seek a friendship, or to provoke a war. Even the ceremonial visit was used to discuss state business. Missions were sometimes sent to conclude trade agreements, for example, to buy grain at a time of shortage (the shipment of grain from surplus to deficiency areas has remained necessary in China ever since). Sometimes they were sent to plan military expeditions against other states or defense against a feared attack, or to ask permission to send a messenger or forces across the territory of another state. One state would always send a messenger to notify an ally of an intended military action, and later send another to announce the result. The large-scale alliance thus came to dominate the structure of relations within the area of each.

As time went on, the alliances and leagues played a more important part in international relations. Multilateral treaties sometimes provided for joint enforcement of their provisions, so that if one state violated the treaty, all the rest would combine to attack it. In other cases bonds were given in the form of hostages, or cities placed under the control of the allied power as a pledge of conformity. Oaths were sworn.[5] Despite all these securities, natural and supernatural, treaties were regularly broken within a short time of their signature. The *Ts'o-Ch'uan*, after recording a case in which hostages had been forfeited by a ruler who resorted to war, added piously that "hostages are of no use if there is no good faith in the heart."[6] At this time there was (unfortunately for the hostages) little good faith around.

Increasing use was made of the system of leagues (see p. 71 above) as a means of stabilizing the society. This operated through two separate processes. On the one hand each league, at least in theory, acted as a regulating force within the area of the alliance. Each state acquired some degree of immunity from attack from the league leader in return for assisting it against the common enemy. Members were also inhibited from quarrels with neighbors. In practice this stabilization was not always effective, both because the league leader, especially Ch'u in the South, sometimes abused its position and attacked a smaller state, and because allies sometimes defected and were in turn attacked by the hegemon in retribution. Nonetheless the system probably did serve to secure a greater degree of security and stability within the area of each league than would otherwise have existed.

4. Legge, *Chinese Classics,* V, 798.

5. The signing of treaties was usually accompanied by a sacrifice (not a usual feature of modern treaty-signing ceremonies). The treaty itself was smeared with the blood of the sacrificial animal, as were the lips of those taking part in the ceremony. A copy of the treaty was buried with the sacrificial beast while other copies were kept by the signatories. The religious sanction secured in this way was used as a means of enhancing good faith among states and securing more stable relationships.

6. *Ts'o Ch'uan,* V, I, III, 13.

Second, the league system helped to stabilize relations *between* the leagues (again in theory) by creating a pattern of deterrence. The northern league was formed with a view to uniting some of the Chou states against the aggressive policies of Ch'u. Ch'u then formed its own league in retaliation. Mutual dissuasion may have led to a genuinely more stable society for a time. But the aggressive appetites of the larger states, especially Ch'u, and the new states such as Wu and Ch'in, were such that often the leagues did not deter effectively. Moreover, sometimes they were used as *aggressive* rather than defensive alliances. Thus even in the period when the leagues were at their peak, warfare remained endemic.

This was thus a regulatory mechanism of competing alliances. Sometimes miscalled a "balance of power" system, it is in fact the opposite, since the whole basis of a genuine balance of power system is that there are uncommitted powers, balancers, which can switch their support to the *weaker* side and so maintain the equilibrium. In the ancient Chinese system, though there were one or two balancing states (Cheng and Sung, for example), they were so weak that they did not significantly affect the relationship between the two main leagues. The Chinese system was really rather a "sphere of influence" mechanism, with great powers exercising leadership in a particular geographically defined area. Insofar as their dominance was effective, it was a viable mechanism within each region. But, like other sphere of influence systems, it inevitably gave rise to disputes at the borders of each region. And because of fluctuations in power and strongly expansive motives, it could not guarantee peace *between* the two leagues as a whole.[7]

While therefore there developed patterns of interaction which together can be categorized as a "system," these were adopted for self-interested, not cooperative, reasons. They presupposed continuation of conflict, not attainment of peace. They could not serve as a mechanism for stabilizing the society as a whole.

## 10.2 The Greek City-States (600–338 B.C.)

The society of Greek states between 600 and 338 B.C. consisted of an unusually large number of separate units. There are some difficulties in quantification, both because some small cities were only semiindependent and because some of the cities of Italy and Sicily were only marginally within the system. It is known, however, that there were about 150 cities paying tribute to Athens around 450, while in 425 this number is supposed to have been 300.[8] Even this excluded most of the states of the Peleponnese, Italy, and Sicily. Thus there were probably altogether between three and four hundred separate city-states in regular contact and intercourse with each other.

Communication among them was by a relatively well-developed diplomatic

7. There were, however, probably longer periods of peace at the time when the leagues flourished than in the later period when they had disintegrated.

8. N. G. L. Hammond, *A History of Greece to 338* B.C. (Oxford, 1967), p. 327.

system. Though there were no resident diplomats, embassies and messengers were frequently dispatched from one city to another to discuss many matters, ranging from questions of peace and war to commerce, debts, and tribute. Thucydides and Herodotus give many accounts of official visits of this kind. The conference described by Thucydides at the opening of the Peleponnesian War, in which the allies of Sparta urged her on to war against Athens, and in which even Athenian delegates were permitted to state their views, is one example. The well-known embassy of Themistocles to Sparta in 478, in which he deliberately sought to prevaricate and delay discussion to allow the construction of Athenian fortifications, is another. The famous messenger who ran from Marathon to Sparta, covering 150 miles in two days, to seek Spartan help before the battle of Marathon is an example of less formal communication. The short distances involved made such contacts relatively simple. Thus it came about that, by the fifth century, B.C., "these special missions between the Greek citystates had become so frequent that something approaching our own system of regular diplomatic intercourse had been achieved."[9] Because the purpose of such missions was often to plead and persuade, skill in oratory, the ability to deliver compelling speeches, was one of the main attributes required by diplomats within the system. For example, according to Thucydides, Archidamus, the Spartan king, urging the Spartans not to rush into war at once, suggested they should send to Athens "some ambassador, who would remonstrate with them in terms neither too suggestive of war, nor too suggestive of submission"[10]—a task clearly requiring considerable linguistic subtlety.

In some cases officials were permanently posted in one state by another. One type of official frequently sent was the prostartos, or trade representative, sent from one state to another to look after the commercial interests of his state and its nationals. There was also a kind of consul (proxenos) who was responsible for looking after the interests of one state and its nationals within the territory of another: for example, if they were involved in legal or other disputes. These might themselves be citizens of either state. Thucydides records that the family of Alcibiades "had looked after Spartan interests in Athens—a post which his grandfather had given up, but which he himself wanted to take on again."[11] Finally, of course, there were also continuing contacts between states which were members of the same alliance, and still more so among members of a tight-knit empire such as the Athenian.

But there were other types of organized relationships within the society. There were the regional associations. The cities of Boeotia, for example, had especially close links with each other, and had developed a form of federation before the middle of the sixth century. There was a close sense of fellow feeling, leading eventually to a loose political organization, among the states of Achaea, Arcadia, Thessaly, Aetolia, and other regions. Though formed originally usually for defen-

9. H. Nicholson, *Diplomacy* (London, 1939), p. 8.

10. Thucydides, *The Peloponnesian War*, V, 43.

11. Ibid.

sive purposes, these associations were used for the discussion of commercial and political problems as well. Increasingly, therefore, the system became one not of individual states alone, but of groups of states superimposed above them.

However, the structures which primarily influenced international relations during this period were those that reflected the prevailing concern with ideology: the two great alliances, part geographical, part racial, but primarily ideological, led by Athens and Sparta. These, as in China, exercised a mutual deterrence and operated, as we saw, within states as well as between them. As in China too, this was not a balance of power system, but rather one of competing alliances. Once the external threat of Persia was removed, the ideological imperialism of Athens, and the fear it inspired among others, brought the confrontation to a head. As it developed, nearly all states were obliged to throw in their lot with one or the other. After the Peloponnesian War, when Sparta sought to impose her ideology, the process was reversed. A political counteralliance now formed around Thebes.

This structure of alliance confrontation, with the middle and small powers occasionally defecting from one side to the other, led, as in China, to a primitive type of sphere of influence system. This was natural to an ideological society. Both the dominance of the two major powers and the prevailing ideological division (as in the modern world) promoted such a system: it combined strategic convenience with ideological solidarity. So long as the power of Athens was not too overwhelming, Sparta was prepared to tolerate her domination in North Greece and Ionia, just as Athens for long tolerated Sparta's in the Peloponnese (and just as today the U.S. tolerates Soviet dominance in East Europe and the Soviet Union that of the U.S. in the Caribbean.) The understandings between Athens and Sparta, in which the interests of their allies were largely ignored, or in which certain powers were forced into neutrality regardless of their own wishes, were one expression of this system of regulation by ideological superpowers.

As always in a sphere of influence system two basic problems emerged. One concerned the marginal areas at the borders of each sphere (say, Yugoslavia or Southeast Asia in the modern world). Was Argos in the Athenian or Peleponnesian sphere? Did the colonies of Corinth, such as Potidea, for example, owe prime allegiance to their mother country, Corinth, or to their league leader, Athens? Was Platea in the Athenian or Theban sphere? The second concerns the problem when one of the smaller states refuses to accept the domination of the major power in its own area. This occurred with Megara in relation to Athens, Platea in relation to Thebes, and Argos in relation to Sparta (just as it has occurred over Cuba and Albania in modern times). Finally, the viability of a sphere of influence policy was affected by the existence of traditional local rivalries disrupting a natural alliance among neighbors, as did rivalries between Corinth and Megara, Mantinea and Tegea, and Thessaly and Phocis (just as long-standing local rivalries—between Turkey and Greece, Hungary and Rumania, Vietnam and Cambodia—may disrupt ideological alliances today).

Nor did the confrontation between the two great alliances bring about any effective balance of power. In general there was not sufficient flexibility of alliance to allow the balance to be maintained. Middle powers such as Corinth and

Thebes did sometimes shift their loyalty against the most powerful superpower of the time, as is required in such a system, but this was not itself sufficient to deter the superpower. Athens, in its period of aggression, was quite undeterred by the lineup of forces against it, even adding eventually a totally unnecessary commitment in Sicily. Moreover, these middle powers themselves sometimes became important focuses of power which might threaten stability, as Thebes did in the fourth century, when she was often a source of conflict and destroyer of the balance. Finally, even small powers were not necessarily kept in line by their own alliance and frequently engaged in private conflicts of their own, quite uninfluenced by the overall balance. Whether or not a balance of power can ever be, in itself, an effective stabilizing force, therefore, two relatively evenly balanced alliances did not provide it in Greece at this time.

Nor was there in any exact sense a sphere of influence system. The structure of allegiance did not correspond totally to geography. Thus there were democratic and pro-Athenian states in the Peloponnese, just as there were oligarchic and pro-Spartan states in mainland Greece, and even in Attica. Still less was there the mutual *recognition* of zones which is the essence of a proper sphere of influence system. On the contrary, there were continual efforts by one superpower to take over cities in areas controlled by the other, either by revolution or, less usually, by war.

This was then a particularly complex international structure, with a large number of units, wide disparities of power, strong transnational forces between states, and sporadic intervention by external powers such as Persia. All this was superimposed on what was for much of the time basically a system of bipolar alliances. Because of ideological and other rivalries, however, even a rough balance between the alliances, when it was achieved, could not prevent a state of increasing confusion and ever more ruthless warfare, culminating in the overthrow of the entire system.

## 10.3 The Age of Dynasties (1300–1559)

The international society which emerged in the later middle ages in Europe shared certain features with both of those that we have considered. Here too the total number of units involved was large: it is impossible to calculate the number exactly because of the difficulties of definition. In Germany alone there were at least three or four hundred separate political units, from large self-sufficient states, such as Bavaria and Brandenburg, to tiny principalities, free cities, and bishoprics, nominally belonging to the empire but in practice largely independent. Even within these there were areas where local knights, or leagues of knights, exercised independence in their own spheres. In Italy there were a large number of separate and independent communes at the beginning of the period, though, with the progressive expansion of the larger states, especially Milan, Venice, and Naples, the number declined as time went on.[12] By the mid-fifteenth century there were five major units, Venice, Milan, Florence, the Papacy, and Naples, and a dozen or so minor cities engaged in a constant diplomatic minuet. In West Europe, too, there were many units of varying size: in Spain several independent kingdoms including the Arab state of Granada in the south; in France a number of independent fiefdoms including Brittany, Provence, Flanders, Artois, Brittany, Lorraine, and Savoy; in Britain Scotland was independent, Wales and Ireland only half-subdued, while other areas, such as Northumberland, were virtually ruled by local lords. Finally, in the East such countries as Bulgaria, Serbia, Wallachia, and Transylvania (not to speak of Byzantium) appeared and disappeared according to Turkish military fortunes.

All this inhibited the establishment of an organized system of relationships. This was made increasingly difficult, as in China, by the large distances involved (in terms of traveling times). To travel from Germany to Italy, from Vienna to Paris, whether for an army or an ambassador, might take several weeks. Notions of distant lands were thus inevitably indistinct and inaccurate. Though all formed part of the nebulous entity called "Christendom," neither peoples nor sovereigns had much knowledge of, or fellow feeling with, those of distant lands speaking incomprehensible languages. While distance did not deter activity *against* other states, where dynastic interests or rights dictated such actions, it did inhibit any effective control of such lands from afar. More significantly, it inhibited the type of communications a viable structure required. Only in Italy were relatively compact and efficiently administered units created, capable of organizing their foreign relations on a rational and carefully calculated basis.[13]

> In terms of commercial intercourse or military logistics or even of diplomatic communication European distances were perceptibly greater in the 14th century than in the 16th, and remained greater in the 16th than they were to become by the 18th. In the 14th and 15th centuries, the continental space of western Europe still impeded any degree of political organization efficient enough to create a system of continuous diplomatic pressures. Rulers might indulge themselves in foreign adventures out of vain-glory or greed or spite: they were not yet compelled to continuous vigilance and continuing action beyond their own frontiers by constant, unavoidable pressures.[14]

Because of the more advanced political structures and the relatively shorter distances, it was thus in Italy that a more developed international structure emerged. A new system of communication among states was developed, which represented an advance over the diplomatic systems of all earlier societies. At first

12. "Big cities ate smaller ones. The boundaries of the victors widened ominously towards one another. From 1300 on, the number of independent communes dwindled. Florence took Arezzo and then Pisa. Milan absorbed Brescia and Cremona. Venice annexed Verona and Padua. And these victims had been powerful cities, the conquerors of their smaller neighbors, before they were conquered in their turn." G. Mattingly, *Renaissance Diplomacy* (London, 1955), p. 54.

13. "It was otherwise in Italy. . . . Italy was beginning to become such a system of mutually balanced parts in unstable equilibrium, as all Europe was to be 300 years later, a small-scale model for experiments with the institutions of the new state." *Ibid.*, p. 56.

14. *Ibid.*

a system of special ambassadors to undertake particular missions—negotiation of a treaty, arrangement of a marriage—was instituted; this was not unlike the systems used in ancient China and Greece. In 1436 Bernard Rosser wrote a "Short Treatise About Ambassadors" which showed that widely recognized conventions concerning the conduct of diplomatic missions and their treatment had already been developed. By that time an ambassador would be especially "accredited" and would be accorded a privileged diplomatic status during his stay. By 1450 there was a big step forward: Italian states began to station ambassadors on a *permanent* basis at each other's courts,[15] to report to their own sovereign (sometimes every day, as Machiavelli did from Paris) and to represent him on important occasions at the foreign court. By the end of the century this example was being copied all over Europe. In addition, a large number of unofficial or semiofficial agents were sent abroad to undertake tasks ranging from those of a messenger to those of a spy. Consuls came to be appointed to look after commercial matters: beginning in the twelfth century, some of the Italian merchant communities in the Levant had elected or appointed consuls to represent them before local authorities or to determine disputes. From the thirteenth century European monarchs, such as those of Aragon and England, sent procurators to represent them, especially on legal, but sometimes on political, questions at the Vatican in Rome.

The ambassadors, as we saw, were here the *personal* envoys of the ruler who sent them. He himself gave them their instructions and the "powers" with which they negotiated. Similarly, they were accredited not to the government of the receiving state but to its court. They were sometimes supposed to have dealings only with those of royal blood. They were in the nature of personal messengers, reporters, and representatives. This reflected the overall authority of the rulers in a dynastic age, their personal control of foreign policy. Though a permanent network of communications among the states of the society was thus established for the first time, it was a system for linking only the topmost points of each state.

In a few cases something like a foreign office developed, under the authority of the ruler, to control foreign policy. In Milan

> the great Duke was his own foreign minister, but . . . an organized Chancery performed at least some of the functions of a modern foreign office. It seems to have drafted official documents, prepared instructions for ambassadors, collated reports from different parts of Italy, acted as a buffer between the duke and foreign envoys, and begun the systematic keeping of records without which a coherent foreign policy is inconceivable.[16]

The other large Italian cities also set up organized chanceries which required written reports from their agents and kept comprehensive records.[17] In France,

15. The first resident ambassadors had been sent a century earlier, from Mantua to Louis the Bavarian in 1341.

16. Mattingly, *Renaissance Diplomacy*, p. 69.

17. *Ibid.*, p. 95.

Francois I established something like a permanent diplomatic machinery.[18] But more often the disorganized and amateurish personal control described earlier in relation to Ferdinand of Aragon was the system employed.[19]

Perhaps because it was a society of self-willed and autocratic dynasts, despite this new diplomatic framework no organized system of relationships among states developed. No consistent balance of power principle operated. As always, powers competed for allies when they faced a conflict (as England and France competed in Flanders and Bavaria during the Hundred Years' War, or the pope and Milan among the Italian states during the French wars in Italy), and this mutual competition inevitably led on occasion to a balance of a kind. But the response to such approaches depended normally on chance sympathies or diplomatic bargainings rather than any conscious attempt to establish an overall "balance." At least till the sixteenth century, it is impossible to find a case where one nation joined the weaker side to prevent a stronger from prevailing (the hallmark of a genuine balance of power system).

During the sixteenth century this situation began to change in a double sense. As usual the system adopted reflected prevailing ideology and motives. The intense personal rivalry between the Hapsburg and Valois kings served to create a de facto balance of a sort, since these were the two strongest powers. Second, England began to pursue unilaterally a balance of power between her two great neighbors for her own purposes (fluctuating several times, for example, between France and the Empire between 1515 and 1545). But this was merely part of the opportunistic shifting and hedging of Tudor foreign policy, and it could not secure a balance within the system as a whole. The Italian states and the pope switched in a similar way, calling on Charles V to expel the French and on the French to expel Charles, but this, too, was a purely self-interested policy which did not achieve balance in the wider world. Such policies were more the spasmodic response to the chances and inducements of the moment than a systematic policy to secure stability. Only among the five main states of Italy between 1430 and 1494 was a balance of power policy more deliberately pursued: Florence shifted her alliance from Venice to Milan, for example, when Milan became weaker and Venice became the main threat. There were nearly always three powers ranged against two during this period. But whatever the benefit for individual powers that resulted, it scarcely secured peace for the system as a whole: there were six wars among the main Italian states during this brief period. This frequent recurrence of war, as we shall see, is a feature of most balance of power systems.

Nor can there be said to have been any sphere of influence system. The

18. While in the Greek system orators had been required as ambassadors to persuade the listening assembly, now *writers* were required to draft clear and well-phrased reports and orations. Thus such writers as Dante, Petrarch, Boccaccio, and Chaucer were sent as ambassadors. In a few cases merchants who had to travel on their own business were appointed: Venice appointed two of its merchants permanent ambassadors in London in 1496.

19. See p. 123 above.

transnational character of dynastic claims, advanced without regard to any geographical logic, the universal competitiveness, and the arbitrary and opportunistic character of alliances prevented any durable groupings of states within a particular area under the hegemony of the strongest. On the contrary, small states in the shadow of the big ones were often eagerly sought as allies by those outside: England found allies in Flanders, Brittany, Artois, Burgundy, and Navarre in the Hundred Years' War, while France found them in Scotland and the Welsh marshes. Francois I allied himself with Milan, Venice, and the German Protestant princes against Charles V, while Charles found support in Savoy, Provence, and Denmark against France.

Nor were alliances dictated by ideology any more than by geography: Catholic France sought allies in Protestant Germany and infidel Turkey, Catholic Spain was allied with Protestant England in the 1540s, shortly after Henry VIII had defied the pope and cast off his Spanish queen. Alliances remained based on dynastic whim and interest, rather than any concept of geographical or ideological blocs. This was scarcely a basis for an organized or stable system. Neither bipolar alliance, balance of power, nor sphere of influence was consistently used as a regulating mechanism.

This then was a loose and highly flexible structure. The deterrent to war was the cost and the distance involved, rather than any automatic mechanism developed for establishing equilibrium. That deterrent was only rarely effective, at least among the major powers. Such countries as France, England, Aragon, later Spain, and the major cities of Italy were involved in wars every few years, often with a different ally and sometimes against a different antagonist each time. The only constant factors were the traditional rivalries between England and France, between Luxembourgs and Wittelsbachs, between Genoa and Venice, between Hapsburgs and Valois. Such recurring feuds were among the few consistent patterns that can be found in this society. Occasionally rivalry created mutual deterrence. But in general the decline of traditional relationships based on feudal or religious ties, and the increasing concentration of power in the hands of the dynasts, left the way open to a personal and arbitrary structure based on dynastic and national rivalries alone.

If the dynastic principle had itself been clear-cut and free from ambiguity, it might have served as a regulating principle—territory would have been distributed according to the rules of the system which all would have accepted. Since those rules were ambiguous and disputed (see pp. 83–84 above), no effective regulatory principle existed.

## 10.4 The Age of Religions (1559–1640)

The structure of society in the succeeding period was wholly different. Relations among states came to be determined by beliefs, above all the beliefs of rulers, rather than by traditional alliances or immediate calculations of state interest. Rights to territory were attributed to states on religious as much as dynastic grounds. Bohemia was judged as the emperor's by Catholics, as Frederick of Palatine's by Protestants; the Netherlands was accorded to United Provinces by Protestants, to Spain by Catholics, and so on.

One important change was that diplomacy became far less important in communication among states. The division caused by religious antipathy was such that often there was no desire for personal contacts with heretics and infidels, whose good faith could not be trusted anyway, and who might use their own diplomatic establishments to spread heresy and sedition at home.

> As the continent divided into two warring camps it became increasingly difficult to maintain the traditional international courtesies, or to continue the dialogue between sovereign states. In a world in which the papacy frowned on diplomatic relations between catholics and heretics, it was inevitable that the normal exchange of diplomatic intercourse should shrink and that embassies, where they survived, should become centers for religious propaganda and political subversion at the heart of alien territory.[20]

Permanent embassies, which had become relatively common in the previous age, now declined again. There was a reversion to the use of unofficial agents in place of resident embassies.

> In diplomacy the effect of the ideological conflict was most obvious in respect of the new institution of resident ambassadors. . . . Residents had always been the object of a certain amount of suspicion. The schism in Christendom hardened that suspicion to a certainty. . . . Since there could be no peace, no real truce even, with the powers of darkness, what purpose could the residents of an infidel power have in the realm except espionage and subversion? . . . Where these pressures did not lead to a complete rupture of diplomatic relations, as sometimes they did, they made the surviving resident ambassadors extremely uncomfortable.[21]

One of the problems concerned embassy chapels. The intensity of religious feelings was such that there was a reluctance to countenance the devotions of a heretic faith even within the private confines of a foreign embassy.[22] Moreover, where embassies did exist, they were generally felt to be nothing but centers for spying and intrigue, which indeed they often were: Wooton's famous description of an ambassador as a good man sent abroad to lie for his country, though it aroused the indignation of James II, was generally felt among most in the age as a not unflattering definition.

The primacy of religion affected the regulatory system adopted. As in all ideological ages a genuine balance of power system—the adoption and abandonment of alliances at short notice to maintain a consistent equilibrium—became impossible, since the ties of ideological commitment prevented the flexible inter-

---

20. J. H. Elliott, *Europe Divided, 1559–1598* (London, 1968), p. 41.

21. *New Cambridge Modern History,* III (1968): 161–62.

22. Ibid., 162.

change of partners that system required (just as corresponding ties do in the modern ideological age). Individual powers sometimes sought to balance their enemies against each other, but this did not amount to the same thing. Both the two leading powers, Spain and France, were Catholic. Smaller powers, whether Catholic themselves (like the Papacy, Venice, or Savoy) or Protestant (like England), might play them off against each other to their own advantage, as has been done in every age. But this did not establish a balance of power *system*. The situation was rather that of two relatively stable ideological blocs, the Protestant lands mainly in northern Europe and the Catholic lands mainly in the south, whose membership did not fluctuate very much. The only important maverick was France, which finally aligned herself with the protestant powers to settle old scores against the Hapsburgs. But the effect of this was certainly not to maintain the balance; the outcome was to achieve for France an ascendancy as powerful as that of Spain had been in the preceding period.

The balance, such as it was, was thus rather one of ideologies than of nations. Here there was perhaps in a more real sense a self-balancing mechanism. The ideological offensive of one side promoted the ideological defense or counterattack of the other. The reformation provoked the counterreformation, and the counterreformation provoked the protestant revolts in the Netherlands and Bohemia. But ideological bipolarity did not secure peace (as, to a considerable extent, it has done in the modern period); the continent of Europe was perhaps more continuously at war during this century than at any other time in her history. Like modern ideologies, each religion had a proseletyzing, that is an *expansive,* zeal, which in itself inevitably led to conflict. At the same time (or for that reason) each faith felt itself to be threatened by the other: the Catholics by the rapid spread of Protestantism throughout Europe, the Protestants by the offensive to crush heresy which they believed Spain to be leading. So the Inquisition stamped out Protestant infection in Spain while Elizabeth stamped out Catholic propaganda in England. The Evangelical Union was set up to preserve the Protestant states in Germany, while the Catholic League was established to protect the Catholic faith there. In the end, each faith successfully resisted the other, except in Bohemia and Austria (where faiths had always been mixed), so that the balance of the two religions was not very different at the end of the period from what it had been at the beginning.

The main difference between this system and the bipolarity of the modern ideological age is that in the age of religion the alliances were much less firm and cohesive than in recent times. There always remained doubt in particular situations which particular states would support their own cause. There were no clear-cut pledges of mutual support, as among NATO and Warsaw Pact countries today: the northern Protestant states of Germany for long remained indifferent to the cause of Bohemia and the Palatinate in the south, just as Savoy and Venice stayed largely aloof from the Catholic coalition. Even important states, such as France, remained unpredictable in their responses. The situation therefore more closely resembled that between the two World Wars than after them, when the democratic states could not be relied on to support each other, as in Czechoslovakia; and important states, such as the Soviet Union, or lesser ones, such as Italy, Poland, Hungary, and Rumania, remained unpredictable in their allegiances and actions.

It might therefore be more accurate to regard this as something like a sphere of influence system, with the leading powers of each side intervening to resist encroachments within their own area. Intervention is thus primarily defensive rather than evangelizing. The emperor, Spain, and Bavaria felt it necessary to intervene to resist the takeover of Bohemia by the Protestants, while Denmark and Sweden felt obliged to intervene to prevent a takeover in North Germany by the Catholics (as Western states did in Greece and Vietnam or the Soviet Union in Hungary and Czechoslovakia in the modern world). Eventually the two sides settled for a draw largely on the basis of a geographical partition, the principle first laid down in the Peace of Augsburg and ultimately reaffirmed in 1648, in a way which preserved a rough division between a Protestant sphere in the north and a Catholic one in the south. As always in a sphere of influence system, it was on the margin between the two spheres that the main conflicts arose: between the north and south of the Netherlands, in the Rhineland, in Bohemia, and in parts of Germany. The intervention of France to promote her own national interests in this margin, while contrary to France's religious convictions, helped to preserve the status quo between the two religious spheres of influence.

This then was a structure very different from anything which had preceded it in Europe. The traditional forms of contact through diplomatic representation declined. The role of unofficial movements, churches, and preachers increased. Transnational influences—Jesuits, Calvinists, religious volunteers—were powerful. Insofar as any stability within the system was secured, it was through the operation of a (tacit) sphere of influence policy, that is, the determination of each religion to resist the expansion of the other. This did not secure peace (any more than a balance of power or bipolar alliance system has ever done). But it did fulfill the function for which (consciously or otherwise) it came into existence: to preserve religious diversity. If freedom of conscience was not yet possible within a single state, at least peaceful coexistence among rival religious faiths in different parts of the same continent was guaranteed.

The principle of *cujus regio ejus religio,* which was reaffirmed in the final settlement of the conflict, reflected a reverence for princely power and a contempt for individual conscience typical of the age. But it at least formulated a principle of a sort, and so established a system for governing interstate relations in an age of ideological conflict. Certainly, after it was adopted and formalized in the Peace of Westphalia, international religious conflict in Europe ceased. This may or may not have been cause and effect. But it is striking that it was almost the same principle which was adopted 300 years later for another ideological age (in the Truman, Eisenhower, and Brezhnev doctrines and their mutual acceptance) and which then proved equally successful in maintaining peace.

The fact is that there are only three systems capable of maintaining peace among two mutually contradictory faiths in a multistate system. The best is total toleration, within states as well as between them. If this is not conceded, an alternative is a system of live-and-let-live between clearly defined areas or states where one faith only may be practiced. This has represented the chosen principle for regulating the two most recent ideological ages. The third alternative—letting each state choose its own creed or political system without interference even from close neighbors—has yet to be put into effect.

## 10.5 The Age of Sovereignty (1648–1789)

The structure of the society that emerged after the Peace of Westphalia in 1648 was quite different. The transnational character of the previous age—with religious movements transcending national boundaries, widespread concern over events within other states, the prevalence of civil war and foreign intervention, alliances based on ideology—all this was replaced by a society of separate and hermetically sealed sovereign states, autarchic in a political as well as an economic sense, each formulating its own policy on the basis of its own interests, little influenced by ideology or traditional associations.

The area covered by the society had expanded. Russia for the first time became in the full sense a part of the system. Turkey, from being a vaguely menacing external force, began to be thought of as a member of the society with which other members might become allied without shame (as Sweden and France were for part of the time). In the 1780s Pitt even declared in the British House of Commons that Turkey now formed a part of the European balance, and so justified British assistance to her (against the criticisms of Burke and others) as a means of balancing Russian power in that area.[23] But the extension of the society went far wider than this. Since the European powers came to compete not only in Europe but overseas as well, the balance established had to be extended to North America, India, and the Caribbean.

Diplomacy, after its decline in the age of religion, now rapidly revived and became the generally recognized method of communication among states. Some of the rules surrounding it were laid down in the Peace of Westphalia, and others were elaborated in the succeeding years. Louis XIV had ambassadors at the courts of all the leading states except Russia, and even in less important states, such as some of the principalities of Germany and Italy, he had "residents." Intense competition for precedence among states began to develop (Louis XIV, though he succeeded in securing precedence for his ambassadors in most capitals, was obliged to send to Vienna an Envoy Extraordinary because the Austrian government insisted on according precedence to the Spanish ambassador there). The main type of diplomatic official were at first the ambassador, the envoy, and the

23. That dispute was the equivalent of debates in recent times on whether the U.S. was justified in intervening in Vietnam to resist communist encroachment there, or whether that area was outside the legitimate sphere of U.S. concern.

resident. Eventually a fixed rank order became established: ambassador, papal nuncio, extraordinary and ordinary envoys, minister plenipotentiary chargé d'affaires, resident minister, internuncio, consul, and diplomatic agent. There was moreover now a generally accepted international language, French, which was used at nearly all international meetings and conferences, between ambassadors and foreign ministers, and in most official documents for the next 200 years.

A society of totally sovereign, self-interested, and nonideological states, with little law or morality to govern it, adopted a regulatory system quite different from the previous age. The system was organised on the basis of ad hoc alliances formed on a flexible basis, so that the power of some states could be mobilized to check that of others. Absolute sovereigns had almost total control over national policy. They were not inhibited by long-term commitments, whether on grounds of ideology or of traditional friendship. They could adjust alliances at short notice according to the needs of policy. Each maneuvred to his own individual advantage, since all wished to prevent the dominance of any other. This acted to preserve some stability within the system by preventing any violent fluctuations in the balance of forces and restricting the scale of territorial transfers.[24] The system therefore normally worked to prevent an undue accretion of power by any one state, above all by France in the late seventeenth century, against whom most of the rest combined to that end.

From the end of the seventeenth century this system was increasingly described as the "balance of power" system. The invention of the concept came to be attributed in Europe to William III and Queen Anne of England, because of their organization of the coalition against Louis XIV. The House of Commons in 1697 expressed its thanks to William the III for restoring to England "the honour . . . of holding the Balance of Europe," and Queen Anne's declaration of war in 1702 explicitly declared that the grand alliance against France had been established "in order to preserve the liberty and the balance of Europe and to control the exorbitant power of France." Often the term was used as a rationalization for state interest. Large coalitions ranged against France in 1689, and against Spain between 1717 and 1725, did not seem to influence those countries; war still occurred. Because power was difficult to calculate, a nation with acquisitive aims, even if the balance was against it, was tempted to chance its arm. In some cases private and immediate quarrels took precedence over maintenance of a balance. Thus on balance of power grounds alone, England should certainly not have joined France against Spain in 1658, nor against United Provinces in 1672. The emperor should not have agreed to the Partition Treaty with France in 1668. These actions were taken for the sake of the immediate advantages which such policies could procure, and the overall balance was disregarded.

Sovereignty found another regulatory mechanism to match this. One of the

24. "The major impression which the observer receives from the state system of 1648–1792 is one of relative stability. . . . Wars, an all-too-familiar disfigurement of the 17th and 18th centuries, repeatedly ended in restoration of either the status quo or a close approximation to it." E. V. Gulick, *Europe's Classical Balance of Power* (Ithaca, 1955), p. 39.

corollaries of the concept of a "European balance" was the doctrine of "compensation." If one great power was to receive advantages in any particular settlement, others, it was held, could claim a corresponding advantage, even if at the expense of a third party; alternatively, if one state was to make concessions to another, it might demand corresponding gains at the hands of the third. An example is provided by the negotiations at the conclusion of the war of Polish succession, when the French claimant to the Polish throne was "compensated" for renouncing it by receiving instead the territory of the duke of Lorraine; he in turn won "compensation" by being given Tuscany and the hand of the Austrian heiress. Austria justified the seizure of Galicia from Poland in 1772 as "compensation" for the seizure of Silesia from her by Prussia, thirty years earlier. The doctrine was seen in its most rigid form during the Napoleonic Wars, when French officials calculated with precision, carefully measuring territory, population, and resources, the compensation to be granted to Austria for the loss of the Austrian Netherlands. Though it could be used to justify almost any territorial acquisiton desired, this too, like the balance of power concept, at least paid lip service to a community interest (the need to secure a balance of interests within the society) and introduced some conception of "equity" to replace the idea of brute force as the sole arbiter in international relations.

The system of spheres of influence, on the other hand, could not operate effectively in a society dominated by the principle of sovereignty. First, each sovereign power asserted total independence in his own territory and would not acknowledge the right of even the most powerful neighbor to a dominant influence there. Second, power was distributed too evenly to allow any hegemony of this sort: even France, the strongest power of the age, though she could sometimes bully Savoy-Sardinia or even Spain, was defied by both of them at times, and almost always by United Provinces, which she might logically have claimed to be within her sphere. Russia, though she extended her own borders, was for long defied by her neighbors Sweden, Poland, and Turkey. Still less was there any clearly defined sphere around Prussia and Austria. Power could not in this age be sufficiently quickly mobilized and maintained outside a nation's own borders to make a consistent policy of dominance in large areas a practical proposition. The system of flexible alliances, on which the system largely rested, was indeed in logical contradiction to one in which large areas were permanently under the domination of the neighboring superpower.

The principles that were applied—the balance of power, compensation, the European system—reflected the needs of a society of sovereign states, each promoting its own interests; almost any policy could be justified on the grounds that it was designed to "restore" the "balance of power," which was always subjectively perceived. The ascendancy of French power and the aggressiveness of French policy during this period genuinely made necessary a mobilization of forces to resist it, and so gave the phrase somewhat more substance at this time. But the policy pursued here is perhaps better described as one of *reactive coalition*, a coalescence of forces against the dominant power of the day, a process which has been common in every known international society, and obviously corresponds to the interests of most states, as well as of stability in the system.

This represents in a sense a kind of primitive collective security system (that is, a system under which the majority combine to resist an aggressor). Vattel, the international lawyer, declared that if any state "should betray unjust and ambitious dispositions by doing the smallest wrong to another state, all Nations may . . . together join forces with the injured State, in order to put down the ambitious Prince."[25] Even Fenelon, though a subject of Louis XIV, declared that "there was a mutual duty of defense of the common safety against a neighboring state which became too powerful."[26] Walpole declared that "it is by leagues well concerted and strictly observed that the weak are defended against the strong. . . . By alliances . . . the equipoise of power is maintained."[27] For the first time a regulatory principle was devised, as an abstract concept, to help maintain stability within the system, rather than simply to promote short-term national advantage.

But the difference from a proper collective security system was that in this society there was no *preexisting* obligation to come to the defense of the attacked. And it was in practice only when one power was so dominant as to be a menace universally feared, as between 1680 and 1713, that a considerable number of states saw their national interests in resisting it. A publication in England in 1741, entitled *Europe's Catechism,* described "the Balance of Power" (attributed to "the immortal King William, the Dutch and other wise men"), as a system under which "when any Potentate has arrived at an exorbitant Share of Power," the rest ought "to league together in order to reduce him to do his due Proportion of it." Under this conception power is a limited asset, to be weighed out in the scales, like butter, so that nobody gets more than his fair share. For this purpose rival alliances might need to be established to secure a balance, so when France allied with Prussia, Britain must ally with Austria, and when France joined Austria, Britain must join Prussia. The doctrine's importance was that it encouraged the sense of a *community* interest, rather than a purely national interest, in the maintenance of a balance. For the first time there was an attempt, in theory if not in practice, to consider the needs of the society of states as a whole, a society having its own rules and principles of interaction to which every member owed certain obligations. Thus the Treaty of Utrecht declared one of its aims to be "to secure and stabilise the peace and tranquility of the Christian world by a just equilibrium of power (which is the best and most solid base of mutual friendship and desirable harmony)."

The principle alone, however, was not sufficient to secure peace. Even when it was desired and achieved, a balance could not necessarily deter war. Between 1740 and 1756, for example, when two almost exact balances between the major powers of the continent were established in turn, two major wars resulted; far from

25. Vattal, *The Law of Nations,* III, 250.

26. Quoted in Gulick, *Europe's Classical Balance,* p. 79.

27. A. F. Kovacs, "Development of the Principle of the Balance of Power," unpublished ms., quoted in ibid., p. 20.

deterring conflict, the alliances were made for the purpose of waging it. Each state was concerned to preserve its independence by preventing gain of excessive power by another. This at least implied taking a more long-term view than before about state interests. A state might have an interest in the long-term stability of the system, which overrode the immediate advantage to be gained by a particular action. It might be better advised not to ally itself with a very powerful neighbor, despite the benefits this could provide, if this would overturn the balance in that neighbor's favour. It might be better to sacrifice the immediate pleasures of neutrality in order to join in deterring the threat against the independence of another state. In the words of Lord Brougham, describing the system in a later age: "All particular interests, prejudices or partialitites must be sacrificed to the higher interest. . . . No previous quarrel with any given state, no existing condition even of actual hostility must be suffered to interfere with the imperative claims of the general security."[28] It was this growing sense of the needs of society as a whole (which the concentration of power in the hands of a limited group of like-minded sovereigns assisted) that represented the most important advance of the age in devising a viable social structure. The system might not be able to secure peace; indeed, wars occurred with monotonous frequency. But the system could moderate the gravity and consequences of war and prevent the ascendancy of a single power. And its merits could be further developed in the age to come.

## 10.6 The Age of Nationalism (1789–1914)

The structure of the society that followed once again reflected the character of the society.

It was now, for the first time, a worldwide society in the sense that, though the headquarters was in Europe, the conflicts of the European powers were fought out all over the globe. Paradoxically it was also a smaller society, in that the total number of units involved was less. With the virtual disappearance of the ministates of Italy and Germany, by 1870 a society of twenty or so significant European states was left, varying greatly in power, with five of major importance dominating all the rest. The states of America, North and South, though they were in increasingly close contact, were never effectively a part of the system; there was, for example, no war involving European and Latin American states, and the U.S. played little part on the world stage until 1900. China was slumbering in semisubjection, while the autonomous British dominions and independent Siam were only marginal forces. Elsewhere, almost every country was under European rule. Only Japan, in the final years, played a world role as an independent state.

The society was smaller in another sense. Distances between states had become far shorter. With the steamship, the railway, and better roads, most

28. Lord Brougham, *Works,* VIII, 72.

European capitals were now only hours rather than days apart. The telegraph reduced communication times still further. This had two effects on diplomacy and international relationships. Personal contacts were much more frequent. Summit meetings were even more popular than today: William I of Prussia met Alexander II at Breslau in 1859, Victoria at Coblenz in 1860, Napoleon III at Compiegne in 1861, and so on. Holidays were often made the occasion for a personal encounter, as when Napoleon III met Prince Albert and Palmerston at Osborn in 1857, when Bismarck went to see Napoleon III at Biarritz, and when Alexander II visited Wilhelm at Ems in 1879. Foreign ministers were often still more diligent travelers than their sovereigns, and their vision was probably correspondingly broadened. The important decision makers had far greater knowledge of foreign countries and their leaders than in previous ages. Knowledge of the intentions and interests of other states increased. The often-mentioned notion of a "European system" was no longer altogether Utopian.

Diplomacy was affected in another way by the decline of distance. Instructions to ambassadors took less time to reach them, especially after the invention of the telegraph. And they could more easily be recalled for consultations. Although some, such as Stratford Canning in Constantinople, continued to be accorded substantial personal authority, in general the personal responsibility they wielded declined.[29] At the same time diplomats became more professional, more skillful, and more assiduous. The number of messages exchanged expanded dramatically. The perpetually changing demands of diplomacy made necessary a constant flow of information in each direction. Every dinner table conversation might have significance and might need reporting to the capital immediately. This increased the total volume of information on which decisions were reached, and so facilitated understandings. Certainly there were many more meetings, and more conferences which ended in agreement. Only when there was never any intention of compromise, as in the wars of the mid century, or when insufficient time was given for negotiation, as in 1914, was it impossible to arrive at a resolution of differences.

There was another important change. In an age of nationalism, diplomacy like everything else was nationalized. Ambassadors became the representatives of national governments rather than of sovereigns. They reported now to foreign ministers, not to rulers. Foreign offices grew: from having been small and haphazard groups of officials often associated with the court before the French Revolution, to substantial departments of state manned by permanent civil servants, by 1914. The permanent official, such as Holstein in Germany, Nicholson and Sir Eyre Crowe in Britain, Cambert in France, could have a powerful influence on government policy. Just as the authority of the sovereign had been increasingly

---

29. This did not apply to remoter parts of the world. When Captain Elliott was negotiating on behalf of Britain after the war of 1839 the instructions took many months to reach him, and he could not consult on the offers that China made. The Chinese representatives were not much better off. The consequence was that the peace terms finally arrived at between them were considered unsatisfactory by the British and Chinese governments alike, but could not be revised without reopening the war once more.

circumscribed, even eliminated, by the foreign minister, now that of the foreign minister began in turn to be circumscribed by his officials. So the system became both more professional and more institutionalized.

The reduction of distance affected the structure of the society in other ways. Warfare no longer necessarily involved long and complicated campaigns with sieges and baggage trains. Armies could be moved much more quickly. Wars themselves became much shorter. Thus the Austro-Prussian War was effectively over in three weeks, the Franco-Prussian War in six (after this the war concerned only the terms, not the outcome), the Bulgarian-Serbian War of 1885 in a fortnight, and the first Balkan War virtually in a month. There was no really prolonged war (more than two years) between 1815 and 1914. This made the first military move an act of profound importance, since an effectively planned campaign could be enough to secure outright victory in the first weeks. So surprise was at a premium. This made the structure even more unstable than in the previous age. Continental nations lived in a state of military insecurity unknown in previous ages, when military campaigns took months to launch. It was only World War I which shattered the myth of instant victory, and even there it was attempted in the strategy of the Schlieffen plan, designed to secure for Germany a lightning victory in France before she need turn to Russia, with her slower rate of mobilization. When that plan failed, so did the myth of instant victory (which had formerly reduced the terror of the idea of war). The protracted slow murder of trench warfare gradually destroyed the glory and glamour which war had retained for many in the age of nationalism.

The final and most important effect of shorter distances was the far greater frequency of international conferences for resolving international differences. This made possible a wholly new regulatory mechanism. Almost every other year, on average, at notice of a month or two, it was possible to call a major international conference attended by foreign ministers or at least by ambassadors. A far more regular and systematic multilateral scrutiny of the affairs of the continent was thus possible. The concentration of power among five or six great "powers" assisted in this. Regular meetings among these introduced a new oligarchic regulation.

The system applied by this oligarchy was not one of spheres of influence. That concept *was* used, and explicitly, in relation to the world outside Europe. Such areas could be shared out relatively easily, since the available space was large and conflicting interests small. But within Europe it was impossible to agree exactly what was within whose sphere. There was no neat dividing line, as emerged after 1945. Britain claimed an interest in the affairs of the Straits on the other side of Europe, as Russia did in those of Spain and Naples, or France in the Levant and Poland. All wanted an influence in what should be done in the way of a response to a revolution anywhere. Even if there had not been this general concern over the events of the continent (which the system of multilateral consultation encouraged), there were rivalries which induced conflict over any division of spheres. So France and Britain had rival interests in Belgium, France and Germany rival interests in Alsace-Lorraine and the Rhineland, France and Austria in Italy, Prussia and

Austria in Germany, Russia and Austria in the Balkans. Even when some kind of clear dividing line was tentatively established in such areas, as between Russia and Austria in the Balkans in 1897, this could not prevent conflict arising again when new developments occurred there (as in Bosnia-Herzegovina in 1908 and in Serbia in 1914).

Nor was the system applied in a proper sense one of balance of power. Of course that concept continued to be used; any action by an opponent that was disliked was denounced as having upset the "balance of power." But in fact, though the "European balance" was frequently referred to, measurements of power were never clearly made,[30] and were certainly not the main influence on policy. Thus though Germany was clearly the strongest military power of Europe from 1870 onward, far from causing nations to rally against her, it rather attracted them to join with her. Not only did Austria, so recently her enemy, and Italy join her partly on these grounds; even Britain, until after the turn of the century, contemplated an alliance with her, thereby joining together the leading naval and the leading land power of Europe. This negligence of the overall balance could come about only because Britain, like Italy, was more concerned about *local* rivalries with France and Russia—in the Near East, the Far East, and Africa—than she was with the overall power of Germany in Europe. Even Russia did not voluntarily leave Germany on balance of power grounds; she was deliberately rejected by the German kaiser. So the concept of the balance was used more as a slogan than as a serious system for regulating society.

The structure was rather a *balance of interests* system: In each settlement everybody should get something, and nobody should be too disadvantaged. So the affairs of Greece, Belgium, Egypt, Schleswig-Holstein, and Luxembourg were disposed of in turn, in a gentlemanly way that offered no great advantage to any major power. So at the Congress of Berlin, at Algeciras, and in the disposal of colonial claims in Africa and elsewhere, interests were carefully balanced out in each separate settlement. But this process could not in itself restrain the naturally growing power of an individual nation such as Germany. In each settlement she might gain only her fair share, yet she might still grow by *natural* processes: by increases in her industrial strength, her population, and so her power. A system of methodically balancing interests could resolve some of the frictions that arose, but it could not halt the overall competition for dominance.

Applying the principle of a balance of interests, the Concert of Europe was able for much of the period to resolve many of the major conflicts which arose, more successfully perhaps than in any subsequent period. That principle, even more than the balance of power principle, implied a conception of community purposes to supplement purely self-interested ones. Frequent references to "Europe," the "European system," or the "general system of Europe" implied an acknowledgement of obligation by each nation to sustain it. Admittedly, this concept could

---

30. This was less true in the naval field, where from 1870 exact comparisons were made among nations' fleets.

often be used, like the "balance of power," merely as a device for justifying national demands or denouncing those of others: Bismarck had a point when he said that "I only hear a statesman use the word 'Europe' when he wants something for himself." But the fact that the word was used at all, the fact that justifications in terms of a common system were thought necessary, was itself an important advance. However hypocritical the homage which vice paid to virtue, the fact that it bothered to pay homage at all was a new event.

New restraints on national conduct thus emerged from the need to justify policies in terms of a fair balance of advantage. This was the essential regulatory principle used in this age: the principle appropriate to an essentially oligarchic society, in which nonetheless competing national ambitions had to be appeased.

## 10.7 The Age of Ideology (1914–1974)

The following age saw a society of quite a different structure. The number of units steadily increased. At the beginning of the period there were little more than fifty, and of these nearly half played virtually no part in the dominant system, which was based firmly in Europe. With decolonization, ten or so were added between the wars, and another ninety after them, creating a society of roughly 150 states of widely varying size and power. Together with this growing size in number went a diminishing size in distance. No state was now more than a few hours apart from any other. All became subject to the same influences, the same political movements, the same strategic developments and economic trends, wherever they were situated. All for the first time were absorbed in a single world community.

The reduction of distance had other effects. Insecurity became still greater. Every member of the society became more vulnerable than ever before. All were within easy reach of the strategic weapons held at the opposite side of the world. All could be almost totally destroyed within minutes. Geographical remoteness (which previously kept Latin America largely isolated, for example, and protected North America from attack from Europe) was no longer any protection. Every major power now had an interest in events in every part of the world; so the U.S., for example, saw events in China, Southeast Asia, and the Middle East, as well as Latin America, as vitally affecting her security. In such a world neutrality no longer provided much safety. In World War II Germany violates the neutrality of Norway, Denmark, the Netherlands, Belgium, and other countries, while the allies violate that of Iran, Iraq, and Egypt. And after that war such countries as Laos, Cambodia, and Hungary find that adoption of a neutral status does little to preserve them (even when it has been internationally agreed).

Against this, the reduced size of the world, with its division into ideological blocks, provides some security of another kind. Almost every state is to some extent under the protection of an ideologically sympathetic power, and the reduction of distance means that such support is of far greater value than in any earlier time. Between the wars, guarantees by France or Britain to Czechoslovakia or Poland were a mere gesture, a promise to fight to recover their territories once conquered; after that war, a defense agreement with a similar power could provide for any small nation a considerable measure of reassurance, and significantly deter attack from elsewhere.

The structure of the society is often described as bipolar. This term is ambiguous. It can be taken to refer either to the division of the world into two conflicting *camps,* or to the existence of two main *centers of power* which in turn influence most of the rest of the world from their centers of gravity. In both senses the term is misleading. At no time is the whole world even nearly divided into rival camps. For a period in the 1950s most of Europe and North America belonged to one or the other of the two armed camps, while a number of other countries were linked, by ties of alliances or sympathy, to one or the other. But already by 1955 the Bandung Conference revealed the existence of a substantial "third world" that belongs to neither grouping. As time goes on, this third camp (itself highly varied in political viewpoint) becomes larger, while the cohesion of the two main camps declines. China breaks away altogether from the Soviet camp, while France and Rumania disengage themselves to some degree from their alliances. In the second sense too the term is misleading. Significant centers of strategic power develop outside the U.S. and the Soviet Union, especially in China, West Europe, and Japan, and the experience of Vietnam shows that in any case strategic power, however great, is not always decisive. So far as political and economic power are concerned (often quite as significant as military), there were always rival centers of influence to dilute and dispute that of the two superpowers.

If there is no genuine bipolarity, what was the system for regulating the society? As in the age of religions, the dominance of ideology prevents a balance of power system from operating effectively. That system depends on the willingness of states to change alliance relatively flexibly, according to shifts in the power balance. But ideological commitments, binding like-minded states on a long-term basis or inducing unshakeable hostility to opponents, now prevent adjustments of this kind. Thus in the years before World War II the Western powers and the Soviet Union are unable to reach an accommodation when this is required to balance the growing power of Germany. After that war China lurches suddenly from a pro-Western to a pro-Communist position on grounds of political sentiment alone, and in so doing radically disrupts the balance. Again, as in the ancient Greek world, the power of the superpowers is sometimes used deliberately to prevent a change detrimental to their interests in a way that ignores overall equilibrium. For example, it is arguable that if Soviet missiles had been established in Cuba in 1962 to match those held by the U.S. in Turkey and other areas, a more even balance of power would have been achieved. But because U.S. power would have been diminished, that outcome was prevented. In a general sense a kind of balance between East and West was established after 1945 (with the new world brought in to redress the balance of the old) and helped maintain the peace. But this merely resulted from unilateral defensive actions on both sides. It did not represent a true balance of power system, with shifting alliances used to maintain the balance, as in the eighteenth century.[31]

There is a more important reason why the balance of power could not operate effectively in such a society. Threats to the order, as we have seen, were now not mainly external but internal: civil conflicts, sometimes aided and abetted from abroad. Military balance in such situations does not depend on the overall equilibrium between the alliance, but on the balance of forces disposable on the spot. That balance is largely a domestic factor which is only marginally influenced by the power available to outside nations (where these do become involved). In this age, therefore, stability depended as much on *political* balance within a state as on the external balance of power. And it is when this *internal* balance breaks down, in Greece, in Lebanon, in Cuba, in the Congo, above all in Indo-China, that the international order is most acutely threatened. That order does not depend on the balance of forces generally or on balance of power policies. It depends on the order that exists within states.

Theoretically the system of regulation applied is that of collective security. Under this, all were to recognize a common interest in the defense of the status quo, that is, they would offer their help to defend any member of the community under attack from another. So in the Covenant of the League all undertook to take steps to preserve fellow members against threats to their territorial integrity or political independence. Since in practice, despite the undertakings, no effective action of this kind was taken by any member, an attempt was made after the next war to establish a somewhat stronger system. Under this it was for the Security Council to "decide" the action to be taken by member states for this purpose, and all members were placed under a specific obligation to obey that decision. But again in practice the Security Council almost never made such a call upon the members. It never made any call for armed action against a state; even when it made a mandatory call for sanctions (against Rhodesia) the call was deliberately and openly flouted by one or two members, against whom no action whatever was taken. In practice, therefore, a proper system of collective security was never put into effect.

In fact this was the type of age *least* able to implement a collective security system. For that system, like the balance of power, depends on a willingness to fulfill commitments regardless of ideological loyalties, an indifference least likely to be present in such an age. UN action in Korea came closest to implementing the principle. But this can more accurately be regarded as action by members of one ideological alliance against those of another. In practice security, such as it was, depended rather on alliances of that kind, multilateral and bilateral; even if *general* support from the world community could not be hoped for in case of attack, the

31. A one-for-one balance is highly unstable, and vulnerable to small shifts such as the defection of one power from one side to the other. So the double defection of China radically altered the power balance. The fact that it did not materially reduce the stability of the system only shows that that stability was not mainly dependent on power balances.

support of certain specific members (the ideological allies) could at least be counted on.

This, however, could not order conflict *between* the alliances. Thus the society is governed far more, like other ideological ages, by the sphere of influence principle. As before the Peleponnesian War, or after the wars of religion, the two main blocks are willing to partition much of the world between them. Provided that they can each maintain considerable areas subject to the influence of their own ideology (and therefore their own power), they are prepared to renounce spreading it to territories controlled by the other. These aims receive concrete expression in the various "doctrines" of the age (comparable in effect to the Peaces of Augsburg and Westphalia in the previous ideological age). The Monroe and Brezhnev doctrines are each designed to keep areas close to the superpowers immune from hostile influences. The Truman, Eisenhower, and Nixon doctrines seek in different ways to preserve more distant areas from the influence of the opposed ideology. This system of partition works well enough where the spheres are reasonably well defined, as in East Europe and the Americas. But its aim is not easily achieved on the fringes between the two zones: in Berlin, Korea, Southeast Asia, and the Middle East, that is, in areas strategically valuable to each side but not automatically belonging to the sphere of either. So, just as the old national empires competed for influence and power within fringe areas such as the Balkans, so now do the new ideological empires compete in the marginal areas of the middle world.

Difficulties arise particularly where the strategic convenience of the major powers is in conflict with the political desires of the small nation concerned. A considerable proportion of the conflicts of the age, in Indo-China, East Europe, and Latin America, arise from threats to a sphere of influence by the emergence of governments ideologically hostile to the former overlord. This leads the major powers to seek to impose their strategic interests on local governments resistant to their wishes (Guatemala, Hungary, Cuba, Czechoslovakia). The system will only work effectively if a spirit of mutual forbearance is shown on both sides when governments emerge that are hostile to the prevailing allocation of spheres. The politically perverse government must refrain from pursuing any serious military threat to the neighboring superpower; in return the superpower must refrain from intervening militarily against it. So a Cuba, an Albania, or a South Korea must be permitted to utter purely verbal pinpricks against the neighboring superpower. But unless their actions create a serious strategic threat to these countries, they are not seriously threatening the stability of the entire system.

Once again the type of system applied followed from the general character of the society and the dominant motives within it. A large proportion of states had relatively firm ideological ties to other states, often including superpowers, which provided them with a greater measure of defensive support than has usually been enjoyed. In return the superpower enjoyed a sphere where its influence dominated. Whether or not for this reason, the society provided for a considerable proportion of states after 1945 a greater degree of peace than in any earlier ages, though at the cost of some loss of independence. The instability that existed now occurred primarily *within* states, especially within poor nations. For it was there that the competitive struggle of the two great ideologies was most destablizing.

So the structure of the international societies we have examined has varied widely. Some have been very large in terms of total number of members, even if relatively small in area covered (ancient Greece). Others have had a relatively restricted membership, even if they have effectively covered most of the world (the age of nationalism). Some have had relatively effective institutions and an advanced diplomatic system (mainly the more recent societies). Others have had only rudimentary facilities for integration (the ages of dynasties and of religions).

More important, perhaps, in terms of our analysis is the comparison among the different systems used for regulating the society and achieving stability within it. As we have seen, there have been three main methods employed.

One has been the so-called "balance of power" system. We have already tried to show some of the ambiguities and difficulties in that phrase. It may describe a self-interested policy (by one nation), or a social strategy (by a set of nations). In the correct sense the object is to secure a long-term balance throughout the society, rather than to maximize the short-term power of the individual country concerned (that is, it will often be more rational to ally *against* than with the strongest power). At certain times this has been an explicit aim, especially in the age of sovereignty and in the ancient Chinese system. More often alliances and coalitions formed to promote short-term national interests have been idealized as promoting a balance. This latter type of balancing has existed in almost every age.

The system is most typical of societies with highly independent units. The principle, even if strictly applied, does not necessarily act as a stabilizing force; often the quickest way to peace would be to allow the domination of a single power (as in the Roman Empire). Even if a balance is achieved, it will not necessarily deter war, as the examples of 1756 and 1914, when alliances of almost perfect symmetry were ranged against each other, amply demonstrate. This is because motivations, the psychological disposition toward war, the consciousness of a wrong, the demand for a territory, the urge for revenge, are usually far more powerful than any assessment of military balance in influencing decisions concerning war. In other words, the effect of the balancing principle is strictly limited to its main aim: to maintain some long-term equilibrium and prevent the domination of a single power. The principle has not, as the record shows, had much success in securing stability or a peaceful international society.

In marked contrast to this is the next regulating strategy: the system of spheres of influence. This system is most typical of ideological ages. The balancing principle demands above all a flexibility in policy, a readiness to shift alliances, to turn rigidly from friendship to hostility to maintain the balance. Traditional loyalties and friendships must count for nothing. This flexibility is impossible where ideological commitments are strong. In the sphere of influence system alliances are determined by geography and so cannot change quickly. The whole of a particular area, and all the nations in it, are placed permanently under the dominant influence of the major power of a region. This may spread its ideology together with its power. Other powers deliberately refrain from challenging it there. This system so clearly corresponds to the self-interest of dominant powers that it too has been applied at least to some extent in almost every international society. As we saw, it operated during the earlier part of the Chinese society, among Athens, Sparta, and Persia in ancient Greece, between the Catholic and Protestant powers at the end of the age of religions, and in various parts of the world outside Europe during the age of nationalism. Perhaps most clearly of all, it has been applied in the modern world, where there has been a tacit understanding between the U.S. and the Soviet Union that neither will intervene in a military sense in the areas adjoining the other.

This principle, consistently applied, has a somewhat greater chance of securing peace: If every major power keeps the peace within its own area, and refrains from intervening in the areas of others, major (interregional) conflicts at least will be prevented. In practice it has rarely worked so well as this, since, as we saw, there are always marginal areas between the spheres which become subject to dispute (as the Balkans did between Austria and Russia, or Korea and Vietnam between the U.S. and China); or there are individual powers which wish to *extend* their own area of dominance (as Germany did before World War I). In the modern world the system may have helped to preserve peace in Europe and North America, but could not prevent conflict in the disputed margins, such as Southeast Asia, the Middle East, and elsewhere. This too, therefore, is certainly not a universal panacea. It has, moreover, a more significant defect. Success can only be achieved at the cost of almost total loss of independence for smaller states within each region. This can only be avoided (then only in part) if the doctrine is interpreted in a negative sense: outside powers will refrain from intervening anywhere within the area of another, but the dominant power will not use its own power against rebels within the region unless the rebels actively threaten its own security.

The third alternative strategy is the system of the balancing of *interests*. This is a system especially likely to appear in an oligarchic society with a few dominant powers. Something like it was applied during much of the age of nationalism. Under this system the major states agree among themselves about the way to resolve the major problems which arise, seeking each time to secure a balance of advantage among themselves. This at least should secure satisfaction for all the main powers and so prevent a sense of serious grievance among them. The difficulty is that it may not always be possible to agree on a settlement which has this effect. While it worked reasonably well for most of the nineteenth century (see p. 329ff. below), and especially so outside Europe, during the last twenty years before World War I it was no longer possible to make the system work effectively; wherever there exist rapidly rising powers demanding concessions (as Germany and Japan were then) they may not always be willing to accept the settlements which will satisfy the *declining* powers. In the modern world the system has been applied in some cases, as in reaching settlements over Trieste, Austria, Laos,

Berlin, and even Cuba. But it was not possible over Vietnam or Korea. Even if the great powers themselves are appeased by the settlements so reached, others affected may not agree. Success therefore depends on a considerable degree of compliance among smaller states. Partly because of their weakness, this compliance existed in the nineteenth century and in the first twenty years after 1945, but not in the periods following. Only if the smaller states can themselves be brought into the process of finding accommodation is the system likely to work well over the long term, for otherwise they may rebel against the oligarchy.

Finally, a more theoretical system, often demanded but almost never actually applied, is that known as collective security. This depends on the willingness of all states to rally to defend any other that is attacked. It was supposed to be implemented by voluntary undertakings in the League, and by mandatory obligations in the UN. In neither case was it applied in practice except on isolated occasions (as over Korea in 1950), and its effectiveness cannot be rated high on the record so far. All that can be concluded is that it is a difficult system to put into operation since it assumes a willingness among governments to frame policy in accordance with an abstract principle (assistance for any victim) rather than on the basis of immediate national interest. To make the system work, governments must take no account of loyalties, national or ideological, nor relate the costs to be borne by taking part in an action to the possible *national* benefits to be gained, which may be small. This is a willingness which few nations have so far been known to possess.

Which of these systems have been employed in a particular international society has depended on a number of factors. It depends partly on rational choice, as when the balance of power system was chosen in the 1690s, or when the collective security system was adopted in 1918 and 1945. It is dependent partly on the national interests of major powers, as when the system of the balance of interests was adopted in the Concert of Europe. But it depends above all on the general character of the age: a sphere of influence system in an age of ideology, a balance of power system in an age of sovereignty, and so on. The sphere of influence system favors the maintenance of ideological stability; the balance of power system favors the maintenance of independence by sovereign powers; the balance of interest favors the continued dominance of major powers; and so on. Even in this field, therefore, we find that the "system" employed is often an effect rather than a cause. Here, too, it is often the general character of the system—its "ideology"—that is ultimately decisive in determining other factors.

# 11.  Roles

Among sociologists it is sometimes held that social relationships are determined by mutual *expectations* concerning actions and attitudes demanded in particular situations. These together establish social *roles:* parts to play and places to occupy within a particular society or social situation.[1] Members of society are distinguished partly by the different roles they play, medicine man, war leader, village elder, which may impose corresponding roles on others.

Within an international society too, the relationships in which nations engage represent sets of mutual expectations concerning behavior, rights, and obligations. And here too the expectations define the roles to be fulfilled by each nation within such a society. Some of these roles are imposed: that of satellite, colony, or outcast. Others are *universal* roles, in the sense that they are supposed to be played by every member of the society; for example, that of member of an international organization, or the socially cooperative member of the society. Others are self-chosen, yet still define the place of a nation within the system: that of neutral (as played by Sweden or Switzerland at present); that of maverick and rebel (as played by Albania and Cuba today); or that of guru and preacher (as played by India in the 1950s).[2]

But a role is usually at least partly socially determined. An individual may unilaterally decide what role he *wishes* to play, and this will affect the role he objectively performs within society. Yet this aspiration itself will in part be socially conditioned: the citizen who wishes to be lord mayor or prime minister, the housewife who wishes to be a fashion model or a society hostess, acquire these ambitions largely because society instills them. And insofar as each succeeds in attaining his or her ends—in other words, secures recognition by others of the role which they want for themselves—the role *becomes* a social as well as a personal one.

In other cases a role is adopted, not because it is chosen, but because it is inherited or imparted by others. The landowner who inherits the position of

1. P. S. Cohen, *Modern Social Theory* (London, 1968), chap. 1. For discussion of roles in smaller-scale societies, see Talcott Parsons, *The Social System* (New York, 1951), pp. 24 ff.

2. For a somewhat different analysis of national roles in international systems, see K. J. Holsti, *International Politics, A Framework for Analysis* (Englewood Cliffs, N.J., 1972), pp. 150–52.

country squire is half-forced into performing that role; he can evade it only by disappointing the expectations placed in him by family and friends as well as by local society. The juryman chosen as leader of the jury, the resident elected as chairman of the residents' association, the officer promoted to general, virtually have to fulfill those roles even though they did not themselves choose them, and may not have wanted them.

Roles vary also in the extent to which they are individual, or widely shared, or even universal. Only one person in each society can play the role of king or prime minister. But the role of the head of a family is very widely shared. And that of citizen is universal. Every member of a society is thus in practice playing many roles, some shared, some individual. And it is the particular combination of roles each one acts out that will effectively determine his place within society.

Certain roles are *reciprocal:* the playing of one role demands the playing of another in response. This is true, for example, of father and son, employer and employee, minister and civil servant. In a sense one role implies another: the role of landlord implies a corresponding role of tenant. In international societies, likewise, there exist such reciprocal roles: superpower and satellite, colinizer and colonized, mutual rivals, mutual friends.

What is important for our purposes is that societies vary one from another in the whole *set* of roles that are demanded within them. Some of the roles which are important in one society may be absent altogether in another. Thus among domestic societies the role of priest may be important in one, but have only a minor place in another. Moreover, even where it is important a role may be played in many different ways and therefore perform different social functions. The priest may be a performer of ceremonies, an interpreter of doctrine, a social leader, a confessor, a preacher, a spiritual adviser, or any combination of these. Thus societies vary from each other not only in the total mix of roles that they demand, but in the way each *individual* role is to be performed.

Within every international society we shall find that there are certain roles which have been filled by one or more powers at any one time. The total set of roles here too gives each society its particular shape and structure. Though some of the roles will be similar within all systems, others take particular forms according to the character of the society. Others *only* appear in certain types of society.

## 11.1 The Chinese Multistate System (771–221 B.C.)

One role that we shall find in different forms in many societies is that of superpower. A strong state may win domination over neighbors in return for providing protection or other services. In the ancient Chinese system this is seen in the role of hegemon (pa). This entailed specific rights and duties. The hegemon had the right to a considerable degree of direct control over other members of the society. That state "directed punitive expeditions, acted as arbiter of differences between the feudal rulers, punished those who disobeyed the orders and received the revenues which had formerly gone to the king.''[3] It could call meetings of the other rulers within the league (in the *Ts'o Chuan* the hegemons are frequently distinguished according to the number of times they called such meetings, clearly reckoned as a measure of power). It could intervene in the territory of its allies. When Ch'i held the position in the seventh century she intervened to restore order in other states of the league, including Chin, an extremely powerful state in its own right. In return she offered protection to her allies "which never failed."[4]

But the role of superpower here took a special form. The religious reverence surrounding the Chou dynasty was exploited to expand the superpower's influence: "By force of arms and persuasion it builds upon what is left of feudal ideals to control the other barons."[5] But this was only a veneer. Because it was a society of territorial expansion, in time the role became merely a cloak for expansive aims: "By the fifth century B.C. hegemony is often the professed goal of one or another of the seven remaining states, but outright territorial conquest and subjugation is what is actually involved."[6]

This is a role unlike any found in recent international societies. The power and influence of the hegemon went beyond that held by the superpower and bloc leader in the modern system. It was somewhat analogous to that held by Athens in the Delian League in ancient Greece, but Athens retained those powers largely by brute force, rather than by tradition, and in Greece the system only lasted a relatively short space of time. In China it had a widely accepted legitimacy and continued in one form or another for two or three centuries. There is perhaps some resemblance to the role of the Holy Roman emperor in medieval Europe, who also called meetings and resolved disputes. There was usually a greater disparity of power between the emperor and his vassals than existed in China, but the social function of the role was similar; the system in both cases provided a degree of security for small and disputatious states within a violent and uncertain environment, and more stability within the system as a whole.

Another role peculiar to this society was that of *legitimizer:* the state which accorded institutional or religious authority to particular actions. This was performed above all by the Chou state, originally the fount of all authority, and later to some extent by the states of Lu and Wei (whose rulers were related to the Chou royal line), which shared some of its aura. When the various hegemons called meetings of the states, these were given legitimacy by the presence of the Chou king or one of his representatives. Even in the Warring States period this legitimacy was still theoretically acknowledged; it was not until the third century that Ch'in finally took over the nine tripods which were the symbols of Chou authority. That this was thought worthwhile doing at all is an indication of the role the tripods

3. W. G. Creel, *The Birth of China* (London, 1936), p. 244.
4. H. Maspero, *La Chine Antique* (Paris, 1927), p. 252.
5. J. I. Crump, *Intrigues* (Ann Arbor, 1964), pp. viii–ix.
6. K. S. Latourette, *The Chinese, Their History and Culture* (London, 1946), p. 49.

possessed—they symbolized the continued sanctity of the Chou line. Lu benefited in a similar way: "During the Spring and Autumn period the prestige of the Duke of Chou was very great, and the state of Lu found the descent of its rulers from him to be a practical asset which it exploited to the full. Although Lu was relatively small and weak, its goodwill was valued by states that were far more powerful." [7]

Institutionalized roles of this sort are, of course, as in smaller societies, always liable to be counteracted by the more arbitrary and deliberately chosen roles of individual members of the society. In a territorial society there is the role of self-made man, upstart, rebel, *chief expander,* or threat to the peace: the state whose territorial ambitions represent the chief menace to other states at any one moment (the role of Germany and Japan in the interwar period). In the seventh century in China, Ch'u occupied this position: it swallowed up a large number of smaller states, first barbarian and later Chinese, creeping from the Yangtse Valley toward the Yellow River. Later, after its decisive defeat by a coalition of smaller states, its position was taken by Chin, which then became almost equally rapacious. Later Wu and Ch'in held similar positions as the expanding power and major threat. As such they inevitably provoked strong alliances against them, and until Ch'in finally absorbed all other states, the rest were often capable of resisting and eventually overcoming the dominance of the chief expander.

Then there is the role of *balancer.* This is the role said to have been exercised by Britain in Europe in the nineteenth century: the nation able to remain detached from the hurly-burly and to throw its weight where most required. In the Chinese system the balancers were mainly the states situated geographically in the middle of the system, limited in their power but strategically placed to hold the balance. For much of the period Cheng and other small states of the original Yellow River civilization, such as Sung, Wei, and Lu, performed this role. The way such states swung could determine the balance among the largest states. When Ch'u emerged as a serious threat, most of these states, after some vacillation, were willing to accept the protection of Ch'i to withstand that threat. Sometimes the smallest states of all would simply offer their alliance to the likely winner. As an officer of one of the smaller states declared, "Chin and Ch'u make no effort to show kindness [to smaller states] but keep struggling for superiority. There is no reason why we should not take the side of the first comer. They have no good faith: why should we?" [8]

Next, in all systems there is the role of *ally.* The importance of this will depend on the degree of insecurity and the relative size of states. In China the relatively small state was almost always obliged to remain in alliance with one of the bigger ones. This was not an easy part to play. It meant having to perform certain symbolic acts of deference, such as the regular missions which were supposed to be sent to the leader of each alliance. It involved being subject to strong pressures,

7. Creel, *Birth of China,* p. 217.

8. Quoted in R. L. Walker, *The Multi-State System in Ancient China* (Hamden, 1953), p. 28. As the author says: "It was the duty of their statesmen to determine which way the wind was blowing and get on the right side regardless of prior treaties or agreements."

intimidation, and even intervention; there are many accounts of states intervening against one of their own allies, sometimes to prevent it from switching allegiance to another greater power. The converse of the dominance of the hegemon was the subordination of its allies. They could be bullied into war, or have their quarrels with one another settled, with or without their consent. In other words, there was no real conception of sovereignty, of independence for each state, however small. The demands of the greater powers for a position of superior power and influence often forced the smaller powers into a situation of dependence.

Some roles emerge from local relationships, such as rivalry or friendship with a neighbor. The long-standing rivalry between Sung and Lu or Chin and Cheng, for example, inhibited membership of a common alliance. Conversely, the traditional association of Lu and Wei with the Chou royal line inhibited them from joining with a barbarian ally against the Chou states: in 587, when Lu was contemplating abandoning the alliance of Chin for Ch'u, the ruler was disuaded because the latter were not "kin." On the same grounds the Chou states in general had special roles of friendship with each other.[9]

Reciprocal to this was the role of the barbarian states, on the outside looking in, at first an external threat, but increasingly desiring to become members of the system and eventually to dominate it.

The character of the roles here reflects the values of the society. Some of the roles derived from traditional culture and belief (such as those surrounding the ancient Chou dynasty). Others derived directly from the struggle for power and dominance within the system (such as the role of hegemon). These two principles, the traditional and the new, that based on status and that based on power, are always liable to find themselves in conflict in any society. In ancient China they were in perpetual conflict, and the roles which emerged reflect their constant interaction. Similarly, there was conflict between the ideal roles for states laid down by Mencius and Confucius, peace-loving and benevolent, and those actually adopted, power-loving and aggressive. Those which finally emerged both reflected and intensified the character of the society as a whole: individualistic, competitive, Dionysian.

## 11.2 The Greek City-States (600–338 B.C.)

Since many of the same roles reappear in different international societies— superpower, ally, neutral, balancer, and so on—what counts is not simply roles themselves but the way they are played within each society. Just as, in narrower communities, the role of father, uncle, elder, priest, or medicine man may occur in one form of another almost universally, and the significant point is therefore the

---

9. See H. G. Creel, *Statecraft in Ancient China* (Chicago, 1972), p. 209: "States whose rulers were descended, or at least claimed descent, from the Chou royal house formed a group with ties that were considered especially close."

way each is interpreted and understood, so equally in international societies it is the way a national role is interpreted and acted out that may determine the character of the society.

So, for example, with the role of superpower. Among the Greek city-states, as in early China, an important part is played by the hegemon (this is indeed where the word originated). There were a number of resemblances in the form the role took in the two societies. Both in China and Greece the hegemon could call meetings of all the league members. In Greece too, it could recommend action of a particular kind to its allies. It could normally expect to exercise a considerably measure of command in the field in any military operation which might be authorized. It could, at least in the case of Athens, exercise considerable domination over its allies: Athens not only held the treasury of the alliance in her own hands, she placed military garrisons and cleruchies among her allies, and used force against some which presumed to decide for themselves whether they would join a particular operation. Sparta, however, played it differently: she "did not owe her leadership to force. In politics she favored oligarchy, but she did not impose an oligarchic government on her associates by the use of garrisons and political residents."[10]

But there were also a number of differences between the way the role was interpreted here and in China. First, in Greece the position did not circulate from one state to another as in China. The same two powers remained heads of their respective alliances for a large part of the period. The process in Greece was rather that new powers emerged, controlling new leagues, as Thebes in the fourth century became leader of a group that included some states previously acknowledging the leadership of Sparta or Athens. Second, the role was not, as in China, bolstered through association with a preexisting royal authority to which all paid allegiance by tradition (it was thus more comparable to the role of Ch'u in the southern league in China than to that of the northern hegemon there). The only comparable factor, in the case of the Delian league, was that it was bolstered by at least a nominal devotion to a common religious cult and institution (the temple at Delos, the traditional center of Ionian religion, was headquarters of the league). Finally, the dominance of the hegemon within each league was perhaps even greater than in China, reflecting the greater preeminence of power which the great powers wielded (a situation again more similar to that in the southern Ch'u league in China than to that in the north).

Because this was a society of very many, very small states, there was also the role of *local* hegemon. The leaders of the smaller leagues, Thebes in Boeotia, Argos in the Argolid, Elis in the western Peloponnese, and so on, were in effect hegemons within their own areas, often exercising a domination little different from that enjoyed by Athens and Sparta within the wider world. The relationships they established within such groupings varied. Democratic Thebes developed a relatively democratic structure for the Boeotian federation, but her own superiority

10. N. G. L. Hammond, *A History of Greece to 338* B.C. (London, 1967), p. 310.

in power was so overwhelming that there could be no question of resistance to her will on most questions. The Aetolian league also acquired a relatively tight federal structure, as Aetolia became more involved in international politics and more vulnerable, with a central system for electoral and military purposes. The structure of the leagues thus depended to some extent on the role each played within the international society. The Achaean league, for example, remained the most loosely organized because it was more isolated from the normal currents of Greek interstate warfare.

The role of ideological hegemon demanded its complement, that of ideological ally (or satellite). The way this was conceived obviously depended on relative power. The powerful ally could less easily be bludgeoned into following a particular ideology or policy by the hegemon; it might not always be relied on to remain within the alliance at all. Thus the more powerful Argos could threaten to leave Athens (as in 419); Corinth could desert Sparta (in 394); Thebes could afford to offer its favors to whichever power was less of an immediate threat. The smaller ally, however, had little choice but to remain in close obedience to the great power of its choice: as the Euboean cities did to Athens, Mantinea to Sparta, Tanagra to Thebes, Nautila to Argos, and so on. This dependence was particularly acute when, for whatever reason, a small power had a traditional enmity with one of the big powers. Because Plataea was totally hostile to Thebes, it was obliged to remain totally dependent on Athens; because Mantinea had historical disputes with Tegea, she was especially dependent on Sparta; and so on. On the other hand, the cities were less restricted in choice of alliance by geography than the states of the modern world, where most middle and smaller powers are considerably dependent on the neighboring great power. Ideological commitments of nations in the modern world thus conform fairly closely to a clear-cut geographical pattern, with communist states in one area, democratic states in another (though it is questionable whether this is cause or effect). In Greece all distances were small, yet democratic and oligarchic states often lay cheek by jowl.

The role of *balancer* in this society was often played by the external power of Persia. Persia and her satraps skillfully played off the rivalries of Athens and Sparta, usually trying to ally themselves with the weaker against the stronger, and occasionally deliberately delaying and withholding help even to an ally in order to weaken both powers. Persia tried to win the support of Sparta against Athens in 459, supported Sparta again in the closing stages of the Peleponnesian War, threw her support to Athens soon after that war in 399, and then back again to Sparta a few years later (in return for recognition of her overlordship in Asia Minor). The value set on Persian support is indicated by the price that was paid to get it: in the case of Athens the introduction of an oligarchy, and in Sparta the renunciation of freedom for the Greek states in Asia Minor, a freedom she had twice fought to protect. Corinth too sometimes performed the role of balancer and was geographically well placed for this: she sided with Athens in the days before Athenian ascendancy (for example, against Megara and Aegina), with Sparta between 440 and 404, and turned against Sparta again when Sparta enjoyed total dominance.

Boeotia followed a somewhat similar course, being neutral in 435, then joining Sparta against Athens during the Peleponnesian War and Athens against Sparta from 395. Even a very small state such as Megara, with its delicate strategic situation on the isthmus, was obliged to pursue a difficult balancing operation between Corinth and Athens (against Athens before 460, with her in the next decade, and against her usually from 431 onward).

The ultimate form of balancing is *neutrality*. As we saw, this was not a role that was recognized in China at all. But in a polarized society it may be a role required to insulate certain areas from rival claims, external and internal. In the ancient Greek society certainly it was important, and even sometimes *enforced*. Argos was *made* neutral in the treaty between Athens and Sparta in 446 (just as Switzerland was made neutral by the great powers in 1815, Belgium in 1840, and Luxembourg in 1867). Plataea was held to neutrality under a treaty made by Sparta after the Persian War, and this was charged against her fifty years later when she aligned herself with Athens. Under the treaty between Athens and Sparta concluded in 421, six cities were prevented from aligning themselves with the Spartan alliance irrespective of their own wishes. Against this, small powers were sometimes *prevented* from choosing neutrality. Athens, for example, refused to allow its own allies to opt for neutrality; this was seen in the ferocious punishment meted out to Melos for precisely this lapse. In other words, the role of neutrality, and indeed the whole structure of alignments among states, was related to the general bipolar situation: It was sometimes imposed by the great powers rather than being the effect of individual choice. In other cases, roles might be imposed by geographical or strategic necessity: Megara, as we saw, was forced to play a balancing role because of its vital strategic position on the isthmus.

For the individual state neutrality could provide the same obvious benefits and risks as in other societies. The main benefit hoped for was noninvolvement in the main conflicts of the day as well as freedom from tribute paying. It is scarcely surprising that when the people of Camarina were being wooed by both Athens and Syracuse during the Sicilian campaign, they felt it wisest to join neither in the hope they might be left in peace. Neutrality could also lead, however, as in other systems, to a situation of extreme vulnerability. As the representative of Corcyra told the Athenian assembly: "We used to think that our neutrality was a wise thing, since it prevented us being dragged into danger by other peoples' policies; now we see it clearly as a lack of foresight and as a source of weakness."[11] In a society so lawless that a neutral might be set on at a moment's notice on whatever pretext, neutrality often proved a somewhat dangerous luxury. From the point of view of the whole society, however, neutrality could, as in the modern society, provide increased security even for the dominant powers by removing the risk that a neighbor would go over to the enemy.

The roles adopted in this society, therefore, were determined by the unusual degree of dominance exerted by two or three superpowers. In a number of cases roles were *imposed* from without, whether by imperialism, as when Athens forced

11. Thucydides, *The Peloponnesian War*, I, 32.

allies back into line, or by superpower diplomacy, as when Athens and Sparta decided between themselves which other states would be neutral (this might be compared to the decision among the Big Four that Austria should be neutral in 1954, or between the U.S. and the Soviet Union that Laos should be so in 1962, regardless of those countries' own wishes). Imposition of roles in this way may work for a time if the two superpowers concerned can remain in agreement, and if the proposed role is not totally unacceptable to the small state concerned. It is not feasible in the long run if that role becomes unacceptable to the ruling elite of the small power concerned, or if the strategic interests of the great powers change. Such examples, however, are sufficient to show how roles in an international society (as in a domestic one) are partly determined by the needs of the society as a whole, rather than by the deliberate and autonomous choice of its individual members.

Here too it is not simply the existence of particular roles—super-power, satellite, and so on—but the way they are played that betrays the character of the age. The position held by Sparta, Athens, and Persia derived partly simply from their power or prosperity. But the way they saw the role—as implying a political commitment, as sometimes demanding political intervention rather than external attack, as leadership of an ideological rather than a merely military alliance—was determined by the ideological character, the ethos, of the society as a whole. Similarly, the role of satellite, though it existed equally in other societies, for example in the Chinese society existing at the same period, was played in a quite distinct way among the Greek city-states. It required here a deference to the ideological views as well as the strategic interests of superpowers. So each role, though it may be repeated in many different societies, is molded and adjusted to the needs and character of each.

## 11.3 The Age of Dynasties (1300–1559)

The European society of the late Middle Ages demanded a different set of roles. Since policy was in the hands of rulers pursuing goals that were essentially dynastic, the roles played were now mainly personal rather than national.

Thus the role of top dog, the holder of maximum prestige, was held by the leading dynasty of the age, rather than by superpower, master race, or superior political ideology. The image in the minds of contemporaries was that of a struggle among ruling families—Wittelsbach or Luxembourg, Lancastrian or Yorkist—for prestige or glory. The international successes attained, whether in foreign wars, territorial gains, or dynastic marriages, were those of the dynasty itself, and only by association of the nation it ruled. In the contest between Hapsburg and Valois in the first half of the sixteenth century, it was for the glory of their royal houses as much as of their nations that they chiefly struggled (what, after all, was the "nation" of Charles V—the Netherlands or Spain, Naples or Burgundy?).

The role of ally was equally now a personal one. Alliance depended not on considerations of national interest but on personal regard or kinship ties between the rulers. Edward III felt bound to assist the king of Castile, Pedro the Cruel, despite his universal reputation for tyranny, because he was a cousin and old comrade in arms. Charles V was in alliance with Denmark when his brother-in-law was king there, but turned to enmity when his brother-in-law was turned out. Charles the Bold gave assistance to Edward IV partly because they were related by marriage. But personal whim also played a role. The effect of this personal element meant that there was for example very little consistency about alliances. There were no long-term traditional alliances, based on geography or ideology, of the kind we found both in China and Greece (the only possible exception was the alliance between Portugal and Britain which, though it lasted for 500 years, was mainly a sleeping partnership). In general, princes would abandon allies and seek new ones with remarkable facility, as when Burgundy fluctuated between England and France in the early fifteenth century, or Henry VIII between France and Spain a century later, or when the Italian cities rearranged their alliances every few years without apparent difficulty.

Similarly, the role of antagonist or *rival* was often seen in personal terms. It was the personal rivalry of Edward III, not national or racial antagonism, which spurred him to contest with the French kings for the crown of France. It was the personal rivalry between Henry VIII and Francois I which dictated their competitive display at the field of the Cloth of Gold; personal rivalry that dictated competitive patronage of the arts among Italian dukes. Above all, the contest between Hapsburgs and Valois was widely seen as a *personal* competition between the current rulers.

The role of *neutral* also changed again. It now once more played little part. There was no conception that it was open to a state deliberately to opt out of the normal rough and tumble of international politics through studied withdrawal. The Papacy perhaps came closest to occupying the role of the neutral, especially in functioning as peacemaker. But increasingly the popes were absorbed in the general struggle for power, and in the fifteenth century were secular rulers like any other. Most rulers had no wish for neutrality; they wanted nothing better than to participate in the great competition for territory and glory. Even if they did not, they were not necessarily allowed to opt out. Small and ineffective states such as Flanders, Savoy, and Portugal found themselves forced into the general competitive struggle, either because of the demands of others on them, or through the positive desire of their rulers to plunge into the fray.

The other feature of this age was the amorphous structure of society, with few permanent contacts between the members. So many roles were now somewhat ill-defined. Traditional roles were modified. The lurking *outsider* was no longer, like Persia, a balancer or kingmaker, but an unpredictable incursor like the Turks. The chivalric tradition created the role of *champion*, like John of Bohemia battling for France, the Black Prince of England for Portugal. The religious environment created that of *crusader*, like Hungary under Hunyadi or Cyprus under Pierre de Lusignon, campaigning against the infidel. The dynastic spirit established the role of the *adventurer,* chasing after crowns, like Hungary under Lewis, Aragon from the time of Alfonsus V, England under Edward III. One can almost identify a role of *victim,* passive sufferer from the ambitions and acquisitiveness of others: such territories as Flanders, Naples, Savoy, or Navarre, strategically valuable but militarily negligible, or the smaller Italian cities, which found themselves the prey or the stamping ground for the struggles and rivalries of others.

Nor, because of the fluidity and unpredictability of alliances, did any nation consistently play the part of the *balancer.* Perhaps closest to playing this role were the popes. Not only did they secure their own survival among the Italian states by balancing one against the other, but after 1494 balanced France against Spain by calling in one against the other. Florence consciously adopted the role of balancer between Milan and Venice. The constant maneuvering of Burgundy between France and England, or of Maurice of Saxony between France and Spain in 1546–1552, could perhaps charitably be interpreted as a balancing policy, though it can perhaps more accurately be described as blatant opportunism. England, with equal opportunism, did initiate the policy of conscious balancing with which she is sometimes associated by joining the empire against France in 1511 and then changing sides four times within the next twenty years.

Thus each of the roles played in this period had a somewhat different character from what they had in other societies. The most characteristic feature is their personal quality: They were the roles of dynasts or individual rulers rather than of nations. But because of the importance of the dynasties within the society as a whole, the roles in effect involved, emotionally if in no other way, most of the general populace. Feudal roles derived from domestic society—those of emperor, overlord, vassal—had their influence on international relations. Here too, therefore, a certain type of ideology imposed its own roles, relationships, and expectations on the society.

## 11.4 The Age of Religions (1550–1648)

The roles adopted in the international society existing between 1559 and 1648 again reflected the character of that age: that is, an age preoccupied by religion.

One important role required at this time, for example, was that of patron, national champion, or protector of a particular faith. This transformed the role of superpower in that it was invested with a spiritual or moral character not present at other times. Spain's rulers, especially Philip II, felt themselves to have a divine calling to maintain the purity of the Catholic faith, to stamp out heresy, and to assist Catholic minorities (such as those in England and France) against oppression. Coligny declared that the aim of the king of Spain was "to make himself the monarch of Christendom, or at least to rule the same." It is true that God's purposes here, by a happy chance, coincided with the interests of Spain, but this does not mean that the latter was the only true motive for action. Many rulers felt a genuine moral obligation to promote the cause of their own faith. The Elector Palatine and Gustav Adolfus of Sweden on the Protestant side, Ferdinand II on the Catholic side, felt a divine call to preserve their own religion against its enemies. Such a role is perhaps closest, among other societies, to that of Sparta and Athens, defenders of particular ideological beliefs in classical Greece, or that of the superpowers championing ideological blocs today. But it was here associated with a degree of moral fervor not known in either of the other periods.

Other roles were inevitably transformed in the new situation. The pope, for example, could no longer perform his traditional function of mediator and umpire, the conscience of all mankind (a role somehwat comparable to that of secretary-general of the United Nations today), as he had at times before. His authority was no longer recognized by half of Europe. A pope who celebrated the massacre of St. Bartholomew with the ringing of bells and the singing of a special mass, and who excommunicated Protestant leaders such as Elizabeth of England, the Elector Palatine, and Henry of Navarre because of their beliefs, could scarcely any longer be regarded as an impartial figure, standing above the conflicts of the age. Instead his role became rather that of cheerleader and patron saint for one of the main international factions. In presiding over the Council of Trent he gave the lead to the forces of the counterreformation: just as once he had inspired and incited crusades against Moslems, now he did so against the Protestants.

On the Protestant side there was no equivalent role. Gustav Adolfus held the role of military leader of the Protestant forces, but there was no acknowledged spiritual leader. The role adopted by France as "protector of the Germanic liberties" was different again. She was a *patron* in a political rather than a religious sense, more like the role of a superpower to its client states in the modern world. She was able to exploit the intervention of the emperor in the affairs of the client states to secure allies against the Hapsburg interest. Since her own religion was different from that of most of her clients, she could not lay stress on the religious aspect. But she could present herself as the defender of the ancient constitutional rights of the princes within the empire, and so as the defender of the established order and the status quo.

The role of *ally* also took on a different character in this age. Alliances, as we saw earlier, were entered into largely on religious grounds. The two unions of provinces in the Netherlands and the two religious leagues in Germany are the clearest examples of this process at work. But the same tendency can be seen in the alliance policies of England, Sweden, and Denmark, which were bound, either through the preferences of their rulers or the pressures of public opinion or both, to ally themselves exclusively with Protestant powers. Moreover, the function of an ally in a religious age was not the same as that of an ally in the traditional sense. It implied a readiness to intervene to protect a particular faith, rather than to guarantee frontiers or to win victory for a particular government. It might involve alliances with religious minorities having no independent sovereign status, and insistent requests for intervention in support of such minorities, both from abroad and at home. Common religious sentiment lent a greater degree of solidarity and fellow feeling, as well as a greater permanence, to associations of this kind. Finally, there was the difference that a change in the religious views of a people or a ruler could make necessary a change in alliance, as when the Transylvanian leader, Bathori, defected from one side to the other during the Thirty Years' War, according to the change in his own religious views.

The role of *neutral* also changed. In an age of religions it was difficult for any state to remain neutral. Everybody had religious views of a kind, and so could scarcely be impartial where religious issues arose. Even if rulers themselves were relatively unmoved by such issues, they might be obliged to act because of the sentiment of their peoples, or because of insistent demands from abroad. Thus Gustav Adolfus declared: "I tell you frankly I will not listen to talk about neutrality. His Excellency [i.e. the Elector of Brandenburg] must be either friend or foe. . . . If he wishes to hold with God, good; he is on my side. If, however, he wishes to hold with the Devil, then in truth he must fight against me. There cannot be a third way, that is certain." For this reason in the Thirty Years' War virtually no European country was fully neutral; almost every nation was involved at one time or another. One effect of this situation was that it was often very difficult to find acceptable neutral mediators to resolve disputes between different religions. At the Peace of Westphalia Denmark and Venice, each of which had been involved in different phases of the Thirty Years' War, had to act as mediators, while Sweden and France, which had been heavily involved, had, in practice, to mediate between their own allies and the emperor.

Again the role of *balancer* was transformed. Such a role, as we saw, implies a readiness to switch alliances on a flexible basis according to movements in the balance of forces. But in an age of ideological commitment this willingness is usually not present. Even England, which had adopted the role spasmodically in the previous age, could now, whatever her own interests, never give military support to the Catholic cause. Only a very small state, such as Savoy, whose security was vitally dependent in playing off one power against another, was willing to throw in its lot with its religious antagonists for the sake of maintaining a balance. France, it is true, intervened on the side of her religious opponents; but this was not so much to maintain the balance as to overturn it in her own favor. In other words, there was now no power whose main task it was to throw its weight into the balance on the weaker side in order to maintain a general equilibrium.

All the roles of this period, therefore, were at least marginally affected by the special character of the age. The emergence of a global confrontation between the forces of the reformation and the counterreformation transformed the context in which they were adopted. New roles emerged, such as that of religious patron or religious ally, to meet the needs of the age; old ones were modified for the same reason. Some of the new roles, like the old, were complementary, such as that of protector and protected, ally and superpower. Because the whole society was seen in a different way, with a less rigid division *between* the units, but a much sharper one *within* them, the significant roles were often transnational as much as international, toward minorities and peoples as much as toward governments. A new set of relationships, and assumptions about these relationships, flowed inevitably from a new way of seeing the society as a whole.

## 11.5 The Age of Sovereignty, (1648–1789)

With the emergence of a new type of society among states after the Treaty of Westphalia, new kinds of role began to be required.

The role of superpower was transformed in subtle ways. With the end of the age of religions, it was of course no longer associated with the patronage and support of a particular religious faith. It was associated with a more self-conscious striving for status and for the acknowledgment of superior power by others, as manifested, for example, by Louis XIV's demands that his ambassadors be accorded precedence all over Europe, and that the ships of other nations dip their flag to French vessels. This was the role of the great *magnate,* the nobleman to whom the ordinary mortal must doff his cap.

But the dominance which such a figure might acquire was strictly limited by a new role: the humble but independent *citizen,* the ordinary member of society. The concept of "sovereign equality" meant even the smallest and weakest ruler was now sovereign in his own domain, and protected by the invisible walls which the concept of sovereignty created. Thus the type of domination, including the right of military intervention, which had been the prerogative of the superpower in the previous age—as shown in Spanish policies then, for example—could no longer be exercised. Occasionally threats of coercion from without could be used (by France against Genoa, Luxembourg, and Savoy), even an all-out external attack (as in the devastation of the Palatinate). But these provoked condemnation and retaliation from the whole world. And most of France's neighbors, including Savoy and the United Provinces, in their new role of sovereign states, defied her with impunity.

For the same reason, the complementary role of *satellite,* or long-term ally of a superpower, disappeared. Flexibility in alliance was an essential part of the system, and especially important for the small and vulnerable state. States such as Savoy, Lorraine, and Tuscany, and the smaller German states, now avoided as far as possible a relationship of long-term dependence on a neighboring superpower. Instead they sought to maximize their own bargaining power by playing off one major power against another. After the death of the short-lived League of the Rhine, the German Protestant princes broke away from their long-standing association with France and were now often in opposition to her (only the fairly consistent partnership between France and Catholic Bavaria showed some elements of a consistent patron-client relationship). For the most part even the small powers, though their military strength was limited, used the conventions of a society of free competition and free bargaining to maximize their own advantage.

The role of *ally* changed too in a world of sovereignty. An essential feature of the period is that relationships are short-term rather than long-term: alliances are essentially immediate matches of convenience, which may be abandoned within a few years when a more attractive partner turns up. The role of ally thus entails the minimum of commitment, sympathy, and loyalty, and the maximum of caution, mistrust, and opportunism. This is shown in the tendency of members of an alliance to seek a separate peace with enemies, irrespective of their allies' views (as Savoy did in 1696, Britain in 1712 and 1762, and Prussia in 1742 and 1745, for example). This heightened mutual suspicion and increased the temptation of others to do the same thing, only quicker, to beat their allies to it. The ally was a contractual partner for a very specific purpose which was clearly laid down; once the conditions were fulfilled (sometimes even before) all commitments were at an end.

In such a competitive society the role of *rival* becomes important. It is now not so much rivalry between great dynastic houses, Hapsburg and Valois, or between Catholic and Protestant champions, as rivalry between emerging sovereign states, acquiring an increasingly self-conscious national pride, that is significant. This is an essentially competitive society in which the competition is for status and prestige as much as for victory for its own sake. It now becomes possible for France, for example, to ally herself with Austria, in defiance of the traditional rivalry of their houses, to enable her to compete more effectively with her new national rivals, Britain and Prussia. In such a contest the rivals compete especially in the weak border areas between the great centers of power. So Prussia and Austria contest for power in Germany, Russia and Austria in East Europe, Britain and France in the Low Countries—competitions that continue to preoccupy them for the next two centuries. But just as the role of ally in such a society must be flexible and temporary, so must that of rival. So Britain and Prussia must be prepared in 1756 to abandon their previous conflict to fight on the same side again against their former allies. So Prussia and Austria a few years later, having only just completed their own conflict, must join hands in dismembering Poland. And so on. Some of the roles are temporary and ad hoc rather than stable and prolonged.

In such a society the role of *neutral*—in the sense of a power permanently outside the main competition—has little part to play. Any nation might remain uninvolved in a particular conflict. But even here

> the notion of neutral status remained somewhat nebulous . . . because the practice of the times had blurred the line separating war and peace. A neutral abstained from direct acts of hostility; but he could send auxiliary troups to a belligerent . . . without compromising his neutrality, and could allow the troops of a belligerent "innocent transit" through his territory to attack the enemy.[12]

(For example, neutral Spain did not resist the passage of French troops across the Spanish Netherlands in France's war against United Provinces in 1672). Again, particular areas could be declared neutral, in which belligerents would agree not to fight.[13] But in general, since all the major nations were involved in the general

12. *New Cambridge Modern History*, VI (1970): 174.
13. Ibid., 175.

competition for status and power, no member considered the role of long-term neutral as acceptable. Nor could one power easily remain neutral in particular wars: one of the striking features of this era (distinguishing it sharply from the next) is that most of the major powers are drawn into every war.

The role of *balancer* is also transformed. Because commitments are short-term, and alliances perpetually changing (and sometimes secret), it would have been impossible for any nation consistently to play the role of middleman, shifting its weight to the side that appeared weaker at any one time. Britain was not so far outside the mainstream of European conflict that she could perform that role, as she was sometimes thought to do in the next century. The lesser powers, in rallying against France in the seventeenth century, might be said to have played a balancing role, but in effect this was a reaction to France's own aggressive policies. When power became more evenly distributed in the eighteenth century, each nation was too preoccupied with the pursuit of its own particular interests to spare much thought for maintaining a long-term balance, however much they proclaimed that objective. Savoy-Sardinia pursued its traditional policy of opportunism, changing sides with bewildering facility, but this was for her own purposes and she was in any case too small to affect the balance significantly.

It is perhaps not altogether fanciful to trace again the role of *victim,* the relatively small power that is used, at the convenience of other powers, to assist in their own struggles for preeminence or to balance their own interests. Such a role perhaps appears readily in a society where the wishes of populations count for nothing. The role is of course in this case not chosen but, like that of scapegoat in domestic societies (Jew or immigrant), imposed by more powerful forces in society. The increasing concentration of power among five or six main powers meant that the weak became relatively weaker and more at the mercy of the great. Typical examples of this are the treatment of territories such as Tuscany, Sardinia, Parma, or Lorraine, passed around from one ruler to another and finally extinguished to satisfy the interests of the powerful. Saxony was nearly forced into the same role by Frederick the Great, and Bavaria by Austria. But perhaps the classic case of the victim was Poland, progressively devoured by her avaricious neighbors, as much to deprive the others as to benefit themselves.

Again, therefore, the roles adopted in this age are adjusted to the needs of society as a whole. The roles of great power, client state, ally, victim, become those which correspond to the all-pervading demands of sovereignty. A more structured society, more contacts between states, and a greater consciousness of status promote more clearly defined national roles than in previous times. The great play a role distinctly different from the small. Sea powers such as Britain and United Provinces, concerned over trade and colonial possessions abroad, play a different role from the land powers; rising and aggressive powers, such as Prussia and Russia, play a different role from the declining states of Spain and Austria. These are the variations. But every role is modified by the new ideology of sovereignty, and all nations increasingly follow a universal role, the generally accepted model of the independent, highly competitive, national, sovereign state.

# 11.6 The Age of Nationalism (1789–1914)

In the age that followed there were new modifications of the parts to be played.

A new role—marginally lower than that of superpower—was that of the "powers," as they came to be known. These had both rights and responsibilities (mainly the former). Their main right was that of reaching decisions among themselves over many matters which often affected other and smaller nations even more closely. Enjoyment of that right was one for which certain qualifications were thought necessary. There was an understandable doubt whether Turkey was really equipped to undertake the role in 1856 when she was admitted to the Concert. But it accorded clear-cut privileges:[14] Once admitted Turkey was invited to send delegates to every general conference until 1914, like the other "powers." It was thus in a sense comparable to permanent membership of the Security Council later: the right of the largest and most important states to participate in the discussion of *all* major questions that arose within the system, and not only those concerning themselves directly. It was perhaps therefore comparable to the role of *elder* or magnate in domestic societies.

But the role also implied certain responsibilities. The chief one was that of respecting the joint decisions reached.[15] Every power became in a sense accountable to the rest. So Russia was not permitted in 1870 to alter unilaterally the Black Sea clauses which were imposed on her in 1856; a new agreement had to be reached among all the powers to ratify the change. Turkey, in becoming a member of the Concert, was obliged to enter into certain undertakings in respect of her treatment of her Christian subjects. Finally, the powers had to take the responsibility for insuring that their decisions were applied. Britain and France had to send forces to secure the separation of Belgium from the Netherlands, force was used in the Balkans to enforce the decisions of the Congress of Berlin, commissions were sent to insure satisfactory treatment by Turkey of her Christian subjects, and so on (see p. 331 below). In brief, the powers jointly adopted the role of "world policemen," comparable to that which the U.S. is said sometimes to have adopted in recent times.

This implied a complementary role for the smaller states: the deferential *yes-man*. The smaller states were required to conform to the wishes of the powers as a whole. In extreme form, an individual small power became virtually a satellite of a single larger power, which became its big brother. Serbia was in this situation

14. Cf. F. H. Hinsley, *Power and the Pursuit of Peace* (Cambridge, 1963), p. 234: "The great powers had more responsibility and more rights than the other states: and they tended to emphasize their rights more than their responsibilities."

15. Ibid., p. 225: "It was from this theory that the states derived the principles underlying the Concert, that the great powers had a common responsibility for maintaining the territorial status quo of the treaties of 1814, and for solving the international problems. . . which arose in Europe: but when the status quo had to be modified, or a problem had to be settled, changes should not be made unilaterally and gains should not be made without their formal and common consent."

in relation to Austria in the years after 1878. In the abject letter he sent to the Austrian government in 1881, Prince Milan was obliged to commit himself to total conformity with Austrian wishes, undertook to enter into no treaty with another government without Austrian consent, and even agreed to make a secret declaration "in whatever terms you care to notify me." Similarly, in 1887 Russia asked Germany to accord Russia exclusive influence in Bulgaria, entirely without reference to Bulgaria's own wishes (which were at this time in fact anti-Russian). In other words, the role of protector was often taken unilaterally and without the consent of the protected; the role of the small power was to be seen and not heard. So Tunisia and Morocco had to accept the "protection" of France, and in doing so surrendered all control over their foreign affairs, just as Egypt did in relation to Britain.

Even if they were not under the tutelage of one of them, the smaller powers had a general duty of deference to the greater. Since the essential was to preserve the balance of interests among the powers, this meant that the wishes of the smaller fry had often to be ignored. If the Netherlands was ordered by the powers to give up Belgium, Turkey to give up Greece, Montenegro to give up Scutari, Bulgaria to be subdivided, they were expected to conform, regardless of their own wishes, or even the wishes of the people most concerned.

Nationalism altered roles in other ways. It sharpened the intensity of the competitiveness within the society. The role of *rival* took a national rather than personal form, as in the competition for colonies, or economic success. More than in any previous age, perhaps, there was a desire not only to keep up with the Joneses, but to compete with a particular Jones: so Italy had to compete with France, Germany with Britain, Serbia with Bulgaria. Sometimes rivalry was concentrated in particular regions: between Russia and Austria in the Balkans, between Britain and France in Egypt and Southeast Asia, between Italy and France in North Africa, between Britain and Russia in Turkey, Central Asia, and the Far East. An essentially competitive society promoted competitive roles.

Nationalist ambitions also gave rise to the role of *opportunist:* the independent power which sold its favors to one party or the other, to maximize its own advantages. This part had been played in the past many times, as by Savoy and Sardinia. It was now played for a time by Italy, desperate for allies to support her in her various Mediterranean ambitions, and not too disturbed whether the various undertakings into which she entered in return were mutually compatible. Japan seized each opportunity which presented itself. In another sense Britain, from her position of strength and isolation, was sometimes able to throw favors to one side or the other, to suit her own ends (rather than to achieve a balance, though sometimes it served both purposes).

Another role is that of the *arm-twister,* or extortioner, normally a weak ally holding a stronger partner by the short hairs. It has often been noted that in economic relations the debtor is more powerful than the creditor: the latter can do nothing against the debtor since he may only default altogether, but the debtor can always extract further concessions from the creditor, because these may be necessary if the latter is to get any money at all. Similarly, the weak ally always has its stronger partner at its mercy: it has little to offer its ally itself, but it can always strengthen its own position, even in reckless adventures, through the power with which its ally invests it. This was seen in this period at its clearest in the relation between Austria and Germany. Germany sought always (until 1914) to restrain Austria-Hungary in the Balkans, an area in which Germany herself had little direct interest. But Austria-Hungary was always able to overcall its own hand, in the certainty that Germany would come to her aid. So in 1908, and again in 1914, she could take action unilaterally in the certainty that Germany had no choice but to back her in the final resort. A similar role was played by Turkey in 1854 in declaring war on Russia, relying on Britain and France to pull her chestnuts out of the fire. Here it is the weak which have the strong by the nose, rather than vice-versa.

Nationalism also changes the role of *neutral*. A nation may have its neutrality thrust upon it (like Belgium and Luxembourg) to suit the purposes of the "powers." Even so, it may subsequently discover in the event that the status is not of much value to it in a crisis, as Belgium and Luxembourg found in 1914. In an age of ruthlessness, self-defense is the only true protection.

Nationalism also creates the role of the *social climber*, the middle power sometimes arriving late in the field and determined to become greater, like Japan, testing its newfound strength against China and Russia; or like Italy, determined to catch up to those who had already acquired great power rank before her. It also created the role of *avenger*, like France, determined to take revenge for the defeat of 1870 and recover Alsace-Lorraine; or of Bulgaria, seeking to vent her spite on Serbia for her failure in the First Balkan War.

These then were a varied set of roles dictated by the needs of a highly competitive and status-conscious society. The dominance of an oligarchy meant that a few powers were able to impose roles of dependence and even subservience on the lesser (see pp. 219–222 above). They could dictate neutrality, "autonomy," or "protected status." The strength of nationalist feeling meant that many of the roles were associated with attitudes of great emotional intensity. The rivalry between Russia and Austria, France and Italy, Germany and Britain, Serbia and Bulgaria, affected attitudes in many fields, political, economic, and cultural, as well as military. But the nature of the society was such that it was the military relationship which ultimately dominated all others. So Britain's political rivalry with Russia in Persia and the Far East, her cultural rivalry with France in Africa and the Near East, could be quickly transformed to friendship to enable them to unite against the greatest *military* challenge of the day. Conversely, the racial affinity with Germany which so impressed Chamberlain, the economic link with her which influenced the businessman, the cultural admiration of her which affected the intelligentsia, all these had to be abandoned in the interests of confronting her in her role as the main military threat in Europe and to Britain's status in it. It was national competition which exercised the dominant influence on roles.

## 11.7 The Age of Ideology (1914–1974)

In the age of ideology there are further changes in typical roles. The universal ideological struggle, the decline in distance, the emergence of nuclear weapons, and other factors transform relationships once more.

The role of *superpower* reappears. Superpowers exist in the first place, as in other ages, simply by reason of the size and military technology of particular nations. But their *role* is established by the demands placed on them by the system. They now require to unite and coordinate strategy for their own group, to supply armaments and manpower, to be a source of economic and other aid. They come therefore to represent a powerful center of gravity, leading many others to cluster around them. Potential military dangers are now more widely spread because of the decline in distance, and this in turn causes more states to nestle firmly in the shelter of the nearest superpower. On the one hand, ideological groupings require a leader to give guidance and support. On the other, the increased military vulnerability produced by the new weapons increases the need among smaller powers for protection and patronage.

The complementary role is that of ideological *ally*. This is usually a relationship more or less dependent on the superpower. The degree of dependence will vary, not only according to how far an ally is militarily threatened, but how far it is internally vulnerable. So the governments of Indo-China, are far more dependent on the U.S.' aid and succour than those of Western Europe, since they cannot survive without them. The role demanded of the dependent nation is one of general support for the superpower, verbal as much as military, in the confrontation with the opposing alliance. Thus East European states are expected to vote with their Soviet ally within the UN and other international organizations, whatever the subject being discussed. Even in the Western world, though a greater independence of action is allowed and taken, there is a limit to the degree which can be shown: limited, for example, by the demand for the retention of U.S. forces in Europe. Even where direct military dependence of this sort is not present, it may be replaced by a form of economic dependence that is equally inhibiting.

The role of *neutral* also changes. Those who are ideologically committed demand an equal degree of commitment from all other states. Thus "neutralism" acquires a pejorative flavor: Mr. Dulles condemns it as immoral. Neutrals are renamed the "nonaligned" (implying that alignment is regarded as the normal state). Nonetheless, the totally noncommitted powers, at first relatively few (since they forfeit the economic and military benefits of alignment), acquire a specific position within society. Sweden, India, Ireland, and so on, provide the forces for UN peace-keeping operations; provide mediators (such as Count Bernadotte and Ambassador Jarring) in disputes; provide all four secretaries-general of the UN (Norway was still regarded as a neutral at the UN's foundation). And they have a more general role in breaking the logjam in relations between the major blocs. Thus the nonaligned group in the Geneva disarmament talks succeeds sometimes in launching new initiatives which prevent deadlocks there; individual nonaligned countries, such as Yugoslavia, India, or Sweden, often have an important role as middlemen and compromisers in the overall struggle between the blocs.

The role of *balancer* also reemerges in a new form. In a political sense the third world, as its name implies, represents a balancing force between the two blocks. Such countries as India and the UAR exploit this key position to some advantage. But most of the rest, instead of using their power by a self-conscious act of balancing, are willing to remain passive until wooed for their political support. In a military sense such powers are insignificant in affecting the balance. Only China, as she emerges to significant military power and detaches herself from the Soviet Union, begins to become a counterweight to the two main superpowers, able to throw her weight to one side or the other as circumstances dictate. This maximizes the power she can exert. Indeed, all three of the great powers have an interest in showing themselves capable of friendship with either of the other two, and so increase their bargaining power. If either showed itself irrevocably committed to hostility to any other, the third can increase its own power by balancing between the two. Each must thus show itself as flexible and ideologically uncommitted as possible. This helps from the late 1960s onward to break down the antagonism between the U.S. and Russia and between the U.S. and China. So it comes about that instead of China balancing between the U.S. and the Soviet Union, it is rather the U.S. which balances between the other two (between which the division lies deepest). Similarly, though to a lesser extent, the increasing detachment of West Europe from the U.S. can enable that region (insofar as it pursues a united policy) to balance between Russia and the U.S. or between both and China.

Another change in this age is the increasing importance of economic relationships. Some of the important roles adopted relate to these. The roles of *aid giver* and *aid recipient* are obviously complementary. Sometimes they give rise to a relationship of dominance and dependence, but this need not be so. Sweden, Canada, and the Netherlands are generous donors without being seen as acquiring dominance over the small. Even with larger powers influence is not necessarily the outcome of generosity. The increasingly widespread concept of a moral duty to give aid robs the donor of some of his leverage—even transfers it to the recipient. A recipient who is politically or strategically valuable may be able to twist the arm of the donor which is unable to see a particular government collapse or defect. Sometimes more effective influence, though less visible, is acquired where capital is provided in private form. Transnational cooperations and other private firms may begin to acquire a dominant influence over whole sectors of an economy, and this may eventually restrict the freedom of action of the recipient nation. Thus wholly new economic relationships begin to be established; differences of economic status in particular affect political relationships more than at any earlier time.

As in other societies there exist the *rebels,* the deviants, and similar antisocial groups. In the previous age these had been the extreme nationalists—Germany, Italy, and Serbia, for example. Now it is those that are ideologically extreme or perverse—for example, Albania, Cuba, or Libya. These act outside the normal international system to promote radical and unconventional views and policies. They tend to goad and denounce the "establishment" of the international society, just as rebels and radicals do within national societies.

In a somewhat different category are the *outcasts,* such states as South Africa and Portugal (till 1974), which violate the norms established in the society as a whole, and are almost universally condemned in consequence. More than in most earlier ages, standards of internal government influence the attitudes of the international community as a whole to particular states. Increasingly, relationships are determined not by power factors alone, or even by conduct, but by good name, and this is measured partly in terms of reputation in domestic affairs.

Thus the primacy of ideology dictates new changes in the traditional roles. The great power becomes the ideological leader, the ally becomes the ideological supporter, the balancer the ideological balancer, the rebel or outcast the ideological rebel or outcast. With the change in the underlying concern, there is a subtle change in every role. A new network of relationships emerges.

It is scarcely surprising that the main types of role we have identified are found in some form in almost all the societies we have examined. This is because such roles reflect—like those of father, priest, or elder in smaller societies—basic features of international social life that are almost always present in every age. They express basic attitudes and tendencies within international societies: the desire to dominate other states, the desire to band together against common dangers, the desire to withdraw from the dangers of the hurly-burly, and so on. The essential point is the variation in the way each role is viewed and performed in different societies, and these variations, as we have seen, represent adjustments to the essential character of each society. So the role of superpower is different in ancient China from what it is in ancient Greece; that of ally is different in the age of ideology from what it is in the age of nationalism; and so on.

What is the relationship between a particular type of international society and the way the roles are performed? To some extent it is self-evident; thus in an ideological age the role of superpower is in part that of ideological leader, fount of doctrine, and guardian of doctrinal purity. But this does not tell us enough. What accounts for the different ways in which the role has been performed in *different* ideological societies: in ancient Greece, the age of religion, and today? In every case the superpower is concerned with the defense of the ideology and of those regimes which share it. But the strategies used vary widely. The superpower today demands in some ways a more absolute conformity than in the age of religion. Then it wanted only the widest possible practice of one religion rather than another, not the right to control particular territories. Today a superpower wants more specific assurances about particular areas: It is not prepared to tolerate, for example, the possibility that any part of East Europe or the Caribbean will defect to the rival faith, and will unfailingly intervene to prevent this. This demand in turn implies the role of satellite, involving a degree of submissiveness rarely demanded of neighboring states, even in ideological ages, before.

Apart from the basic ideology, there are many factors which may influence the particular roles performed. For example, changes in *means* may influence the way a role is performed. The superpower today, having modern communications media at its disposal, is more concerned with propaganda than its predecessors in other ideological ages. Such extraneous changes can even bring altogether new roles into existence. The development of a more clear-cut conception of international morality in modern times creates a place for the role of moralizer or preacher, as played, for example, by India at one time, or by Sweden today (a role that perhaps, despite its widespread unpopularity, has its place in a viable society).

There is no exact correlation between a particular type of society and the existence of particular roles within it: superpowers, neutrals, allies, and victims are found in almost every society. But, as we have seen, the way they are played varies widely from one to another. The roles are adjusted and molded in different ages so that they best conform with the general character, that is, the ideology of the society as a whole.

Like many of the other specific features we have examined, the roles adopted in a particular society represent an integral component part of the social structure as a whole: one of the means by which a particular type of society maintains itself. In international, as in domestic, societies, members have to be taught the parts they must play if the entire structure is to be held together.

# 12.  Norms

Every society, narrow and wide alike, requires to develop means of securing orderly relations among its members, and of containing violence and conflict. Two main means have been used: rules to influence behavior, and institutions to resolve disputes. Each has a role to play in most societies. Both have been used in international societies for the same purpose.

All domestic societies of which we have knowledge have developed *norms*— traditions, rules, and practices—to act as restraints on arbitrary and antisocial individual conduct. Any group, however, small and temporary, will usually develop accepted modes of interaction, even if there exist no formal institutions to enforce them. It is thus not surprising that international societies, where institutions are weakest, have often evolved rules of mutually acceptable conduct to regulate behavior.[1]

Norms are more uncertain than institutions as a means to influence conduct. They are uncertain since their capacity to influence depends on the socialization process—the methods used within a society to instill particular attitudes and rules of conduct—and this varies in effectiveness. The process may take place early in life or late, through explicit instructions or implicit pressures. It derives from parents, peer groups, or the society generally, and the instructions given from these different sources may be self-consistent or conflicting. Thus the effect will vary from person to person, according to innate disposition and the way the pressures are encountered. While some may be fully conditioned into adopting the code demanded, others will be more resistant and less influenced, and may become deviant or even delinquent. All this is, of course, equally true of international norms of conduct. Here the code is still more uncertain and disputed, since it is instilled later in life for most individuals, derives from an even greater variety of conflicting sources, and is powerfully counteracted by other influences seeking to

1. There is thus no basis for the frequently expressed assertion that international society, until today, has existed in a state of perennial "anarchy." A surprising number of those writing in the field of international relations, and even of historians, continue to make unsupported generalizations to this effect. The fact that there exist no authorities with absolute power over states does not mean they are not subject to other types of restraint on conduct which, as in smaller societies, may be ultimately more powerful.

glorify the independent authority of the state and its freedom from international rules.

But, though uncertain, norms may ultimately be even more influential than institutions in influencing conduct since, if the socialization process is successful, the required attitudes and norms are more deeply instilled and become *internalized*. They then appear to be self-imposed; instead of being a response to "you must" or "you should," they become "I must" or "I should." Instead of the fear of some external authority, the compulsion of *internal* desire or sense of duty becomes the driving force. This can exercise a more reliable compulsion to conformity than fear of an external power. This applies especially in international societies, where external authorities (international organizations) have in all ages been weak in relation to national power and have had a small influence on national conduct. Nations can thus be induced to behave in a more socially responsible way only by causing them to *want* to do so. To achieve this, all international societies of which we know have established expected norms of behavior comparable to those which operate in domestic societies.

The problem is that norms may be uncertain and disputed. This is especially so in international societies, which are so loosely integrated and have no clearly recognized means of establishing rules.

In both domestic and international societies norms can take a number of forms of varying degrees of precision or power: ad hoc practices, customs, moral rules, and laws. It is for debate whether the final category has existed in any international society: although we often speak of "international law," law in a strict sense implies a body of rules which acquire their force from the knowledge that they can be enforced. This has not existed in any international society, and what is known as international law is perhaps better thought of as a body of rules or customary practices. The other categories are even looser. But all are norms of a kind. And it remains true that every international society of which we know has devised some such rules to influence the conduct of states. How far they have been observed in practice is of course a different question (just as domestic societies sometimes lay down rules that are violated).

The fact that norms exist at all is the significant fact, and in general we shall find that, as in domestic societies, most such rules are observed most of the time. The fact that war occurs does not contradict this fact. In many societies war may not be against the rules at all (this was so in all ages until recent times). Even if it is, wars may occur rather as aberrant delinquincies, much as crime within the state, rather than as the normal conduct expected of a state. Or they may occur because, while certain forms of warfare (aggression across frontiers) are taboo, other forms (armed assistance to the parties in a civil war) are not covered by the rules in any clear-cut way—this is roughly the situation in the modern world.

Thus we shall be concerned here not only with the differing influence which the rules may have in different international societies, but with the varying character of the rules, what they say, and above all, what is their relationship with the prevailing international ideology.

## 12.1 The Chinese Multistate System (771–221 B.C.)

In the Chinese multistate period, some of the norms established derive from the traditional ceremonial rules of the Chou dynasty. At the beginning of the period some of the rules were designed to express the obligations of feudal lords to their overlord, or to each other (for example, the order of precedence among them), rather than the type of rules to be observed by sovereign *states*. But these rules lost force with the decline of the old order: "Within a few years after the beginning of the Ch'un chiu, the ranks of the rulers of the various states derived from the previous feudal system were without any practical significance."[2] But ceremonial rules continue to represent a part of the customary law of the system: The respects to be paid by one state to another, for example, on on the death of a ruler, or a marriage, for a state visit, and so on, were among the most clearly established and widely observed norms. The *I-Li,* one of the most famous classics of the Confucian ideology, describes in detail the rules to be observed in receiving visits from other rulers, or their representatives, and we saw earlier the importance attached, for example, to the number of dishes served at a banquet in identifying the degree of respect being paid to a visiting dignitary. The special honors due to the Chou monarchy, the obligation to pay him special visits or even tribute, and the special position enjoyed by such states as Lu and Wei all represent part of the heritage of these old feudal relationships.

New rules were developed to replace the old. As in most systems, these grew out of the experience and practice of relations among states. As contacts and commerce increased, a growing body of customary conduct emerged which became accepted as *normal,* as the *appropriate* form of behavior among states (this reflected the basic ethic of propriety contained in Confucian teaching). The development of law within states perhaps encouraged a readiness to develop similar rules for the system as a whole (as the same process did in Europe in the seventeenth century). The proliferation of treaties between the states, to which appeal was frequently made, provided a statutory basis for some of the undertakings and obligations proclaimed (as occurred in nineteenth century Europe).

But some of these treaties were multilateral in form and laid down general rules. For example, under a treaty signed in 562, twelve of the Chou states agreed "not to hoard up the produce of good years" (in other words, to be prepared to send grain to states in distress). They agreed "to aid one another in disasters and calamities" and to have "compassion to one another in seasons of misfortune and disorder" (in other words, to accept some of the obligations to international aid accepted in the modern world). And they agreed "not to protect traitors" and "not to shelter criminals" (in other words, not to give covert support to revolutions

2. R. L. Walker, *The Multi-State System in Ancient China* (Hamden, 1953), p. 75.

elsewhere, as is equally demanded today), though this obligation came into conflict with another tradition according the right of asylum.

Some of these undertakings probably represented general good intentions rather than hard and fast obligations, but they at least give an indication of the *standards* of good international conduct which were current at this time. Other rules were made for the individual leagues of states, binding among the members of that league, and sometimes enforced by the pa or hegemon. Together these represented a considerable body of doctrine. And for this reason "there is little reason to doubt that the patterns of interstate intercourse which developed did constitute a rudimentary system of international law."[3] The fact that the system did not have the effect of preventing war is of course irrelevant, for the rules did not prohibit war as such. Such a rule would have been wholly contrary to the prevailing spirit of this power-hungary age. The law rather set out the rules for *making* war.

One rule held that a well-behaved state should not attack another state whose ruler bore the same surname as its own; the commentaries in the Lu annals strongly condemn Wei for its attack on Hsing in 635 on these grounds. Again, it was against the rules to attack a state in the year in which its ruler had died, and occasional cases where this rule was violated also come in for adverse comment. The fact that violations of such rules are reported does not indicate that the rules were not of significance. On the contrary, the very fact that breaches were reported and with such force is an indication that, generally speaking, the rules did have some influence.

Some of the other rules bore a closer analogy to those of recent times. One, for example, laid down that a state should not be attacked in the year in which a revolution had occurred there. This might be compared with the obligation, under traditional international law in Europe, that states should remain neutral in case of a civil war in another state, and give no assistance to either side. The Chinese rule was no doubt designed to moderate the frequent examples of intervention by one state on behalf of a pretender in another. How far it was successful in this aim (any more than the similar Western rule has been in recent times) is difficult to judge. Though there were frequent examples of intervention, there may have been other cases where intervention was deterred by knowledge of the rule, and of the bad name which would be acquired by a state which violated it.

As in most other societies, there were strict rules concerning the safe conduct of messengers and other diplomatic staff (even in time of war). These rules were essential to maintaining the communications without which the society could scarcely be viable. Here again the rules were not invariably kept. There are reports of cases where a foreign messenger was deliberately put to death in order to provoke a war; or, even more complex, a messenger sent in the knowledge that he would very likely be put to death, in order to justify retaliation against such an action. Here too the fact of retaliation in such circumstances is an indication that

3. Ibid., p. 74.

286 THE KEY FACTORS IN INTERNATIONAL SOCIETY

the rule was widely known and respected. Other rules and conventions, especially in the early part of the period, derive from the tradition of chivalry mentioned earlier. It was a breach of etiquette, for example, to take advantage of an enemy in a vulnerable strategic situation or to take him totally by surprise; victory was supposed to emerge from a set battle, or a complicated competition in maneuver.[4]

The rules may have been marginally influenced by the moral teachings of the philosophers, who, as we saw, in many cases occupied positions close to the rulers and were often consulted by them. Confucius, without being a pacifist, was clearly opposed to militarism. While he accepted, for example, that for good government sufficient weapons, sufficient food, and the confidence of the people were necessary, he argued that if one of these had to be abandoned it should be weapons. He believed that if a truly virtuous and enlightened ruler came to power somewhere and followed the doctrine of benevolent government he preached not only would that ruler bring peace to his own land but his example would assure peace elsewhere. Similarly, Mencius spoke against warlike conduct, saying "even if it was only a question of taking territory from one state to give it to another, a benevolent man would not do it: how much less when it is done through the slaughter of men."[5] And he reproached the ruler of one of the states for his armaments on the grounds that "to collect the equipment of war endangers the soldiers and officers and excites the resentment of other rulers."[6] Such teachings, even though frequently disregarded, may have served to spread the idea that foreign policy should be conducted according to certain recognized principles. At the very lowest, moral concepts of this kind provided a rationalization to justify a foreign policy. During the Spring and Autumn period, "war between the feudal states [was] carried on in large part according to recognized rules. Moreover, in theory it did not have as an aim the destruction of the army but the punishment of the guilty and giving effect of the judgment of heaven!"[7]

Thus there were a number of forces influencing the form of rules: ancient religious concepts, the teachings of the philosophers, the requirements of the multistate system. But possibly as important as any of these was self-interest. There was general recognition of the need for some good faith and stability in mutual relations. A reputation for straight dealing "was important in attracting allies or in gaining the support of one of the great powers in a treaty of mutual assistance. The great powers themselves were especially anxious for a reputation for good faith, for it could sometimes be the basis for choosing between them and their rivals."[8] But against this was the self-seeking, mutually competitive character of the society. The pressure for aggrandizement was such that in many cases the rules were simply flouted. Even if without scruples such a state normally would

4. W. G. Creel, *The Birth of China* (London, 1936), pp. 257–59.
5. *The Works of Mencius*, VI, 8.
6. *Mencius*, VII, 17.
7. K. S. Latourette, *The Chinese, Their History and Culture* (London, 1946), p. 51.
8. Walker, *Multi-State System*, p. 86–87.

not attack a fellow member, both because it was not in its long-term interest to weaken the league and because it might bring retaliation from the leader or other members. It would not attack a member of another league as this could bring retribution for the league as a whole, Only large powers could be oblivious of such considerations: "In general the great powers could and did act with less consideration of rules. . . . If the penalties for nonobservance outweighed the advantages to be gained by nonadherence, then the law was obeyed. . . . In their struggles with each other the big powers seldom found it advantageous to hold to the rule."[9] Such unscrupulousness, as we saw, increasingly became the norm.

Thus the rules developed in this society to some extent were rules of convenience, designed to moderate, if only marginally, the unscrupulous competitiveness of traditional interstate behavior. Though frequently violated, they undoubtedly did affect expectations of normal state conduct—and so expectations of what was acceptable for one's *own* state. "Throughout the period, there was the overall expectation that the state which adhered closely to the rules had a better than even chance against another state of comparatively equal power which violated them."[10] Against this, the increasing unscrupulousness of the members, the cutthroat competition, and knowledge that others might default brought in many cases a readiness to plead *raisons d'état* for breaking the rules. As the Ch'u general Tzu Fan declared, "When we can gain the advantage over our enemies we must advance without any consideration of covenants."[11] There were a few exceptions: Duke Wen of Chin is often cited as the example of a statesman who, while expanding the power of his own state, was scrupulous in his regard for principle (he refused, for example, to annex Yuan by force when he had the opportunity). In time, however, the attitude of Tzu Fan came to prevail over that of Duke Wen. And this breakdown of the rules, with the violence that went with it, eventually brought in its train the breakdown of the entire system.

## 12.2 The Greek City-States (600–338 B.C.)

Within the society of Greek states, almost contemporary to that in China, there emerged quite a different set of principles and understandings concerning the way relations should be conducted: rules that conformed to its own social needs.

Even in earlier days, during the so-called "dark ages" from the twelfth century onward, there had probably been in Greece some kind of code of personal chivalry governing the conduct of warfare. From the sixth century there emerged a set of principles often referred to under the name of "Hellenic law and custom." The rules that developed were partly associated with the religious associations and

9. Ibid., p. 93.
10. Ibid., p. 92.
11. Ibid., p. 88.

cults, especially the so-called amphictyonies. These were associations originally designed to preserve the purity of religion and the temples, and to organize common festivals and sacrifices. Thus one of the earliest rules was the rule of a truce during the celebration of festivals. Oracles, shrines, festivals, and games were to be guaranteed against attack. When Aegina failed to observe a truce during a festival in Potideia in 506, this was sufficient to cause Sparta to withdraw support from her. Thucydides records how Boeotia complained against Athens "that the Athenians had done wrong and transgressed against Hellenic law, since it was a rule established everywhere that the invader of another country should keep her hands off the temples in that country."[12] The Olympic games, associated originally with the cult at Mount Olympus and attended by representatives of nearly all the cities, were the occasion for a truce in any war then occurring.

There were also international rules concerning sanctuary, which were again semireligious in character. Anybody who found refuge within a temple was normally given sanctuary, since killing within it would have defiled the temple. When the Spartans, after Pausanias had taken refuge in a temple, allowed him to starve almost to death, this was regarded by many as having brought a curse on the Spartans, and was used by the Athenians as one of the many justifications for the Peleponnesian War.

There were other rules affecting the conduct of war between the states. Heralds and envoys were to be inviolable. The dead were not to be mutilated or denied burial: often a truce would be observed immediately after a battle during which the dead of each side could be buried. Members of the Amphictyonic league undertook that in secular wars they would not raze cities or cut off water supplies.

Again, the oaths of a treaty were supposed to be binding. The contracting parties to the Thirty Years' Truce in 446 bound themselves by religious oaths to keep the treaty. Copies were inscribed at Olympia so that they should obtain divine authority and sanction. Similarly, when Elis and Heraea made an alliance, they agreed that if it should be breached they would pay a fine to Zeus. In this way a divine sanction was obtained for international law. Finally, the oracles themselves, in their own pronouncements, established a corpus of tradition concerning acceptable behavior among states.[13]

But this was a society torn by ideological dissent. Passions were such that enemies were felt not to deserve the protection of the rules. It is easy to find examples in Thucydides of ambassadors being killed, oaths being violated, and Hellenic law being forgotten. But the very fact that these cases were regarded as shocking is an indication that the rules sometimes had some force. They were sufficiently well known and widely regarded for an appeal to them to be thought a powerful argument. When the Plataeans were calling to the Spartans for mercy after their city had been captured, they declared, "To spare our lives ... would be

12. Thucydides, *The Peloponnesian War*, IV, 97.
13. See N. G. L. Hammond, *A History of Greece to 238* B.C. (London, 1967), p. 169.

a righteous judgment.... We surrender to you voluntarily, stretching out our hands as suppliants, and Hellenic law forbids killing in these circumstances."[14] The same passage makes clear that it was felt that a country which violated the rules would pay heavy sacrifice in terms of public respect: "Beware lest public opinion condemn you, however superior to us you may be, for passing an unworthy sentence on good men and for dedicating in your national temples spoils taken from the Plataeans who have done such good service to Hellas in the Persian War."[15]

Some of the rules, as one might expect in a society beset by ideological and transnational warfare, concerned civil conflict and the obligations of outside powers in such a situation. For example, if a colony revolted against its mother country, no other state was supposed to intervene. Thus the Corinthian delegate at the conference preceding the Peleponnesian war declared: "What you ought not to do is to establish a precedent by which a power may receive into its alliances the revolting subjects of another power."[16] Other rules on intervention were more hazy. External involvement tended to be denounced when practiced by the other side, justified when practiced by one's own (in other words, the situation was exactly as today). But it is clear that there was a general feeling that in such cases the citizens of each state should decide their own affairs for themselves, a feeling that found expression in the widespread demand for "autonomy." Thus intervention, however blatant, paradoxically was often justified, especially by Sparta, in the name of "autonomy" (a situation which again finds many parallels today when external powers intervene to establish a government that is "truly representative").

The treaties among the states established the basis of a kind of international law. This applies particularly to the main alliance agreements, which set out the relationships and behavior to be expected among the members. There were also bilateral agreements between states, granting personal rights, protection of property, and the right of acquiring land to the citizens of another state. The rights granted could include those of intermarriage or special rights while attending public games. In some cases (where "isopolity" was established) a complete equality of rights among the citizens of the states was established.

Similarly, commercial treaties established trading rules which were observed among a number of states, at least within an alliance. Other treaties were concerned with currencies, or laid down the way in which legal disputes between citizens of the states concerned should be determined. There was even a small body of maritime law. So eventually rules developed which covered a much wider field than peace and war, or respect for shrines alone. But they tended to have greater force among ideological allies bound by the same treaty. The rules of opponents were frequently flouted.

14. Thucydides, III, 58.
15. Ibid.
16. Thucydides, I, 41.

Development of this system of rules, as in China, did not go far to preserve peace among the states. They could not prevent wars, for the rules themselves did not prohibit war as such. They merely regulated its conduct in certain respects. It was generally taken for granted that in certain situations an act of war against another state was one of the policy options available. This does not mean the rules were without influence. The commercial law, and the rules relating to the observance of shrines and games, were generally regarded, and no doubt acted as integrating factors. Above all, the very existence of rules promoted the conception of a wider international (Hellenic) society with its own morals and standards. Against this, the effectiveness of the rules for many purposes was weakened by ideological divisions circumscribing the area where they were observed. So the underlying nature of the society influenced the nature of the established norms.

## 12.3 The Age of Dynasties (1300–1559)

The international society which developed between the fourteenth and six-teenth centuries in Europe was an age of personal rule, and it was thus the personal code existing among the rulers which was of the greatest importance in influencing the conduct of states. This code derived from a number of different sources.

One of these was the laws of chivalry. These dictated, for example, often in theory rather than in practice, the behavior to be adopted on the battlefield, the respect to be accorded to heralds, the observance of truces and treaties, the treatment of prisoners, and other questions.[17] The challenge to a battle was regarded like a personal challenge to a tournament. For example, Froissart tells how Edward III discovered himself in the vicinity of the French king's forces and felt it a question of honor to do battle immediately, sending a herald to the French king, who then named the battle day. This tradition is shown equally in the rules concerning the declarations of war through the issue of "defiances": Froissart describes how Edward and his allies agreed to send their joint defiances to the French king "to the intent that the war should be more laudable," and how the Bishop of Lincoln delivered this defiance to Paris "in such manner that he could not be reproached or blamed," and was given a safe conduct for the purpose.[18] It is seen in the importance of the word of honor among princes and knights: when the French king John pledged his honor for the payment of a ransom to Edward III and this was not paid on time, he felt himself bound to give himself up voluntarily to be a prisoner in London, where he died a captive. But these rules of chivalry only

17. "The laws of chivalry described the proper conduct of the feudal class in peace and war, regulated precedents and the etiquette of intercourse in all situations undetermined by direct feudal obligations, and laid down the tabus to be observed and the courtesies to be extended...." G. Mattingly, *Renaissance Diplomacy* (London, 1955), p. 29.

18. Froissart, *Chronicles,* I, 34.

applied among the chivalric classes, and in other respects the conduct of war and standards of honor were often barbarous.

> Savagery in medieval warfare—during and after battle—with its incredible excesses of revenge and bloodthirstiness has often been depicted. Humanitarian rules comparable to those developed in modern international law were practically absent. . . . Chivalry, whose rules were based on honor rather than law, somewhat counteracted the barbarism and perfidy of the period, but it was observed only in combats between knights.[19]

But it was not only an age of chivalry, but of deep religious faith. Though the authority of the pope and the Church generally were declining, the Church had a major role in developing new rules of international conduct. The second Lateran Council in 1139 forbade the use of the crossbow as "deadly and odious to God" (though this has been interpreted as a means of preserving the supremacy of the mounted knight). The third Lateran Council prohibited making slaves of Christian prisoners of war (Muslims and other infidels were of course beyond the law). An attempt was made to outlaw "feuds" and private wars by declaring "truces of God"; the third Lateran Council forbade such feuds except between sunrise on Mondays and sunset on Wednesdays. The pope's moral authority was also important in that he could legitimize a conquest, giving it his authority; for example, Pope Nicholas V gave the king of Portugal authority to keep all countries to the west of a line drawn westward of Cape Badajoz through Guinea. Conversely, the threat of excommunication would be used to ban a war. Treaties were often confirmed by a sacred oath which subjected the obligation contained in them to the jurisdiction of the Church; violation of its terms might then call down sanctions in the next world as well as this.[20] Finally, in a general sense, papal pronouncements might be seen as a source of obligations in international as in other matters.[21]

But the church's influence was not only through direct pronouncements. Canon law and church doctrine also exercised an indirect impact on the practice of international relations. The doctrine of the "just war" was widely discussed in theological circles. Originally devised by St. Augustine in the fifth century, this sought to reconcile war with theological theory by declaring that to participate in a war could be legitimate, provided that the cause of the war was just. War should not, for example, be waged out of a desire for revenge, or for the sake of power alone. This theory was developed by St. Thomas Aquinas in the thirteenth century, who declared that war was justifiable if it had been authorized by the prince, if there was a just cause, and if the intent was to promote good or to avoid evil.

---

19. A. Nussbaum, *A Concise History of the Law of Nations* (New York, 1947), p. 35. See also the *New Cambridge Modern History,* I (1957): 288–89.

20. The Church also possessed the power to grant dispensation from such oaths, an eventuality which could reduce the value of a treaty. Thus in a treaty of 1477 Louis XI and Charles The Bold mutually agreed not to seek dispensation from their oaths from the pontiff.

21. Cf. Nussbaum, *A Concise History,* p. 23: "In theory . . . there existed authorities entrusted divinely with the task of ruling the rulers and of protecting the right on earth. According to this notion there was no need for war or for international law."

Naturally most dynasts, in promoting their own cause, had little difficulty in convincing themselves and their subjects that their war was just, and it may thus be doubted if this general rule exerted much influence.[22] It was rather the more specific prohibitions of St. Thomas, as of lies and broken promises, or of war strategems, which may have had some influence on policy. Certain jurists held, for example that the killing of women and children was not "just" and should be prohibited, and this came to be a fairly generally accepted doctrine, though not invariably applied.

A third important source of international rules was the tradition of Roman law. The classical conception of a *jus gentium,* a rule of the peoples, was revived with other features of Roman law. Bartolus and his followers, in the fourteenth century and later, devised doctrines which foreshadowed modern conceptions of sovereignty: a king was "emperor within his own realm" and the city was *sibi princeps,* lord in itself, that is, under no other authority. The Bartolists continued throughout the fifteenth century

> his efforts to assimilate into civil law the teachings of the church and the customs of the Italian cities and of the trans-Alpine peoples, so as to provide a single rational body of doctrine for the legal relations of the western world. . . . Officials employed in foreign affairs were expected to be trained in civil and common law. Indeed, down into the last decade of the seventeenth century men usually spoke of the civil law as if it were what we now call international law.[23]

In a more general way Roman law, from the very fact of being widely accepted among European countries, served to bring about some uniformity in the legal principles accepted during this period.

> In what we may call the international law of the 15th century Roman law was the most important element—the warp on which the legal garment of the great society was being constantly woven. In part this was because Roman law appealed to the rulers of the west . . . as a generalized and rational system, adapted to the needs of a civil society, to secular authority and to pecuniary interests. In part, it was because of the familiarity of the maxims which had served the canonists since the 12th century and the lawyers of the feudal kings since the 13th.[24]

Finally, a fourth strand in the emerging international rules of the period was the developing code governing international commerce. Reciprocal treaties were signed (such as the famous Intercursus Magnus between Henry VII and the Duke of Burgundy in 1495) according mutual protection and commercial rights to the citizens of the two countries concerned: for example, the right to buy and sell

22. "The Church, . . . by admitting that it was permissible to wage a just war . . . had in effect sanctioned all wars. The criteria of a just war, it was generally agreed, were that it should only be waged on the authority of a superior, for a just cause and with righteous intent, and the satisfaction of these criteria was not hard save for the most recalcitrant conscience." *New Cambridge Modern History,* I (1957): 259.

23. Mattingly, *Renaissance Diplomacy,* p. 22. See also B. Hay, *Europe in the Fourteenth and Fifteenth Centuries* (London, 1966), pp. 82–86.

24. Ibid., pp. 21–22.

freely, subject only to normal dues, to occupy warehouses and other buildings, to bring ships into all or specified ports, to be free from arbitrary arrest, and so on. Such rules began to become generalized rights for merchants trading elsewhere. Some treaties included the most-favored-nation clause, in use ever since, by which a commitment was made not to grant any other nation rights or terms superior to the rules laid down in the treaty, but this usually referred at this time to the personal rights of merchants rather than to tariff rates.

Rules of maritime law also began to be developed. Some were based on the ancient Greek Rhodian sea law. For example, the Rolls of Oleron, the rules of commerce established in the island of Oleron, became widely acknowledged in many parts of northwest Europe. Similarly, in the Mediterranean a set of rules developed in a Barcelona court became generally acknowledged as the accepted international law governing shipping, freight, and documentation, and especially the rights of neutral ships in time of war. It thus established some kind of international standards in this field. Treaties on monetary questions created common standards of coinage, and laid down which coins were legal tender in the countries concerned. There also emerged commonly accepted rules concerning negotiable instruments, an essential advance to sustain the rapid growth of international trade and credit in this period.[25]

A particular code required by this society of personal rulers related to diplomatic privilege and immunities. For centuries writers on canon law had elaborated rules on the treatment to be accorded to papal legates. With the development of diplomacy rules began to be devised concerning the rights that should be accorded to ambassadors, whether special or permanent. For these were seen as the personal representatives of their master; an offense to them was one to him. To strike or injure an ambassador, for example, was held to be punishable by death. An ambassador could not be sued in a court, nor could legal action be taken against him for debts, even those contracted before the beginning of his embassy. He was exempt from all taxes and customs duties. All authorities were bound to protect and assist him in every possible way. And these immunities applied not only to the ambassador himself but to all regular members of his suite.

These rules were not merely theoretical, but seem to have been fairly widely observed. "With remarkably few exceptions ambassadors, and even minor diplomatic agents, did enjoy the privileges and immunities to which theory said they were entitled."[26] Here was a relatively uniform set of norms, accepted all over Europe, in which the honor of the ruler was felt to be engaged, and which accordingly were in general fairly scrupulously observed. They began to become an essential part of the fabric of international society.

Thus from a number of different sources—the traditions of chivalry, Roman law, canon law and religious doctrine, commercial and diplomatic practice—there emerged some embryonic conceptions of the rules of conduct to be observed

25. Nussbaum, *A Concise History*, pp. 28–33.
26. Mattingly, *Renaissance Diplomacy*, p. 43.

among states. Many were only sketchily observed. Even specific undertakings between rulers were not necessarily held binding, by them, still less general rules (some fully agreed with Machiavelli's advice: "A prudent ruler ought not to keep faith when by so doing it would be against his interest and when the reasons which made him bind himself no longer exist"). But the significant point was the increasing acknowledgment that some set of rules of state behavior was required. The form the rules took—the laws of warfare, the chivalric code, and so on—was influenced by the nature of society, by the style and ambitions of dynasts. Since those engaged in the practice of international relations, mainly the dynasts themselves and their advisers, were relatively small in number, there was at least the chance of some mutual understanding on such matters. But against this, since personal distrust among these was widespread, and competition intense, there were still in practice many violations of the newly emerging code.

## 12.4 The Age of Religions (1559–1648)

In the age which followed new rules had to be developed, related to the problems and needs of a different type of society.

The international conflicts of this time mainly concerned religion and the rights to be enjoyed by the adherents of different faiths. So new rules had to be formulated here. An initial attempt of this kind was made in the Peace of Augsburg of 1555. That Peace laid down a principle of a kind: the right of the ruler to determine the religious rights of his subjects. This neither prescribed nor forbade toleration within the borders of each state or city of the empire; the ruler could himself determine how much toleration, if any, was to be allowed, and what faith should be practiced. Though some rulers allowed the peaceful coexistence of different faiths, most permitted only their own. The basic norm adopted here to cope with an era of religious discord was thus not toleration but partition:[27] the sharing out of Germany between the Lutheran and Catholic faiths (Calvinism was originally excluded from its terms, though within twenty years the Elector Palatine applied the same principle in respect of Calvinism within his own lands). Even this norm therefore implied the toleration of opposed faiths in *other* lands (provided they were Christian). Eventually this principle, first devised for Germany, came to be that adopted in Europe as a whole. Most states tolerated the religion of the ruler but no others. France, perhaps because of the numbers and power of her Protestant community, was for a time a conspicuous exception, but she too followed the general rule from 1685. And the general principle laid down—that the king, or the

27. Toleration was an abomination to many on both sides. Since both thought they knew the only true faith, to permit any other was to encourage heresy and error. Thus Pope Clement VIII greeted the edict of Nantes as "the worst edict that can possibly be imagined . . . an edict that permits liberty of conscience, the worst thing in the world."

government, should decide what faiths should be practiced within each realm—continued to be applied throughout most of Europe for the next two centuries.

A lesser, but related, issue for which rules were required in an age of religious conflict concerned rights to church property. If a kingdom changed faith, did church property belong to the old church, the new one, or to the kingdom as a whole? Since church property was a large part of all property, the issue was not without importance. Here too the Peace of Augsburg attempted to lay down a principle: the naming of a date after which all further "secularization," i.e., seizing of church property, was regarded as illegitimate. It was, however, difficult to define and to enforce, and only gave rise to further conflict in the future. In a sense this too became the norm adopted elsewhere: Church property was widely seized by Protestant rulers in the early stages of the reformation, but after a certain date this became less frequent.

In theory, support for revolution elsewhere, plotting and conspiracy by ambassadors, and certainly assassinations, were impermissible. But there was no attempt to lay down clear-cut rules. In an ideological, transnational society, the need for the rule was great, the temptation to break it greater. Certainly the general practice allowed such conduct. Under the Treaty of Cateau-Cambresis, Elizabeth was pledged to nonintervention in Scotland, but she violated the undertaking the following year. There was no more surprise that Spain intervened to assist the Catholics in France than that England and the Palatinate intervened to assist the Protestants in the Netherlands. Even the growing writing on international law sometimes reflected the assumption of religious solidarity. Thus Gentili supported the right to send aid not only to an ally, but to any nation similar in religion, blood, or race which was involved in conflict.[28]

The violence of the age provoked a new attempt to devise new rules: the so-called birth of international law. But there was a considerable gulf between the rules laid down in these theoretical writings and those accepted by rulers and statesmen, often almost totally ignorant of such writings. Among the former, the concept of the "just war," which went back to classical times, was now elaborated, combined often with the concept of "natural law," an absolute standard of justice which men could apprehend with their reason. No war that was undeclared, nor any private war, according to Grotius, for example, could be a just one. On the other hand, a war fought to right a wrong or remedy an injustice, even if that wrong had not involved the use of force, might be just. One consequence of.these somewhat loose and generalized terms was that any government (insofar as it was concerned at all with questions of international law, which was unlikely) could nearly always show that its own cause was a just one. It was not difficult, for example, to show that almost any war was fought to "right a wrong" and so within the absolved category of just wars.

There was a further difficulty in defining the rules even in this theoretical

28. Nussbaum, *A Concise History,* p. 79.

sense. This was the strong religious feelings of the international lawyers them-selves, often theologians in origin, who reflected the prevailing religious preju-dices of their own society. Thus while the Catholic lawyers supported the concept of papal supremacy and papal arbitration, this was inevitably rejected by lawyers of Protestant religion. Similarly, Catholic lawyers such as Suares, the Jesuit, held that a "just" cause of war was interference with the propagation of the gospel or opposition to the Christian faith, and that Saracen prisoners might be indiscrimi-nately killed, and their wives and children committed to slavery. Thus the fact that Spanish kings and officials, it is said, were influenced by these writings (and on one occasion stopped to consult the clergy before declaring war) by no means self-evidently ensured that they were thereby deterred from ruthless action. Gentili and Grotius, on the other hand, both Protestants in countries that had once been Catho-lic, were inevitably more sympathetic to toleration in matters of religion: Grotius, for example, held that a conquered people should be granted autonomy on reli-gious questions. So, inevitably, in a bipolar world, the views expressed on inter-national law tended to reflect the two alternative religious views of the age.

New rules began to emerge to confront the new needs of the age. Some concerned the conduct of war. Possibly no wars in history give rise to such brutality as those of religion, and those of this age, especially the Thirty Years' War, were among the most brutal of all. This provoked the first mild attempts to lay down a more civilized code. Gentili held that the duties of a belligerent in respect of prisoners, booty, and other questions remained the same, irrespective of the religion of those involved or the "justness" of their cause. Grotius held that property should not be destroyed except for reasons of military necessity, that hostages should not be put to death unless they had done wrong themselves, that the conquered should be killed only when necessary to save the life of the conquerors or because of undoubted crimes by the conquered, and that some liberty should be left to vanquished peoples. Though these precepts were not necessarily accepted with alacrity by governments—and indeed were probably not even known to many of them—they were evidence of the increasing recognition within the society of a need for rules which might moderate the excesses of international conduct at this time: a recognition which perhaps partly accounts for the huge acclaim accorded to Grotius in his own time.

Another issue on which rules were increasingly needed concerned the use of the seas. Three developments made this increasingly urgent: piratical activities by English and Dutch privateers off West Europe, and by the corsairs off North Africa; the purported partition of the oceans, as well as the lands, of the Americas between Spain and Portugal, which aroused understandable indignation elsewhere; and the assertion by a number of nations, especially England, of sovereignty over extensive areas of the sea up to 100 miles off their own coasts (which aroused the same hostility among foreign sea powers as equally extravagant claims by Latin American countries in recent times). In general, the writings of international lawyers reflected the interests of their own states (again not unlike the situation today). Grotius, the Dutchman, defended the freedom of the seas as vigorously as the Dutch government. Seldon, the Englishman, defended the cause of closed seas as passionately as his government. It was only at the end of the seventeenth century, when the sea powers became dominant all over the world, that the doctrine that the territorial sea ended only three miles from the coast began to be generally accepted. But in this area too increasing legal controversy at least reflected a recognition that some kind of mutually acceptable rules were required.

Another field where new rules were needed was that of commerce. The increasing resort to protection of home industry, special charges for foreign trade, reservation of colonial trade to home nationals, and similar policies evoked the need for new rules concerning mutual commercial rights and duties. France and England in 1606 concluded a treaty ''for the safety and liberty of commerce,'' providing for the public advertising of tariff rates a limitation on internal taxes, and reasonable treatment for the merchants of the other state. The principles of nondiscrimination and reasonable tariffs began to be more widely recognized. The concept of ''most-favored-nation'' treatment, with one state given the right to treatment at least as favorable as any other state, began to be more widely accepted.

In general, an age of contending religions was not favorable to the development of common norms and standards of international conduct.

> The shared assumptions and attitudes of a united Christendom were no longer available to provide the foundations required. In the later Middle Ages Europe had had, as far as it needed to have, a common legal system. . . . Then in the half century after 1559, it melted away and had become in another hundred years so completely forgotten that men could talk as if the interstate relations of the Middle Ages had been an anarchy subject only to jungle law, and as if the rule of reason in the conduct of European affairs was a discovery of the age of reason.[29]

In the interval between, there existed neither the generally accepted value system nor the mutual trust which could assist in the establishment of common rules.

But despite this missing consensus and the undoubted brutality of the age, there did begin to emerge, among some at least, a realization that at least elementary rules of conduct were required within a viable international society. The sharpness of the religious divisions and the brutality of the wars encouraged this. The growing volume of writing, and increased interest, in international law reflected that concern. In doctrinal terms this was seen in the increasing tendency to conceive of *jus gentium* as a law *among* nations, a set of rules made by nations and established among them, derived from custom or from treaties, rather than as a law *of* nations, part of the natural law governing all human activities, important though that might be as well. Victoria, Gentili, and Grotius each in turn extended this distinction and so moved a little nearer toward the concept of positive law, a law deriving from the express consent of governments, which became widespread in the age to follow.

But the hostility and distrust of a divided world made such agreement, so long

---

29. *New Cambridge Modern History,* III (1968): 167.

as this age lasted , difficult to achieve. Some hoped that the settlement reached in the final year of the period, in the Peace of Westphalia, might provide the foundation for a more orderly age to come.

## 12.5  The Age of Sovereignty, (1648–1789)

But the norms which emerged in the following period reflected the purposes of an equally competitive society.

The primary principle now was that of sovereignty. That doctrine strongly influenced expectations of behavior among states. It influenced, above all, attitudes to the very notion that a state might be "governed" by rules. In the eyes of many, the essential character of a sovereign state was that it was governed by nobody and nothing outside itself. The effect of this is seen clearly in the *theory* of international law: above all in the doctrine of "positivism." International lawyers in this period came increasingly to abandon the notion of "natural law," a law inherent in reason and eternal principles of justice, as the basis on which all action, in the international society as in the national, should be governed. It was replaced by the idea of "positive law," the international customs and treaties to which governments had positively given consent.[30]

Already in 1650, two years after the Treaty of Westphalia, the English international lawyer, Zouche, declared that international law was the law "accepted by customs conforming to reason among most nations, or which had been agreed upon by single nations."[31] Subsequent writers—the German Pufendorf, the Dutchman Bynkershof, and the Frenchman Vattel—went further in restricting the scope of law to the treaties governing particular states and the relatively few customs recognized as having a universal character. *Jus gentium,* the law of the peoples, was now transformed into *jus inter gentes,* a law among peoples, that is a created law, subject as much as domestic law to the will of the sovereigns themselves.[32]

The influence of conceptions of sovereignty is also seen in the development of the doctrine of "sovereign equality," or the equality of states. This was the logical extension of the idea of sovereignty itself. If rulers or governments were fully independent within their own territories, it followed that they were equal in that independence. Only if power could be extended beyond the borders of one state into the territory of another did variations in the size and power of states have significance; and it was this right which the doctrine of sovereignty prohibited. The

30. Even Grotius, immediately before this age began, had declared that the law of nations "derived from the will of all nations or many nations."

31. R. Zouche, *Juris et Judicü Fecialis,* p. 1.

32. The same tendency to exalt the role of the state in relation to law is shown in the doctrine of "the fundamental rights of states" elaborated by Vattel and the German writer Wolff. The rights of states in this age were emphasized almost as much as their duties.

sovereigns themselves might vary in splendor and power, as the many battles over precedence demonstrated. But by the very fact of being sovereign, each authority and state acquired a similar status: that of legal independence (just as equality before the law came to symbolize "equality" among individuals within states, however unequal their real condition). And because of the greater distances dividing states, independence was then genuinely more real for small states than it was to be later. The norm was of course especially stridently asserted by small states, but it was accepted as valid by the entire international community.

Something of the same influence is seen in the widely accepted principle of the duty to respect the "European balance of power." The ambiguity of this phrase has already been shown (p. 245 above). But the very fact that it was so generally acknowledged, however variously interpreted, was significant. It represented one important advance in that it recognized the *common* interest of all in maintaining stability in the system. But it was also revealing in the way it conceived of that mutuality: The balance to be achieved was not one of "advantage" or of "interest," but of "power." States were conceived as interacting primarily, if not exclusively, in terms of power relationships. An individual member of the society might make secret agreements that frustrated the policies of a third state, commercial agreements that damaged the trade of another, or even plot to divide the territory of a weaker victim, such as Poland or Tuscany. What the member must not do is to threaten, as Louis XIV appeared to do, the basic power relationships existing within the society. This was now held to be a basic rule of the system.

The preconceptions of a world of sovereign states were reflected in a number of the specific norms and rules which emerged in this period. Thus in general war was now to be permitted only as long as it was made by sovereign states (was "public"), but should be outlawed if made within states (was "private"). The law of the territorial sea, as it finally emerged in the eighteenth century after many disputes—that national rights extend as far as the range of a cannon shot from the shore—equally symbolized the demands of sovereignty: national rights could be asserted as far as could sovereign power. Neutral states were now to be permitted to pursue their own business in peace in time of war, without being subject to the arbitrary interference of the belligerents, as they had been in previous times (a doctrine enforced by Frederick the Great in demanding that Britain compensate him for the destruction of Prussian merchandise when Prussia was neutral). An advance of another kind was achieved in the attempt to humanize, if only marginally, the treatment of prisoners and the wounded in war. Yet again this was done so far only through *bilateral* agreements among international sovereigns or sovereign states, rather than through any multilateral agreement (which had to wait until the following society).

Trade rules reflected similar attitudes. In an earlier age Victoria had advanced the doctrine of the "natural" liberty of trade. Now this view was repudiated everywhere. It was generally accepted that sovereign states had the right to interfere in the free flow of trade by tariffs, bounties, taxes, and many other means, to promote the advantage of their own state. Mercantilism was the supreme expression of sovereignty. Moreover, with the acquisition of new empires over-seas, these barriers are transported overseas as well: foreigners are prevented from selling to colonials, while colonials are prevented from selling to foreigners. And where, occasionally, the barriers are broken down, it is again only through bilateral agreements among sovereign states wishing to show each other special favors, as in the famous Methuen Treaty between Britain and Portugal. No general principle of nondiscrimination is yet accepted. In 1786 the British parliament refused to accept a commercial treaty negotiated with France until the most-favored-nation clause it originally contained was removed to allow the special position of Portugal to continue. The prerogative of all sovereign states in making special arrangements with other such states was not to be interfered with. And though internal duties began now to be abolished and custom duties imposed on a more regularized basis at the frontier, this only served to emphasize the power of that barrier between states which sovereignty upheld.

Here too, therefore, the norms reflected the general character of the society. Despite the frequenty of wars in this period, it is possible to discern some slight advance in the standards of international behavior generally demanded. The doctrine of sovereignty imposed duties as well as rights. The age is characterized by some degree of restraint both in means and ends (see p. 95 above). The actions of France after 1680, especially the bombardment of Genoa, the coercion of Savoy, the seizure of Luxembourg and Avignon, and the devastation of the Palatinate, genuinely shocked the opinion of the age in a way that the barbarities of the Thirty Years' War had not done in the previous age. The idea of the "European balance" encouraged the conception that some state actions threatening it were unreasonable, and not to be tolerated.

But the new rules were only those acceptable to the sovereigns of the new sovereign states. What emerged was indeed a conception of generally civilized conduct among sovereigns rather than a doctrine of "international law" in any explicit sense (few statesmen had read the outpourings of the international lawyers). "It is hardly possible to speak of international law. . . . The term international practices seems more appropriate, for there existed as yet no body of law with any authority other than the forms of international life."[33] But those forms began now to be regularized. The norms were still loose and imprecise, but they were an advance on anything which had gone before.

## 12.6 The Age of Nationalism (1789–1914)

In the society that followed nationalism had emerged as the dominant force within the system, threatening in many cases to disrupt or destroy the old estab-lished sovereignties: in Latin America, in East Europe, in Germany and Italy, and

33. *New Cambridge Modern History,* V (1961): 201.

other areas. The basic principles which had governed the previous era, sovereignty and legitimacy, were under threat. Norms of a new kind were now required to take their place.

A basic issue of principle now concerned the legitimacy of the new claims of nationalism against the old claims of sovereignty. Increasingly, among public opinion everywhere, there was sympathy with the new spirit of nationalism (at least if it was directed against other sovereignties) and acceptance of its legitimacy. So Russians sympathized with Slav nationalism, French with Polish, English with Greek, German with Italian, and so on. But it began to be understood also that a general acknowledgment of such claims must involve the dissolution of the old order everywhere. So, within the emerging international institutions, there was much discussion of the rival demands of revolution and legitimacy. In general the Western nations, Britain and France, were more sympathetic with revolution and the national principle, and the Eastern with legitimacy and sovereignty. But there was no clear consistency: Britain demanded respect for popular wishes in Greece but not in Ireland, France in Poland but not in Savoy, Germany in Holstein but not in Alsace-Lorraine, Russia in Bulgaria but not in Poland. There was an increasing readiness, as time went on, to accord certain rights to any people who showed, through their actions, a consciousness of national identity, and a determination to preserve it against traditional masters.

Thus the question became not so much whether the national principle had any legitimacy, but *when* it should prevail over traditional sovereignty. This was the issue underlying most of the international conflicts of the day, including the greatest of all in 1914. At the Congress of Vienna nobody had even thought of consulting populations about the transfer of sovereignty. But by 1870 Gladstone regarded the transfer of Alsace-Lorraine without consulting its people as ''a crime against the conscience of Europe.'' And by 1916 it came to be widely accepted that the principle to be applied above all in the forthcoming settlement was that of ''self-determination.'' So a new norm emerged which had played a role in no previous intellectual society but became increasingly important from this time on.

This itself raised another principle of international conduct: what *right of intervention* existed for outside powers, whether for or against revolutionary forces, when they threatened to ovetthrow the existing order? This issue also arose many times in the early years of the Concert of Europe. Here too the attitude of the powers was by no means consistent, each sometimes favoring intervention both for and against revolution, according to national interests. The conservative powers were generally thought hostile to revolutionary movements and the liberal powers sympathetic. Yet conservative Prussia and Austria favored intervention *for* revolutionaries in Schleswig-Holstein, as conservative Russia did in Greece and Bulgaria, while liberal France and Britain favored intervention *against* it in Spain and Piedmont respectively.

Then the question arose: who had the right to intervene in such cases? There was increasing recognition of the dangers of unilateral intervention in either case. So there was joint action by Britain, France, and Russia in Greece, adopted by each to prevent unilateral intervention by the others; and by Britain and France in Belgium, for much the same reason. In 1876 it was not the fact that Russia supported the Bosnians and Serbs against Turkey which aroused concern elsewhere but that she took unilateral action for this purpose. Thus another of the important principles which emerged in this period was the need for *multilateralism*, joint action and joint consultation over situations of this kind.

This emerging sentiment in favor of multilateralism applied not only to civil disturbances elsewhere but to every issue that arose. It led to a new sense of public *accountability*, perhaps the most important single principle to emerge at this time. The fact that the European settlement in general had been established by international treaty at Vienna implied, in the eyes of many, that any subsequent change needed the consent of all parties. It was on these grounds that Prussia was prevailed on to withdraw from Schleswig-Holstein in 1852, even though she had complete military control there; that Russia agreed to a substantial modification of the terms she had already reached with Turkey in 1877, to her own disadvantage, at the Congress of Berlin; that Britain, after the occupation of Egypt in 1882, felt obliged continually to assure other powers she was on the point of departing, to regularize her position by securing the consent of the sultan and the dispatch of an Ottoman commissioner-general, and even to make significant concessions to other powers in other parts of the world in recompense. It was on the same grounds that Britain complained, after the Austrian annexation of Bosnia-Herzegovina in 1908, against the "arbitrary alteration of a European treaty" by some powers "without the consent of the others." The basic principle was that every nation had an obligation toward Europe and the "European system" which must qualify its pursuit of national interests. This was expressed in explicit form in the protocols of the London Congress on Belgium in 1831: "Each nation has its own right; but Europe also has its rights, which the needs of social order have imposed." And even the archconservative Metternich wrote:

> We must always view the society of states as the essential condition of the modern world. . . . What characterizes the modern world and distinguishes it from the ancient is the tendency of states to draw near each other and to form a kind of social body based on the same principles as human society.[34]

This feeling of accountability encouraged the growth of a more general sense of international *morality*. War itself was not necessarily illegal. In some cases it was certainly still consciously planned. But it is significant that even in those cases there was usually an attempt to force the opponent to make the actual declaration of war, as was achieved by France and Savoy in 1859 and by Prussia in 1866 and 1870. This would not have been the case in the previous century and reflected a recognition that aggressive conduct was now to be regarded as antisocial and reprehensible. France after 1850 and Germany after 1900 were widely considered as dangerous threats to the international order whose conduct did not conform with

---

34. *Memoirs of Prince Metternick*, to Mrs. A. Napier, London, 1880–82, I, 30.

the standards of reasonableness and moderation generally recognized. Statesmen congratulated themselves on the long periods of peace which had been attained before 1853 and after 1878, as they would not have done so fervently in the previous age.

It is true that in a nationalistic age such scruples could nearly always be overcome if it could be shown that what was at stake was a vital "national interest" (for example, the Kaiser assured Austria privately in 1912 that if "vital national interests" made it necessary for Austria to precipitate war, Germany would stand by her). Nearly all nations made an exception of questions in which the vital interests, independence, or "honor" of their state were engaged when committing themselves to settle disputes by legal procedures (p. 334 below). But in general it was more honorable to be peaceful than warlike. Disraeli, in claiming he had obtained "peace with honor" at Berlin, assumed that this was a matter for congratulation: which would not have necessarily have been so a century earlier. Unprovoked or "preventive war" were no longer regarded as justifiable. When France publicized the indiscretions of a German statesman implying the possibility of such action in 1875, she knew that this was likely to discredit Germany.

The traditions of sovereignty were breached in another way. In the previous age everything that occurred within the borders of one state was beyond the concern of another. It began now to be accepted that some intervention in the affairs of other states might be legitimate if it was for the protection of *basic human rights*. After a revolution in Poland or atrocities in Turkey, expressions of concern, even direct intervention by other states, became normal. The provisions of the Treaty of Vienna on slavery, weak though they were, and subsequent international conventions on slavery and the slave trade, the perpetual remonstrances by the powers to the Porte to reform its administration and treatment of Christians, the demands by the Concert for a reform of the administration of the papal states, and the Notes delivered by Britain and France to Russia about her treatment of the Poles in 1863, are all examples of this tendency. For all the concern of nationalism to build powerful and independent states, the collective principle established by the Concert meant that states became more accountable to others for their behavior than ever before: they were indeed more so then than they are today (France and Britain issue no diplomatic notes to the Soviet government about the treatment of minorities in Russia now).

There was also a development of international law in the strict sense: generally accepted obligations undertaken by all, or a majority of governments, affecting their relations with each other. The number of treaties of all kinds increased rapidly (there are said to have been 16,000 entered into between 1815 and 1924).[35] A number of these were multilateral conventions in which many countries accepted *general obligations* in particular fields. The subjects on which rules of this kind developed included diplomacy and diplomatic privilege (the Vienna Treaty, the protocol of Aachen of 1818); the principles of maritime law, neutrality, blockade,

---

35. Nussbaum, *A Concise History*, p. 191.

and contraband (Treaty of Paris, 1856); free navigation and international waterways, such as the Elbe, the Rhine, the Danube, and the Congo (conventions of 1821, 1831, 1856, and 1884); abolition of the slave trade, including eventually a provision for multilateral enforcement and mutual inspection (Brussels, 1890); copyright and patents (Berne, 1866, and Paris, 1883); rules of warfare (the Hague, 1899). Bilateral treaties established widely accepted principles on extradition, consular rights, railway freight and insurance, fishing rights, and monetary affairs.

Though there was greater lip service paid to the obligation to comply with "international law," the force of nationalism continually worked the other way. There is little evidence that many statesmen had much direct knowledge of writings in this field, or even of the substantive provisions of international law, such as they were. Moreover, increasingly widespread acceptance of "positivist" doctrines, confining the law to principles explicitly acknowledged by states (so excluding all principles derived from "the law of nature" or general principles of equity), meant that international law was less likely to be regarded as an inhibition on a state's freedom. Abstract ethical or legal doctrines were held to be binding on a state only insofar as they were formulated or codified in formal treaties, signed and ratified by it according to the proper constitutional procedures. The sovereign body, whether monarch or parliament, in reserving the right of ratification, was at the same time reserving the right to limit and circumscribe the extent of a state's obligations.[36]

This reservation of ultimate power to the nation gave a special importance to treaties. One norm that was almost universally acknowledged now was that *pacta sunt servanda:* treaties are to be observed. Some theorists even contended that this represented the sum total of international law—the law was what was in treaties. Certainly the conference system, which was the principal instrument for resolving the main international issues of the day, would have been of no value unless there was a general presupposition that the undertakings reached there would be observed. Just as the law of contract and contractual relations generally became the dominant legal principle in domestic affairs (indeed, according to some, the characteristic feature of the contemporary society), so now contractual law came to dominate international relations equally.

This was then an age when the norms reflected the purposes of a few powerful nation-states pursuing enlightened self-interest. General acceptance of the principles of multilateralism and accountability, the principle that nations should not bring about important alterations to the status quo without the consent of other powers, the accepted need to pay regard to the "European system," even to the principles of "international law," the developing concept of basic human rights,

---

36. Cf. M. Kaplan and N. Katzenbach, *The Political Foundations of International Law* (New York, 1961), p. 64: "National identification . . . reached its ultimate philosophical statement in notions of state will. . . . According to the new theories, the 19th century corporate sovereign was "sovereign" in a quite new and different sense from his historical predecessors. He no longer sought to find law; he made it; he could be subjected to law only because he agreed to be. There was no law, domestic or international, except that willed by, acknowledged by or consented to by states."

the increasing resort to mediation and arbitration, made this society more concerned with social obligations than any that had gone before. There was probably a
wider body of norms of conduct, which were in turn more generally observed, than
at any earlier time.

But against this rebelled the new and rising force of nationalism, stimulating
populations and governments to behavior that was more self-interested, less
moderate and restrained, less concerned with the needs of the system, than even in
the previous age. As the century progressed this force increasingly weakened
the effectiveness of the new civilizing influences. The civilizing influences were
successful in securing longer periods of widespread peace than in any earlier time
(two stretches of almost forty years). But the new norms could not withstand the
explosive force of nationalism, which ultimately brought the society to an end in a
conflict of a savagery and scale never previously seen in human history.

## 12.7  Age of Ideology (1914–1974)

In the age of ideology that followed there were substantial changes in the norms
influencing behavior.

One of the effects of the overriding concern with ideology was abandonment of
the traditional justifications of realpolitik and *raison d'état*. Since the state was no
longer the be-all and end-all, its reasons were not necessarily overriding. National
interest alone was not always sufficient justification for any action a state might be
tempted to undertake. This change already began to be apparent during World War
I: "Great popularity attached to the concept that competition for power and
concrete interests was evil, that moral ends alone could justify the struggle. . . .
The revolution in Russia and the influence of the U.S. worked at the time to much
the same effect."[37] Each of the two great powers that emerged to dominance at this
time proclaimed, for different reasons, the end of the old system of naked power
struggle and the need for a new international society ruled by moral principles: in
the case of the U.S., respect for the rights of nationalities and small nations, for the
principle of democracy, and open diplomacy; in the case of the Soviet Union, the
principle of the illegitimacy of imperialism and great power arrangements, and the
superiority of "socialist internationalism" over old-style nationalist ambitions.
U.S. foreign policy alternated for the next fifty years between periods of high
idealism and crusading zeal (Wilson, Roosevelt, and Kennedy) and periods of
introspection and withdrawal (Coolidge, Hoover, and Nixon) which, though less
morally exhilarating, were sometimes more favorable toward realistic accommodations. Soviet foreign policy showed a more steady return from an ultrapolitical
and ideological concern for world revolution during the twenties to an ultrarealistic

---

37. R. A. Albrecht-Carrié, *Diplomatic History of Europe Since the Congress of Vienna* (New
York, 1958), p. 348.

and cautious concern for strictly Russian national interests in the latter part of the period.

The growth of moralistic attitudes during this time was reflected in the development of international morality. It was shown first in changing attitudes toward the legitimacy of war. While war did not at first necessarily become less common, it was more generally regarded as an aberration, a moral crime, or at least a "great illusion" which, it was said, could bring no benefits even to the victors. In an ideological age, external war in any case was less relevant to purely political ends, to securing the *internal* changes which were most fervently desired. At such a time, when propaganda became of the first importance, all alike sought to show that their own aims were peaceful and those of their enemies warlike. Nor was this only show, for the horrors of the two world conflicts which did occur induced a real revulsion from the idiocy of war among the vast majority of the public, as among their governments. For the first time, therefore, international law and international doctrine generally, which had before always conceded that war could be legal in certain circumstances—for example, to defend "vital interests" or "national honor"—began now to lay down, at least in theory, the inadmissibility of resort to war.

The provisions of the Treaty of Versailles, declaring the war guilt of Germany and her liability to pay reparations, though unilateral in form, served to establish the principle that the deliberate preparation of war was regarded as an international crime. The war crime trials which were instituted after both World Wars I and II asserted the same notion in more dramatic form. The Treaty of Versailles declared that the German kaiser was "publicly arraigned for a supreme offense against international morality" and the sanctity of treaties, and would be tried "with a view to vindicating . . . the validity of international morality." And the trials after World War II sought to make the planning and preparation of war against other states a new crime in international law. The covenant of the League, while it did not outlaw war as such, by committing all members to assist any other that was attacked reaffirmed the principle that such an attack was a violation of the principles of the society, which all must join in putting down. The Pact of Paris of 1928, which was signed by almost all governments of the world, explicitly condemned all resort to war. Finally, this principle was stated even more clearly in 1945 in the Charter of the UN which, in its opening articles, explicitly committed all members to refrain from the "threat or use of force." None of this, of course, prevented force from being used, or war deliberately resorted to. But it did serve to reflect a widely held view, not maintained in any previous age, that the deliberate use of force among states was illegal and immoral. "Aggression" (whatever it was) became, more than in any previous time, a generally condemned offense against the rules of society.

In itself and undefined, such a norm was inevitably crude and imprecise. Which warlike acts were "aggressive," which were in self-defense? When nations did take action by force, like Japan in 1931, Italy in 1936, North Korea in 1950, Britain, France, and Israel in 1956, or the U.S. in Vietnam in 1965, it was always in "self-defense," against the actions of others, or for other generally approved purposes. Soviet actions in Hungary and Czechoslovakia were claimed to be necessary in defense of the "socialist commonwealth." U.S. action over Cuba in 1962, which involved a forcible violation of free navigation on the high seas, was widely hailed, and not only in the U.S., as legitimate self-defense against an action said to threaten the security of the U.S. (even though precisely similar actions had just previously been taken by the U.S. against the Soviet Union).

So intense ideological conflict produced almost as many attempts to bend the rules as intense national conflict in the previous age. There were some attempts to define somewhat more certainly what constituted aggression. In the 1930s, and again under the UN, committees considered the definition of aggression almost continuously. But it remained impossible to find a description that was satisfactory to all. Even when eventually, in 1974, such an agreement was reached, it was widely rejected as unsatisfactory. Most nations now came to accept that the first use of force against another was normally impermissible. But there remained considerable differences about detailed application of this principle. It was not always easy to say, when large-scale hostilities did occur, who had the greater responsibility for starting them (as in the Arab-Israel conflicts of 1956 and 1967, the two Indo-Pakistan wars of 1965 and 1971, and in Vietnam). Each side could always justify itself, like squabbling schoolboys, by saying, "you started it."

External attack in its most overt form did become less common, at least from 1945 onward.[38] In an ideological age it was not territory but human hearts which were the target. There remained more ambiguous forms of conduct which in effect involved the use of force or assistance in their use, yet could scarcely be condemned as overt aggression: external assisstance in civil wars, aid for coups and countercoups, aid to colonial revolutions. Many new justifications emerged for intervention in particular cases: to maintain respect for international undertakings (over Suez in 1956); to aid an ally against a rebellion assisted from abroad (Vietnam and Cambodia); to protect a country's own nationals (in the Dominican Republic in 1965); to restore a government overthrown by "reactionary" forces (Hungary and Czechoslovakia). In an age of ideological struggle intervention of this kind was the main danger. Yet no accepted rules on such questions were established.

In some areas more firmly established norms began to develop. The concept of certain basic human rights which every government was under an obligation to accord and which the international community had the right to protect became even more widely acknowledged. This principle was no longer applied only to a few European states, but in the world as a whole. The Universal Declaration of Human Rights of 1948, which was unanimously adopted, laid down some of the more basic rights, though in somewhat woolly form. A series of international conventions elaborated them in greater detail, and imposed more specific obligations on

38. For statistics, and a more detailed elaboration of this point, see Evan Luard, *Conflict and Peace in the Modern International System* (Boston, 1968).

governments. In a few cases, as in the case of the labor conventions negotiated in the ILO and the Convention on Racial Discrimination negotiated in the UN, these obligations were accompanied by machinery designed to insure that they were adequately applied. By this process new *standards* were set which became widely demanded of governments everywhere. These reflected a more widespread public concern about standards of government in other countries, brought about by closer contacts. The standards also intensified that concern by providing a yardstick, a measure of attainment, by which all governments should be judged (they could also, if desired, be used as a stick to beat ideological opponents).

These new standards, and the concern they reflected, probably did serve, if only marginally, to influence governments. Slavery and white slavery were virtually abolished. Minority peoples began to secure somewhat better treatment than before. Religious discrimination almost disappeared. Even governments which held large populations in considerable subjection, such as those of South Africa and the Soviet Union, were sometimes induced to make marginal adjustments (for example, in their treatment of African workers and Jews respectively) in response to external pressures. Here, therefore, new norms began to be established whose validity, if not formally endorsed, was almost nowhere wholly rejected.

There began too to be increasing acknowledgment, at least in theory of the legitimacy and authority of international organizations. During the League period that authority was still challenged and even explicitly denounced (for example, by Italy, Germany, and Japan). After the UN was founded, no government wholly repudiated its authority. Membership became virtually universal. Only one government decided to leave that organization, very briefly, and she returned within two years. While UN resolutions were widely flouted and ignored, governments usually sought at least to pretend they were complying (for example, over sanctions against Rhodesia, which had not been the case over the sanctions against Italy in 1936), or to justify their noncompliance in acceptable ways. Financial support for international organizations increased steadily; there was no defaulting (as there had been in the League). Their total revenues rose to nearly a billion dollars by the end of the period, and even voluntary contributions rose rapidly. Governments sought so far as possible to avoid being condemned by UN bodies, which were taken to reflect in some vague sense "world opinion." They even attempted to avoid being left in a small minority in UN votes. Here was a new norm: the duty to stand reasonably well with general opinion, as expressed within such bodies.

Finally, the network of international rules and obligations was extended into wholly new areas where, with increasing contacts, regulation at the international level became necessary. Rules on trade restrictions, which had been developing slowly since the eighteenth century, became, after a brief period of nationalism in the 1930, more detailed in scope and more internationalist in purpose than ever before. New obligations concerning air navigation, sea transport, posts and telegraphs, health regulations and standards, radio frequencies, patents and copyrights, industrial standards, and many other subjects came to be widely accepted. New rules had to be evolved for previously undiscovered areas, such as space and the seabed, to regulate activities there. New laws were framed relating to diplomatic and consular relations, the making and validity of treaties, the law of the sea, and other matters. As always there were governments which failed to accede to the new instruments, and others who violated them after they had acceded. But in general such rules have normally been observed. And certainly the accumulation of this increasing body of international rules had an important psychological impact in creating greater consciousness everywhere of an obligation to the international society as a whole.

Another new development was the increasing willingness to make individuals, as well as governments, a subject of international law. After World War II German leaders were tried, condemned, and hanged for the commission of "international crimes," as the court itself defined them (such as genocide and the planning of aggressive war), irrespective of the laws of their own country. This was a radically new principle, though not pursued in subsequent international legislation.

So the total *volume* of rules developed in this period was greater than ever. A great proportion of them inevitably were in the least contentious areas of technical and commercial cooperation. On the most vital issues they were sometimes ambiguous (as over intervention in civil wars) or ineffective (as over externally inspired coups and countercoups). Nonetheless, the taboos against war became probably stronger than in any earlier age. Support emerged for the idea of "insulation" of conflict areas from great power rivalry: the U.S. and Soviet Union kept their troops from the Congo and Cyprus, restrained the temperature in the Middle East, and, eventually, even moderated their activity in Southeast Asia. There was a general consensus in favor of "restraint" and wise statesmanship, rather than ruthless national competition in the handling of world problems.

While for a period ideological conflict led to a state of international tension as great as at any time in history, this in turn led eventually to the emergence of a new code designed to contain those tensions and conflicts, to make possible the peaceful coexistence of rival political creeds. So again the development of a new type of society leads to the emergence of new norms appropriate to its needs.

The process by which societies evolve their own norms of conduct is complex. Even in domestic societies norms are not usually *created* by a process of deliberate decision. They emerge gradually out of the experience of the society, the recognition that certain rules are necessary to allow it to operate effectively and without violence. It may be long before they are expressed in any written form: before conventions become rules, before common law is turned into statute law.

In international society these difficulties are even more obvious. There exists no central authority or accepted leadership to formulate the rules. Contact between the members may be only spasmodic. The need for common laws may not be generally accepted. There is not even an integrated society, with common values and assumptions, still less a common language, within which the rules can evolve.

Conceptions of the norms required will thus vary widely. International rules for this reason at first are weak or disputed, and certainly have a very limited authority in relation to those of the domestic society.

Nonetheless, every international society has had rules of a sort. None have been genuinely anarchic. Most members have observed most of the rules most of the time. But there has sometimes been dispute or ambiguity about the content of the rules. The sanctions against breaking them (even the nonmaterial sanctions) have always been weak and uncertain. And therefore violations have been frequent. Indeed, it is arguable that it is the lack of a fully developed and fully accepted system of norms (rather than of more powerful institutions) which, above all, has prevented any fully integrated society of states, comparable to a domestic society, from coming into existence.

In a certain sense there has been a progressive development. As communications have improved and contacts developed, ever more complex norms have been established. In the ancient Chinese society, though there were effective rules concerning diplomatic intercourse, rules in many other fields were ineffective or nonexistent. The situation was little different among the Greek city-states, though religious taboos perhaps played a somewhat greater role there. During the last six centuries, though there have been periods of retrogression, gradually an increasing range of rules has been established. Though these have not abolished conflict (and there is always conflict of some kind in every society) or wholly abolished warfare (and questions of peace and war are by definition those where effective norms are hardest to establish, because they are the questions on which men feel most passionately) they have done something to harmonize activities in many fields. These range from the law of space to that of the sea, from the treatment of diplomats to the organization of postal services, from trade rules to the validity and duration of treaties.

However, this increasing range and effectiveness of norms is not the only factor which counts. The *type* of norms existing within each society is equally significant in determining its character. Like the other factors we have examined, this is one of the elements which goes up to make up the fabric of the international society as a whole. So in the age of dynasts the norms established are related to the rules of inheritance, chivalry, and knightly combat; in the age of religions they are concerned with religious observance and the resolution of the conflicts occurring on that subject; in the age of sovereigns they relate to diplomatic precedence, the rules of war among states, the law of neutrality, and similar questions; in the age of nationality to finding accommodation among the major nations, distributing spheres of influence, and defining the national principle; in the age of ideologies to laying down the ground rules for competitive coexistence; and so on. This relationship is not surprising. New norms must be adjusted to the types of conflicts and behavior which require to be restrained. Today new rules have to be formulated for outer space, satellite communications, biological weapons, and so on, to take account of *technical* changes. But they are also needed in a more general way to order a world of ideological conflict, with relatively rigid frontiers and a high degree of interpersonal contact. In other cases a change in the norms may reflect a change in the character of the elites. Thus the world of chivalry, in outlawing the crossbow or gunpowder, legitimizes, however ineffectively, the conventions and assumptions of chivalry, where power rests in the horse; a world of sovereigns, in removing these prohibitions and banning instead the destruction of civilian populations, substitutes new ones of its own, reflecting the social structure of a new international society, where the sovereign needs power independent of his knights.

In international as in national societies, norms are a way of regulating and ordering society with the minimum threat to free will. They induce conformity without imposing it. Rules are indeed always the ultimate rulers: They regulate society by securing *regularity* in behavior and therefore making it more predictable. They have a special importance in international societies, where there exists no supreme authority able to secure conformity by coercive means. Within such societies, as our examples have shown, they evolve in response to a changing environment. As in narrower societies, they are molded by the prevailing preoccupations and needs of the society as a whole. But they secure their full effect only if accompanied by institutions capable of defining and enforcing them.

# 13. Institutions

The other main means societies have used to regulate the conduct of their members are institutions to discuss common problems, resolve disputes, or establish rules. This method too has been attempted in international as in national societies.

Let us then, finally, consider the types of institutions developed in different international societies to secure some degree of order in the relations among their members.

The word "institution" is used in the social sciences in two quite distinct ways. Anthropologists use it to refer to relatively stable practices and customs within any particular human society, such as the institution of slavery, child marriage, totem religion, or war. Political scientists use it to refer to specific bodies usually meeting on a regular basis to discuss or decide questions of a particular kind: a parliament, a law court, or a church. The term "international institution" has usually been used in the second sense, that is, to refer to such bodies as the League of Nations, the International Court of Justice, or the International Labor Organization. But studies of international society are also legitimately concerned with the other aspect of the term, for example, with the institution of diplomacy, international arbitration, or warfare among states. And though in this chapter we shall be mainly concerned with institutions in the second sense—international bodies—we shall also consider institutions and traditions of a wider kind: stable practices designed to influence relations among the members of a particular society (such as diplomacy).

In both senses institutions can be regarded as stabilizing factors within society. The very word implies a practice, or a body, that is firmly established and which commands widespread support. The institution of marriage in any particular society refers not to any kind of marriage, but a particular kind, solemnized in particular ways and practiced according to set conventions. Religion as an institution implies not any religion but *the* religion of the society, whose importance is as a source of common belief.

Institutions hold society together in two separate ways. On the one hand they hold them together in time; they link the present to the past and the future. They are relatively stable factors and insure that the society at one time is not too different from what it was ten years before, or even 100 or 1,000 years before: in other

312

words, they save a society from violent change and the conflict which may accompany it.

But they also hold a society together in space. They represent a common focus, a common belief or practice, a common authority, which is *shared* by all of those, in however wide an area, who are members of that society. Institutions in the second sense we defined, bodies or authorities, are particularly important for this purpose. They may even determine the definition of the society. Members of the same society are those who owe allegiance to particular authorities: a chief, a council of elders, a national government. Those who may share many similar beliefs but recognize different authorities will not, under most definitions, belong to the same society. Political authority will ultimately determine the boundaries of a society, partly because it will also determine many other things which are held in common. Thus the most important institutions of all are those which constitute some form of political authority.

Even in national societies, and still more in international societies, the most basic problem for institutions of this kind is how they can or do command authority. In a fully integrated society this is no problem. The very fact that they are acknowledged and traditional institutions of the society will automatically accord them authority. The chief is obeyed *because* he is chief; his own personal qualities are irrelevant. It is the office and not the person which commands authority. In a less integrated society, a society subject to change, a society where the traditional ways are under challenge, or a society only beginning to emerge as a community (like almost all international societies), this will not be so. Institutions, in the sense of collective bodies, will be new. And they will thus need to create their own authority, to win for themselves the respect in which authority resides. Only institutions in the sense of customary practices—such as diplomacy—are old enough to command universal authority. In a decaying society even an old institution which once commanded authority may do so no longer, may come under challenge. It will no longer command authority simply because it is an institution. Institutions, in the sense of collective bodies, are thus not necessarily effective focuses for collective loyalty or effective authorities within society. Especially in international societies a new kind of society may require a new type of institution.

Institutions in international societies take many forms, representing different degrees of social integration. They may be nothing but occasional *contacts* to discuss mutual problems. They may be regular *conferences* among some or all members. Finally, they may be a system of international *organizations* concerned with a wide range of international problems, and eventually carrying some degree of centralized authority over the separate units of the society. In many cases the different types of institutions exist together and the question is the balance maintained among them. That balance depends partly on the level of integration, the degree of contact and communication among the members. But it also depends partly on the ideology of the society. It is especially this question, the relationship between the form of institutions and the ideology of a society, which we shall need to examine.

## 13.1  The Chinese Multistate System (771–221 B.C.)

Among early international societies traditional ceremonies or religious practices have sometimes represented primitive international institutions. For example, in the Chinese multistate system the institution of greatest importance originally was the Chou monarchy. The rulers of each state at first held their fiefdoms from the Chou ruler, and could be made accountable to him. Traditional ceremonies served to symbolize and reinforce the obligations and duties which the feudal lords were in theory supposed to undertake. At one time the system may well have really operated in this way.

> The control by the Chou court . . . had been maintained through a system of ceremonial functions. . . . The linking of the ceremonial aspects of political subservience with a primitive religion allowed the Chou rulers to mobilize the opinion of other feudal lords against any individual or group which did not conform to the pattern. The premium placed upon the practice of proper court conduct by the various members of the aristocracy enabled the Chou court to maintain its existence and to receive the support of the various princes long after it had ceased to be a military power.[1]

Thus these traditional institutions were used to maintain a specific type of international order. Relics of this system remained in the first part of this period. The Chou court continued to undertake ceremonial functions and to convene occasional meetings of the Chou states. These were the only officially accepted central institutions of the system. But as the hegemons, from the early seventh century, increasingly usurped many of the powers of the Chou kings, even while paying lip service to their authority, the vestigial effect of these older institutions disappeared.

They were in time replaced by the institutions of the *leagues,* under the leadership of the hegemons.[2] These took over the important task of calling together the rulers to discuss common problems: it is recorded, for example, that the Ch'i rulers did this thirteen times in the relatively short space of under fifty years that they were hegemons. These meetings therefore served as the primary institution of their age, in which the states were able to exchange views and deliberate on future policies.

> Assemblies of the league were not held at stated intervals, but, whenever need arose, the heads of the allied states were convoked by the president. Some were convened for the purpose of undertaking a joint war, and were attended by the feudal chiefs with all

1. R. L. Walker, *The Multi-State System in Ancient China* (Hamden, 1953), p. 6.
2. Confucius and Mencius never acknowledged the term hegemon (pa), because they did not recognize the authority of these leaders to usurp the Chou power.

their armed contingents. Others with peaceful purposes did not bring together so large a body of men.[3]

They met "to plan mutual defense, to strengthen ties of friendship, or to keep each other posted on their activities."[4]

By 652 such a meeting of the more powerful states was even able to decide on the succession to the Chou throne. This has a double significance: it shows that the institution of the Chou monarchy no longer had any effective power since the monarch was dependent on the choice of other states. Second, it shows that the chief states were able, despite their differences, to reach agreement on a contentious question of this kind. Such meetings may have been often dominated by the views of the hegemon of the day, but at least the principle and the precedent of regular interstate conferences came to be established. An effective institution for consultation had thus been created.

Parallel to the institutions of the leagues there developed the practice of diplomacy: regularized contacts on a prearranged basis to discuss common problems. We have already described the way this was organized (p. 204–5 above). It is important here to recognize how highly developed were the traditions and techniques established. It was not simply a question of occasional messengers being exchanged between normally isolated rulers. It was a system of diplomacy operated according to very strict rules. There were many occasions when diplomatic visits were obligatory: assumption of a throne, burial of a former ruler six months after death, marriage of a daughter to another ruler. Again, "it could be considered almost a legal requirement that the states send envoys to each other to acknowledge more formal missions. Failure to do so was considered a serious breach of propriety."[5] Very often such occasions were used, after the formal ceremonies were over, to discuss interstate affairs.[6] Here is a perfect example of the way in which the formal and ceremonial aspects of diplomacy came to be used to perform a *structural* purpose for the society: the discussion and negotiations of interstate problems and differences. Such an institution was especially required in such a competitive and warlike society.

There also existed a system of conference diplomacy. In addition to the meetings *within* the leagues (which occurred on average every one and one-half years between 681, when the Chou league was founded, and the end of the Spring and Autumn period 200 years later), conferences sometimes took place on a wider basis. In 546, for example, a general conference of all the major states of the system was held to discuss a proposal for general and complete disarmament. Such conferences were large state affairs; each delegation might number a hundred members. The record of this particular meeting is reminiscent of some recent discussions of the same subject:

3. K. S. Latourette, *The Chinese, Their History and Culture* (London, 1946), p. 48.
4. Walker, *Multi-State System*, p. 80.
5. Ibid., p. 81.
6. Ibid., p. 78.

At the meeting there was a great amount of haggling about the text of the agreement and, when the wording was finally determined, there was a dispute about whether Chin or Ch'u should sign first. Ch'i and Ch'in did not sign at all. The document contained only a general agreement for abolishing warfare. . . . Throughout the conference there was an intense air of distrust; the Ch'u representative even wore armor. . . . The conference was a total failure from the point of view of its original objective. The states went on their way, distrusting each other more than ever, and increasing their armaments.[7]

There were also some institutions for arbitration and peaceful settlement of disputes. These operated especially within the leagues. Sometimes the leader of the league acted as arbitrator between two members, since it had, of course, a direct interest in resolving a quarrel between two of its allies.[8] In rare cases the Chou ruler, as the titular head of the Chou alliance, served as an arbitrator. When the dispute concerned the leader of the league, a third state, also a member of the league, sometimes offered to mediate (as Ch'en did between Chin, then the hegemon, and Wei in 625 B.C.).

Besides these formal institutions there were more informal traditions and devices designed to maintain peace among the states (institutions in the broader sense defined above). There are many recorded examples of combined action against a state that was attacking or had attacked another state, a kind of primitive collective security system. In some cases this took place *within* the leagues, for example, when one member had attacked another. Sometimes it occurred *between* the leagues: The main northern league was indeed established as a means of combining against the threat from the expansive Ch'u. In the Warring States period, when the leagues had effectively ceased to exist, voluntary and ad hoc combination against the major threat was frequently adopted. For example, when Yen, in the far northeast, was attacked by Ch'i in the fourth century, all the other states came to her rescue. Again, when Ch'in became manifestly the main threat to the peace in the third century, all the other six states combined for a time to resist her, though unsuccessfully in the end.

A number of institutions existed, therefore, within this society, even if of a somewhat primitive character, to regulate its affairs and moderate its violence. Some, such as the leagues, suffered from the obvious defect that they were only partial: while they might reduce conflict within each league, they could do nothing to reduce it between them. Even these increasingly broke down from the fifth century onward. The Chou monarchy had lost authority even earlier. Though there was a developed system of diplomacy and of conferences, these were insufficient

7. Ibid., p. 57. See also J. Legge, *The Chinese Classics*, V, 120–121. The chief minister of Sung is reported in the Tso-chuan to have denounced the agreement as a "delusion," declaring that "it is by their arms that Chin and Ch'u keep the small states in awe. Standing in awe, the high and low in them are loving and harmonious and thus the states are kept quiet"—an interesting view of how peace was conventionally maintained within the system, and why the small states favored disarmament so strongly.

8. "The Tso-chuan reports many cases of mediation, arbitration and even intervention within both the Chou and Ch'u leagues. These methods of settlement developed to prevent the disputes which might have weakened the power of either league." Walker, *Multi-State System*, p. 88.

to exert any effective influence on conduct. Collective security procedures were too spasmodic to make much impact.

None of these, therefore, significantly modified the powerfully competitive character of a society of intensely individualistic, power-hungary states. The sense of obligation toward them was too weak, at least in proportion to the powerful aggressive motivations of the states toward each other and their appetite for territory. Against those powerful forces, the embryonic institutions of the age proved wholly inadequate.

## 13.2  The Greek City-States (600–338 B.C.)

The institutions established among the society of Greek city-states had some resemblance to those established at the same time in China 10,000 miles away.

In Greece as in China, religious institutions influenced international relations. The religious Amphictyonies had certain political functions. ''Although the main purpose of these conferences, and of the permanent secretariat which they maintained, was the safe-guarding of shrines and treasures and the regulation of the pilgrim traffic, they also dealt with political matters of common interest and as such had an important diplomatic function. . . .''[9] In 356, for example, Thebes forced a resolution through the Amphictyonic Council demanding the payment of fines from Sparta (for violating sacred land and seizing the Cadmea) and another one declaring a sacred war against Phocis. The oracles, providing widely respected judgments, and the Olympic games, securing universally accepted truces, were institutions derived from the past, shared among many states, that continued to perform an important function for the international society of later days. The organization of each required a considerable degree of cooperation among the states.

These are both examples of the way institutions originally devised for other reasons and for other purposes can come to perform valuable social functions for an international system. They can do so only when religious and traditional values are shared and still have a powerful hold on all men's minds. This is less likely to be true in ideological ages. Later, in the Middle Ages, some religious bodies, and the popes in particular, were able to use their religious authority to help solve international disputes, acting for example as mediators (see p. 323 below). In that sense the papacy became a form of international institution. Thus common religious beliefs of a religious age can sometimes serve to make accommodations easier and mutual trust (for example, in oaths) somewhat greater. But where religious beliefs diverge widely, the scope for religious ceremonies or authorities to promote compromise is obviously reduced. So when the age of religions replaced the age of dynasties, the pope was no longer able to perform a mediating

9. H. Nicholson, *Diplomacy* (London, 1938), p. 19.

function. And in general, religious or traditional practices have played a continually declining role in later international societies.

The most important institution in Greece, as in China, was the large-scale league or alliance. As in China these were sufficiently comprehensive in scope to include a large number of states. But here they were joined together by common ideological sympathies rather than geographical propinquity—indeed, they often contradicted the logic of geography.

These associations could entail not only the joint discussion of common problems, but obligations and undertakings of considerable importance, so that they could effectively modify state behavior. The main alliances met together to discuss what action might be required in certain situations. Just as the Chou league in China developed relatively advanced arrangements for discussing action against the encroachments of Ch'u and other powers, so the states of the Peleponnese met together, in the sixth century in Greece, to discuss joint action against the tyrants of that time: those of Athens, Samos, Thasos, and other places. This Spartan league developed increasingly formalized arrangements for joint discussion of such matters. Originally Sparta was in alliance individually with each of the other members, while they were not necessarily so with each other. From 506 (when Sparta failed to win support for joint action against Athens) a new system was instituted. Under this Sparta on the one hand, and all her allies by majority vote on the other, met and voted separately on each proposal; only if both sides agreed was the action obligatory. In effect Sparta was given a veto, like the great powers in the Security Council today, in deciding on enforcement action.

Just as establishment of the Chou league in China stimulated the formation of another still more closely knit and autocratically organized alliance against it, so in Greece the existence of the Spartan league stimulated the formation of the Delian league to the north, dominated by Athens and soon transmuted into an Athenian-run empire. Originally justified by the war of resistance against Persia, it became in time an organization for promoting Athenian power, economic as well as military. The original obligation to provide ships for joint defense was commuted in most cases to an obligation to pay substantial tribute. The alliance had its own treasury, eventually simply taken over by Athens for her own purposes. As in the Spartan alliance, there was a bicameral constitution: Athens on the one hand, and the Synod of the allies on the other, met separately to reach a decision. In the conduct of war Athens was given command of the forces, and even disciplinary powers over the troops of other cities. Thus each of the two alliances become relatively close-knit and formal international institutions, dominated by a single superpower.

The league or alliance is indeed, we shall find, particularly typical of ideological societies. Thus we find it again in the age of religions, when the religious leagues, though their scope was less wide and they were less dominated by a single power, reflected the same tendency. It is seen again even more clearly in the most recent age of ideology, when again the two major blocs develop elaborate machinery for joint consultation. In such ages there is often a superpower, the ideological leader, dominating and organizing the group. The common faith and common strategic interest of the members (together with the great power interests of the leader) establish between them institutions of their own, more close-knit than exist among the society as a whole.

Nonetheless in ancient Greece, as is natural in a society of very many, very small states, there were also regional institutions. There was an increasing number of federal arrangements among neighboring states. The major cities of Boeotia (which had often themselves absorbed some of their smaller neighbors) joined together before the middle of the sixth century in the Boeotian league. This was based on religion as well as geographical links, but especially on the need for joint defense against Thessaly in the west and Athens in the east. By around 550 it was issuing its own federal coinage, which became current throughout the league. About the same time the states of Phocis formed a union, calling themselves "the Phocians," and they too issued their own federal coinage. Later there developed a large number of local leagues: the Acarnanian league in west Greece, the Arcadian league in the northern Peleponnese, the Achaean league, the Aetolian league, and the Thessalian league. A somewhat looser arrangement was the pact among Ambracia, Amphilocaia, and Acarnania, under which they made a defensive alliance for 100 years, so securing some freedom from intervention by the big powers. Still looser was the "Ionian" league in Asia Minor, with its own Council of Ionians. This had no dominant city but, as during the Persian wars, it planned campaigns, organized the raising of ships and money, and even had its own joint coinage.

There were a few wider institutions. The Pan-Hellenic oath, occasionally taken at the isthmus, was supposed to symbolize the unity of the Ionians and Peleponnesian worlds. During the Persian wars in 480, thirty cities, previously often in conflict, agreed to sink their differences temporarily to meet the common threat. They decided on a common strategy, agreed on the allocation of forces, and decided to accord the leading role and command in the field to Sparta, which was deputed to raise and allocate money and to conduct diplomatic negotiations. This loose association was based on an oath and a covenant of alliance which officially remained in force until 461. It styled itself "the Greeks" and it linked Dorians and Ionians in a single alliance.

Almost as broadly-based was the coalition of leagues formed by Boeotia around 370, joining the leagues of Aetolia, Acarnania, Thessaly, and Arcadia. This reached joint decisions on peace and war, but was manifestly dominated by Boeotia, which enjoyed military command in the field. The only nearly comprehensive organization was the League of City-States, established briefly after the battle of Mantinea in 362. With the single exception of Sparta, every city of any importance belonged to this. It had its own federal court and probably a federal treasury. It was able to reach joint decisions, for example, not to help the Ionian states of Asia Minor, once again threatened by Persia. It had, however, a very short life, being fatally divided by the effort of Athens to build up within it an alliance against Thebes.

Another institution, more highly developed than in China, was that of arbitration. Already around 650 B.C. a dispute between Andros and Chalcis was settled by arbitrators chosen from three other states. Later five Spartan arbitrators settled a dispute between Athens and Megara on the possession of Salamis, and a single arbitrator was appointed to decide the dispute between Athens and Mytilene over Sigeum. Sometimes overlords arranged the arbitration to maintain order: Persia, after the Ionian revolt, arranged a system of arbitration and mutual nonaggression pacts among the Ionian states, to help them to regulate their affairs and reduce the continual conflicts among them. Similarly, Athens arranged within her own empire for disputes, including those between herself and the colonies on financial matters, to be settled by arbitration, or by a decision of the Athenian courts, which were generally accepted as impartial in such questions. Such institutions had some moral authority. Athens gained at least a debating point over Sparta at the beginning of the Peleponnesian War by offering to submit the questions that had arisen between them to arbitration under the Thirty Years' Truce of 446. And the force of such appeals is indicated by the demand of the Spartan king that the offer should be accepted: "We should not forget that the Athenians have offered, in the crisis over Potideia, to give us legal satisfaction. It is against the law to treat as a criminal a country which is prepared to offer arbitration."[10]

Some of the institutions of this society, therefore, were somewhat more developed than those existing in the contemporary society in China. This was probably partly the effect of the shorter distances in Greece, which made easier the calling of meetings among the alliances, amphictyonies, and federal institutions. The relatively small size of the society and greater cultural homogeneity may also have contributed to establishing a greater sense of fellow feeling among the Greek peoples than existed within the vast spaces of China. But whatever the value of these institutions for resolving particular disputes, they were ineffective in resolving most conflicts of a political kind within this ideologically divided society. Indeed, nobody expected they would resolve harmoniously all the disputes arising within this warlike society. The only effective institutions were the leagues, designed to enable the ideological allies to make war on each other more effectively. The role that institutions could play was inevitably determined by the expectations and ethos of the society: in a word, the ideology that dominated.

## 13.3 The Age of Dynasties (1300–1559)

In both these two societies, therefore, there did exist some common institutions, especially relating to diplomacy and the settlement of disputes. But the most

10. Thucydides, *The Peloponnesian War*, I, 85. A more unusual procedure for settling disputes was that of a challenge to a battle between so many warriors of each side. A dispute between Sparta and Argos had been settled by such a battle between 300 warriors of the two states, which each claimed to have won. In 419, when Argos and Sparta were negotiating for a treaty, the representatives of Argos proposed that the same procedure be used once more to settle the problem of the Cynurian land, a border district between the two states, if either side would wish to make such a challenge.

effective were partial bodies that served to divide the society rather than to integrate it. The institutions of the international society existing in Europe in the late Middle Ages were in many ways even less advanced than those of Greece and China.

There were no permanent alliances holding regular interstate meetings at which common problems could be discussed, such as we have seen in both of the earlier societies. Possibly the closest to these were the great church councils, such as the Council of Constance. These discussed problems affecting the churches, but they had only a limited impact on international relationships, and were attended by church rather than by state officials. Occasionally a pope called a special congress, such as that convened by Pius II at Mantua to consider a crusade against the Turks; this came nearest to the meetings of permanent leagues to consider common action which took place in China and Greece. There were also sometimes large-scale congresses, called to conclude the terms of a peace, in which many nations might take part. The meetings at London in 1518 and at Cambrai in 1529 even purported to lay down the terms of a general peace to prevail in Europe for years to come (an expectation rapidly deceived in both cases).

In an age of personal relations and personal decisions, the most characteristic institution, as might be expected in a world of dynasties, was the *summit:* the personal meeting between two or more sovereigns seeking to resolve their differences on a personal basis. In 1520, when there was already a danger that the Treaty of London would break down, a series of personal meetings and interviews between rulers to discuss common problems took place: first a meeting between Charles V and Henry VIII at Sandwich, next the confrontation between Henry and Francis I at the field of the Cloth of Gold, and finally yet another meeting between Charles and Henry at Gravelines. The outcomes of such meetings determined the course of events, and the chances of peace, over the next few years. In Italy in 1451 the great diplomatic revolution, the switch in Florence's alliance from Venice to Milan, was the result of long-term personal acquaintance between Cosimo Medici and Francesco Sforza, the newly established Duke of Milan.

Such meetings had some of the same drawbacks sometimes attributed to modern summit conferences:

> Generally undesirable was the excessive publicity which inevitably accompanied them, making their failure far more damaging than any other kind of failure, and so tempting both parties to impracticable commitments, and ambiguous agreements, and a willingness to accept vague, partial solutions, which often led to grave subsequent misunderstandings. Besides, there was the likelihood that two mature politicians with incompatible aims, having discovered that neither would bend to the other's will, would end by dislking each other more bitterly than before, so that Commines advised princes who wanted to keep friends with one another never to meet.[11]

Like modern leaders, however, rulers were prepared to brave these risks:

> Such is the perennial optimism of politicians and the indestructable confidence of rulers in their own sagacity, that 16th-century princes continued to seek personal interviews,

11. *New Cambridge Modern History,* III (1968): 152.

just as they continued to exploit all the other traditional means of diplomatic action. . . .
Both Francis and Charles were able to persuade themselves that in personal conver-
sations . . . they had found solutions which had eluded the patience of other negotiators
and the dexterity of the Pope.[12]

The development of permanent embassies and a more continuous diplomacy
was an important institutional advance. This enabled sovereigns, in an age of
constantly shifting alliances and fast-moving events, to keep more consistently in
touch with each other than in most earlier ages. Diplomacy eventually became the
primary institution employed to resolve differences (see pp. 237–38 above). It developed, however, only slowly, and mainly toward the end of the period.

Because of the society's scattered character, regional institutions played an
important part. In Germany the empire represented a kind of regional organization,
though its effectiveness was minimal. The formal constitution provided for an
imperial diet in which 30 princes, 100 prelates, 150 lords, and the representatives
of 80 or 90 towns came together to discuss some common problems. This could
pass ordinances to be applied throughout the empire, though they were frequently
ignored. Occasionally differences between states, or between a state and the
emperor, were discussed there, but this was relatively rare. It was open to the
emperor to call for an imperial army or to place a ban on a particular state, but this
too was not often undertaken. Thus the diet was not an effective peace-keeping
institution. In general it was the emperor who decided, unilaterally, whether to call
for the support of his vassals in any particular case. By this time

> the central administration and jurisdiction [of the Empire] were hardly existent. Such
> authority as the king possessed rested upon the territorial powers which he held
> independently of his kingship. His nominal vassals—ecclesiastics, lay-princes,
> knights, and cities—enjoyed practical independence. If they quarreled with each other,
> they fought the quarrel out as if they had been independent states. If the emperor
> intervened it was as partisan rather than as arbiter.[13]

*Within* the empire there were still more restricted leagues and groupings, such as
the Swabian league and a similar league on the Rhine, but these were alliances of
like-minded states against the pretensions of the emperor rather than institutions to
resolve quarrels among their own members.

In Italy somewhat more effective regional bodies began to emerge, though for
a relatively short time. In 1443 the last Visconti, Filippo Maria, proposed the
calling of a congress of the major Italian powers for the settlement of all outstanding political questions among them and the exchange of mutual guarantees. The
congress met, but it was poorly attended and finally came to nothing. But in 1454,
under the Peace of Lodi, a new and comprehensive organization was established.
A Most Holy League was set up, first among the three main northern powers,
Venice, Milan, and Florence, but later including almost all the other states of Italy,
who were invited to accede. Any member who attacked another was immediately

12. Ibid.
13. R. Lodge, *The Close of the Middle Ages* (London, 1957), p. 183.

to be expelled and disciplined by common military action. "The general object was to guarantee permanent peace within the closed Italian system."[14] Under the treaty all members were to consult immediately in case of war, and subsequent negotiations were to be jointly conducted. The exchange of ambassadors was extended throughout the league to make possible rapid consultation. The league, however, was scarcely effective.

> Although they had all ratified the solemn declarations of the League of Venice, the four powers had each sound reasons for supposing that the other three had not really renounced all thought of future aggrandizement, since each knew his own state had not. . . . Neither within nor without the peninsula did the League perform its expected function. Instead of the stable equilibrium of confederation, Italy arrived only at an unstable balance of power, a precarious counter-poising of the conflicting interests of jealous sovereign states.[15]

As in subsequent international organizations, sovereignty was not effectively restrained by the new institution however solemn the undertakings made to the contrary.

A brief attempt was made to implement a similar and more ambitious system for Europe as a whole. The Treaty of London, drawn up by Wolsey in 1518, was designed to establish a general league, not only to defend Christendom against the Turks but to preserve peace in Europe. Intended to include any European nation which might wish to join, it contained provisions for arbitration of disputes and guarantees against aggression, which all signatories must unite to resist. In the case of an attack by one state against another, there would be consultation among the parties to decide the joint action against the attacker. The proposals were greeted by humanists and others all over Europe as a hugely important advance in statesmanship, implementing at last the dreams of earlier seers and thinkers for some kind of international organization. In this case too, however, the objectives were never to be realized. Within three years most of Europe was at war again, and the recurrent campaign in Italy had been renewed. Once again promises alone were not enough.

The institutions of mediation and arbitration were occasionally employed in this period, though not well developed. The pope was sometimes asked to mediate.[16] He tried unsuccessfully to do so between England and France in the Hundred Years' War (just as his predecessor, Boniface VIII, had negotiated peace between England and France in 1298). Wolsey sought to mediate between Charles V and Francis I in 1521, and Pope Paul III did mediate between these two in 1538. Peace conferences between two countries were nearly always attended by mediators from a third, who were supposed to bring the two parties closer together.

The more formal institution of arbitration (in which the parties pledge themselves to accept the judgment of the arbitrator) was sometimes used to decide on disputes concerning territory and other questions, especially among the lesser

14. G. Mattingly, *Renaissance Diplomacy* (London, 1955), p. 82.

15. Ibid., pp. 83–85.

16. "It is the proper function of the Roman Pontiff, of the Cardinals, of Bishops and of Abbots," wrote Erasmus in 1514, "to compose the quarrels of Christian princes.'

rulers. In one or two cases there were permanent arrangements for the arbitration of disputes, as that between Denmark and Sweden in 1343. Often in such cases a tribunal or team of arbitrators and conciliators was appointed: in the agreement between Denmark and Sweden twenty-four were named, twelve to be appointed by each party.[17] In general, however, these procedures had little impact on the normal conduct of international relations. There existed no generally acknowledged court for arbitration, nor even any universally respected authority. The pope, while he might be acceptable to certain rulers at certain times, was in sharp conflict with many of them during much of this period, and was not therefore always accepted as an impartial judge of their disputes.

The institutions of this period were thus somewhat sketchy and ill defined. There were no automatic procedures which all knew could be invoked in case of dispute or war. A meeting between sovereigns, a congress, a call for arbitration, could be put in motion on occasion, but only if mutually agreeable. The only well-established institution was that of diplomacy, conducted by the servants of the princes. Contact and correspondence among sovereigns was the most widely employed means for resolving differences. In a word, the institutions employed reflected closely the ideology of an age of personal rulers.

## 13.4 The Age of Religions (1559–1648)

International institutions, like national, are adjusted to changing values. In the international society which followed, prevailing preoccupations with questions of religion, and the discussions that resulted, atrophied almost all the institutions of earlier periods.

In an ideological age the summit conferences and congresses typical of the previous society become less possible. When they took place at all, it was almost exclusively among rulers of the *same* religion (for example, the famous conference at Bayonne in 1565 among Catherine de Medici, the Spanish queen, and the Duke of Alba, which was generally believed to have planned a new drive against protestantism throughout Europe). Between rulers of different religions, suspicions and hostility were so intense that it was not felt proper or desirable to have any personal contacts (just as in the modern ideological age from 1917 to the late 1950s a visit to Moscow by Western leaders, except in war, was regarded as wholly taboo). "The era of personal interviews between sovereigns closed abruptly. Queen Elizabeth never left England. Once he got back from the Netherlands, Philip II never left Spain. . . . Similarly the age of great European congresses seemed over. . . ."[18]

17. Cf. A. Nussbaum, *A Concise History of the Law of Nations* (New York, 1947), p. 34: "Generally the Middle Ages preferred large arbitral tribunals, and an even number of arbitrators, both features indicating an approximation of arbitration to conciliation; in fact, the latter task was sometimes expressly imposed upon the arbitrators."

18. *New Cambridge Modern History,* III (1968): 154.

The vast religious gulf meant too that mediation, traditionally performed by the pope and other Catholic prelates, was no longer an acceptable procedure. Foreign sovereigns were now more likely to be called in aid for this purpose. Maximilian II arranged a peace conference between Sweden and Denmark in 1568, which finally secured agreement between them. James I of England successfully mediated between the same two countries in 1613, and (with France) between Sweden and Russia in 1616. He also helped to mediate over the Cleves-Julich dispute in 1613–1614. To bridge the religious gap a team of mediators including those of both faiths sometimes operated. The king of Denmark acted, together with representatives of Venice and the papacy, as mediator during the prolonged negotiations before 1648. Even so, religious differences could represent a fatal barrier: It is inconceivable that Spain, for example, would have accepted a Protestant mediator to resolve her disputes with a protestant power (still less with a Catholic).

The more formal device of arbitration became still less common. Here too, in such a society, ecclesiastical arbitrators would rarely be acceptable to both parties. In such an age, in any case, the disputes were not of a kind for which most rulers would have been prepared to accept judgment. Willingness to go to arbitration implies a willingness to compromise, to accept an adverse judgment in the final resort, and on many of the religious issues which now arose this willingness was not present, since it would imply a willingness to compromise on vital matters of conscience. The issue of ecclesiastical property in Germany, or that which arose in Cologne in 1580 concerning the right of a bishop to continue to exercise his functions despite his declared wish to marry, were of a sort that in other ages might have been resolved by a papal judgment. In this age, since they aroused the passions and loyalties associated with two great religious causes, they could certainly not be settled in that way; in the final resort they could be resolved only by war.

Again, and for the same reason, because of the religious division diplomacy was used much less than before. Embassies were distrusted and often closed, if only because an alien religion was practiced there.

> Instead of widening, the area of diplomatic contact constantly narrowed. . . . Throughout the second half of the 16th century, diplomacy declined because an ideological issue, the difference between catholics and protestants, divided Europe into two camps more bitterly irreconcilable and more firmly alienated than any that had ever rallied behind Hapsburg and Valois. As religious issues came to dominate political ones, any negotiations with the enemies of the faith looked more and more like heresy and treason. The questions which divided catholics and protestants had ceased to be negotiable. Consequently, instead of increasing . . . diplomatic contacts diminished. Special embassies continued to go back and forth from time to time between powers in opposing ideological camps, but they were less frequent and instead of expanding, the network of resident embassies actually contracted.[19]

In such an atmosphere of distrust it is not surprising that the effort to build more permanent international institutions became still more modest: this is a difficulty

19. Ibid., 154–157.

facing every ideological age. The grand visions of the treaty of London in the previous period, even the modest regional arrangements envisaged in the Peace of Lodi for Italy or in the imperial idea in Germany, thus had no place in this divided world. At the wider level Sully's ''grand design'' for a European confederation, with its own arbitration court, seems to have been a private dream of his own or his master, rather than a concrete proposal that either expected to discuss seriously with other states. At the regional level, Italy was now largely under Spanish occupation and the main peace-keeping force was Spanish military power. In Germany religious differences were making imperial institutions increasingly ineffective. In such an age, when conflict was endemic and passions bitter, the establishment of organized arrangements to keep the peace seemed more utopian than ever. The nearest approach to them was made at the end of the age in the terms of the Peace of Westphalia. These included provisions for joint enforcement: all the parties to the two treaties agreed to watch over their execution, to seek to insure their observance, and in the final resort to use force to maintain them—quite a revolutionary obligation, occasionally recalled in later years, but never fulfilled.

So, in general, international institutions collapsed with the collapse of a united Christendom. As always the institutions of the age reflected its general character and beliefs. The religious division which bisected Europe left its mark on almost all the arrangements for organized intercourse between governments which had been slowly emerging in the preceding period. Mediation, summit conferences, diplomacy, and more formal international institutions all were inhibited in their development through the suspicions and mistrust that religious differences generated. To resolve these differences themselves, institutions alone would not have been sufficient. What was required was mutual trust, goodwill, and above all tolerance and a willingness to compromise. These were just what were lacking. Only at the end of the period, when a new, more integrated type of international society began to emerge, was it possible once more to seek to establish new institutional arrangements in which some measure of mutual trust could be assumed.

## 13.5  The Age of Sovereignty (1648–1789)

The following international society required different institutions again: those which best served the needs of a society concerned with the aims of sovereignty.

One of the hallmarks of sovereignty was the independence of the individual state. But such states, now closer to each other than ever before, nonetheless required the means of reconciling their interests and resolving their differences. It was not possible to restore the authority which religious and other traditional institutions had enjoyed in earlier times—the pope, the church councils, the Empire, the religious leagues. Though the age of acute religious conflict was past, the continent remained divided and would recognize no common religious authority. Religion in any case counted for less. Yet some common institutions and procedures were more than ever necessary in a society so long divided against itself.

The most important was that of diplomacy, now for the first time formalized as the established system of communication among governments. The system was made uniform through the terms of the Peace of Westphalia (which was in many other ways the basis of the international order). Diplomatic rules were further elaborated and developed as the era progressed, through agreements between two or more of the members. Organized foreign offices were established in almost every capital. The system of consulates for looking after the interests of traders and other citizens abroad was developed (especially by Colbert). For the first time a substantial specialized class emerged whose function it was to seek to resolve differences among states. Governments were thus better informed than in any earlier time about the intentions and wishes of other states, and better equipped to signal their own intentions and desires to those states.

Diplomacy served the needs of the society of sovereignty in a number of ways. First, it provided a regular and permanently available means of communication among the sovereigns who, by their very nature, were largely self-sufficient and independent.[20] Second, it provided the channel for those deals and secret undertakings which were the essential element of state policy in this period. Finally, it provided the instrument through which the settlements at the end of conflicts were eventually arrived at. In the jargon of sociology, it could be said that diplomacy performed here the functions of communication and conflict resolution which every society requires.

But the world of sovereignty required other institutions too. Occasionally diplomacy was supplemented by large-scale international meetings or congresses. The Congress of Cambrai in 1724, for example, was called not to end a particular war or settle a particular issue, but to consider the problems and conflicts of the continent in general. The Congress of Sissons is 1727 had an almost equally wide mandate. These can perhaps be regarded in a sense as anticipations of the congress system as employed in the next century.

There were other anticipations of the age to come. Sometimes the big powers arrogated to themselves a peace-keeping role. The Quadruple Alliance of 1718, in which four of the great powers of Europe joined to suppress Spanish aggression, foreshadowed the Quadruple Alliance of a century later, in which the great powers joined to prevent threats to the peace at that time (even to the extent that in each case the country against which the alliance was originally formed—Spain and France respectively—were finally permitted to join it to make a general peace-

20. See Nicolson, *Diplomacy,* pp. 60–61: "Louis XIV and, to an even greater extent, Catherine II and Frederick the Great, retained the conduct of foreign policy . . . within their own hands. They were the 'sovereign authority,' not in name only, but also in fact. Inevitably under such a system diplomacy and policy became inextricably mixed; negotiation became an intimate problem of personalities; and it was highly important that an Ambassador should secure the confidence, and if possible the affections, of the sovereign to whom he was accredited."

keeping organization). There thus began to emerge not merely, as we saw in discussing the structure of the society, a new conception of an established international order—the "European balance," the general interest of Europe, even the "public good"—which had to be maintained by joint action, but the idea of an oligarchy, or self-appointed junta, whose task it was to achieve this. An alliance of big powers occasionally became a self-appointed police force for international society as a whole. Similarly, the alliances against French aggression at the end of the seventeenth century can be seen as a primitive collective security system.

As before the religious partition, procedures for settling disputes reemerged. One was by the method of conciliation. In the League of the Rhine in 1658 the members pledged themselves to resolve their disputes by conciliation. Ad hoc mediation by one government between two others became relatively common. Britain and the United Provinces mediated to bring peace among Sweden, Poland, and Denmark in 1660, and between Sweden and Denmark in 1700 (they had a keen interest in both cases in opening the Sound to their shipping). Britain mediated between the Turks and the Holy League in 1689; Britain and France mediated between the Empire and the Turks in 1717–1718; Sweden mediated between France and her enemies in 1696; and the Western powers mediated between Turkey and Russia in 1710. Louis XIV, when at his lowest extremity during the War of Spanish Succession, called on the pope and the Swedish King Charles XII to mediate between himself and his enemies. Mediation indeed represented the legal procedure most appropriate to a world of sovereigns: It committed the sovereign state to no absolute obligation, yet might suit the convenience of both states.

Arbitration was also used, though more rarely. The 1655 treaty of friendship between Britain and France provided for arbitration to settle the question of the Arcadian forts, taken by the English colonists from the French, and to assess damages for shipping losses to the two states. A number of Netherlands treaties provided for arbitration in cases of commercial claims and debts: A treaty with England in 1654 provided that the arbitrators "should be shut up in a room separate from all other persons, without fire, candle, drink or other support till they had agreed." But in general the absolute commitment required in arbitration was unacceptable in a world of sovereigns. Thus "arbitration fell off sharply . . . the emphasis on sovereignty characteristic of the period was not favorable to submission to international tribunals."[21]

New institutions in a more theoretical form were devised. The Abbé St. Pierre published in 1713 a "project to secure perpetual peace in Europe" which provided for a federation of states, with a permanent assembly of delegations which would decide on all disputes between nations; if necessary, a party refusing to accept a decision would be coerced by war. In this assembly only the greater states would enjoy a vote, while the smaller would vote in groups, with one vote for each group. Though not altogether unlike the international institutions which developed two

21. Nussbaum, *A Concise History*, p. 90.

centuries later, such ideas were wholly unsuited to the age of sovereignty, where rulers were concerned above all to maintain their own independence, and were therefore generally regarded with some amusement at the time. More hardheaded was Kant's vision of "perpetual peace," in his book of that name, which foresaw the gradual abolition of war through elimination of the conditions which encouraged it, including standing armies, trickery in international dealings, absolutist constitutions, and the total sovereignty of states. Most of these conditions were, however, inherent in the state system as it then existed, and Kant's writings thus had no more impact on the practice of international relations than those of the Abbe St.Pierre. Similarly, Rousseau's belief that war could be eliminated by abolishing the authority of personal rulers and substituting more representative governments inevitably came into conflict with the most firmly established institution of the day, the government of sovereigns. In all these cases, the theoretical international institutions demanded were incompatible with the reality of the individual units as they then existed.

Inevitably in this age there was a conflict between the demands of sovereignty, which prevailed everywhere, and the need for more effective international institutions which must curtail this sovereignty. The most powerful ideology of the age proclaimed the total independence of states, whereas almost any effective international institution, mediation, arbitration, collective security, or fully fledged international organization must restrict that freedom in some measure. Nor was this conflict to be confined to this society alone. For the doctrine of sovereignty was a powerful heritage which continued to influence attitudes in the international society which was to follow. It continued there, too, to inhibit the development of effective international institutions. But it could not prevent significant developments in the new climate then prevailing.

## 13.6 The Age of Nationalism (1789–1914)

The following age saw a dramatic advance in international institutions, perhaps more dramatic than has occurred at any other time.

For the first time a system was established under which governments met together at frequent intervals to resolve the problems of the continent even, later, of the world. The ad hoc *bilateral* settlements of the previous age were now to be replaced by *multilateral* arrangements and joint decision making. While settlements of this kind had been attained before in the aftermath of war, now they were to be arrived at whenever a crisis occurred. Moreover, every great power took part in each settlement, whether or not it was directly involved. As Louis Phillippe put it, the ideal was that "no change, no alienation of territory would take place without the concurrence of all the powers . . . an entente of the five powers for the solution of all the great political questions." This was not achieved in every case. The Prussian wars and the war of Italian unification, for example, were followed only by bilateral settlements, but these covered only German and Italian territory and so could almost be regarded as internal questions. In general, during this age even minor alterations in the status quo, such as a change in the status of Luxembourg or of the Black Sea, or a settlement of the Balkan wars, required the endorsement of a general European conference, representing all the powers, however little their direct interest or involvement.

The basis of the system was set out in the Vienna settlement. Under the second Treaty of Paris of 1815 periodic meetings of the great powers were to take place, not only "to secure the execution of the present treaty" but for the "consideration of those measures which . . . shall be considered the most salutary for the repose and prosperity of the nations and for the maintenance of the peace of Europe." Summit meetings, to be attended by sovereigns or at least foreign ministers, were to be held at "fixed periods" (though the period was never laid down). "Congresses" of the kind originally intended were held only for the first seven years. But there continued throughout the century, at intervals of every two or three years, a long succession of conferences among the "powers," and sometimes other interested nations, to discuss, and in many cases to settle, the major issues of the day. The fact that these were called "conferences" rather than "congresses," that they were not always attended even by foreign ministers but sometimes only by ambassadors, and that they were usually called ad hoc to discuss particular subjects rather than for a general overview, made little fundamental difference (in many cases conferences called to discuss one subject considered others as well). It remained the case that a new type of international system had been established. In the words of Castlereagh, the congress system was "a new discovery in European government, at once extinguishing the cobwebs with which diplomacy obscures the horizon . . . and giving the councils of the Great Powers the efficiency and almost the simplicity of a single state."[22] The system served to secure a period of uninterrupted peace among the European powers until 1854, a striking contrast to the previous century, when wars had been recurrent, and helped to secure a similar period of peace among the major powers from 1871 to 1914. In almost every case, after the divided 1820s, unanimous agreement was reached among the powers. In general the decisions taken were effectively implemented. And in a number of cases joint action was taken, including armed force. This is a record that compares favorably with every subsequent age.

The settlements reached fall into a number of categories. A number were concerned with jointly establishing *new states*. In 1830–1831 the London conference established the independence of Belgium (so revising one of the major provisions of the 1815 settlement), and eventually secured agreement on its new frontier with the Netherlands. The same conference, under the London Protocol of February 3, 1830, established the independence of Greece and again determined the boundaries of the new state (reducing them from those established in the conflict). The independence of Luxembourg was jointly determined in 1867. The

22. Castlereagh, letter to Liverpool, 20 October 1818.

"autonomy," or the independence, of the principalities (1856 and 1860), of Serbia (1856 and 1878), of Montenegro (1878), of Bulgaria (1878), of Crete (1897), and of Albania (1913) were also jointly agreed on in this way. There was even agreement on the sovereigns to whom the crowns of the newly established nations should be offered. In other words, instead of such arrangements being made, as in later times, in private dealings between the leaders of the emerging people and the previously sovereign power, it was accepted that the creation of new states was a question to be jointly determined by the concert of powers managing the affairs of the continent as a whole.

In other cases there were group decisions for the *neutralization* of certain areas. The Treaty of Vienna established the neutrality of Switzerland and obliged all signatories to guarantee it. The London Conference of 1839 established the permanent neutrality of Belgium, which all countries undertook to respect—a decision taken not by Belgium herself, but by the "powers," in order to reconcile their own interests. Similarly, when Luxembourg was given independence by a collective decision in 1867, her neutrality was established and guaranteed by the powers as a whole. The guarantees given in this way anticipated the principle of collective security so much discussed in the following century: if a country was too weak to defend itself, then others should join in undertaking to protect it against attack.[23]

Third, joint decisions were reached on *peace-making* and *peace-keeping*. At the London Conference of 1852 a resolution of the conflict between Prussia and Denmark over Schleswig-Holstein, based on a return to the status quo, was brought about largely through the decisions and pressures of powers not directly involved. Similarly at the Congress of Berlin in 1878, third parties, such as Germany and Britain, played the major part in defining the settlement reached, though neither had been in any way involved in the conflict before. Perhaps most remarkable of all was the case of the Balkan wars of 1912–1913, where the settlement was reached in London, far from the scene of conflict, at a conference attended and dominated by all the "powers," not one of which had been in any way involved in the preceding war.

Equally striking was the development of collective *enforcement* of such settlements, once reached. The Battle of Navarino in 1827 was in effect a multilateral enforcement of a common decision in favor of Greek independence by uninvolved great powers (though in this case Prussia and Austria did not take part). Britain and France acted, on the express authority of the powers as a whole, to impose on the Netherlands by force the decision of the London Conference of 1831 in favor of Belgian independence. A joint naval blockade was used in an attempt to prevent the unification of East Rumelia and Bulgaria in 1885. A four-power naval expedition was used against Greece when she demanded territorial concessions from

23. The neutralization of the Black Sea, agreed to in the Treaty of Paris in 1856, was in a somewhat different category, being *imposed* as the effect of a war, and for this reason was fairly easily reversed fifteen years later when Russian power was restored. Even here an international conference was needed to endorse the reversal.

Turkey in 1886. One or more of the powers acted to enforce collective decisions in a number of other cases: to compel Mahommet Ali to withdraw when he was threatening Turkey in 1839; to make Turkey give Crete autonomy in 1897; and to insure the evacuation of Scutari by Montenegro after the Second Balkan War. In still other cases, one of the powers claimed the authority of the rest to take action in particular areas, as when Austria sought and was generally given authority to intervene in Naples and Piedmont in 1820, or when France sought and obtained authority to use force in Syria in 1861.[24] Finally in China, after the Boxer Rebellion, a fully international force was established to take part in a form of peace-keeping operation there.

In other cases the powers engaged in collective *rule making*. The conferences of the powers were sometimes designed to make rules, or establish regimes, which would be of general validity, and would bind even nations which had no part in forming them. The London Conference of 1840–1841 reached agreement on the rules to govern navigation through the Straits, and though both Britain and Russia sought on occasion to challenge or reinterpret these to their own convenience, it remained widely accepted that they could be changed only through multilateral agreement. At the Congress of Paris in 1856 international rules were agreed on concerning privateering, the right of blockade, the right to confiscate neutral or enemy goods under neutral flag, navigation on international rivers, and other questions; rules which it was held had thereby become part of "the public law of Europe" and should therefore be recognized by all other countries. At the Conference of Berlin in 1884, rough and ready rules concerning the establishment of claims in colonial territories in Africa were agreed on. Finally, at the Hague Conference of 1899, important revisions of the rules of war were held to have been made part of international law.

One effect of this system of collective decision making was the sense that it was necessary to obtain *collective authority* for any attempt to change some feature of any previous settlement. Even revisionist powers—France from 1815 to 1860, Russia from 1856 to 1870, Serbia and other Balkan states from 1878 onward—generally recognized that they could only secure the revision of earlier settlements by agreement. France, though desperately seeking to escape from the settlement of 1815, recognized that she would be unable to achieve this unilaterally (as when Lamartine, declaring in 1848 that the Vienna settlement was overthrown, prudently added that even revolutionary France would continue to respect it). Similarly, when Russia sought to escape from the Black Sea clauses in 1870, she and those who supported her accepted that this could only be legitimately accomplished by a conference of the powers to endorse it, and that conference explicitly laid down, at British insistence, the principle that international obligations could not be changed by unilateral action. And that principle was most explicitly

24. There were still other cases when a power *claimed*, on doubtful grounds, to be acting on behalf of the powers. Britain claimed this in acting against the Barbary pirates in 1816; Russia offered to act for the powers against Egypt in 1840; and Russia claimed to be acting for the powers against Turkey in 1876–1877.

declared by Russia herself in her demand that *all* the powers participate in the settlement between Prussia and France in 1870: "It is impossible that the other great powers be excluded from the future negotiations for peace, even if they did not take part in the war."

An even more remarkable innovation in institutions was the introduction of various forms of international control in particular areas. The setting up in 1821 and 1831 of the two commissions for joint control of navigation on the Elbe and Rhine rivers, with international officials, international boards, and international finances, was an early example; the similar commission established for the Danube in 1856 included representatives of some powers which were not even riparian states. In Shanghai an international settlement, with an international police force, and international court, and its own finances, was set up in 1860. A form of joint control of the Congo Basin, to insure free navigation and trade there through an international association, was established in 1884. Joint commissions were set up to apply the provisions of the Treaty of Berlin in the Turkish provinces, and to inquire into the atrocities in Armenia in the 1890s. Forms of *international inquiry* were instituted. For example, an international commission was set up to supervise elections in the principalities in 1856, to decide whether they wished to be united. A commission of all the powers was established to look into the uprisings in Bosnia in 1875. In 1913 an international commission was set up to establish the frontiers of Albania. The tradition of setting up joint international bodies became firmly established.

Similarly, international institutions were set up in the economic field. Britain, France, and Italy acted together to set up a triple financial control in Tunis in 1869. Britain, France, Germany, and Austria established joint financial control in Egypt in 1866, subsequently replaced for periods by the dual control of France and Britain. In Turkey innumerable commissions and committees of the Western powers were established to supervise the financial system there, and to take almost complete control of tax collection and other revenues.

Finally, perhaps most revolutionary of all was the beginning of the "public international unions," the first fully international organizations. For the first time international bodies were established on a permanent basis, open to all nations, with international secretariats and internationally financed. In 1868 the International Telegraph Bureau, now known as the ITU, was set up, followed in 1874 by the General Postal Union, later called the UPU. An international bureau of weights and measures was established in 1875. International health offices were set up in Havana and Vienna in 1881. In 1901 the International Labor Office, a precursor of the ILO, was set up in Berne. The first significant regional organization (if the Concert of Europe is excluded) was the International Union of American Republics of 1890, replaced by the Pan-American Union in 1910. Altogether by 1914, thirty or forty intergovernmental bodies for specialized purposes had been established.

The "powers" also sought to develop some of the traditional institutions for resolving conflicts. The Treaty of Paris in 1856 specifically expressed the desire of "the plenipotentiaries . . . that States . . . shall before appealing to arms have recourse, so far as circumstances allow, to the good offices of a friendly power." Mediation, in a formal and informal sense, thus became common in this period, usually undertaken by one or another of the "powers." Britain and Russia mediated between Turkey and Greece over Greek independence in 1825. Britain and France offered mediation between Austria and Sardinia in 1848. Austria mediated between Russia and the Western powers over the Crimea. France in effect mediated between Turkey and Greece over Thessaly in 1880–1881. So old institutions were adopted to an oligarchic world.

Arbitration too became more common. In the early nineteenth century sovereigns were frequently asked to arbitrate between other states, especially on frontier disputes. In practice, in a world of nations rather than sovereigns, this was normally undertaken by commissions appointed by the governments concerned. Again the great powers played a dominant part. Chile and Argentina turned in 1881, not to a fellow Latin American state, but to Queen Victoria to arbitrate concerning their common frontier. This system became increasingly institutionalized. In 1873 the Institute of International Law was established to promote and formulate the rules for international arbitration. And at the first Hague Conference in 1899 a permanent court of arbitration was established, consisting of panels of judges who were available to be called on to settle international disputes. This was used in one or two important cases, including the Dogger Bank dispute between Russia and Britain, resulting from the occasion when Russian warships fired on British fishing boats near the Dogger Bank in 1905.

Thus a wide range of new institutions began to emerge. There was a paradox about this. Intergovernmental institutions had never before developed so fast. There was far greater effort than at earlier times to reach joint decisions on matters of common concern. Yet precisely while this new institutional framework was developing, so too were the pressures within the social structure it had to contain. The strength of nationalism—the rise of nationalist governments, and popular support for them—was being built up as fast as or faster than the strength of international institutions. Internationalism was growing, fast, but nationalism grew faster still.

This affected all the institutions we have been describing. The system of regular consultation in the Concert was weakened because of the increasing determination of some governments to go their own way, or to reach bilateral accommodations rather than multilateral agreements. From 1878, and especially from 1890 onward, the number of conferences declined and bilateral agreements came to predominate. Most of the colonial issues, though they were successfully resolved, were settled by bilateral rather than multilateral means. Similarly, the procedures of mediation and arbitration became, in an age of intense nationalist rivalry, increasingly difficult to use effectively. In ratifying the convention establishing the new court of arbitration, and in the many bilateral agreements on the subject reached in this period, most governments insisted on excepting all disputes in which the "vital interests, the independence or the honor" of the state were involved; in other words, precisely those most likely to lead to war. Where national honor was at stake, nationalism was not prepared to renounce the right to appeal to the final arbitrament of brute force.

So too national ambitions, armed with the traditional doctrine of sovereignty, carefully and deliberately limited the authority and powers of the new public unions and other international organizations being set up. They were thus still basically only forums for consultation and discussion of common problems. Any amendment to the systems established, such as for posts or telegraphs, had to be ratified by each government, so any one of them could refuse to apply any change in the system of which it disapproved. In a word, the national state still ruled supreme: it accepted only those international arrangements which it found con- venient and which represented no real threat to its own power.

Though new institutions, new forms of cooperation and mutual consultation grew perhaps faster than ever before in this period, therefore, they still had to be subordinated to the overriding requirements and aspirations of the age. The way the institutions operated was limited by the ideology of the society as a whole.

## 13.7 The Age of Ideology (1914–1974)

In the folllowing age institutions changed yet again. The form these now took were affected by changes in communication, by changes in the power structure, but above all by the decline of nationalism and the growth of ideology as the main concern of the society.

The Concert of Europe had reflected the social relationships of the previous age, the dominance enjoyed by a small group of major European powers and the need for understandings among them if order were to be maintained, both in Europe and elsewhere. These relationships now changed. The dominant powers were no longer European; the U.S., the Soviet Union, and later China and Japan became the major powers who had to play the main part in any new system, for example, in the institution of superpower bargaining. At the same time the society became worldwide, so a voice had to be found for smaller powers from all parts of the world who wanted to have a share in the discussion of common problems in world bodies. There was, in a sense, (corresponding to the growth of democracy within states) a democratization of the international system by which, on the surface at least, a larger voice was given to smaller powers than in any earlier time. But all these new worldwide institutions were fatally split by the all-pervasive division among ideologies.

Even before the end of the previous age the Hague conferences had included representatives of almost every state in the world, including many outside Europe. After the second conference they were to become regular affairs. World War I prevented the third such meeting, but at the conclusion of that war it was decided that the system of regular meetings, with almost universal attendance, should be put on a more systematic basis. The League of Nations was therefore set up as a permament institution, to be, so far as possible, representative of all states, however small, and general in scope. But at first many relics of a nationalist world were retained—in the rule of unanimity, under which every government represented must agree to a decision if it were to be binding (so maintaining the tradition of the nineteenth century conference); in the right guarded for each nation to decide for itself what action it should take in case of a breach of the peace; in the doctrine of "sovereign equality," which continued to be asserted; in the absence of any general prohibition of war; above all, in the weakness of the central institutions, which could recommend the action required to help a threatened state, but no more. Even an institution on these lines might have represented a significant advance if it had been used with resolution. But it was fatally weakened by the split among ideologies. The totalitarian states quit altogether, denouncing the League and all its works. The only communist state was for long excluded and was finally expelled. As a result the membership at all times excluded most of the major powers, and the organization's effectiveness was nullified.

At first sight the institutions established after 1945 represented an advance, since they reflected more accurately the changed structure of society. The UN was more genuinely a world body; it came to include large areas of the world effectively left out as dependencies before, and by the end of the period virtually no united state remained outside it. The veto power was now confined to the five largest nations instead of being universally enjoyed. The organization was given the power of "decision" over its members to keep the peace. It was also provided with widespread functions in the economic and social field. Gradually some of the defences previously erected by nationalism began to be broken down. Exclusion from discussion of matters within the domestic jurisdiction of states was weakened even in theory, and eroded still further in practice: such questions as colonialism, apartheid, and other human rights questions were now regularly discussed internationally.

All this made the UN a more significant factor within the society than any previous international institution. But like its predecessor it was fatally weakened by ideological conflicts. One side abused the veto power to prevent any decision it disliked. The other abused its majority position to manipulate the organization in the direction it favored. In consequence the organization was never able to perform the role laid down for it. The Security Council's power of "decision" was almost never used. The UN became a forum for ideological warfare rather than for the resolution of conflicts; a means of scoring points off opponents rather than negotiating settlements. Reflecting the ideological character of the age, the world institution conducted its affairs through public debate rather than private negotiation, and was used as the instrument of propaganda rather than of diplomacy.

There were, however, some institutional advances. For example, peacemaking and even peace-keeping capabilities, far more significant than in any previous society, now emerged. In a number of cases international forces were established to patrol and pacify disputed areas, or to keep separate the forces of hostile nations. This began even in League times. The League set up an international force to supervise the plebiscite in the Saar in 1935, and established a tiny force to administer the disputed area between Peru and Colombia in 1935. The UN established six such forces: to keep the peace between the Arab states and Israel from 1957 to 1967; to reestablish law and order and central government control in the Congo between 1960 and 1964; to supervise the transfer of authority in West Irian in 1962–1963; to keep the peace between Greeks and Turks in Cyprus from 1964 onward; and to occupy two areas of disengagement among Israel, Egypt, and Syria in 1974. In addition, the UN sent observers to try to keep the peace in Palestine after 1948; in Kashmir from 1949 onward; in the Lebanon in 1958; in Yemen from 1963 to 1965; and on other occasions. It sent mediators to resolve a number of disputes. But here too, where the conflicts concerned the great ideological blocs—over Berlin, Hungary, Vietnam, Czechoslovakia (precisely the most dangerous conflicts in such a world)—the organization was powerless.

New legal institutions were also set up. A permanent International Court of Justice was established in 1919, to be replaced by the present International Court in 1945. This extended the system of legal adjudication established earlier. The court, with elected judges, was relatively permanent in membership and served over the years to lay down a considerable body of international law. Its function was no longer simply mediation or even arbitration, but could now be "judicial settlement": final decission, irrespective of a formal request by both parties, comparable to the decisions of a domestic court. Usually governments needed to be committed in advance to accept its jurisdiction for the type of cases concerned. But some governments undertook to accept automatically the jurisdiction of the court in a dispute with another such state (though even these governments often excluded certain types of case). This was an advance on the legal institutions of any earlier age.

The court was able to resolve a number of contentious cases. These were, however, not those of the greatest importance to states. Disputes that were held to be political, or "nonjusticiable," governments preferred to resolve by more brutal but decisive means. But these were precisely those of greatest importance. It certainly cannot be said that the existence of the court, as had been hoped, allowed law to replace war as a means of resolving disputes within the society. But it perhaps served to establish in the general consciousness that there could exist a more civilized means for resolving international disputes than the traditional crude resort to armed force.

More significant perhaps was the emergence of new institutions in the economic field. The League initiated some small-scale activity in this area, providing assistance, for example, in the rehabilitation of some countries in East Europe. This was hugely extended after 1945. An International Bank, to channel development funds to poorer countries, was established, and later became the single most important source of aid for developing countries, some of it on concessionary terms. A Monetary Fund, to provide short-term assistance to countries in balance of payments difficulties, was created, and later this issued its own international currency, in the form of special drawing rights, to replace national currencies as a measure of value and source of reserves. Neither of these, however, were joined by communist powers. The UN established its own development program which planned projects to be executed by more specialized agencies. In the trade field, two new bodies were established: GATT and UNCTAD. Here too, however, communist powers played little part. The most close-knit institutions of the age were probably those joining ideological allies: COMECON, EEC, OECD, NATO, and the Warsaw Pact—scarcely international institutions in the proper sense.

Regional bodies acquired a new importance. In many regions special common markets were established which provided an increasing degree of economic coordination. The erosion of distance and closeness of economic political and personal contacts meant that there was now a greater interdependence and mutual interest among the nations of a particular geographical area. Regional cooperation could be fostered by ideological sympathy. It could also *reduce* dependence on superpowers. Thus the members of Comecon, the EEC, even the OAS and the OAU, became linked together by ties that sometimes predisposed them to common political as well as economic action.

New agencies emerged too, within the framework of the UN, to organize or coordinate world services in a wide range of specialized fields. Beginning in 1918, but far more rapidly from 1945, a whole family of these agencies appeared. The subjects they dealt with included labor standards and working problems, health, education, agriculture, air transport, sea transport, meteorology, posts, and tele-graphs. More than at any earlier time problems which had been dealt with before only at national level now needed and obtained international administration as well. The new agencies provided the coordination which a shrinking world increasingly required, gave assistance to individual governments, and in some cases ran common services. New problems, the environment, population, drug control, refugees, the seabed, made necessary still further international institutions to cope with them. Thus innumerable new bodies continually emerged, both among governments and among individuals, to study or administer these specialized problems and activities. These too, however, were continually weakened by political conflicts between rich and poor or between East and West.

More important, in a world of ideologies and superpowers, were the less formal institutions which the improved communications now made possible. Summit conferences, bilateral meetings between heads of state or prime ministers, innumerable travels by foreign ministers, regional meetings, contacts within the UN, brought governments together far more frequently than in earlier times. Sometimes such contacts provided the means of reaching agreements which could not be attained in the public environment of international organizations.

So once again the general character of the age affected the institutions established. The main feature of this age was the bitter struggle between rival ideologies. The effectiveness of all the institutions we have described was diminished by these conflicts. The League was rent by disputes between the Western democracies and the totalitarian systems (which quickly abandoned the organization altogether). The UN was split, for at least the first twenty years of its existence, by intense disputes between the Western world and communism which erupted on virtually every issue discussed, and later by conflicts between different communist powers. The effectiveness of the legal institutions was diminished by the reluctance, of communist states particularly, to submit important disputes to their judgment; the verdict in one important case was deliberately flouted by such a government. The new economic institutions were weakened by the same conflicts and the consequent reluctance of communist states to contribute. Communist states, being in a minority were opposed to aid programes through UN institutions they were unable to control, and refused to join the World Bank, the IMF, or to contribute to UNDP. They opposed the conduct of peace-keeping operations, for example in the Congo, and refused to pay the cost of those undertaken elsewhere. Even regional organizations were affected: Europe was largely split between communist and noncommunist communities; the only communist member was expelled from the OAS. And communist China was prevented for years from joining the UN. So ideological divisions crucially weakened all the apparent institutional advances. The most effective and close-knit institutions were partial, joining ideological allies: OECD, EEC, and COMECON.

Everywhere, while new institutions emerge and grow, their effectiveness is impaired by the new concern which comes to dominate men's minds. Just as diplomacy, as an institution, was weakened and almost eliminated, as we saw, by the universal religious schism of the sixteenth century, so now diplomacy, negotiation, international organization, and other institutions were weakened by the antagonism of ideologies. In a few cases the new institutions helped to overcome the barriers that ideology established. The UN could sometimes bring better contacts and a greater understanding than would otherwise exist. But for much of the time the institutions served only as the sounding boards and megaphones through which the ritual political slogans and catcalls of the main political factions could be yelled. Certainly they were ineffective in bridging the main ideological conflicts themselves.

There have thus been a wide range of different institutions in the various international societies we have been examining.

At first sight one can trace a consistent growth over time in the strength and number of institutions set up. This is partly a direct result of the improvement of communications. Because contacts among the Chinese states were relatively tenuous, institutions linking the states were necessarily embryonic. Because today contacts of every kind—personal, commercial, technical, and political—are so profuse, it is both easier and more necessary to establish effective arrangements for consultation or joint decisions. But the growth in the *number* of organizations is not a measure of their effectiveness or the degree of influence they can attain over governments, though it is probably a sign of an increasingly *integrated* society. It is indeed not unreasonable to conclude from this growth that international societies have become progressively more integrated over time.

This is not in itself either good or bad; integration can sometimes entail an unacceptable loss of diversity even while creating more harmonious relationships. Nor is it synonymous with greater peace; a society may be closely knit yet marked by frequent conflict. For this reason it may be that better institutions alone will never abolish war from the world, any more than they can abolish crime from smaller societies. They will succeed only insofar as they influence attitudes and motivations among the members, that is, transform the ideology.

There has also been an extension over the years of the size and universality of membership, culminating in the UN and its various functional agencies which are virtually universal. This has not necessarily made them more effective. Indeed, universality in membership and authority may well vary in inverse proportions, since universality also brings greater diversity. There may be a choice between small and strong or large and weaker international bodies.

More significant is the contrast in the *types* of institutions favored in different kinds of international society. In the ideological societies (ancient Greece, age of religions, age of ideologies) we find the most important bodies have been partial: leagues, religious alliances, ideological blocs. Universal organizations have been prevented, or divided, by ideological disputes. In the age of dynasties all the dynasts share common assumptions and are able to share the common institutions of summit conferences, mediation, and diplomacy, institutions which reemerge for similar reasons in the age of sovereignty. So too the age of nationalism, though now an olioligarchy, develops common institutions which for a time at least all are willing to respect. For the same reason, while all societies have made some use of legal procedures, mediation, arbitration, and so on, they have varied considerably in the emphasis placed on them and the extent they have been obeyed. Even the most widely used of all institutions, diplomacy, which has existed in some form in every international society, varies in effect with the context; it is used for different purposes in different types of society.

Thus the clearest conclusion is that, though some of the same institutions have existed in many societies, the type of institution employed and the part that it plays is crucially affected by the ideology of the society as a whole. So in the age of religions many institutions are affected by the religious character, alliances become religious leagues, arbitration declines and can no longer be undertaken by the pope or other religious figures, and diplomacy takes place only within, but not between, religions. In the age of sovereignty diplomacy between sovereigns assumes a new importance, mediation is favored over arbitration, and the power of institutions over states is generally weak. In the age of nationalism the major powers, through the Concert of Europe, are able to negotiate accommodations among each other, which they can sometimes impose, but cannot always contain the nationalism of lesser states, and still less, finally, their own. In the modern world smaller distances promote stronger functional organizations, but ideological divisions weaken the power of political bodies while the dominance of superpowers places a new emphasis on negotiation between the great.

These differences between the *types* of institutions favored in different types of society are more important than the apparent progressive development of international institutions generally. Even where the institutions are the same, they perform different functions in different types of society. Once again we find the character of society as a whole influences the character of any particular feature within it.

# PART 3

## Conclusions: The Structure of International Society

# 14. Future International Societies

We have now looked at a variety of international societies. We have seen that they have varied in the types of elites which have exercised dominant power within them; in the foreign policy motives which have inspired those elites; in the means they have employed to attain this end; in the system of stratification within them; in the methods of communication and mutual adjustment which have been evolved; in the national roles adopted; in the norms of behavior demanded among the members; and in the institutions they have established. But we have seen that they have varied above all in the underlying ideology, that is, the ethos, the value consensus, the beliefs, attitudes, and expectations prevailing in each society, which in many cases influenced many of the other factors.

It may be useful, having examined past societies, to consider possible societies of the future: the various ways in which the present international system might evolve. In examining these possibilities, we shall be concerned (as in the previous chapters) with contrasting *types*, none of which probably resembles the international community that will in fact develop in the next fifty years or so. This will probably possess features of each type. But a consideration of the different categories may assist in clarifying analysis.

Let us consider the possibilities in turn.

## 14.1 The Transnational Society

One type of international society that could emerge would be one in which one feature of the contemporary world—the progressive erosion of national boundaries—would be greatly intensified. The nation-state might be largely dethroned from its present position of authority, and the barriers between states thrown down. Transnational forces would operate freely, untrammeled by restrictions placed at natural boundaries. Ideas, political movements, people would travel freely from one area to another. Trade would pass without restriction. Capital would move easily to those places where it could be most effectively

345

employed. For many purposes the world would become similar to a single, large, and undivided state.

Here the structure will be entirely different from any society we have considered. In this world the important political groupings would not be those among nations, but between classes and pressure groups within all of them. National alliances would count for little; groupings and associations of common interests or viewpoint scattered among all countries would replace them. These would be organized for action internationally far more effectively than they are today. Here the significant elites, for the first time, would be private individuals, not members of governments. International unions, international political parties, international groups of women or conservationists, with members in many countries all over the world, would become the significant international actors. Their activity would be designed to influence international and regional organizations as much as national governments. For a large range of functional fields, these multinational associations would take over the role of national governments. And it would thus be their decisions which would most need to be influenced.

Because of the ease of movement, frontiers would cease to be of much importance. Thus frontier and other territorial disputes would decline or vanish. Similarly, the national sentiments which nurture such disputes would be far weaker. Most conflicts would be in a sense civil disputes, with both sides receiving assistance from outside (as sometimes occurs today). Since similar social and economic problems might arise in many different states, political movements would be carried on simultaneously in a number of different countries. International strikes, called by the international unions, could develop into prolonged economic disputes between managements and workers in many countries, affecting large parts of the developed world. Racial conflicts, between black and white or other groups, might be reproduced in a number of different countries simultaneously. Revolutionary elements of many sorts might increasingly coordinate their activities to strike in many areas at the same time. The dominant motives will be political change in the world as a whole.

Means might thus become quite different too. Terrorist activities, such as those undertaken by Palestinians and the IRA, Croats and Basques today could become widely adopted. Hijacking, kidnapping, and assassination might be the normal weapons in such conflicts, and this could pose wholly new problems of national and regional defense. The permeability of states, deriving now more from the freedom of personal mobility than from the development of missiles and other weapons, would be intensified. In consequence, assistance to police forces and secret services would be more important than alliances, antiriot techniques more important than arms programs, as methods of defense.

The ideology here is that of *individual transnational competition*. The elites are no longer the representatives of regions or nations but individual leaders, in industry, political parties, and social movements throughout the society. The motives too are not collective ambitions for nation or region, but those of private individuals or commercial organizations in competition with each other. The means are the same in the wider society as those traditionally employed by such forces in individual nations: political and commercial pressure, intrigue, and manipulation. The stratification is highly diversified and unequal and the structure one of interpenetration. The institutions are those of the society as a whole, but now directly representative of individuals rather than states.

The mobility of capital in this society, and the decline in national authority, would probably lead to an increasingly powerful role for large-scale international corporations, operating in many countries of the world and controlling an ever larger proportion of world economic activity. Economic operations would increasingly become transnational, multinational, or even nonnational. International banking insurance and other financial institutions might extend their tentacles ever wider, operating on a world rather than a national level. These international corporations would cease to become identified with any particular nation, would establish themselves in whatever state would provide the most favorable tax opportunities, and in practice become as important as sovereign states. Thus effective power might cease to be wielded by governments and instead become concentrated in the elites controlling such organizations. Governments might need to deal with great deference with such powerful organizations, sometimes having larger incomes than the governments themselves.

Norms would be adjusted accordingly—the principle of noninterference in free economic activity would be valued so highly that no attempt to control such organizations, at national or international level, would be pursued. Under the prevailing ideology of an uncontrolled nonnational free-enterprise world, the role of public authorities of all kinds would be deliberately restricted. For this reason the role of international organizations would also be limited. Just as many capitalist states until recently deliberately favored a restricted role for government as a means of promoting a "liberal" economic system, so now at the world level the role of international authorities would be limited for the same reason. Economic "rationality," it would be held, demanded the minimum interference in the working of autonomous transnational economic forces. This might be claimed even as a means to *promote* the internationalization of the world, through the transcendence and blurring of frontiers, and so create a more peaceful society (an argument already sometimes heard today). The countervailing forces against such organizations would thus be not so much international organizations as international workers' unions or international consumer associations.

Since governments would play little role here, the basis under which international relations are conducted would be changed. Superpowers, large-scale alliances, international conferences, international negotiations would all count for less. Now the great issues would be the *internal* problems of a single world community: the price and availability of materials, the distribution of investment among rich and poor regions, monopolies among producers, international levels of employment, relative wages in different parts of the world, communication systems, and similar matters. These might be dealt with by direct negotiations between the interests immediately involved (world capital and world labor) or by market forces; occasionally perhaps by functional agencies established for the purpose. Thus institutions would be diverse and lacking in power in this society. Authority would be concentrated neither at international, regional nor national level, but still lower, among individuals and organizations within states, or in specialized transnational agencies established for specific purposes.

There would be some attractive features about this world, including some which could appeal to radicals. For example, there would be a decline of authority of every sort, both national and international. Warfare might be eliminated in its organized form, though possibly only to be replaced by more irregular and unconventional types of conflict. But against these advantages would be the defects inherent in any ultraliberal society, above all the disequalization which must occur from a natural diversity of wealth, enterprise, and talent, between individuals and regions alike. These disadvantages and the injustices and resentments that would result would, in the eyes of many, far outweigh the advantages.

## 14.2  The International Society

A second type of society would be one in which there was a rapid and substantial growth in the authority of international organizations of every kind.

Here too there would be a transfer of power from national governments, not down to private organizations within states but up still further to the level of international bodies. International institutions would acquire a much greater authority over both states and individuals. This would represent a continuation of a trend already begun. We have seen the rapid growth of international organizations over the last century in a wide range of fields, especially among functional institutions. That growth could accelerate. So the IMF might become the controller of world monetary policy, issuing its own currency (a process already started) and effectively controlling parities and reserve levels all over the world. The World Bank might become a genuine world development authority, transferring funds from rich regions to poor and influencing investment programs in each region, as individual governments do through their regional policies. The WHO might become a kind of world ministry of health, not only undertaking campaigns to eliminate particular diseases and laying down international medical standards (as today), but itself administering, through the dispatch of doctors, nurses, and equipment, a form of international health service, and so seeking to equalize health standards. The ICAO and IMCO could be regulating agencies controlling air and shipping services as closely as national governments control national services in that field today. The UPU and ITU could extend their administration and control of world postal, telegraph, and telephone services. Agencies concerned with disaster relief, the control of trading in narcotic drugs, the protection of the world environment, and other such tasks might be strengthened and extended to become effective world services.

So the ideology would be one of *world integration*. In such a society new organizations would be established to undertake new tasks. An agency to oversee the use and conservation of the world's declining stock of natural resources would be established. A world energy authority, to husband and extend the world's limited stock of energy sources, might be set up. International administrations to control such areas as the Antarctic, the moon, and other ungoverned regions might be established. An international authority could be set up to undertake control of the seabed, and to secure large-scale redistribution of resources from this source. And so on. In a wide range of fields functions carried out at present mainly by national governments might be taken over by an ever-widening range of international organizations.

In itself this would represent only a sharp accentuation of present trends. But in the *political* field the change required, if the ideology is to be fulfilled, would be more radical. A considerable increase in the powers and authority of the UN would be necessary. Meetings of the Security Council might come to be held on a continuing and regular basis, instead of only in an emergency, and to be attended by foreign ministers or even prime ministers. It could thus come to represent a kind of world cabinet, keeping the world political situation constantly under surveillance. There might be increasing use of UN peace-keeping forces in disturbed areas such as the Middle East and Southern Africa. This could lead to the establishment of a permanent UN force to be called on in any emergency. There would be a corresponding decline in national armed forces, perhaps felt to be less necessary in such a world. Those national forces retained might be largely earmarked for use in international peace-keeping, or in disaster relief when required.

The type of conflict occurring might not be very different from today. Situations of civil war or internal unrest, particularly in developing regions, yet of concern to all great powers; struggles for influence among the superpowers in marginal areas; racial conflicts both between states and within them; economic conflicts between rich states and poor; struggles over the control or disposition of increasingly scarce world resources; disputes on human rights questions; all these would no doubt continue to arise. But under the prevailing ideology the reaction would be different. The immediate effort would be not to promote unilateral solutions, nor to devise partial arrangements among a particular group of states, but to set in motion the *international* procedures or initiatives best capable of resolving them. Conflicts might take place between whole regions of the world, each perhaps increasingly unified and increasingly conscious of economic disparity. But here again the reaction would be to bring in the international bodies which alone could resolve such conflicts, or organize the international redistribution of world resources required. And increasing use of such bodies could eventually create in men's minds the automatic presumption in time of crisis that the immediate recourse was to call in the higher authority whose task it was to confront such situations, and leave it to that body to resolve.

Within such a society the important elites are the leaders within international organizations, especially the secretaries-general and other senior officials. The overriding motive among them, and of much of the public, is to extend the authority of their organizations and so to overcome and submerge national divisions and national conflicts. The main means for achieving this is by continually proposing new areas where authority can be transferred from the national to the international level, and instituting the conferences and other deals among governments to secure this. Stratification among states becomes less important as their own power and authority declines in relation to that of international organizations. The structure is one based on negotiation and maneuvering *within* international organizations rather than relying on bilateral diplomatic bargaining. The institutions are those of increasingly widespread and formalised international organizations, and the norms established are support for and loyalty to these organizations.

Thus while here, as in the previous society discussed, there would be a decline in the authority wielded by national governments, in this case that authority would be transferred upward to international bodies. International politics would therefore take a somewhat different form. For the prime object would usually be not to negotiate with other *governments* to influence their policies, but to influence the policy adopted within the international organizations. So there might emerge within each organization unified blocs and groupings of governments, each committed to the prosecution of a particular type of policy. A kind of elementary party system might occur at this level (comparable to that developing within the EEC) to fulfill this. A conservative group might be ranged against a socialist or progressive group; communist governments against anticommunist governments; rich countries against poor; internationalists against nationalists. The majority group would use its position within each organization to carry through the policies corresponding to its own political philosophy. There might be changes in voting procedures to insure that votes corresponded more closely to the populations represented. For if international authorities were to be more powerful, there would be attempts to make them more democratic as well. Just as a century ago political activity within states was largely devoted to making governments more representative of national populations, so now it would be designed to make the policy of *international* bodies conform more closely with the views of *world* populations.

This is the scenario which many might regard as the most desirable among those we are examining. It would create a more structured, organized, and perhaps more peaceful world society than has ever been seen before. The conflicts and violence so typical of the decentralized world of nation-states where authority is divided might be eliminated in this centralized international society. War between individual states and regions might become as infrequent and unacceptable as civil wars within a modern state. And there could be a further benefit: the authority of national states, once weakened, might not only be transferred upward to regional ,and world bodies, but downward to more independent, diverse, and popularly based local authorities too.

Against this there would, as in all other systems, be certain costs. The benefits of an increasingly peaceful and orderly society could be gained only at the expense of a loss of diversity—not only a decline in national independence, but in the autonomy and variety of individual states and regions. A uniform world society, with a uniform political pattern and cultural life, might emerge and prove incapable of fruitful evolution. A mammoth bureaucracy on a world scale might proliferate in every area of activity. More even than today, the individual might feel himself a tiny, helpless cog in a global machine which, once set in motion, could neither be halted nor put into reverse. A mechanistic Utopia might prove to have eliminated all opportunity for individual iniative or local variation.

## 14.3 The Sphere of Influence Society

Another possible course of evolution would be one where the major powers were each accorded a considerable degree of dominance and control within their own area; a clearly recognized system of spheres of influence would be established.

This also would merely extend a process already begun. Already today East Europe has been largely assigned to Soviet control, by Western powers as much as by Eastern; North and Central America have been accepted, by communist as well as other powers, as a zone where the U.S. exercises domination; China has been generally recognized to have a special interest in the countries immediately bordering her frontiers (North Korea and Indo-China, for example). Neither of the superpowers has thought to intervene directly in areas under the hegemony of another. And their own inaction where the *neighboring* superpower has intervened shows that this division of the world is acknowledged.

Until now, however, delimitation of these areas has been left extremely vague. There have been whole regions—Southeast Asia, the Middle East, and South America—which did not fall clearly within any great power's zone. There have been border countries—Finland, Austria, and Yugoslavia in Europe, Burma and Thailand in the East, Cuba in the West—whose allocation was left in doubt. At the same time geographical areas did not exactly coincide with political sympathies. So Japan, South Korea, Pakistan, the Philippines, Australia, New Zealand, and much of West Europe, though not *geographically* within the zone dominated by the U.S., were so by sympathy, and welcomed her protection. Against this the U.S. regarded some regions—such as the Caribbean or Southeast Asia—as areas in which she had special rights or responsibilities, even when this view was not necessarily acceptable to all the peoples concerned, least of all to other superpowers. It was especially where such uncertainty existed—Greece and Korea in the 1940s, the Middle East and Laos in the 1950s, the Congo and Vietnam in the 1960s—that conflict between the superpowers was likely to emerge (never in the heart of the dominated zones).

Moreover, there was no clear consensus on the rights to be enjoyed by the superpower even within its own sphere. Could it apply a Brezhnev doctrine, involving the use of armed force to protect its own interests, as in Czechoslovakia in 1968? Could it apply a Monroe doctrine, by more indirect means, as used by the U.S. in Guatemala in 1954 and the Dominican Republic in 1965, and attempted by her in Cuba in 1961? Could it demand political and economic, as well as strategic, dominance in the area concerned, as the Soviet Union has done overtly in East Europe, and the U.S. does in practice in Central America?

In recent years some of these ambiguities have lessened. The U.S. is reducing its commitments in remoter parts of the world, and some of its allies have voluntarily loosened their ties with her, so the U.S. sphere has become less widely flung, and in this way better defined. West Europe and Japan have acquired a strength of their own, almost entitling them to be regarded as centers of new zones in their own right. Even developing regions such as Latin America are becoming more powerful, and so better able to defend their own interests without any outside protection.

Such a pattern of distinct and recognized spheres might become established and acknowledged as the foundation of international relations in the next forty or fifty years. The basic ideology in such a system is oligarchy: the control of the society by the few great powers dominating the zones. The pattern is one of domination and deference. The most significant elites are the leaders and decision makers of the superpowers, political and military (leaders elsewhere can only accept and apply the system imposed). The motivation is to acquire and maintain effective control of a significant region of the world, and thereafter to stabilize and defend the status quo. The main means is intervention by the superpowers, political, and if necessary military, within their own sphere, and resistance to intervention by outsiders there. The structure is one of direct dealings among the superpowers to order the affairs of the world (superpower diplomacy). There is a sharp stratification, with effective power concentrated among the small number of superpowers and no power for the rest. The norms are restraint in encroaching on the sphere of others and, for the lesser states, submission to the local superpower. The chief institutions are the wheelings and dealings among the superpowers, and there is little scope for wider and more representative bodies.

Under such a system the distribution of spheres might become more clear-cut. The U.S. would be accepted as the dominant power in North and Central America, the Soviet Union in East Europe and possibly Mongolia. The EEC would dominate West Europe and part of the Mediterranean. Chinese power would extend to East Asia and the northern parts of Southeast Asia. Japan would dominate the Pacific areas including Indonesia and the Philippines. India, which already dominates her subcontinent, might extend her influence around the Himalayas and southern Southeast Asia (here Chinese, Japanese, and Indian influences would meet). Australasia would be a separate world. Even in Latin America, Africa, and the Arab world, while there would be no single power which dominated each area, there might be subregions, each under the control of the most powerful state, say Brazil and Argentina in Latin America, Iran in the Persian Gulf, Egypt in the fertile crescent, Algeria in North Africa, Nigeria in West Africa, Kenya in East Africa, and South Africa in the south. A new type of deferential system might emerge in which the small and weak everywhere had to defer to the magnates within their own area.

Such a system, if fully acknowledged and effectively implemented, can minimize conflict *between* superpowers and between regions. Provided the spheres are clearly drawn, in theory *world* war becomes impossible. Neither major powers nor regional groups would any longer concern themselves with events in any area but their own. Conversely, they would be assured that no other significant power was seeking to interfere with their own region. The system's success thus would demand a considerable degree of *indifference* to events in other areas, including political events such as the overturning of a recalcitrant government by another superpower. In ideological ages (including the most recent era) this indifference has not existed. All have been genuinely and passionately concerned over the political systems established in many parts of the world, even if they were remote. And in such cases—in Greece as in Cuba, in Vietnam as in the Congo—conflict between great powers was always in danger of erupting. Where spheres of influence are firmly demarcated and consistently acknowledged, conflicts of this kind are eliminated.

From the point of view of the great powers themselves, the system has considerable advantages. They become insured against the risks of conflict with any other major power. They acquire a considerable degree of domination within an area close to their own borders. For most other powers, however, the system has many disadvantages. It is true they too are freed of the risk of world war and secured from intervention by a *distant* superpower. But this is only at the cost of easier intervention by the neighboring one. A small nation which finds itself in considerable isolation within a particular region—say Albania in East Europe, Thailand in East Asia, or Cuba in the Caribbean—may find its entire existence threatened because it is now totally cut off from assistance by any great power outside its region; it must either conform to the prevailing allegiance or remain in peril. Finally, any system of *world* collective security, any U.N. action to save threatened nations, for example, becomes impossible if this system is maintained. Every small power is permanently at the mercy of its larger neighbors.

Not only is the security of small powers threatened, but so is their independence. For the great powers (unless their rights within their own region are rigidly circumscribed) in practice will seek not merely strategic but political and other domination within their area. This is what the Soviet Union already demands in East Europe. Even the U.S. in Central America seeks it in a more restricted sense (in that she acts, by force if necessary, to prevent the emergence of communist-dominated governments in that region). In a system of spheres of influence that were more explicitly acknowledged, these dangers would be increased. Whatever the theory, in practice the great power could expect to have its own way on most subjects in its own region. The great powers might seek not only political control but perhaps a considerable degree of economic domination as well. A superpower could seek a monopoly of investment, trade, and aid (so that Romania was prevented from seeking aid in the West or Cuba in the East). In other words, a feature of any sphere of influence system is an erosion of sovereignty for all except the great powers. Stratification is here at its most extreme.

Moreover, such a system implies the effective abandonment of any attempt to preserve human rights on a world basis. Since outside powers would be powerless to intervene in any practical way in the region of another power, and would be known to be helpless, their leverage in protesting about violations of human rights becomes almost nonexistent. In practice they would be expected to avert their eyes whenever any violation of such rights, or even outright atrocities, were committed. If the Soviet Union oppressed its Jews or its writers, the world would have to look away. If South Africa were to intervene to overthrow a government in Malawi or Botswana, her neighbors would be expected to ignore it. Large-scale intervention by the U.S. in Nicaragua or Haiti could be deterred only by the somewhat uncertain power of world opinion—a somewhat fragile restraint.

The viability of such a system (and something like it could easily emerge in the coming years) would thus depend vitally on certain conditions. First, the system would require accurate demarcation of the borders between spheres. In the past conflicts have frequently occurred, as we have seen, at the margins between the spheres of different great powers; examples in the modern world include Southeast Asia, Berlin, and the Eastern Mediterranean. While in Europe a reasonably clear-cut line exists, in some other parts of the world, such as Southeast Asia, establishment of such a border would be much more difficult to secure. One possible way of meeting this difficulty in some cases would be the establishment of "neutral zones," regarded as beyond the sphere of any major power; this principle has already been partially applied in Africa—in the Congo though not in Angola—and could well be extended elsewhere.

Second, for such a system to work without friction, there would need to be some clear consensus on the *type* of domination which a great power might expect to enjoy within its own region. It might, for example, come to be accepted that this should be acknowledged in the military field, but not in the political and economic; in other words, small nations could adopt any kind of government they choose, but could not enter into military arrangements with powers outside the region. While there would be obvious difficulties about securing a general consensus of this kind, its achievement would be necessary if the system were not to produce conflicts between zones on such questions or bring with it a total loss of independence for small states in every field of activity.

The elites here are the decision makers within the superpowers. Superpowers would in a sense negotiate for a whole region. This could raise problems of representation. Brazil would not necessarily be held by all Latin Americans as a valid representative of that group, nor Nigeria of Africa, nor Egypt of the Arabs. Moreover, this diplomatic role could strengthen domination of the great powers over the small even more than the dominance they enjoyed within their own areas. A new Concert could emerge, with the U.S., China, the Soviet Union, Japan, and West Europe coming together regularly to decide the affairs of the world. This would be even less acceptable to smaller powers than the earlier Concert was in the nineteenth century. The authority of world institutions such as the UN, in which smaller powers have a larger voice, would be weakened. And in this and other ways the system would provoke confrontations not merely among the great powers, but between all of them and all the dependent small states.

Against this, effective deals among the great, if they could be attained, would promote stability in the system as a whole. There may indeed be (as in smaller societies) a genuine choice to be made between maximizing representation, or democracy, and the maintenance of stability and effective authority. The system which we have described, though essentially oligarchic, would be more *efficient*, especially in reconciling the interests of major powers, and so possibly in maintaining world peace. But because it would be authoritarian, it would arouse the resentment of lesser powers, both in the world as a whole and in the individual regions where domination would be most visible. While it could solve some problems, therefore, the system would create others which might ultimately be more serious.

## 14.4 A World of Regions

Another possibility is the development of a high degree of *regional integration* all over the world, leading to a concentration of authority at regional level, especially that of the continent, and a reduction of authority at the national and world level.

Under this system each region would to a large extent develop its own regional economy and its own institutions. None would interfere in the affairs of another. Each would be divided from the rest of the world by powerful barriers. But there would not exist *within* each region the domination of a single superpower, as in the society just described.

As a result of this process East Europe, West Europe, North America, Latin America, Australasia, East Asia, Southeast Asia, South Asia, the Middle East, and perhaps individual regions of Africa might become increasingly close-knit associations of states. The association would be largely by voluntary choice, or by force of geographical circumstances, rather than through extension of the power of a dominant nation. Increasing integration in each region would lead in time to an increasing coordination of foreign and defense policy. Each group would thus deal largely *collectively* with other groups, on the basis of joint decisions reached through mutually agreed procedures.

Regional integration would make necessary procedures for agreeing on regional policy. Ideally this would be through a regional assembly, reaching decisions on a joint basis. Or there could be a smaller council for each region providing, like the Security Council, special representation for the larger powers. These regional institutions would have the effect of establishing regional policies and regional decisions on many of the issues decided at present by national governments (the first stage of this process can already be seen in West Europe).

Representatives of each region would them come together to discuss the questions arising *between* regions: the world issues. Individual nations might be selected by election, rotation, or some other means, to act as representatives of the region and negotiate on its behalf. This interregional negotiation would therefore largely replace existing international exchanges. Even discussions in the UN and other world bodies might take place on an interregional basis (as negotiations on the composition of committees and certain resolutions already do at the General Assembly). Votes might be taken on a regional basis, with votes allotted to regions rather than to nations, and perhaps a three-quarter majority required for any resolution to be passed. This would indeed be far more representative and ''democratic'' than the present system, under which nations together representing a fraction of world population can control a majority of votes.

Here the basic ideology is regionalism: the automony of the regional unit. The assumption would be, as in the previous system, that all internal questions of each region are solely its own affair. This would in a sense represent a transfer of sovereignty from the nation to the region. Thus all internal disputes of every region—between Brazil and Argentina in Latin America, between Germany and France in Europe, between Cambodia and Thailand in Southeast Asia—would be decided within each region according to its own procedures. World bodies would have a role in such questions only if specifically requested by a majority of the region, or possibly as a kind of court of appeal for an aggrieved minority. But the main role of world bodies would be in considering conflicts *between* the regions, and the primary institutions would be those at the regional level.

In a sense, therefore, under such a system the region would begin to replace the nation as the basic unit of international society. Besides undertaking a joint foreign policy, it might become responsible (as the European community is already doing) for economic management within the region, and for economic negotiations on behalf of its members. Functional services, for example, for transport, development, energy, and so on, might come to be organized mainly at the regional level. Even culture might become primarily regional: European, African, and Latin American, rather than French, Nigerian, or Mexican.

Here the significant elites are those who control and influence regional policy within the various bodies. The chief motivation is regionalism, an enlarged version of nationalism: pride in regional identity and a desire to promote regional interests. The means are mainly peaceful, at least within regions, and consist, as among nations today, in diplomatic negotiation, political pressures, and economic expansion. The structure consists of a few relatively equal units, the regions, with a number of smaller subregions, and the social system is one of spheres of influence. The institutions are the internal regional bodies and those that bring the regions together. In most parts of the world (except in Asia) the beginning of this process of regional integration is already taking place.

Such a system would have some of the same *benefits* as a sphere of influence society. Conflicts between regions should, if the borders are acknowledged and the system fully applied, be eliminated altogether. Nor, if the basic principle were accepted, should there be any question of interference in other regions. Thus world wars and world conflicts would be prevented. Wars within the region, among the countries of Latin America or Africa or West Europe, could still be of considerable scale and violence, but they would be one degree less serious in their effects than wars which transcended regional boundaries. Each region would moreover be protected, by the tradition of joint regional decision making, from the domination or interference of superpowers (as is not always the case today). Finally, each would have the opportunity to develop regional diversity, its own culture, style, and personality, according to its own individual choice, and avoid the submergence of all within one vast, integrated, global omniculture.

Against this there would, once again, be certain clear costs. As in the previous system there would be a loss of independence for individual nations. Here this should be more acceptable, since a national government could be overridden only on the basis of a majority vote in its own region and according to an agreed procedure. Minority nations and groups within each region could seek, like comparable groups within a nation, to change the balance of opinion, and so the decisions reached, within the region. Because the decision ultimately arrived at would be that of a collective body, it would be more tolerable than that of a dominant superpower. Moreover, large nations would be as subject as small to these majority views. Yet even here it would remain the case that individual nations holding minority opinions would have less opportunity than today to pursue their own independent policies within the world at large.

Second, as in the sphere of influence system, the independence accorded to each region through insulation from other parts of the world could carry its own dangers. The majority in one region might pursue a policy of domination, even of oppression, of minorities within the region. Human rights and freedoms regarded as fundamental in some areas might be systematically denied in others. Under the rules of the system, all other regions would be precluded from intervening. Each region would become increasingly self-absorbed and oblivious of the affairs and destinies of others. Given the scale of interregional contacts and communication, it is not certain that indifference on this scale could be easily promoted.

This difficulty might be diminished if there existed procedures for *discussion* of events in other regions, though not for active intervention; this is not unlike the situation which exists in the UN in relation to *nations* at the present day. It would be possible in this way, to develop worldwide *standards,* for the protection of human rights and other aspects of government, even though it might be impossible to enforce their observance. The increase in intercommunication, while it might arouse *concern* in outside regions, might also promote *receptiveness* within each region to powerfully expressed opinions from elsewhere. *Within* each region at least, it is to be hoped, some effective machinery for enforcement (again the system developing in West Europe represents a precedent) could be built up by which the common standards of the region could be maintained.

Apart from these difficulties, there would be the wider danger of disputes *between* regions. There could, for example, be disputes comparable to frontier conflicts between nations concerning the limits of the authority exerted by particular regions: such as whether Yugoslavia belonged in East or West Europe; whether Sudan belonged in North or West Africa; whether Vietnam belonged in the Chinese or Southeast Asian region; whether the Caribbean was part of North or South America; and so on. Though theoretically such questions should be for the individual nation to decide by its own choice, in practice there might be factions within each favoring either course, and so temptations for the two competing regions to intervene on behalf of one side or the other. There could be interregional conflicts on economic questions, trade barriers, investment, and interest repayments. Finally, there are the conflicts that would probably emerge from the development of world institutions and conflicts of authority between regions there. Only a parallel development of joint *inter*regional economic and other agencies would be likely to relieve this danger.

There might be less risk of conflict between the regions under this system than under one of spheres of influence, in which great powers would be competing for supremacy beyond their own sphere. There might equally be less risk of conflict *within* the regions, since the collective authority imposed there would be more acceptable than that of a single superpower. Against this, there is the possibility that individual regions might fail to establish satisfactory machinery for reaching joint decisions and resolving disputes, so that conflict within the regions was in practice *more* frequent than if a single power could impose solutions for local disputes. Here again therefore there may be a choice to be made: between democracy and efficiency, regional stability and local independence.

## 14.5 The Rich-Poor Society

A final possible future society would be one where the main divisions were no longer geographical, as in the two systems just described, or ideological, as in recent decades, but economic. The world would become divided into two or three clearly differentiated economic classes having sharply diverging interests. They would organize and align themselves on this basis alone. And because economic competition would then become more important than political or military competition, most of the issues of world politics would come to be economic disputes among these groups over such questions as commodity prices, access to raw materials, foreign investment, and multinational companies.

Like all the other societies we are describing, this only represents an intensification of trends which already exist. Relative growth rates might remain much what they are today. Although growth is at present marginally faster in poor countries than in rich, because population growth is faster in the former and because the base from which they begin is so much lower, rich countries still grow far more per year in absolute terms. A growth of 4 percent in rich countries and 5 percent in poor will still cause living standards to grow by far more in dollars a head among the rich. And this will still be so even if population growth becomes equal. The gap between rich and poor would thus continue to grow wider for many decades even after that time. So there would be a high degree of stratification, with wide disparities, measured now in economic terms. These class differences might become increasingly unacceptable, so that more and more countries would think of themselves, and organize themselves politically, in terms of their stage of economic development. Thus confrontation between the groups would intensify.

This would create a new kind of *structure*. Economic factors would come to dominate the political struggle between states (as it already does within them). Poor continents of Asia, Africa, and Latin America would unite to confront the rich continents of Europe and North America (and parts of the Middle East) in demanding greater economic equality at the world level. As in the last society described, negotiation would take place on a group basis. But the groups would now be economic rather than geographical.

Because the main concerns in such a society are economic, the elites would be economic, rather than political, decision makers: businessmen and bankers in the case of a private enterprise world, commercial and finance officials in a state-run world. Dominant motives would be commercial success and penetration of foreign markets and economies (and resistance to such penetration). The means would be those activities that achieved or prevented this: investment, trade, tariffs, economic diplomacy. The norms would be rules for the conduct of economic competition, perhaps intended to minimize conflict (though the radical differences of interest among states might well make such rules ineffective and promote conflict).

The ideology of such a society would be one of economic competition and economic status seeking. New types of conflict would thus emerge. Some would be at the level of private economic contacts. The economic power of the great corporations in the rich countries might grow still further, and could increasingly dominate the economic life of the poor nations. They might control a growing proportion of the latter's natural resources and dominate world trade and investment. By the way they disposed of their investment funds, they could determine the economic fortunes of the poor states. And this dependence would in turn arouse profound resentment among the poorer countries.

Even if the poor states tried to prevent this degree of domination, they would face difficulties. If they imposed protection, increased taxation, passed laws governing the remittance of profits, or nationalized the multinational corporations, they might merely impoverish themselves by cutting themselves off from investment funds and aid. Under these conditions poor countries might find themselves largely unable to compete on equal terms with rich ones all over the world. They might find the only outcome of defiance was that they were cut off from vital supplies of capital, technology, and managerial skills. They might then be faced with the agonizing choice of being poor but independent (like Tanzania today) or prosperous but dependent (like Taiwan)—independent outcasts or rich hangers-on. Either way by far the greater proportion of all economic activity would continue to be dominated and controlled by the rich.

Even if private enterprise were not so powerful, a similar set of conflicts might arise, now at the government level. Disputes could occur, for example, over questions of trade and protection. They could arise over the increasing burden of debts, which poor countries already find difficult to repay. They could occur over trade imbalances in one direction or the other, raw material prices, import controls, and so on. The poor nations as a group might be joined by increasingly close ties of sympathy and support against the rich.

Such conflicts might even conceivably reach the stage of open warfare. A poor state might nationalize large amounts of the property of the rich without compensation, leading to military intervention by one or more rich countries. A whole group of states might take such action, together or in succession, and so provoke a whole group of rich states to take action against them. Or the refusal of adequate trading opportunities, by one group to the other or by individual members, could lead to an attempt to secure these rights by armed force. So in such a society for the first time wars might take place over issues of genuine material consequence, instead of over barren patches of valueless territory or petty issues of national pride, as in the past.

The institutions of the system would be mainly economic bodies. International organizations would become the forum for prosecuting claims and counterclaims. The poor countries, being in a majority, might attempt to use organizations such as UNDP, the IMF, and the World Bank (perhaps under new voting rules), even the UN itself, to bring about larger transfers of funds than the rich were prepared to provide. There would be confrontation concerning the management and control of the seabed, and the rights to resources there (perhaps a majority of those remaining on earth). There would be disputes about fishing rights; about the prices of raw materials such as oil, copper, and tin; attempts to introduce monopoly bargaining in the sale or purchase of such materials; over protection of shipping by flag discrimination; and other matters.

The effect might be that world bodies would be wholly polarized between the two groups. The poor countries would have the votes, but the rich countries the power. The consequences would be deadlock. Both would possess a veto in the Security Council (China using hers on behalf of the poor states, while other permanent members protected the rich). Elsewhere votes by the poor states in favor of a more significant transfer of resources would come up against a point-blank refusal by the rich to cooperate. In consequence loyalties might be transferred to those bodies which represented only one group or the other: OECD and EEC for the rich, regional organizations for the poor. World organizations might be increasingly deprived of all part in international affairs in favor of partial, politically one-sided bodies whose main interests would now be economic.

A society of this kind would contain some features of the world of regions described before. For, by chance, the economic division among nations largely corresponds to a clear-cut geographical division: Europe and North America on the one hand, against Asia, Africa, and Latin America on the other. Because of the confrontation each region might increasingly concentrate investment, trade, and management skills within its own economies, even deliberately cut them off from those elsewhere, so that all the most advanced industries would be confined to the developed world, with the poorer continents confined to primary production and processing. The world would become divided into two economies, one rich and one poor, each becoming increasingly independent of the other.

There are some factors which might prevent the division from becoming total. There is the dependence of the rich states on raw materials and food obtained from the poor; there is the existence of pockets of "richness" among the poor (such as the oil-producing states) which could provide an increasingly important source of investment funds; and there would be the manifest mutual interest of all parties in maintaining economic interdependence. But even if no total division took place, growing confrontation between rich countries and poor would probably develop. Because this confrontation would to some extent correspond to geographical divisions, it would be reinforced by cultural and racial antagonisms. The sense of economic injustice, itself sufficiently bitter, would be intensified by the feeling of a white-race domination of the world and its economy. And the economic imbalance would moreover be accompanied by a military imbalance directly derived from it—and this too would intensify the sense of grievance.

This would therefore be a highly unstable society, beset by intense antagonisms perhaps even more powerful than those of the age of ideology. There would be no effective international authority able to impose order on the warring sides, nor would meaningful negotiation between the divided factions be encouraged in the embittered state of relationships. The only restraint on violence would be the military power in the hands of the richer states—not a very happy or effective deterrent. But for all its dangers this must appear (especially for those who believe economic factors determine all political relationships) as perhaps the model of international society most likely to emerge in the decades to come.

These sketches depict some of the types of international society which might emerge over the coming years. Each of them represent merely a continuation of tendencies already apparent within current world society. All are theoretically possible. All will partially come true. Yet none of them, almost certainly, will materialize in the pure form here described. What in fact emerges will no doubt be a mixture of them all. What counts is the type of mixture: the *balance* among the elements, which of the strands will predominate.

At present probably any variation is equally possible. All will depend on the character of the dominant ideology which emerges and the elites which accordingly prevail. But by outlining each variation in its extreme form, we can see more clearly the implications of each, and the factors which may influence their working. This may be of assistance to us as we now turn to a more general consideration of the character of international societies, and the forces at work within them.

# 15.   The Nature of International Society

## 15.1 The Sociological Approach to International Relations

We have sought in this book to propose a specific method for the study of international relationships: a method that analyzes these as taking place within a society of states, not unlike a society of human beings, and subject to similar social forces. The method therefore seeks to examine what those forces are, using for that purpose concepts and techniques comparable to those used by sociologists and anthropologists in studying smaller societies. And we have attempted to apply that method in relation to specific international societies at various times in man's history.

Before considering whether there are any general conclusions to be drawn from this examination, it may be worth considering whether the method itself is valid, and how far, if at all, it may be an improvement on other systems of analysis which have been used in the past. What are the advantages, if any, of this approach?

The first advantage which may be claimed is that it perhaps corresponds more closely than most other approaches to the *reality* of international relationships. The fact is that there does undeniably exist some kind of social existence among states, however imperfect. From the very moment that there is regular communication between them, as opposed to occasional chance contacts, an embryonic type of society begins to develop. At this moment *expectations* begin to emerge concerning relationships, the responses regarded as normal in particular situations, the type of international behavior that is acceptable. When (as in all the historical societies we have examined) there exists some means of organized communication between governments, such as a rudimentary diplomatic system, these expectations become more firmly established. Relationships and roles begin to be formalized. An embryonic international society then emerges.

This approach does not require, therefore, like many of those we examined in the first chapter, the use of a metaphor (such as that of mechanical systems, games, or economic markets): that is, to transfer to the field of international relations concepts and terms derived from another. There is no need here to strain and force

362

particular words or ideas—"output," "input," "feedback," "equilibrium," and so on—out of the context for which they were designed into another for which they were not, and to introduce distortions in doing so (by assuming there must *be* feedback, or an economic calculation of profitability, or an attempt to score a victory over each antagonist in all bargaining). Groups of nations *are* societies of a kind; there really are national elites, national motives, national roles, international institutions, international norms, and so on. All that is necessary is to show the way they operate in a particular case.

Second, the approach has the advantage of being more *comprehensive* than many others employed, in that it takes in a wider variety of international phenomena. The systems approach, for example, analyzes those aspects of international relations that derive from the relative power of the different units or their method of communication but leaves largely out of account others, such as types of elite in power, motives of the actors, types of institutions available, the system of norms, and general expectations and attitudes within society, which may be just as important. The decision-making approach can study the effect of different ways of making decisions in different institutions on the actions of states, but ignores, or at least underplays, many other factors affecting the decision makers which derive from the wider international environment. The bargaining approach assesses many factors related to a rational calculation of self-interest, but ignores many others which are less rational, but may in practice play an important part. In approaching the international scene as a type of society, the sociological approach necessarily takes account of all phenomena that are "social": from the internal structure of the component states to the types of communication between them, the institutions established, the norms that are current, and so on.

Third, for this reason some of the intangible factors, which are sometimes left out of account, find their place here. This applies to a whole variety of psychological factors related to motives and attitudes. It applies above all to that elusive factor which we have named here as "ideology," the ethos, or spirit, or value consensus of the international society as a whole which gives it its special character. Here, as in the smaller society, the systems of belief which lie behind the institutions are often the essential factor determining the role they play. A sociological approach makes it possible to take adequate account of these.

Fourth, the use of sociological concepts helps, in conjunction with historical evidence, to apply the *comparative* method in a specific way to the study of international relations. It is possible to consider the character of the elites in one society and compare them with that of another, to consider the different systems of stratification among states in different ages, to compare the type and effect of different institutions in different types of society. The insights that sociological and anthropological studies have brought in their own fields may be transferred to the realm of international relations, and in some cases can prove helpful. Though these are not likely to provide all the answers we need in studying international relationships, they may help us to discover some of the crucial variables.

There are a number of criticisms which may be made of this approach that should be examined. First, it could be held that we are guilty here of the very fault that we have criticized in others: that is, of imposing a framework which itself distorts the picture. Under this view, it is no more valid to assume that nations act within a social framework, perform "roles," develop "norms," or evolve a system of "stratification," than to assume they devise a system of "feedback" or a precise and rational method of calculating national profit and loss. In practice, it can be held that even when nations live in a state of permanent interrelationship with other nations, there is nothing like a genuine "society," as there is no means by which any member can be induced into conformity. Normally each goes its own way wholly oblivious of the demands of others, still less of the needs of the society. It cannot be denied that there is some danger of this kind; any system of analysis lays stress on one aspect of reality at the expense of another. This one perhaps fastens attention too exclusively on those aspects of national behavior which are "social." Description of national roles, international stratification, or norms, lays stress on the international context of all national attitudes and actions. So one part of reality is magnified at the expense of others. To this the only reply can be that even if these represent particular facets of reality, they are nevertheless an important part that perhaps needs more emphasis than it customarily receives in the recent study of international relations. The study of international relations is by definition concerned with those aspects of national behavior that have repercussions elsewhere. Our approach merely reflects this emphasis.

A second criticism that could be made is that, even if it is accepted that some form of international society exists and must be analyzed, it should be approached as a society of individuals, in direct relation with each other, or of transnational forces—international movements and parties, international trade and investments—rather than as a society of states, which merely represent artificial agglomerations of individuals and groups associated in them for certain purposes. There is, of course, room for an alternative approach on these lines. Against this, it is undeniable that in practice international relations actually are conducted by governments and the interaction of individuals and groups has been normally mediated through the states to which they belong (see p. 50 above). Even the "transnational actors," though more significant in recent times, are still today held firmly under the ultimate authority of national governments, acting individually or collectively. In general nations do act as fairly homogenous wholes. They enter into collective relationships and roles, set up institutions among *states,* evolve norms for states, acquire state motives, and pursue state policies. It is for this reason that not only this book, but most other books on international relations, concern themselves largely with the relations of states, as if these represented real collective entities. So here too it is possible to defend the approach as reasonably well adjusted to the reality it seeks to study.[1]

A third objection can be offered that even if some *analogy* can be made between an international and a domestic society, this should not be pursued too far.

---

1. Nor are individuals left out altogether, for example, in studying elites.

Some of the features that are essential to smaller societies—an acknowledged system of authority and leadership, firmly based traditions and common beliefs, a continuing rather than intermittent interaction, a common scale of values—do not exist within the international society. Above all, the persistence and the extent of violence which occurs in the international society, and the antipathies between nations which often result, pass beyond the scale which can properly be assimilated in any social organism. In these circumstances, comparisons based on a simple analogy with a small-scale society break down. There may be some substance to this argument—an international society is certainly an undeveloped, diffused, and wholly unintegrated society. But it does not follow that the analogy is false. For the social concepts this approach uses can be applied equally to divided and immature societies as to developed ones. It is not self-evident that the scale of conflict in the international society is altogether beyond the scale that can be tolerated within an essentially social type of organization. Both the existence of violence and the lack of a powerful central authority are seen equally in many primitive societies, which are still able to secure a considerable measure of order most of the time and can usefully be studied by sociologists. This may be a loose form of association, and power within it may be widely diffused, but it is nonetheless a society of a sort. And it is thus not inappropriate to study it by the methods evolved in studying other species of society.

Nobody would suggest that this is the only, or necessarily even the best, way of studying international relations. It is held merely that, since it studies one important aspect of the reality of international life, the approach has something of value to offer. It may supply some understanding of the way nations react to each other, and the way in which they see each other, which will not be provided by any alternative method of approach. There is no more reason why there should only be one way of studying international relations than that there should be only one approach to psychology, or one school of sociology. There is room for a number of varying ways of viewing this, as any other, important area of reality.

## 15.2 Types of International Society

Having tried to justify the type of approach employed, let us turn to some of the wider questions that our analysis has raised concerning the workings of international society.

In earlier chapters we have examined in turn various social forces and factors which have influenced the way particular international societies have operated, and sought to compare the parts they have played in different periods. Let us now attempt a different type of comparison: a series of contrasts between different *types* of international society as a whole. What are the main differences and resemblances among them?

The first contrast we have found was noted earlier (p. 109 above). There is one type of society that is basically *cellular* in structure, in that it is subdivided into units that are separated from each other by a relatively hard surrounding barrier, so that the main influences affecting decisions come from within the state rather than from outside. There is another that is *diffused* or fluid, in that the barriers between the units are much weaker and there is a wide range of cross-influences working on all the units alike. The theoretical extreme of the former kind is the classical "billiard ball" image of international society (which has never existed), in which the units have contacts only through collision between the hard outer casings. There is no direct communication from the center of one to another; if one were to pursue what is an essentially artificial image, one might say the units are impelled always by their own dynamic motion, and are deflected only as a result of a physical confrontation, never through mutual adjustments determined through mutual intercommunication. The theoretical extreme on the other side, that is, of the diffused society, would be the transnational society of the future (which has also never existed), described in the preceding chapter, in which all the main influences cross boundaries freely, so that the world represents in effect a single political community, with the decision-making centers all sharing essentially the same environment.

Among historical societies those which have come closest to the cellular type are probably the ancient Chinese, the age of sovereignty (it could indeed be argued that the concept of sovereignty was invented as a means of strengthening the barriers around states), and the age of dynasties, in that order. In every case there existed some communication and mutual adjustment between the units, but for the most part each unit reached its own autonomous decisions, and domestic influences played the dominant part within them. The societies which have come closest to the diffused type have been the ancient Greek, the age of religions, and the age of ideologies: here communication was easy and there were powerful influences, deriving mainly from the nature of religious or political belief, which operated across the frontiers, influencing the autonomous decisions of each unit. In such societies individuals or organized groups could have an influence that was sometimes independent of the national authorities, while within the cellular society the latter were almost exclusively the sources of decisions and actions. The age of nationalism is an ambiguous case: Although the units, being nationalistic, were by definition highly influenced by internal, self-regarding impulses, there also existed, at least among the larger members, a strong tendency to have regard for the interests of others in reaching important decisions and a sophisticated mechanism for mutual adjustment.

Is there any persistent trend between the two alternative types of society toward a more or less "cellular" society? In world history as a whole it is impossible to trace such a trend. Examples of diffused societies occur in both early and later periods of world history (though the Greek example, covering only a limited number of culturally related states, introduces an element of distortion here— diffusion is clearly more likely in such circumstances). It would perhaps be easier to argue that over the last century or two there has been a trend toward a more diffused international society; that is, developments in communications have brought an increase in transnational influences. Even this, however, is by no means sure. Improvements in communications and large-scale organization have not only improved contacts and influences between states but within them; strengthened national units as well as international understandings. National authorities are more powerful, and perhaps more deeply conscious of strong domestic influences, than ever before. Thus among the possible societies of the future that we sketched in the preceding chapter, three are essentially cellular in type (the sphere of influence, the regional, and the rich-poor) and only two are diffused (the transnational and the international). There would seem no grounds for saying that there is inevitably an overall movement toward a less cellular and more diffused type of society, or even that this is always *desirable* if it brings an increase in cultural and political uniformity and a loss of diversity.

Let us now turn to other types of contrast that can be made, this time based on the characteristics of the units. One is between a society in which the units are *expansive* in their aims, and a society where they are essentially self-sufficient. Expansionism may be of many sorts—military, political, economic, or cultural. But whatever its type, it is liable to lead to a competitive international society, both because expansion by one will normally provoke resistance by others, and because several states may engage in rival expansion in the same areas. But the degree of conflict will depend on the type of expansion. If it is territorial expansion, conflict is especially likely, since resistance to territorial encroachment is almost universal in all known societies. If expansion is economic (as in recent periods), conflict still remains possible but warfare is far less so (since *warlike* conflict is not customary in this field). Cultural or political expansion are also unlikely to lead to armed conflict, though they may evoke resistance of some sort. In practice the great majority of societies have been expansive in some degree; there has been virtually no period when nations were totally self-sufficient and nonexpansive in attitudes or motives. In the modern age territorial expansion has declined but political, economic, and cultural expansionism remain powerful; though rather less likely to cause war, each of these could lead to serious conflicts. It is indeed arguable that, if it is desired to create an international society that is both peaceful and yet diverse, that will combine the benefits of local independence and harmonious coexistence, and create stability without an all-powerful world authority to impose it, it is precisely self-sufficiency in all of these respects, even enhanced sovereignty, which should be made the highest goal of policy.

A more limited contrast can be made between societies where the concern of states is with *territory,* and those where they are concerned rather with political or other *influence*. The ancient Chinese and ancient Greek societies represent examples of societies of each type, the Chinese society being concerned with territory, the Greek with influence. A territorial society is inevitably expansive, and therefore almost invariably marked by frequent conflict. This is because land is finite in quantity, and once all is occupied, more can be had only at the expense of others. If nations all seek to secure wealth, a higher standard of living, or cultural achievement, they are not necessarily brought into conflict because these can be expanded in quantity: all can enjoy increases at the same time (they only come into conflict when they want the *most* wealth or the *highest* cultural achievement, goals which cannot be attained by more than one). It is true that territory is not acquired only by force; for example, it can be gained through marriage and inheritance, as in the age of dynasties. Yet if it is the possession of territory which is valued and which secures status, such a society remains territorial in its attitudes. These may therefore be contrasted with societies in which territory is not desired for its own sake, in which national status is acquired in other ways. In general the ideological societies (ancient Greece, the age of religions, and the age of ideologies) have been those least concerned with territory, while in the others it has always counted for something.

In general it is the ideological societies that are most concerned with influence. The ideological type of society is not necessarily the direct antithesis of the territorial society. It is at least theoretically possible for a society to be both territorial and ideological: territory may be desired, even if only as a means of preserving or exporting ideology. And it is certainly possible for it to be neither (like all our theoretical future societies). But in practice the international societies we know have usually been preoccupied *either* with territory or with ideology, not with both equally. Where there is deep concern with ideology, such as the practice of a particular religious faith, that goal can be achieved without any transfer of territory—by securing a change of government, or an undertaking that a particular faith would be permitted. Conversely, where governments have been less concerned over the practice of a particular faith or political doctrine, ambitions have often been concentrated on securing a wider measure of *national* control or influence, usually through securing territorial power.

A related contrast is that between the types of *status* sought in different international societies: whether, for example, they have seen high status in terms of military dominance, political influence, economic strength, cultural achievement, sporting victories, environmental standards, or way of life generally. This is of course related to the contrast just sketched concerning dominant *aims*. Nations will usually seek the successes which secure them high status: the societies where territory is an important goal will normally be those where high status attaches to territory. However, this identification is not complete; a nation may seek territory or power, even though it knows it will not gain respect in doing so.[2] Thus one could divide international societies according to how closely status is associated with military conquest (as, to some extent, in the age of dynasties); how far with domination and demands for submission (as in the age of sovereignty); how far with economic, scientific, or cultural achievement (as in the present age). It is doubtful whether this would be a satisfactory general system for distinguishing societies; any more than an analysis of the changing concept of a "gentleman"

2. It is partly because of this ambiguity that we have generally avoided use of the word "value"; as used by many writers, it is obscure whether this refers to what is *wanted* or what is *valued*, whether by individuals or by societies—not always the same thing.

would be a satisfactory way of analyzing domestic societies. It tells us something about the societies concerned, but not necessarily the most important thing. It tells us what kind of thing is desired, but not what sort of things are actually done.

A number of other significant distinctions can be made between types of society. One is between a society that is highly *centralized,* with a large degree of authority conceded to some international body, and one that is very decentralized, with the nations acting largely independently. But this is a somewhat theoretical distinction. In practice there has never been any genuinely centralized international society (the only one we have considered is the theoretical international society of the future). Power has always been largely dispersed among the units. In this century there has been an increase in the authority demanded for international organizations, but that effectively given them is still minimal. Probably the *most* decentralized we have examined were the ancient Chinese and the age of sovereignty.

It is thus perhaps more significant to distinguish among the *types* of decentralization which have existed, that is, the degree to which power has been concentrated among individual members of different societies. This is really the kind of distinction we examined in considering stratification. The degree of concentration has varied from the age of the Roman Empire, when there was only one major source of power, to the early sixteenth century, when there were two; the present age, when there are three; and so on (see p. 59 above). However, except in the case where there is one single all-dominant power, it is doubtful whether these categories really distinguish societies which are genuinely distinct in their general character; in other words, it is questionable if this is an important type of distinction.

Again one can make a distinction between a society that is *cooperative* and one that is *competitive*. The ancient Chinese society, the age of sovereigns, and the age of nationalism were highly competitive societies, in that there were strong pressures among the units to vie with others for status or position. The most cooperative society so far is probably that of the present day, judged, for example, by the scale of joint activity in specific functional fields, the number of international organizations and arrangements in operation. But the difference is only one of degree. In practice nearly all societies have been largely competitive, with a limited degree of cooperation in certain narrow fields (today's society is intensely competitive in economic growth, sports, and technology). And it is perhaps doubtful, therefore, that this contrast can be used as a fruitful tool of analysis.

Can one, finally, order these different societies according to the degree of *integration* achieved? This is a test frequently applied in the study of smaller societies, and in a general way it might no doubt be used for international societies as well. If homogeneity and understanding among the units is what is meant, then perhaps the age of sovereignty would come highest in the scale. If freedom from armed conflict is the answer, then perhaps the present age would come highest, at least for large areas of the world (Europe, North America, Latin America, and most of Africa.) But the concept of "integration" is complex and ambiguous. It is seen by many as an ideal, though it is arguable that the most integrated society is sometimes the most static and least adaptable. International societies have in general been so loosely organized that the concept may not have much revelance here. It would in any case need careful definition before it could usefully be applied.

Thus the most useful categories to apply to international societies are perhaps those dividing the cellular and diffused societies, the territorial and ideological types of society; and societies with expansive or self-sufficient units. There is, of course, a relationship among the three pairs of alternatives. In general, the first of each pair are more likely to be associated together, as are the latter halves. But there are some exceptions. A society can have an expansive character without being territorial, as where expansion takes economic or political forms. Self-sufficient units are at least as likely or more likely in a cellular society than in a diffused society; the fact of cross-border influences is likely in the long run to reduce self-sufficiency. But the relationship among the categories is not the most important point. The categories are useful if they point to important distinctions arising within different types of international society.

There may well be other distinctive types which could be drawn, even from the descriptions contained in this book. Once categories of this kind have been developed, it may be possible to go further and determine why a particular society belongs to one category or another. Our main conclusion remains that the essential distinction among societies is between the different *ideologies* that govern them, in the sense employed in this study. For this determines not only the general character of the society but many of the individual factors within it.

## 15.3 Structure and Function in International Society

So far we have been seeking to compare *different* types of international society. Let us now go on to consider certain questions common to all these societies: What are the processes by which they function, develop, and decay? What determines their evolution?

In analyzing domestic societies, social anthropologists in recent years have made much use of two key concepts, structure and function. These have given their names to the theories of structuralism and functionalism.

While there are many varieties of structuralism, they share in common the belief that various elements and institutions of a society should be examined and judged, not in isolation, but always in their relationship with each other and with the structure of society as a whole. It is the interrelationship among the parts, rather than the mere existence of one feature rather than another, which is the key social factor. What is important, if the structure is to be viable, is that there be a consistency and compatibility among the various elements, so that if one social feature is changed (say a new system of agriculture borrowed from elsewhere), some modification of other features of the society may need to be made to maintain a consistent structure. Thus each particular feature is better examined and explained within the context of the social organism to which it belongs, rather than looked at in isolation. A study of the evolution of each specific feature (marriage, kinship system, totem cult, and so on) among different societies, as was once fashionable, may therefore be meaningless, since the surrounding context of each society will be ignored. In particular, any worthwhile study will need to make clear how the particular institution performs not only its *apparent* function within the society, but others that are less obvious, especially the underlying one of maintaining a sense of solidarity and cohesion in the society as a whole. In a word, the society must be regarded as a complex and interrelated structural whole, and the meaning and social significance of one feature cannot be understood except in its relationship with others.[3]

Related to this view, but somewhat broader in its approach, is that of functionalism. This view is concerned with analyzing the *needs* which must be fulfilled in all societies—such as the establishment of effective authority, maintenance of social stability, resolution of disputes, rules of property and succession, a recognized marriage and family system, shared myths concerning the origins of the people and the forces of nature, and so on (the needs that are postulated vary widely)—and with considering how these may be fulfilled in particular cases. The assumption is that if a particular institution or social practice has been adopted, the underlying reason, if not consciously understood, is because it can fulfill a function, a *purpose* for that society. The aim of the social scientist will then be to examine and understand more clearly what that underlying purpose is and how it is achieved through these particular social features.[4]

Each of these closely related views has been profoundly influential in modern social science. Each has been subjected to substantial criticisms both of method and aim. Some of these criticisms are not unlike those already made here in relation to the systems approach to international relations. To analyze societies in terms of structural interrelationships, to examine institutions according to the functions each one performs, is to beg a large number of questions. The structuralist approach tends to take for granted at the outset that a structural interrelationship does, even must, exist among social features and institutions; the functionalist assumes that institutions always perform some clear social function. Both tend merely to find in any particular society the evidence which will support these views. They thus underplay the roles of chance, cultural borrowing, irrational

3. The true originator of the structuralist viewpoint is A. R. Radcliffe-Brown, since he originated the name for it. But the description could be used to cover a wide range of modern social anthropologists who are especially concerned with the *interrelationship* among the different features within a society. A similar view in the field of the social sciences generally goes back to Comte.

4. Though here once more a large number of anthropologists in recent times fall broadly into this school, the one who invented its name, and is perhaps most closely associated with it, is D. Malinowski. A somewhat similar view has been applied to the social sciences generally by Talcott Parsons, among others.

beliefs, or personal influences in determining social features. In addition, by assuming that every society, from the mere fact of existing, must have achieved a kind of internal harmony and consistency among the parts, they seem to underplay the role of conflict within society and the degree of internal tension which may in fact exist. By assuming institutions have a structural or functional role, such theories imply they have a positive purpose: if they are features of the society, they are performing a useful role. In other words, both approaches have a distinctly conservative bias, since they seem to assume that whatever is, is right. If a feature exists in a certain society, there must be some good reason for it: though it may not be right for other societies, it must at least be right for this one.

Provided these limitations are borne in mind, there is clearly some value in approaching a society as a delicately interrelated whole, and in considering the functions which may be performed within it by particular institutions. Such approaches have their application to the international societies which we have been examining in this book. It could be said that there must be some kind of adjustment among the constituent elements of each such society if it is to hold together, and that there are particular functions which need to be performed within each one (say, communication between states), making necessary the institutions (say, diplomacy) appropriate to that task. Thus it could be argued that in all the societies we have examined there was a kind of structural interrelatedness among the parts which was partly the result of the common underlying ideology, the common expectations, which we considered in Chapter 5. These expectations in turn influenced and so harmonized other social features. Thus we tried to show how the assumptions of the age of dynasties affected many aspects of that society, including motives, means, institutions, and norms; in this way they helped to bring such aspects into reconciliation with each other. Similarly, it would be possible to see the emergence of the doctrine of sovereignty in the seventeenth and eighteenth centuries as performing a clear functional purpose: it served to rescue the society from the dangers of frequent and excessive intervention by one state in the internal affairs of others, which had almost destroyed the society of the age before. A general rule of "keep out" had the effect of minimizing interference of this sort throughout that age. Again it could be said that the Concert of Europe had the functional purpose in the following age of containing and limiting the conflicts among the great powers by providing the machinery for resolving most of their disputes. Or it could be held that the sphere of influence system, as it has begun to operate in recent years, has a functional purpose in restricting conflict among the major powers by reserving to each large areas of the world which are subject to their dominance.

There is no doubt that there is some validity in these applications. To some extent these are tautologies rather than explanations. The Concert of Europe was devised to resolve disoutes, so it is not surprising that it often served that purpose. It is not difficult to show that some features of each society—such as the balance of power system, the establishment of international organizations, or the adoption of national roles—have a clear social function, and often that the features are logically interrelated. But some of the same difficulties occur here as in the application of these theories to domestic societies: the approach begs many questions. For example, though the doctrine of sovereignty *could* be explained in the way suggested, it is more simply explained as resulting from the desire of the sovereigns and their advisers to protect the power of the sovereign in their own domains; in other words, from the *self-interested* aims of each, rather than the *social* aims of all (certainly the degree of conflict that occurred in that age shows the doctrine did not *fulfill* its assumed function). In many other cases, while arguments can be found to show that a particular social feature—such as diplomacy, the balance of power system, even warfare—exists to perform a "social function," it can often equally well be argued that its function is sometimes antisocial. Diplomacy was a means by which the strong tried to manipulate the weak, the balance of power a means by which the medium-sized sought to outwit the strong. Warfare is more plausibly seen as a means by which individualistic nations compete with each other, and so as a divisive and antisocial factor (insofar as it has a function it is in integrating nations rather than in integrating the international society as a whole), than as a social force insuring the survival of the fittest among nations (as both Hegel and Herbert Spencer sought to show).

Here, therefore, even more than in the case of domestic societies, such theoretical approaches need to be handled with extreme caution. The assumptions of the structuralists that there always exists an "integrated," well-adjusted social system is especially hard to maintain here, since all international society is manifestly riven by internal conflict. The belief of the functionalists that particular needs of a society are performed by the adoption of a particular institution or custom is even more suspect, for there is even less agreement on the nature of the required functions and whether they are effectively performed in a particular case, though the same tautological arguments can be used to support them (for example, that conflict resolution is required in every society and this must therefore account for the existence of international organizations today). It seems more reasonable to maintain that there are some features of each society which perform a clear social purpose and have in many cases been adopted for precisely these reasons, but that others have come about by chance, or to promote the sectional interests of individual members or groups, and may be antisocial in their final effect. Conversely, there may be many functions which ideally should be performed and which are not in fact performed in many societies.

Both of these theories tend to assume the subordination of most aspects of society to social purposes, and perhaps can only satisfactorily be applied to simpler societies where this is sometimes the case. For international societies where the situation is normally the reverse, they may have a much more limited application. In most societies, both simple and complex, there usually exists at least implicitly a conflict of interest and desires among the members. Sometimes, especially in simpler societies, norms, institutions, and values have been developed which successfully contain or mask a large proportion of these. But in large-scale and complex modern societies they are rarely successful in fully resolving the conflicts and dissatisfactions which exist. And this is still more the case in international society, where divisions of interest are so manifest and the socializing influences so weak.

One feature which almost invariably emerges, within both the fragmented modern state and the international society, is some system of mutual accommodation: procedures for seeking at least some reconciliation of essential interests among the members. It is the study of these methods of *interest adjustment* which should perhaps hold the key position in the study of society. Such a system may take many forms, in which power may be more or less evenly shared, and accommodation more or less willing on either side. There may be oligarchies, democracies, or plutocracies at the international as at the domestic level. The initial situation, economic, political, or military, from which those engaged begin is not always equal, in international as in national societies. Thus procedures themselves do not always give equal weight to different sections of society: just as the parliaments of a century ago were dominated by the privileged classes, the international society of the last century was an oligarchy controlled by the dominant powers of the era. But in practice such arrangements are rarely totally one-sided. There is usually some give-and-take, no matter how unevenly the dice are loaded.

For example, in the society of the age of nationalism, the dominant oligarchy, the "powers," though certainly not notably sympathetic with the force of nationalism among the smaller states, in practice made consistent concessions to it throughout the century in almost every settlement reached. Superpowers today, which wield unchallengeable power, economic and political as well as military, cannot in practice simply impose their own views on the international proletariat with which they deal without making some concessions in return. In the negotiations through which most international decisions are arrived at, many factors have influence, including external opinions and pressures, desire for good name, even willingness to compromise, as well as the balance of military power (just as the balance of economic or political power is not always exclusively decisive within states). Thus over most issues most of the time, some kind of accommodation must be arrived at, a deal must be done, between states as within them. It is in its ability to adjust and resolve diverging interests in this way, not necessarily without conflict, but without creating totally unmanageable stresses—rather than in "structural" interrelatedness or "functional" performance—that a society's viability is best judged. The process by which an accommodation of interests is achieved is thus the key factor to be studied.

This may be relevant in helping us to answer another problem which has preoccupied those who study societies: the reasons for change within them. Why did the age of sovereigns come to an end, to be replaced in turn by the age of nationalism in 1789, and why did this in turn disintegrate entirely in 1914? If we are right in judging the capacity for securing mutual accommodation as the essential test of a viable society, we must look to the threats posed to each of these societies by the events at their end. If the French Revolution had remained a purely internal phenomenon, it might not have destroyed the age of sovereigns. But it was never purely internal in its effect, both because other sovereign governments, especially Austria, Prussia, and Russia, felt the need to challenge it; and because the revolution itself quickly spread, or was spread, first to Belgium and later to the Netherlands and northern Italy, and finally grew into the attempted conquest of Europe by France. Though this was resisted and finally reversed, a new spirit of nationalism emerged which was incompatible with the whole system of a mutual balancing of interests among sovereigns—regardless of popular wishes—which had previously prevailed. Mutual accommodation among the new forces and the old was no longer possible. So an entirely new system had to be invented which could take greater account of the rising nationalist movement as well as resolve disputes among the big powers themselves—a function which the Concert of Europe performed. Similarly, in the following period, though the Concert worked reasonably well at first, and succeeded in adjusting to the new force of nationalism in many parts of Europe, by 1914 the combined force of the frustrated nationalism of the southern Slavs and the expansive nationalism of some of the powers themselves, above all Germany, could no longer be contained within the old system. The procedures for adjustment which had served for a century thus now broke down. And so once again, when the immediate conflict was brought to an end, a new type of society had to be established, with a new system for mutual accommodation. Each time new social forces emerged that the old system was no longer capable of containing. So an entirely new method of interest adjustment had to be devised.

Thus the one function which any society, national or international, *must* perform if it is to survive (as opposed to those which it may usefully perform) is the mutual accommodation of conflicting interests, at least among the important actors of the society. Where new forces emerge which need to be reconciled, a new system of accommodation needs to be developed. Every international society of which we have knowledge has provided some mechanism of this sort, even if it is only an elementary diplomatic system. But such procedures, even though they exist, are not always effective. Especially where a totally new ideology arises—a concern for nationalism replaces concern for sovereignty, ideological fervor replaces nationalist fervor—the old procedures may break down and the international society itself may be unable to survive in the old form. It must be replaced by another, better able to respond to the challenges and divisions which bring its members into conflict.

## 15.4 Social Theory and International Society

The argument of this chapter so far has been, first, that international relations are best examined within the framework of a study of international societies, each with its own individual character and ideology; that such an examination reveals the differences among many different categories of society of varying types (cellular or diffused, territorial or ideological, and so on); and that within these structures the most important single function determining survival is the system for accommodation of interests among its members. We are now faced with a wider question: is there a general theory or principle that will tell us how international societies are formed and held together?

Those studying societies of a narrower kind have evolved various theories concerning the foundations of social existence. And once again it may be worth considering how far these are relevant, if at all, to the study of international societies.

One of the oldest and most pervasive theories of this sort, going back through Pareto and Marx to Hobbes, Plato, and Han Fei-tzu, is that ultimately the force holding society together is *coercion*. Holders of this view point to the fact that there exist in the hands of those who govern in most organized societies instruments by which the rules of society, or their own personal interests, may be enforced. Usually only a few are in a position to influence these law-enforcing agencies and the rules they apply. The great majority obey because they must. Order in society exists because of the power of some to command the compliance of others. Less tangible means of securing enforcement, a body of customary *rules,* or an *ideology* to buttress the existing authority of the state, may be built up in support, but ultimately the reason why the laws of society are obeyed, and why rebellious groups and opinions are repressed, is because those in authority possess powers of enforcement. Thus the means of securing a more orderly society, according to such thinkers, is not to secure greater conformity by the authority to the wishes of the people, but greater conformity by the people to the wishes of the authority. This may be in the interests of the citizens as much as of the rulers. For by securing conformity in belief and behavior, and by reducing dissent and disorder, the authorities can assist the citizen by reducing uncertainty and insecurity.

This type of theory at first seems to have little relevance to international society. International societies have never possessed the kind of central authority with coercive power which is the key assumption of the theory. Whatever is the basis of social order there, it clearly cannot, in any easily foreseeable age, be coercion of this sort. In this respect international societies are more akin to certain primitive societies which have no central power of enforcement. Such enforcement as exists is brought about in both cases by intangible procedures—the subjection of all members to group pressures, supported perhaps by group revenge, feud, and self-help—rather than power at the center. It is a key weakness of the whole coercion explanation of social order that it fails to explain the existence of order in such a society, where there is no central power and sometimes no means of enforcement (this perhaps results from the fact that those who have held the theory have been mainly political thinkers rather than anthropologists). Nor does the thesis account for the fact that most members of a society usually conform not out of any sense of fear of sanctions, but *voluntarily,* whether by habit, indifference, or choice. It is the fact of persistent *willing* obedience within society, rather than of unwilling conformity, which most requires explanation.[5] But if coercion is not the basis of authority even in domestic societies, it is still less likely to be the basis of order within the international society.

The theory might be applied to the international society in a somewhat different way. For in such societies coercion *can* be applied by an oligarchy, a few major powers which wield superior force. Acting together, these can sometimes secure the submission of others, as the Concert of Europe was often able to do, or the two superpowers sometimes do today; or a few states may combine to punish an aggressor (as in World War II) or a threat to stability (as in the wars against Louis XIV). Even powerful members of the society can thereby be constrained through force to conform with general social rules. In this sense a form of coercion is still at the root of the social order, even though it is somewhat unpredictable and arbitrary in its application. The difficulty is that power exerted in this haphazard way could hardly be said to provide an adequate basis of order. Nor does this version account for the fact that many states conform for much of the time even though never threatened with coercion, and that to a large extent even the very powerful obey the general rules of the society. Moreover, in practice, it can be held, it is precisely in those fields of international activity, from rules of navigation to trading rights, diplomatic practice to international frequency regulation, where the use of force is least to be expected or feared, that the most widespread and willing conformity is obtained.

Altogether, therefore, the coercion theory seems to provide an explanation of social order which is even less satisfactory at the international level than it is at the domestic. Other theorists, especially modern social scientists, are more inclined to explain social order as the result of a general *consensus* concerning values within the society. This both reduces the scale of conflicts that occur and secures acceptance of the procedures laid down for resolving them when they do occur. But though somewhat more satisfactory than the last, this theory too cannot be considered altogether convincing, at least for societies beyond a certain stage of complexity. In most modern societies there exists in fact little consensus concerning many basic value questions. In general, people totally opposed in religious, political, social, and economic opinions nonetheless coexist in society relatively peacefully most of the time. Moreover, insofar as there exists any consensus, it may be held, this is the *effect* of society rather than a condition; it is manufactured by those in authority to bolster their own power, or is slowly created by common institutions and a common culture. There is a certain *negative* force in the theory—social order is certainly strengthened when a degree of consensus exists about fundamentals. This applies particularly to agreement concerning the means for *resolving* conflicts. Where minorities do not agree on the procedures laid down

5. A further defect in this argument is that, as Hume pointed out long ago, force is always on the side of the governed, not of authority, even in authoritarian states. A government can usually be overthrown by the generals, the generals by the common soldiers, and the soldiers by the mass of the population. The fact that the latter usually obey the former must therefore be explained on the basis of some bond other than force alone.

for this purpose, social disorder is likely to result; one of the strengths of democratic societies, for example, is that consensus, in this form at least, is usually present (since it is difficult to justify the use of violence against decisions introduced by authorities demonstrably ruling with the consent of the majority).

What then is the relevance of this theory to the international society? It is sometimes held that there can never exist any genuine social order in international society precisely because consensus is lacking there. Yet, as we saw in Chapter 4, this argument is often based on a fallacy, for it often confuses the *type* of consensus which is in question. The fact that there is no consensus concerning principles of internal government—that some believe in communism and some in democracy, for example—is quite irrelevant in considering whether those who hold such views can coexist at the international level. The type of consensus necessary here is consensus concerning the principles governing international society, that is, concerning behavior and relationships among states. Even here only a bare minimum may be required. It might be held, for example, that a belief in the nonuse of force against frontiers was almost the only essential condition of peaceful coexistence. Even this is not necessarily essential to the existence of a society of a kind; in some cases, as we saw, war has been an acceptable institution of an international society in the past, and not incompatible with order of other kinds. Others might hold that at least the total destruction of other states is incompatible with a social order. Even this is not certain, since in a number of the societies we have considered individual states have been eliminated. But it is perhaps true that if such mutually destructive behavior is used to the limit, as in the ancient Chinese society, and no restraints on annexation imposed, this must ultimately lead to the destruction of the society, for only one state will eventually be left. In a broader sense, a worldwide commitment to abide in a general way with the traditions and rules of the society might be held to be a condition of social existence among states. But the theory of *value* consensus implies more than this: a commitment to specific values and ideas in common. And this is not essential in international societies any more than in domestic.

In many of the international societies we have examined a social existence of a sort takes place even if there is only the barest minimum of consensus concerning the basic principles or norms which should govern them. Most states, like most individuals, are often willing to settle for a reasonably peaceful coexistence with neighbors for most of the time, even without any clear consensus concerning values. They have, like members of a domestic society, a built-in *interest* in a reasonably stable coexistence with their neighbors which is more likely to be the main basis of order.

This leads us to a third and the most plausible explanation of the existence of social order. It can be argued that the basis of social order is neither an intellectual commitment to common values nor the brutal power of coercion, but rather habit, sloth, indoctrination, and passivity. Society exists because it exists, and most who are born into it become sufficiently a part of it, sufficiently socialized by it, that they have no wish or need to challenge it unless forced to do so by the gravest threats to their own well-being. Thus what we have to explain is not why social order exists—this occurs almost automatically from the fact of birth and of upbringing—but why it sometimes ceases to exist.

This theory is in many ways more persuasive than the others we have considered. Yet it cannot explain everything. It does not explain how a social order is established in the first place, or why there is sometimes more social order in some societies than in others. Above all, it does not explain how a social order is changed. For if all found it easiest to accept the social order they inherit, none would challenge it and society would become totally stagnant. Society would never be changed except, in extreme cases, through revolution. How then could one account for disorder? Does the existence of large-scale dissent and violence in the U.S. in recent years mean that no U.S. society exists? Moreover, socialization itself may promote competition and conflict, so that if some kind of order nonetheless exists, it must have some other cause. This would be, in any case, a depressing theory to apply to international society, since here socialization is minimal and the habit of obedience nonexistent, and one would be obliged to conclude that no international society has ever existed, and perhaps never can exist.

Thus while each of these theories contains a germ of truth, they cannot, even together (and none is *automatically* incompatible with the others), explain everything. For what most needs explanation is that in every society personal interests and personal values are often in conflict, yet conflict is normally contained and channeled within acceptable bounds. This leads to the conclusion that social order occurs because a society normally acquires one very specific mechanism: a system for the *adjustment of interests*. The balance of interests established varies from age to age. The balance which is acceptable to one age is often unacceptable to that which follows. A shift in the balance of power, or in the direction of aspirations, creates new demands which will ultimately result in a new balance. Conflicts within the society will exist, but the system for adjustment will either contain them or itself be modified. Insofar as the great majority accept, whether through social conditioning, coercion, or rational judgment (usually a combination), that the system is, if not just, at least tolerable and not incompatible with their essential interests, social order will be preserved. So long as there exists a common pattern of expectations concerning the way of securing a just distribution of benefits— whether of influence, wealth, education, or other rights—the order will be maintained. Only when the expectations cease to be met, when it comes to be believed the existing order not only provides an unjust distribution at present but cannot be adjusted to secure a just one, will the existing order break down. When new expectations arise which cannot be reconciled, when the existing distribution cannot be adjusted to provide a balance which meets the new expectations, the society will need to be remade.

This *adjustment* theory—that social order is achieved only insofar as a society finds a means to balance the interests of its members in a way the great majority accept as tolerable—is also the one that best explains the existence of order at the international level. Here too, as we saw in the last section, the attainment of some system of mutual accommodation to reconcile the interests of its members, is the essential condition of a "society," as opposed to an anarchic association of mutually hostile states. If some kind of social existence among states is to be maintained, some system of mutual accommodation must be established. The strong as well as the weak must recognize that other states have interests of their own which must be taken into account in any settlement reached. This may be achieved through any of the systems we described in Chapter 10 (negotiation, balance of power, competitive alliances, and consultation), through the institutions set up to resolve disputes, as discussed in Chapter 13, or even through the norms we considered in Chapter 12. The essential feature of all these is that they are means of securing settlements which provide some balance of interest among different members of the society.

The willingness to seek *accommodation* is thus the necessary minimum required in a viable society. It will not in itself create a uniformly peaceful society. For this something more explicit is required: establishment of norms of conduct which provide for peaceful coexistence and obedience to those norms. It is not the purpose here to suggest exactly what international norms are required for this.[6] While some are relatively simple and straightforward—for example, a general prohibition of incursions over the frontiers of others—others are considerably more complex—those concerning assistance to one or both sides engaged in civil war, the limits of international action to protect essential human rights, minimum rights in the economic field, and so on. The essential point is that such norms may help to create that adjustment of interests among states which is the first condition of any kind of order, whether within states or between them.

The theory suggested here is not incompatible with any of the others described earlier. Most societies are in practice maintained by a combination of coercion, common values, habituation, and interest adjustment. But they vary considerably in the balance among them. Some early empires and totalitarian states have depended primarily on coercion; some simple and highly homogeneous societies may depend mainly on a consensus in values; some traditional and conservative societies have depended on habituation and passivity. But in the complex plural states of the modern world, it is arguable that it is a system for securing an effective and acceptable accommodation of interests which is of primary importance, both within states and between them. Modern societies usually rest ultimately on a modus vivendi among their various interests, rather than on coercion, preexisting agreement on what represents a "just" society, or the forces of intertia alone. There is a need for a bargain among various interests to be hammered out, and states may need above all to create the procedures for hammering out such bargains. The same is true at the international level. Here, too, a bargain has to be hammered out, and only insofar as mutually acceptable bargains are accomplished does a stable and viable society come into being.

6. For an attempt to suggest a system of norms which might facilitate peaceful coexistence in the modern world, see Evan Luard, *Conflict and Peace in the Modern International System* (Boston, 1968).

If this is so, then the task for man in the modern world is not merely to seek the *principles* on which international society should be based—that is, the norms of conduct which may provide for peaceful coexistence within it—but the *procedures* by which such principles may be formulated and conflicts resolved. Both principles and procedures will need to take account of the interests of all members of the society, small as well as big, poor as well as rich, weak as well as strong, so as to establish an order seen as ''just'' by a majority within the society. For unless they do, they are likely eventually to prove incapable of resolving the stresses and strains within society, and of appeasing the resentments and dissatisfactions of its members. This will require, within the international order today, economic adjustments as well as political (just as an acceptable order within states requires economic as well as political adjustments there). For it must certainly be doubtful if a society in which economic inequalities among states are as great as they are today can prove viable for long.

The inescapable fact is that nations are one of another, just as men are one of another. They are social beings just as men are social beings. And only by accepting this essentially social condition, and by understanding the social forces that operate among them, are nations likely, as are men in their smaller societies, to be able to establish among themselves the order to which, however profoundly they differ, however passionately they dispute, all claim to aspire.

**INDEX**

## A

Accountability, 302
Aggression:
  among states, 306–307
  among individuals, 11, 44–45
Alliance policies, 88, 105, 175, 177, 188–89, 235, 318
Ambassadors, 112, 126, 131–32, 238
"Anticipations" (of international social change), 85, 165
"Approach" theories of international relations, 5, 10–13
Arbitration, 316, 320, 323–24, 328, 334
Aristotle, 44
"Arm-twisters" in international societies, 276–77
Aron, R., 48
Assistance to rebels, 174, 177, 182, 186–87, 197
Authority, in international societies, 53, 313ff
Avengers, in international societies, 277

## B

"Balance of interests" system, 251
Balance of power, policy, 175, 256, 262, 265, 269, 271, 274, 281
Balance of power, system, 230, 233, 235, 241–42, 245–48
Bourgeoisie, 125–26
Bureaucracy, 140

## C

Carr, E. H., 25
"Cellular" international societies, 109, 366–67

Ceremonial in international relations, 231–32
Chivalry, 154, 286, 290–91
Class among nations, 54, 201ff, 218
Class structure and foreign policy, 117–18, 120–21, 127, 139–40, 142–44
Coercion, as basis for social order, 376–77
Collective ambitions of states, 50, 99
Collective decision-making, 119, 140
Collective security, 254–55, 258, 332
Colonialism, 163–64, 166, 207, 220
Commercial class, influence on policy, 114–15
Commercial rules, 292–93, 297, 299, 308–309
Communications, 59, 285–86, 310, 367
"Compensation" among states, 246
Competition among states, 57, 100, 109
Concert of Europe, 217–18, 331–32, 338, 340, 372
Conference diplomacy, 113, 250–51, 313, 315
Confucius, 11, 286
Consensus, as basis of social order, 377–78
Consuls, 195–96, 234
Containment, 169, 198
*Cujus regio ejus religio,* 91, 167
Custom, among states, 284–85, 288

## D

Decision-making theory, 12
"Democracy" in international societies, 226–27, 335
Demonstration (of strength), 194
Dependency among states, 205, 216
Diplomacy, 132, 176, 184, 230–31, 233–34, 237–39, 241, 244–45, 249, 293, 325
Disequalization (among states), 224

385